always up to date

The law changes, but Nolo is always on top of it! We offer several ways to make sure you and your Nolo products are always up to date:

1   Nolo's Legal Updater
We'll send you an email whenever a new edition of your book is published! Sign up at **www.nolo.com/legalupdater**.

2   Updates @ Nolo.com
Check **www.nolo.com/update** to find recent changes in the law that affect the current edition of your book.

3   Nolo Customer Service
To make sure that this edition of the book is the most recent one, call us at **800-728-3555** and ask one of our friendly customer service representatives. Or find out at **www.nolo.com**.

please note

7th edition

Chapter 13 Bankruptcy

Repay Your Debts

by Attorney Robin Leonard

NOLO

Seventh Edition	MAY 2005
Illustrations	MARI STEIN
Cover Design	SUSAN PUTNEY
Book Design	TERRI HEARSH
Editors	STEVE ELIAS
	ALBIN RENAUER
	ILONA BRAY
Index	THÉRÈSE SHERE
Proofreading	ROBERT WELLS
Printing	DELTA PRINTING SOLUTIONS, INC.

Leonard, Robin.
    Chapter 13 bankruptcy : repay your debts / by Robin Leonard.--7th ed.
      p. cm.
    Includes bibliographical references and index.
    ISBN 1-4133-0181-9 (alk. paper)
    1. Bankruptcy--United States--Popular works. I. Title: Chapter thirteen bankruptcy. II.
Title.
    KF1524.6.L46 2005
    346.7307'8--dc22

                                      2005040655

Quantity sales: For information on bulk purchases or corporate premium sales, please
contact the Special Sales department. For academic sales or textbook adoptions, ask for
Academic Sales, 800-955-4775. Nolo, 950 Parker St., Berkeley, CA 94710.

Acknowledgments

The author gratefully acknowledges the following people.

Barbara McEntyre, a bankruptcy attorney in San Rafael, California. Barbara is a smart, competent, and extraordinarily ethical lawyer. Barbara was incredibly generous and gracious in sharing her time and knowledge with me, including meticulously reading the manuscript and sending me detailed comments. I am honored to be able to call her a friend.

Joan and Bob Leonard. Mom and Dad let me live in their house for nearly a month, 3,000 miles from my own home, away from telephone calls, meetings, and the stress of day-to-day work life so I could actually write this book.

Mary Randolph, Senior Legal Editor at Nolo. Mary is the perfect editor. Her ability to take a good, but disorganized submission and turn it into a great and easy-to-use guide made writing the second, third, and fourth drafts pleasurable.

Attorneys Steve Elias and Albin Renauer. Steve's knowledge of bankruptcy and skill in questioning everything he reads made the book even that much better. Albin diligently updated the state exemption charts, among other important contributions.

Terri Hearsh, whose beautiful and user-friendly design makes the book a delight to read.

Table of Contents

8 Filing Your Bankruptcy Papers

9 After You File Your Case

Appendixes

Index

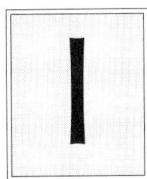

Introduction

Americans learn almost from birth that it's good to buy all sorts of products and services. A highly paid army of persuaders surrounds us with thousands of seductive messages each day, all urging us to buy, buy, buy. Readily available credit makes living beyond our means easy and resisting the siren sounds of the advertisers difficult. But we're also told that if we fail to pay for it all right on time, we're miserable deadbeats. In short, much of American economic life is built on a contradiction.

If for some reason, such as illness, loss of work, or just plain bad planning, our ability to pay for goods or services is interrupted, fear and guilt are often our first feelings. We may even feel we've fundamentally failed as human beings.

Nonsense. There's lots more to life than an A+ credit rating. Our importance to our families, friends, and neighbors should never be forgotten. Nor should we forget that the American economy is based on consumer debt. The guilt we may feel about the debts we've run up must be put in perspective; after all, we live in an age of $500-billion bailouts for poorly managed financial institutions. Large creditors view defaults and bankruptcies as a fact of life and treat them as a cost of doing business. The reason so many banks push their credit cards is that it is a very profitable business, even with so many bankruptcies.

Fortunately, for at least two dozen centuries it's been recognized that debts can get the better of even the most conscientious among us. From Biblical times to the present, sane societies have discouraged debtors from falling on their swords, and provided sensible ways for debt-oppressed people to start new economic lives. In the United States, this process is called bankruptcy.

Bankruptcy is a truly worthy part of our legal system, based as it is on forgiveness rather than retribution. Certainly it helps keep families together, reduces suicide, and keeps the ranks of the homeless from growing even larger.

A. The Basics of Chapter 13 Bankruptcy

Most people think of bankruptcy as a process in which you go to court and get your debts erased. But in fact, there are two types of bankruptcies: the more familiar liquidation bankruptcy, where your debts are wiped out completely (Chapter 7 bankruptcy) and reorganization bankruptcy, where you partially or fully repay your debts. The reorganization bankruptcy for individuals is called Chapter 13 bankruptcy. There are two other kinds of reorganization bankruptcy: Chapter 11, for businesses and for individuals with extremely high debt levels, and Chapter 12, for family farmers (Chapter 12 has been intermittently unavailable, but is routinely reauthorized by Congress on a six-month basis). The names come from the chapters of the federal Bankruptcy Code.

Chapter 13 bankruptcy lets you rearrange your financial affairs, repay a portion of your debts, and put yourself back on your financial feet. You repay your debts through a Chapter 13 plan. Under a typical plan, you make monthly payments to someone called a bankruptcy trustee, who is appointed by the bankruptcy court to oversee your case, for three to five years. The bankruptcy trustee distributes the money to your creditors and collects a small percentage as his fee.

Chapter 13 bankruptcy isn't for everyone. To succeed in a Chapter 13 bankruptcy, you must be able to come up with a feasible plan to repay at least a portion of your debts. If your total debt burden is too high or your income is too low or irregular, you may not be eligible. You may be better off handling your debt problems in another way—such as filing for Chapter 7 bankruptcy, seeking help from a nonprofit debt counseling group, or negotiating with your creditors on your own. (These options are explored in Ch. 1, *Should You File for Chapter 13 Bankruptcy?*)

Here are some important features of Chapter 13 bankruptcy:

- **Chapter 13 is flexible.** In Chapter 13 you may have to pay only a small fraction of your unsecured debts.
- **Chapter 13 bankruptcy is very powerful.** You can use it to stop a house foreclosure, make up the missed mortgage payments, and keep the house. You can also pay off back taxes through your Chapter 13 plan and stop interest from accruing on your unsecured tax debt.
- **Filing your papers with the bankruptcy court stops creditors in their tracks.** When you file for Chapter

13 bankruptcy or any other kind of bankruptcy, something called the automatic stay goes into effect. It immediately stops your creditors from trying to collect what you owe them. At least temporarily, creditors cannot legally grab (garnish) your wages, empty your bank account, go after your car, house, or other property, or cut off your utility service or welfare benefits.

- **You can use Chapter 13 bankruptcy to buy time.** Some people use Chapter 13 bankruptcy to buy time. For example, if you are behind on mortgage payments and about to be foreclosed on, you can file Chapter 13 bankruptcy papers to stop collection efforts, and then attempt to sell the house before the foreclosure.
- **A successful Chapter 13 bankruptcy requires discipline.** For the entire length of your case, three to five years, you will have to live under a strict budget; the bankruptcy court will not allow you to spend money on anything it deems nonessential.
- **The majority of debtors never complete their Chapter 13 repayment plans.** Although most people file for Chapter 13 bankruptcy assuming they'll complete their plan, only about 35% of all Chapter 13 debtors do. Many drop out very early in the process, without ever submitting a feasible repayment plan to the court. If you can come up with a realistic budget and stick to it, however, you should have no trouble completing your Chapter 13 plan.
- **Payments may be deducted from your wages during your case.** If you have a regular job with regular income, the bankruptcy court will probably order that the monthly payments under your Chapter 13 plan be automatically deducted from your wages and sent to the bankruptcy court.
- **Bankruptcy rules vary from court to court.** Bankruptcy law comes from the federal Congress and is meant to be uniform across the country. But when disputes arise about the bankruptcy laws, bankruptcy courts make the decisions—and they don't all decide the issues in the same way. The result is that bankruptcy law and practice can vary significantly from court to court and from region to region. This book highlights the different ways courts have ruled on major issues in Chapter 13

bankruptcy. But this book can't possibly address every variation. If you research a question yourself or hire a bankruptcy lawyer, you'll need to be sure the information you get applies in your particular bankruptcy court.

- **Chapter 13 bankruptcy may stay in your credit file for only seven years.** Most credit bureaus, under pressure from banks to encourage debtors to choose Chapter 13 over Chapter 7, report Chapter 13 bankruptcy for only seven years instead of the usual ten years for Chapter 7. No matter how long reported, after your case is over, you can take steps to improve your credit. In fact, some Chapter 13 bankruptcy courts have established programs to help you do just that. In such a program, if you have paid off around 75% or more of your debts, you may attend money management seminars and apply for credit from certain local creditors. These programs are discussed in Ch. 10, *After Your Plan Is Approved*, Section F4.

B. Do You Need a Lawyer?

By using this book, you can file your own Chapter 13 bankruptcy case without a lawyer. Most of the papers you'll need to file are fill-in-the-blank forms. This book includes all the forms you'll need, and complete instruction for filling them out.

But becoming knowledgeable about Chapter 13 bankruptcy will require a lot of work on your part— Chapter 13 bankruptcy is fairly complex and has no shortcuts. You will need to read every chapter of this book; within each chapter, we'll let you know what material you can skip because it isn't relevant in your case.

You may want to use this book to understand Chapter 13 bankruptcy, but hire a lawyer to actually handle your case. The majority of people who file for Chapter 13 bankruptcy use an attorney, for several reasons:

- The lawyer's fee (typically $1,000–$1,500) can be paid through the Chapter 13 plan. This means that you do not have to come up with all of the money in advance.

- Chapter 13 bankruptcy often requires a lot of negotiating with your creditors and with the bankruptcy trustee. If you'd rather have someone deal with creditors on your behalf, you can hire a lawyer to do it.

- Chapter 13 bankruptcy requires at least one appearance in court before a bankruptcy judge, and you may feel more comfortable having a lawyer speak for you at that appearance. Also, a court appearance may require the making of a legal argument before the bankruptcy judge. You may not have the time to do the necessary research to prepare, or have the confidence that you can handle your own contested matter should one arise in the course of your case.

- Unlike Chapter 7 bankruptcy, which is fairly routine and therefore predictable, every Chapter 13 bankruptcy case has some unique variables. An experienced lawyer can help you understand the specifics of your case, including the types of debts you have and the amount or percentage you must repay on each. The more complex your case is, the more likely you will need the help of an attorney.

- If you disagree with the validity of a debt, such as an income tax assessment or deficiency balance imposed after a foreclosure, you can contest that debt as a part of your Chapter 13 bankruptcy. This is a very complicated process, involving both bankruptcy law and tax, mortgage foreclosure, or other substantive law.

The book flags situations in which you should consult a lawyer. If you file your own Chapter 13 bankruptcy case and have questions, get the professional help you need. Help may involve going to a bankruptcy attorney for advice or representation. Or it may involve hitting the law library and figuring things out for yourself. Ch. 12, *Help Beyond the Book,* discusses how to find the kind of help you need.

C. Can You Propose a Viable Plan?

After cutting through the nuances and all the possible ancillary issues that can arise in a Chapter 13 bankruptcy, you'll find that it involves one basic goal: Developing a viable plan for repaying all or a portion of your debts. It's that simple. If you can't come up with a plan that the bankruptcy judge will approve, very little else matters.

Proposing a viable plan can take a lot of work. You don't want to waste your time pursuing a Chapter 13 bankruptcy that is bound to be rejected. Use the following formula to get a rough idea if you'll be able to propose a viable Chapter 13 repayment plan:

1. Your monthly net income (after taxes Social Security, and other deductions are made)   _____

2. Your monthly absolutely necessary expenses   _____

3. **Difference (your monthly disposable income)**   _____

4. Mortgage arrears   _____

5. Other secured debt arrears   + _____

6. Tax debts   + _____

7. Child support or alimony arrears   + _____

8. **Subtotal I (line 4 + line 5 + line 6 + line 7) (debts you must repay in full)**   _____

9. Divide by 36 (# of months of typical plan)   ÷ __36__

10. **Subtotal II (Line 8 divided by Line 9) (amount you pay each month to repay Line 8 in full)**   _____

11. 10% of amount in Line 3 (trustee's fee)   _____

12. **Subtotal III (Line 10 + Line 11) (minimum amount you must pay each month)**   _____

Does the amount in Line 3 equal or exceed the amount in Line 12?

If not, and the numbers aren't even close, you may have trouble proposing a viable plan. It's possible the court would approve a repayment plan up to five years, if that would help. To figure out if you'll be able to repay your debts if your plan lasted longer than three years, follow the same formula, but divide by 48 (for a four-year plan) or 60 (for a five-year plan) on Line 9. If you're still not close, then don't bother reading this book. You need an option other than Chapter 13 bankruptcy to deal with your debts.

If, on the other hand, your calculations show that the amount in Line 3 does equal or exceed the amount on Line 12—in other words, you have enough disposable income to pay your necessary expenses plus a portion of your debts over a period of three to five years—you may be a good candidate for Chapter 13 bankruptcy. Keep reading to find out more.

Icons Used in This Book

Look for these icons, which alert you to certain kinds of information.

 The "fast track" arrow alerts you that you can skip some material that isn't relevant to your case.

 This icon highlights information for married couples only.

 The caution icon warns you of potential problems.

 The briefcase icon lets you know when you need the advice of an attorney.

 This icon refers you to helpful books or other resources.

 This icon alerts you to a practical tip or good idea.

 This icon refers you to related information in another part of the book.

File Before Harsh New Law Takes Effect October 2005

As this book goes to press, legislation is speeding through Congress that would change the bankruptcy system in favor of creditors and against the interests of most debtors. The new law will go into effect 180 days after the president signs it (except for a few provisions). He is expected to sign in April of 2005, which is why we warn you to file before October. Among other things, the new law would:

- prohibit some people from filing for bankruptcy
- make the procedures more complex and therefore harder to do without a lawyer (and more expensive if you hire one)
- make it harder to come up with a manageable repayment plan, and
- limit your protection from collection efforts after filing for bankruptcy.

By the time you read this, the president will probably have signed the bill. So, to use this book—and to have the benefit of relatively friendly bankruptcy law—you must file your bankruptcy petition before six months have passed since the signing.

Even if you do file quickly, realize that the amount you can claim as a homestead exemption will have been affected as soon as the president signed the new law. For more on homestead exemptions and how they'll change, see Chapter 5 of this book.

To learn about of the status of the new legislation and details of its provisions, check for updates to this book on the Nolo website at www.nolo.com (on the home page, click "View All Products," then scroll down the list and click on this book's title, then, under "Product Details," look for "Updates"). Also check the websites of the American Bankruptcy Institute (at www.abiworld.org), the Commercial Law League of America (at www.clla.org), and King Bankruptcy Media (www.bankruptcyreformnews.com).

Should You File for Chapter 13 Bankruptcy?

f you're considering filing for Chapter 13 bankruptcy, you need to know whether or not you are eligible, what Chapter 13 bankruptcy can do for you, and what the alternatives are. The main alternative to Chapter 13 bankruptcy is Chapter 7 (liquidation) bankruptcy, discussed in Section B, below.

A. Are You Eligible for Chapter 13 Bankruptcy?

Chapter 13 bankruptcy has several important restrictions. Your first step is to see whether or not you are legally allowed to use the Chapter 13 process.

1. Businesses Can't File for Chapter 13 Bankruptcy

A business, even a sole proprietorship, cannot file for Chapter 13 bankruptcy in the name of that business. Businesses are steered toward Chapter 11 bankruptcy when they need help reorganizing their debts.

If you own a business, however, you can file for Chapter 13 bankruptcy as an individual. You can include in your Chapter 13 bankruptcy case business-related debts you are personally liable for.

There is one exception: Stockbrokers and commodity brokers cannot file a Chapter 13 bankruptcy case, even if just to include personal (nonbusiness) debts. (11 U.S.C. § 109(e).)

2. You Must Have Stable and Regular Income

You must have "stable and regular" income to be eligible for Chapter 13 bankruptcy. That doesn't mean you must earn the same amount every month. But the income must be steady—that is, likely to continue, and it must be periodic—weekly, monthly, quarterly, semi-annual, seasonal, or even annual. You can use the following income to fund a Chapter 13 plan:

- regular wages or salary
- income from self-employment
- wages from seasonal work
- commissions from sales or other work
- pension payments

- Social Security benefits (although at least one court has ruled to the contrary)
- disability or workers' compensation benefits
- unemployment benefits, strike benefits, and the like
- public benefits (welfare payments)
- child support or alimony you receive
- royalties and rents
- gifts of money from relatives or friends, and
- proceeds from selling property, especially if selling property is your primary business.

If you are married. Your income does not necessarily have to be "yours." A nonworking spouse can file alone and use money from a working spouse as a source of income. And an unemployed spouse can file jointly with a working spouse. (See Ch. 4, *Calculating Your Disposable Income*, for more details.)

3. You Must Have Disposable Income

To qualify for Chapter 13 bankruptcy, you must be able to establish a steady income source large enough to make periodic payments to the bankruptcy court over a three- to five-year period. How much you will have to pay is determined by the type of property you own and the type of debts you owe. To determine whether you have sufficient income to make payments (called your disposable income), you use a couple of official forms to calculate your net income and actual expenses. We show you how to do this in Chapter 4, *Calculating Your Disposable Income*. Once you compute your disposable income, you then must determine whether it is enough to make the level of payments required by bankruptcy law.

4. Your Debts Must Not Be Too High

You do not qualify for Chapter 13 bankruptcy if your secured debts exceed $922,975. This amount is increased every three years. A debt is secured if you stand to lose specific property if you don't make your payments to the creditor. Home loans and car loans are the most common examples of secured debts. But a debt might also be secured if a creditor—such as the IRS—has filed a lien (notice of claim) against your property.

In addition, for you to be eligible for Chapter 13 bankruptcy, your unsecured debts cannot exceed $307,675. This amount is increased every three years. An unsecured debt is any debt for which you haven't pledged collateral. The debt is not related to any particular property you possess, and failure to repay the debt will not entitle the creditor to repossess property. Most debts are unsecured, including bank credit card debts, medical and legal bills, student loans, back utility bills, and department store charges.

How to classify and total up your debts is explained in Ch. 3, *Adding Up Your Secured and Unsecured Debts*.

B. When Chapter 13 Bankruptcy Is Better Than Chapter 7

There are many reasons why people choose Chapter 13 bankruptcy—and in particular, choose Chapter 13 bankruptcy instead of Chapter 7 bankruptcy. Generally, you are probably a good candidate for Chapter 13 bankruptcy if you are in any of the following situations:

- You are behind on your mortgage or car loan, and want to make up the missed payments over time and reinstate the original agreement.
- You have a tax debt that cannot be eliminated (discharged) in Chapter 7 bankruptcy, but can be paid off over time in a Chapter 13 plan. (See Section 3, below.)
- You want to take advantage of something known as the Chapter 13 bankruptcy "superdischarge." Certain debts cannot be discharged in a Chapter 7 bankruptcy, but can be discharged in a Chapter 13 case. This means that if they are not paid in full, the balance is wiped out at the end. The debts that can be discharged under this super-discharge provision are debts incurred on the basis of fraud, debts from willful and malicious injury to another or another's property, debts from larceny, breach of trust, or embezzlement, and nonsupport debts arising out of a marital settlement agreement or divorce decree.
- You have a sincere desire to repay your debts, but you need the protection of the bankruptcy court to do so.
- You need help repaying your debts now, but need to leave open the option of filing for Chapter 7

bankruptcy in the future. This would be the case if for some reason you can't stop incurring new debt.

1. The Basics of Chapter 7 Bankruptcy

If you file for Chapter 7 bankruptcy, many of your debts will be canceled without any further repayment. In exchange, you may have to surrender some of your property (although most filers do not). The filing fee is $209 and the whole process takes about four to six months and commonly requires only one appearance before the bankruptcy trustee to answer any questions that arise from your paperwork. You can probably do it yourself, without a lawyer.

Under the bankruptcy laws, you must give up your "nonexempt" property, which can be sold to pay your creditors. As mentioned, most people who file for Chapter 7 bankruptcy, however, have no nonexempt property to turn over to the trustee. Common kinds of exempt and nonexempt property are listed below.

At the end of the Chapter 7 bankruptcy case, the debts that qualify for discharge are wiped out by the court. You no longer legally owe those creditors. You can't file for Chapter 7 bankruptcy again for six years from the date of your filing.

Exempt and Nonexempt Property at a Glance

Items you can typically keep (exempt property)

- equity in motor vehicles, to a certain value, generally in the neighborhood of $2,000–$5,000
- reasonably necessary clothing (no mink coats)
- reasonably necessary household furnishings and goods
- household appliances
- jewelry, to a certain value
- personal effects
- life insurance (cash or loan value, or proceeds), to a certain value
- employment related pensions
- equity in a residence to a certain value
- tools of a trade or profession, to a certain value
- portion of unpaid but earned wages
- public benefits (welfare, Social Security, unemployment compensation) accumulated in a bank account.

Items you may typically lose (nonexempt property)

- nonresidential real estate
- second or vacation home
- recreational vehicles
- second car or truck
- expensive musical instruments (unless you're a professional musician)
- stamp, coin, and other collections
- valuable family heirlooms
- cash, bank accounts, income tax returns, stocks, bonds, and other investments.

2. Determining Which Is Better for You

The chart on the next page shows how certain common situations are handled in Chapter 13 and Chapter 7 bankruptcies. Scan it to see how the differences affect you.

Help with Chapter 7 bankruptcy. If you decide that Chapter 7 bankruptcy is the best way to handle your debts, or you just want to learn more about it, look at *How to File for Chapter 7 Bankruptcy*, by Stephen Elias, Albin Renauer, and Robin Leonard (Nolo). That book contains detailed information on dischargeable and nondischargeable debts, exempt and nonexempt property, strategies for dealing with secured debts, along with all the forms and instructions needed to file your own Chapter 7 bankruptcy case.

3. More on Back Taxes

If a large part of your debt consists of federal or state income taxes, what would happen to your tax debts may determine whether Chapter 7 bankruptcy or Chapter 13 bankruptcy is a better choice for you.

You can discharge (wipe out) debts for income taxes in Chapter 7 bankruptcy only if *all* of the following conditions are true:

The taxes are income taxes. Taxes other than income, such as payroll taxes, Trust Fund Recovery Penalty, or fraud penalties, can never be eliminated in bankruptcy.

You did not commit fraud or willful evasion. You did not file a fraudulent tax return or otherwise willfully attempt to evade paying taxes, such as using a false Social Security number on your tax return.

You pass the three-year rule. The tax return for the taxes you wish to discharge was originally due at least three years before you file for bankruptcy. This usually means April 15 of the year the return was due. But, if you filed a request for an extension, then it might mean August 15 or October 15 of that year. If the 15th fell on a Saturday or Sunday, your return wasn't due until the following Monday. That is the date you start counting from.

You pass the two-year rule. You actually filed the tax return for the taxes that you wish to discharge at least two years before filing the bankruptcy. Having the taxing agency file a substitute return for you doesn't count unless you agreed to and signed the substitute return. If you don't file a tax return, you can never discharge the taxes you owe for that year in bankruptcy. You can, however, include the taxes in a Chapter 13 repayment plan.

You pass the 240-day rule. The income tax debt was assessed by the taxing agency at least 240 days before you file your bankruptcy petition, or has not yet been assessed.

If any of the following situations apply to you, you will have to add time to the three-year, two-year, or 240-day rules for your debts to qualify for discharge in bankruptcy.

Comparing Chapter 13 and Chapter 7 Bankruptcy

What happens if...	Chapter 13	Chapter 7
You're behind on your mortgage or car loan.	You can repay the arrears through your plan, over three to five years, and keep the house or car.	You'll probably have to either give the house or car back to the creditor or arrange to pay its full value during your bankruptcy case.
You owe back taxes to the IRS.	The result depends on your circumstances. See Section B3, above.	The result depends on your circumstances. See Section B3, above.
You have valuable nonexempt property. (See Section B1, above.)	You keep all of the property.	You must give the nonexempt property up or pay the trustee its fair market value, or, if the trustee agrees, swap exempt property of equal value for it.
You have codebtors on personal (non-business) loans.	The creditor may not seek payment from your codebtor for the duration of your case.	The creditor will go after your codebtor for payment.
You received a bankruptcy discharge within the previous six years.	No problem; you can file anytime.	You can't file Chapter 7 unless the recent bankruptcy was a Chapter 13 case, and you repaid at least 70% of your debts
You want to keep secured property by paying the creditor its value	You can pay (with interest) over time through your plan.	You usually must pay it in a lump sum or in two or three payments.
Your disposable income is sufficient to fund a Chapter 13 plan.		The bankruptcy court might throw out your case or pressure you to convert it to Chapter 13.
You owe debts for: • **back or prospective child support or alimony** • **student loans, unless repayment would cause you severe hardship** • **court-ordered restitution or criminal fines** • **taxes less than three years past due, or filed less than two years previously, or assessed less than 240 days previously** • **debts for personal injuries arising from intoxicated driving.**	These debts must be paid in full in your Chapter 13 repayment plan or you will owe the balance at the end of your bankruptcy.	These debts cannot be erased in Chapter 7 bankruptcy.
You owe nonsupport debts under a property settlement, agreement, or divorce decree.	If you do not pay them in full during your Chapter 13 bankruptcy, the balance is wiped out at the end under Chapter 13 bankruptcy's "superdischarge."	If your ex-spouse or another creditor objects, these debts are not discharged unless you prove to the court that: • you will be unable to pay these debts after your bankruptcy case, or • the benefit you will get by discharging the debts will outweigh any detriment to your ex-spouse.
You have debts due to: • **larceny (theft), breach of trust, or embezzlement** • **fraud, or** • **willful and malicious injury to another or another's property.**	If you do not pay them in full during your Chapter 13 case, the balance is wiped out at the end under the supercharge.	These debts are not dischargeable if the creditor files a formal complaint against you in court and proves his or her case to the judge's satisfaction.

- You submitted an Offer in Compromise seeking to settle with the IRS for pennies on the dollar. An Offer in Compromise delays the 240-day rule by the period from the time from when the Offer is made until the IRS rejects it or you withdraw it, plus 30 days.
- You obtained a Taxpayer Assistance Order from an IRS Taxpayer Advocate. If an Order was issued preventing the IRS from collecting, the bankruptcy court may require that you add the time collection was suspended to the three-year, two-year, and 240-day requirements. Not all courts require this, however.
- You filed a previous bankruptcy case. All three time periods—three years, two years, and 240 days—stopped running while you were in the prior bankruptcy case. You must add the length of your case plus six months to all three.

Effect of Federal Tax Lien

If your taxes qualify for discharge in a Chapter 7 bankruptcy case, your victory may be bittersweet. This is because prior recorded tax liens are not affected by your filing. A Chapter 7 bankruptcy will wipe out only your personal obligation to pay the debt. Any lien recorded before you file for bankruptcy remains. After your bankruptcy, the IRS can seize any property you owned at the time the bankruptcy was filed. But this doesn't mean that after your bankruptcy case is over the IRS will come and grab your property. Postbankruptcy, the IRS tends to seize only real estate and retirement accounts or pensions. And even then, IRS seizures generally take place only when a taxpayer has made no efforts to otherwise resolve the problem. Furthermore, IRS collectors must obtain approval from their supervisors before seizing a house or pension. The IRS is very concerned about negative publicity.

If you are considering bankruptcy, call the taxing agency (800-829-1040 for the IRS) to obtain a plain English transcript, known as a literal transcript or IMF printout, for each tax year on which you might owe. This free computer printout lists important tax dates—

when the returns were filed, when the taxes were assessed, and the dates of any tolling or extending events. Make sure you check the dates from the IRS transcript before filing bankruptcy.

C. Other Alternatives

In some situations, filing for bankruptcy is the only sensible remedy for debt problems. In many others, however, another course of action makes better sense. This section outlines some alternatives.

1. Do Nothing

Surprisingly, the best approach for some people deeply in debt is to take no action at all. If you're living simply, with little income and property, and look forward to a similar life in the future, you may be what's known as "judgment proof." This means that anyone who sues you and wins won't be able to collect, simply because you don't have anything they can legally take. A creditor can't take away such essentials as basic clothing, ordinary household furnishings, personal effects, food, Social Security, unemployment benefits, public assistance, or 75% of your wages (50% if the debt is for child support).

If your creditors know it's unlikely they could collect a judgment, they probably won't sue you. Instead, they'll simply write off your debt and treat it as a deductible business loss for income tax purposes. In several years (usually between six and ten) it will become legally uncollectible under the state law called the statute of limitations.

Stopping Bill Collector Abuse and Harassment

You don't need to file for bankruptcy just to get annoying collection agencies off your back. Federal law forbids them from threatening you, lying about what they can do to you, or invading your privacy. Under this law, you can also legally force collection agencies to stop phoning or writing you simply by demanding that they stop, even if you owe them a bundle and can't pay a cent. (The Fair Debt Collections Practices Act, 15 U.S.C. § 1692 and following.)

2. Negotiate With Your Creditors

If you have some income, or you have assets you're willing to sell, you may be a lot better off negotiating with your creditors than filing for bankruptcy. Negotiation may simply buy you some time to get back on your feet, or you and your creditors may agree on a complete settlement of your debts for less than you owe. In particular, if you are behind on a mortgage issued by Fannie Mae or Freddie Mac, your lender is encouraged to try to work out an arrangement to avoid having to foreclose or your having to file for bankruptcy.

Dealing with creditors. How to negotiate with creditors and collection agencies, and how to stop bill collector abuse, are covered in detail in *Solve Your Money Troubles: Legal Strategies to Cope With Your Debts*, by Robin Leonard (Nolo). That book covers how to deal with creditors when you owe money on credit cards, student loans, mortgage loans, car loans, child support and alimony, among other debts.

3. Get Outside Help to Design a Repayment Plan

Many people can't do a good job of negotiating with their creditors or with collection agencies. Inside, they feel that the creditors and collectors are right to insist on full payment. Or the creditors and collectors are so hard-nosed or just plain irrational that the process is too unpleasant to stomach.

If you don't want to negotiate on your own, you can seek help from a nonprofit credit or debt counseling agency. These agencies can work with you to help you repay your debts and improve your financial picture.

To use a credit or debt counseling agency to help you pay your debts, you must have some disposable income. A counselor contacts your creditors to let them know that you've sought assistance and need more time to pay. Based on your income and debts, the counselor, with your creditors, decides on how much you pay. You then make one payment each month to the counseling agency, which in turn pays your creditors. The agency asks the creditors to return a small percentage of the money received to the agency office to fund its work. This arrangement is generally referred to as a debt management program.

Some creditors will make overtures to help you when you're on a debt management program. For example, Citicorp waives minimum payment and late charges—and may freeze interest assessments—for customers undergoing credit counseling. But few creditors will make interest concessions, such as waiving a portion of the accumulated interest to help you repay the principal. More likely, you'll get late fees dropped and the opportunity to reinstate your credit if you successfully complete a debt management program.

The combination of high consumer debt and easy access to information (the Internet) has led to an explosion in the number of credit and debt counseling agencies ready to offer you help. Some provide limited services, such as budgeting and debt repayment, while others offer a range of services, from debt counseling to financial planning.

Participating in a credit or debt counseling agency's debt management program is a little bit like filing for Chapter 13 bankruptcy. Working with a credit or debt counseling agency has one advantage: no bankruptcy will appear on your credit record.

But a debt management program also has two disadvantages when compared to Chapter 13 bankruptcy. First, if you miss a payment, Chapter 13 protects you from creditors who would start collection actions. A debt management program has no such protection and any one creditor can pull the plug on your plan. Also, a debt management program plan usually requires that your debts be paid in full. In Chapter 13 bankruptcy, you often pay only a small fraction of your unsecured debts.

Critics of credit and debt counseling agencies point out that they get most of their funding from creditors. (Some offices also receive grants from private agencies such as the United Way and federal agencies including the Department of Housing and Urban Development.) Nevertheless, critics claim that counselors cannot be objective in counseling debtors to file for bankruptcy if they know the office won't receive any funds.

In response to this and other consumer concerns, credit and debt counseling agencies accredited by the National Foundation for Consumer Credit (the majority of agencies are) reached an agreement with the Federal Trade Commission to disclose the following to consumers:

- that creditors fund a large portion of the cost of their operations

- that the credit agency must balance the ability of the debtor to make payments with the requirements of the creditors that fund the office, and
- a reliable estimate of how long it will take a debtor to repay his or her debts under a debt management program.

a. Consumer Credit Counseling Service

Consumer Credit Counseling Service (CCCS) is the oldest credit or debt counseling agency in the country. Actually, CCCS isn't one agency. CCCS is the primary operating name of many credit and debt counseling agencies affiliated with the National Foundation for Consumer Credit.

In most CCCS offices, the primary services offered are the debt management program and budgeting. A few offices have additional services, such as helping you save money toward buying a house or reviewing your credit report. CCCS may charge you a minimal fee for its services. If you can't afford the fee, CCCS will waive it.

CCCS has more than 1,100 offices, located in every state. Look in the phone book to find the one nearest you, visit its website at www.nfcc.org, or contact the main office at 801 Roeder Road, Suite 900, Silver Spring, MD 20910, 800-388-2227 (voice).

b. Myvesta.org

Myvesta.org (formerly Debt Counselors of America) offers budgeting and debt management programs, like other debt and credit counseling agencies. But unlike most other agencies, Myvesta has a financial planning department with Certified Financial Planners and a Crisis Relief Team to assist consumers who are turned

---

Buyer Beward: Abuses in the Credit Counseling Industry

In the past several years, investigations by the IRS, Federal Trade Commission ("FTC"), and U.S. Senate have documented widespread abuses in the credit counseling field, by companies such as AmeriDebt (including the Ballenger Group, Debticated, Debtscape, DebtWorks, CrediCure, and many others), Amerix (including Care One, Genesis, American Financial Solutions, Clarion, and others), and Cambridge (Cambridge-Brighton, Debt Relief Clearinghouse, Brighton Credit, and others). Common abuses include charging high consumer fees, arranging lucrative contracts for "back-office" processing, and taking advantage of vulnerable clients in a host of other ways.

Senator Carl Levin (D-Mich.), noted that, ". . . one key abuse involves debtors being charged excessive start-up and monthly fees by a nonprofit credit counseling agency to set up and administer their debt management plans. For example, instead of start-up and monthly fees of $23 and $14, the average charged in 2002 by credit counseling agencies that are members of the reputable National Foundation for Credit Coun-

seling (NFCC), the investigation found some agencies charging hundreds or even thousands of dollars per debtor. Consumers have also complained of being misled about their initial fee, believing it would go to their creditors when, instead, the money was kept by the CCA. The investigation also found that some agencies were providing little or no individualized counseling to their clients, instead simply directing them to standardized debt management plans."

For further information and transcripts on this critical investigation, go online to www.access.gpo.gov/congress/senate/senate12sh108.html and click on *S. Hrg. 108-545 — Profiteering in a Non-Profit Industry: Abusive Practices in Credit Counseling, March 24, 2004.*

Other excellent resources can be found at:
- The Consumer Federation of America (www.consumerfed.org/040903ccreport.html)
- The National Consumer Law Center (www.nclc.org/initiatives/credit_counseling) offering downloadable brochures on how to select a reputable credit counseling agency.

away by other credit or debt counseling agencies or who have very complex problems. Myvesta is also the first credit or debt counseling agency that is a registered investment advisor. Each week, Myvesta broadcasts a live call-in radio show over its Internet site, where you can also find numerous publications on a range of money issues.

Myvesta has only one office because it offers its services via phone, email, and the Internet. You can contact Myvesta at 800-680-3328 (voice), info@ myvesta.org (email), or www.myvesta.org.

c. Other Credit and Debt Counseling Agencies

Surf the Internet and you'll find many other credit and debt counseling agencies offering a variety of services. Be sure to ask about their services before signing up.

Two agencies with national recognition are as follows:

Money Management International
9009 West Loop South, Suite 700
Houston, TX 77096
866-889-9347
www.mmintl.org

MMI provides credit counseling, debt management, and economic education information by telephone, email, fax, and mail, 24 hours a day. MMI's Internet site includes a debt counseling application and message board where you can send your money questions to "Letters to Susan and Co."

The Center for Debt Management
119 Camp Sargent Road
Merrimack, NH 03054
Admin@Center4DebtManagement.com
www.center4debtmanagement.com

CDM offers several services on its Internet site:
- debt counseling—answers to your questions
- debt management—repayment plan
- publications—topics include bankruptcy, debt consolidation, credit cards, credit bureaus, credit repair, collection agencies, student loans, financial aid, government programs, law, and more
- words of wisdom—words of inspirations and noteworthy quotations analogous to debt, and

- consumer information—consumer alerts and links to consumer protection agencies and other sites of interest.

4. File for "Chapter 20" (7 + 13) Bankruptcy

Chapter 20 isn't a specific section of the Bankruptcy Code. Instead, it's a shorthand way of referring to the practice of filing a Chapter 7 bankruptcy to eliminate unsecured dischargeable debts, and then immediately following up with a Chapter 13 bankruptcy to pay off the remaining debts. This is an excellent strategy for many people, especially if your debts are so high that you don't initially qualify for Chapter 13 bankruptcy or can't come up with a feasible repayment plan.

5. File for Chapter 11 Bankruptcy

Chapter 11 bankruptcy is the type of bankruptcy used by financially struggling businesses—such as Macy's— to reorganize their affairs. It is also available to individuals. Individuals who consider Chapter 11 bankruptcy usually have debts in excess of the Chapter 13 bankruptcy limits, $307,675 of unsecured debts or $922,975 of secured debts, or substantial nonexempt assets, such as several pieces of real estate.

The initial filing fee is currently $830, compared to $209 for Chapter 7 or $194 for Chapter 13 bankruptcy. In addition, you must pay a quarterly fee that is a percentage of your debts (often several hundreds or thousands of dollars) until your reorganization plan is approved or dismissed, or your case is converted to Chapter 7 bankruptcy. Plus, most attorneys require a minimum $7,500 retainer fee to handle a Chapter 11 bankruptcy case. If you want to read more on the pitfalls inherent in this kind of bankruptcy, see *A Feast for Lawyers*, by Sol Stein (M. Evans & Co., Inc.).

Help from a lawyer. You'll need a lawyer to file for Chapter 11 bankruptcy. A Chapter 11 bankruptcy often turns into a long, expensive mess, and many Chapter 11 filings end up being converted to Chapter 7 bankruptcy.

Chapter 11 bankruptcy also offers a fast-track bankruptcy for small businesses with debts up to $2 million. (11 U.S.C. § 1121(e).) However, you will still need an attorney to use the fast-track procedure.

6. Farmers Should Consider Chapter 12 Bankruptcy

Chapter 12 bankruptcy is almost identical to Chapter 13 bankruptcy. To be eligible for Chapter 12 bankruptcy, however, at least 80% of your debts must arise from the operation of a family farm.

Unfortunately, Chapter 12 bankruptcy has recently—and intermittently—been unavailable due to maneuvering going on in Congress.

 Help from a lawyer. See a lawyer if you want to file for Chapter 12 bankruptcy.

D. Converting From Chapter 7 Bankruptcy to Chapter 13 Bankruptcy

Even if you've already filed for Chapter 7 bankruptcy, you can switch to Chapter 13 bankruptcy if you decide it would be better. For example, you might discover that a tax debt you thought you could discharge in a Chapter 7 bankruptcy can't be discharged, but can be included in a Chapter 13 repayment plan.

As a general rule, you have an absolute right to convert a Chapter 7 bankruptcy case into a Chapter 13 bankruptcy case at any time, as long as you did not previously convert this case to a Chapter 13 from Chapter 7. However, you must be eligible to file for Chapter 13 and to prepare a workable repayment plan. You do have to file a written request (called a motion) with the bankruptcy court, send a copy of your motion to each of your creditors, and obtain an order from the court.

Resources for converting from Chapter 7 to 13. To see what a motion to convert your case to Chapter 13 bankruptcy looks like, consult a bankruptcy forms book at a law library. Also, *Consumer Bankruptcy Law and Practice*, written and published by the National Consumer Law Center, contains sample motion forms. Check your local law library for this book or contact the publisher at 617-523-8010 or www.consumerlaw.org.

One major issue that immediately comes up when you convert to Chapter 13 bankruptcy is the requirement that your proposed Chapter 13 plan pay your unsecured creditors as much as they would have received had you stayed in Chapter 7 bankruptcy. Conversions to Chapter 13 often occur when the Chapter 7 trustee discovers valuable assets that are nonexempt. In response, these debtors convert to Chapter 13, which doesn't require surrender of nonexempt property. However, as mentioned, the debtor must account for those assets in the level of payments they propose in their plan.

Another issue that can arise is whether you are eligible for Chapter 13. Your debts must not exceed the limits placed on secured and unsecured debts for Chapter 13 filers.

Courts are split as to whether your eligibility for Chapter 13 bankruptcy is based on your financial circumstances at the time you filed your Chapter 7 bankruptcy or at the time you seek to convert. For most people, it doesn't matter. But it may matter to you. For example, if you had no regular income when you filed for Chapter 7 bankruptcy, you may not be allowed to convert to Chapter 13 bankruptcy if your court bases eligibility on circumstances at the time you filed your Chapter 7 bankruptcy case. In that situation, the court would probably require you to dismiss your Chapter 7 case and refile a Chapter 13 case. You would have to pay a $194 filing fee.

If the court does approve your motion to convert, you must file your Chapter 13 repayment plan within 15 days and start making payments under the plan within 30 days after you file it. ■

An Overview of Chapter 13 Bankruptcy

If you've decided that Chapter 13 bankruptcy seems to be the best solution to your debt problems, you've probably got a lot of questions. How much will I have to pay every month? How long will I have to make payments? When I'm done with my Chapter 13 plan, will I still owe any of my creditors?

This chapter can give you some preliminary answers to these and other questions.

A. The Chapter 13 Process

In Chapter 13 bankruptcy, you must fill out a packet of forms listing what you own, earn, owe, and spend. You file these papers with the bankruptcy court, along with an additional form called the Chapter 13 repayment plan.

The forms you file in a Chapter 13 case are mostly the same as those you use in a Chapter 7 case. The exceptions are that you don't use a Statement of Intention in a Chapter 13 case, and you don't prepare a repayment plan in a Chapter 7 case.

1. The Chapter 13 Repayment Plan

This form is the most important paper in your entire Chapter 13 bankruptcy case. It describes in detail how (and how much) you will repay on every one of your debts. There is no official form for the plan, but many courts have designed their own forms. (Drafting your plan is the subject of Ch. 7, *Writing Your Chapter 13 Bankruptcy Plan*.)

2. When You Can File a Chapter 13 Bankruptcy

You can file for Chapter 13 bankruptcy at any time, even if you just received a Chapter 7 bankruptcy discharge or just completed another Chapter 13 repayment plan. If you file soon after completing another Chapter 13 case, however, you'll be required to pay back a larger percentage of your debts. And a court may reject a subsequent filing if it feels you are not filing for Chapter 13 bankruptcy in good faith. (Good faith is covered in Ch. 9, *After You File Your Case*.)

3. Plan Payments

You must begin making payments under your Chapter 13 plan within 30 days after you file it with the bankruptcy court. Usually, you make payments directly to the bankruptcy trustee, the person appointed by the court to oversee your case. Once your plan is confirmed, the trustee will distribute the money to your creditors. If you have a regular job with regular income, the bankruptcy court may order that your monthly payments be automatically deducted from your wages and sent directly to the bankruptcy court. You must also make the regular payments on your secured debts, such as a car loan or mortgage, although, in many districts, car loans are paid through the plan. (For more information on making plan payments, see Ch. 10, *After Your Plan Is Approved*.)

4. How Much You Must Pay

Typically, you must continue to make regular payments for any *secured* debts, and reduced payments on your *unsecured* debts. (Secured and unsecured debts are defined in Ch. 3, *Adding Up Your Secured and Unsecured Debts*, Section A4.) The exact "reduced" amount you must pay unsecured creditors is based on many calculations that we cover, step-by-step, in Chs. 3, 4, and 5, and in Section B below.) Most repayment plans last three years. After that, any remaining unpaid balance on the unsecured debts is wiped out (discharged) unless the debt is not dischargeable by law. In some cases, the court will approve a plan in excess of three years, up to five years.

5. If You Change Your Mind

You can dismiss your Chapter 13 case at any time. You may want to do this to refile your case if you incur a large debt after you file but before your plan is approved by the bankruptcy court. If you dismiss and refile, you can include the new debt in your plan. (You cannot refile, however, if within the previous 180 days the court dismissed your bankruptcy case for willfully failing to follow a court order or if you voluntarily dismissed your case after a creditor asked the court to remove the automatic stay.)

6. If You Can't Make Plan Payments

If for some reason you cannot finish a Chapter 13 repayment plan—for example, you lose your job six months into the plan and can't keep up the payments—the trustee may modify your plan. The trustee may give you a grace period if the problem looks temporary, reduce your total monthly payments, or extend the re-payment period. If it's clear that there's no way you'll be able to complete the plan because of circumstances beyond your control, the court might let you discharge your debts on the basis of hardship. Examples of hardship would be a sudden plant closing in a one-factory town or a debilitating illness.

If the bankruptcy court won't let you modify your plan or give you a hardship discharge, you have the right to:

- convert to a Chapter 7 bankruptcy, unless you received a Chapter 7 bankruptcy discharge within the previous six years, or
- have the bankruptcy court dismiss your Chapter 13 bankruptcy case. You would still owe your debts. However, any payments you made during your plan would be deducted. On the flip side, your creditors will add on interest they did not charge while your Chapter 13 case was pending.

(Modification, hardship discharge, conversion to Chapter 7 bankruptcy, and dismissal of your case are all covered in Ch. 10, *After Your Plan Is Approved.*)

Chapter 13 Bankruptcy Checklist

In every Chapter 13 case, you will need to do the steps set out below: This book will guide you through the process from start to finish.

1. Evaluate your alternatives and decide whether or not Chapter 13 bankruptcy is right for you. (Ch. 1)
2. Add up your debts. (Ch. 3)
3. Calculate your income. (Ch. 4)
4. Calculate the value of your property. (Ch. 5)
5. Fill out the bankruptcy forms and map out a repayment plan. (Chs. 6 and 7)
6. File your forms and plan with the bankruptcy court. (Ch. 8)
7. Attend two hearings. (Ch. 9)
8. Make the payments under your plan and go back to court if any problems arise during your case. (Ch. 10)
9. Obtain your bankruptcy discharge (congratulations!). (Ch. 11)

B. How Much You'll Have to Repay Through the Plan

The total amount you'll have to repay your creditors over the length of your Chapter 13 case depends on a number of factors, including the type of debts you owe and the philosophy of the bankruptcy judges in your area. You can get a rough idea by filling out Worksheet 1, below. The series of worksheets in Chs. 3, 4, and 5 help you calculate the number for this worksheet.

Line 1. Add up the total value of your "nonexempt" property. This calculation is explained in Worksheet 8 of Ch. 5, *Calculating the Value of Your Nonexempt Property.* To get a rough idea, look at the exemption list for your state in Appendix 1. All property you own that is *not* on that list is considered nonexempt.

Your unsecured creditors must receive at least the value of your nonexempt property. Keep in mind that this amount is the minimum, by law, that you must pay. The court will require you to pay more if:

- Any of your unsecured debts are "priority debts" —such as back taxes or child support—which must be repaid in full.

- Your particular court requires debtors to pay back a high percentage of unsecured debts. If you have little nonexempt property, the amount you calculated will be very low. Your creditors might object to your plan on the ground that you have not proposed it in good faith. There is huge regional variation on this issue, however. Some courts approve Chapter 13 plans in which unsecured creditors receive nothing. Other courts rarely approve Chapter 13 plans unless unsecured creditors will receive 100% of what they are owed. Most courts—and Chapter 13 plans—fall somewhere in between. (See Ch. 7, *Writing Your Chapter 13 Bankruptcy Plan.*)

Lines 2 and 3. Add the amount of missed payments you owe to any secured creditors, such as mortgage or car lenders, whose property you want to keep. In Chapter 13 bankruptcy, you have to make up all the missed payments to keep the property.

Line 4. Some courts require that you add an amount equal to at least three year's worth of interest on the amount in Step 1. There are several ways to figure out the rate you might have to pay; for now, leave this blank or use 10%. This money may be required to compensate creditors for the fact that they're getting their money over a period of years instead of all at once.

Lines 5 and 6. Add the trustee's fee—3% to 10% of each payment you make. (See Section F2 below.)

Line 7. Total all the figures you've listed.

C. Your Monthly Payments

Your disposable income is the amount left over when you deduct your necessary monthly living expenses from your total monthly income. (You'll calculate this amount precisely in Ch. 4.) Bankruptcy law requires that you pay all your "disposable income" into your Chapter 13 plan for a minimum of 36 months.

If making 36 monthly disposable income payments will not be enough to repay the minimum amount required by the court (see Section B, above), you will have to do one of the following:

- Ask the court to approve a plan that lasts more than 36 months. The court cannot authorize a plan that lasts more than 60 months (five years), however.

Worksheet 1: How Much Will You Have to Repay?

1. Total value of your nonexempt property (Worksheet 8), plus any increase for priority debts or to pay back a higher percentage	$ 37,754
2. Amount overdue to mortgage lender (Worksheet 2); add interest if loan was obtained before October 20, 1994	$ 8,075
3. Amount overdue to other secured creditors (Worksheets 2 and 3), or the value of the collateral, plus interest	$ 966
4. Compensation for lost interest on payments on unsecured debts	$ 0
5. Subtotal of lines 1 through 4	$ 46,795
6. Trustee's fee (3% to 10% of line 5)	$ 4,680
7. Minimum Amount You Will Pay Into Your Plan	$ 51,475

- Increase your monthly disposable income. When you submit your repayment plan to the bankruptcy court for approval, the court will look at the budget you used to come up with your disposable income. If there isn't enough to pay your creditors, you will have to decrease your expenses in order to increase the money available to pay into your plan.
- Sell some property and use the money to repay enough debt to bring you within the disposable income level you will need to get your Chapter 13 plan confirmed. For instance, by selling property worth $50,000, you can reduce the level of your required disposable income by over $1,300 a month.

D. How Much You'll Still Owe When Your Case Is Over

It is possible that you will still owe money to some of your creditors when your Chapter 13 bankruptcy case is over. Certain unsecured debts cannot be eliminated in bankruptcy—these are called nondischargeable debts. In Chapter 13 bankruptcy, you have two choices in how to handle nondischargeable debts:

- file an action asking the court to rule that in your case the debt is dischargeable (mainly student loans)
- pay them in full through your plan (which may increase the amount you calculated in Section B, above), or
- pay only a portion of them during your case and owe a balance at the end; to keep your creditors from tacking on interest abated during your Chapter 13, you could file a second Chapter 13 case to pay off the balance.

Ch. 7, *Writing Your Chapter 13 Bankruptcy Plan*, Section J, explains how to go about paying nondischargeable debts in your Chapter 13 plan.

The following debts are usually nondischargeable in Chapter 13 bankruptcy.

1. Child Support and Alimony

Alimony and child support debts generally aren't dischargeable. They may be however, if:

- You owe the debt under a state's general support law.
- You're paying the debt under a voluntary agreement between unmarried people—unless, before the bankruptcy case is filed, the recipient sues you and obtains a court judgment.
- You owe the support to someone other than your spouse, ex-spouse, or child, unless it's owed to the welfare department. Be aware, however, that bankruptcy courts are increasingly characterizing debts to people other than parents, but for the benefit of children—such as attorney's fees or hospital delivery costs—as nondischargeable child support. (See *In re Kline*, 65 F.3d 749 (8th Cir. 1995);) *In re Jones*, 9 F.3d 878 (10th Cir. 1993); *In re Seibert*, 914 F.2d 102 (7th Cir. 1990).)

If a court issued an order setting the amount of alimony or child support, or the welfare department is trying to collect child support from you, the debt is clearly nondischargeable. Some other debts may also be considered nondischargeable child support or alimony. These are usually marital debts—debts a spouse was ordered to pay when the couple divorced—which are really in lieu of support. Obligations that are generally considered support and aren't dischargeable include debts that:

- are paid to a spouse who is maintaining the primary residence of the children while there is a serious imbalance of incomes
- terminate on the death or remarriage of the recipient spouse
- depend on the future income of either spouse, or
- are paid in installments over a substantial period of time. (*In re Goin*, 808 F.2d 1391 (10th Cir. 1987); *In re Calhoun*, 715 F.2d 1103 10 Bankr. Ct. Dec. 1402 (6th Cir. 1983).)

2. Student Loans

In general, student loans are nondischargeable, even if you just cosigned the loan or are a parent who took out a PLUS (Parental Loans for Students) loan. Bankruptcy courts have little sympathy for debtors who want to eliminate their student loans.

In only three situations might a judge let you discharge a student loan:

- Repayment would cause you undue hardship. The court may discharge your student loans if you meet all of the following conditions: (1) based on your current income and expenses, you cannot maintain a minimal standard of living and repay the loan; (2) additional circumstances indicate that your current financial condition is likely to continue for a significant portion of the repayment period; and (3) you've made a good faith effort to pay the debt. Courts rarely discharge student loans on hardship grounds. And sometimes, if the court finds that it would be a hardship to repay the entire debt, the court only discharges a portion of the loan. (Some attorneys believe this is not authorized by the Bankruptcy Code.) For an exhaustive interpretation of the "additional circumstances" requirement in the second factor, see *Nys v. Educational Credit Management Corporation*, (9th Cir. BAP, 2004).
- Your loans are connected to neither the government nor a nonprofit institution. Under the Bankruptcy Code, loans made, insured, or guaranteed by the government, or funded in whole or in part by the government or a nonprofit institution, cannot be discharged in bankruptcy. If you have private loans, you might be able to discharge them if you can show that no nonprofit institution was connected to them. Many private loans are initially made by for-profit institutions, but are sold to nonprofit organizations that collect and process payments and pursue debtors in default. In that situation, the loans would not be dischargeable.
- The debt did not provide you with an educational benefit. This is difficult to prove. But some former students have been allowed to discharge their debt when a school has allowed the debtor to attend classes without signing a promissory note or making tuition payments. The reasoning is that the school did not extend credit and therefore no debt for an educational benefit was created.

3. Intoxicated Driving Debts

You cannot discharge debts resulting from the death of, or personal injury to, someone because you drove while intoxicated by alcohol or drugs. Even if you are sued and the judge or jury finds you liable but doesn't specifically find that you were intoxicated, the bankruptcy court can nevertheless declare the judgment against you nondischargeable if the creditor convinces the court that you were in fact intoxicated. You can, however, discharge debts for property damage resulting from your intoxicated driving.

4. Restitution or Criminal Fine

A bankruptcy court will not let you discharge a criminal fine imposed upon you for violating a law, or a debt for restitution included in a sentence you received after being convicted of committing a crime. Restitution is the payment you are ordered to make to a victim.

E. Filing With Your Spouse

A married person can file for Chapter 13 alone or with a spouse. It rarely makes sense, however, for only one spouse to file. The filing spouse must list the income, expenses, and property of both spouses, and the bankruptcy case will have an impact on both spouses.

However, there are two situations in which you should consider filing Chapter 13 bankruptcy alone:

1. If you are separated from your spouse, have divided your property, agreed to pay the jointly incurred marital debts, and have otherwise ended your financial entanglements (other than paying or receiving alimony or child support).
2. If you meet the following three criteria:
   a. You and your spouse own property together in one of the following states:

   East: Delaware, Massachusetts, Maryland, North Carolina, Pennsylvania, Rhode Island, Vermont, Virginia

   Midwest: Illinois, Indiana, Michigan, Missouri, Ohio

   South: Florida, North Carolina, Tennessee

   West: Hawaii, Wyoming.

b. You and your spouse own this property as "tenants by the entirety" (if you're not sure, see Ch. 5, Section A6).

c. All of your debts are in your name alone—with no mention of your spouse.

If you think you meet all three criteria (a, b, and c), be sure to read Section A6 of Ch. 5, *Calculating the Value of Your Nonexempt Property*. Read and understand this material before you decide whether to file alone or jointly. If you are still not sure, you may need to consult an experienced, local bankruptcy attorney. (See Ch. 12, *Help Beyond the Book*.)

F. The Chapter 13 Trustee

In every Chapter 13 bankruptcy case, the court appoints a person called the Chapter 13 trustee to oversee the case. In most bankruptcy court districts, the same person serves as the trustee in all Chapter 13 cases. In large districts, however, such as Los Angeles, the court has more than one Chapter 13 trustee. The trustee may be a local bankruptcy attorney, very knowledgeable about Chapter 13 bankruptcy generally and the local court's rules and procedures specifically. In some courts, trustees are not attorneys, but are businesspeople with specialized knowledge of finances or personal bankruptcy.

1. Working With the Chapter 13 Trustee

Just a few days after you file your bankruptcy papers, you'll get a letter telling you the name, address, and phone number of the trustee. The trustee will work very closely with you throughout your case.

If, in the course of following your Chapter 13 plans, you have trouble making your payments, the trustee may suggest ways for you to modify your plan, give you a temporary reprieve, or take other steps to help you get back on track. The trustee doesn't do this simply to be nice, although many trustees genuinely want to help debtors. The trustee is doing this because the trustee's fee is based on the amount of money you send the trustee to pay your creditors.

2. Paying the Chapter 13 Trustee's Fees

The trustee's fee can range anywhere from 3% to 10% of the payments you make. In bankruptcy districts with a high number of Chapter 13 cases (this includes various districts in Alabama, Georgia, Louisiana, North Carolina, Tennessee, and Texas, among others), the percentage is often less than 10% because a lot of money flows through the court. In jurisdictions with few Chapter 13 cases (most of the rest of the country), trustees usually charge the full 10%.

As a general rule, the trustee is paid through the plan. Let's say, for example, that you propose paying your creditors $100 each month and the trustee will take 10% as compensation. If the fee is based on the amount the trustee pays to your creditors, then you'll have to pay $110 so that the trustee can keep 10% of $100. Whenever you calculate the amount you'll have to pay in your Chapter 13 plan, remember to include the trustee's fee!

G. Going to Court

A Chapter 13 bankruptcy case requires at least two formal appearances. These appearances aren't anything like full-blown trials; they're usually brief hearings where you appear before the trustee or judge for just a few minutes.

Here are the most common types of appearances; they are covered in more detail in Ch. 9, *After You File Your Case*, and Ch. 10, *After Your Plan Is Approved*.

- **The meeting of the creditors** is the first appearance you (and your spouse, if you filed together) must make. It's fairly routine and usually something you can handle easily without an attorney. Despite its name, usually only a few creditors, if any, show up. The judge isn't present. The trustee and any creditors who come will ask you about information in the bankruptcy papers you filed. Sometimes, creditors may show up and try to negotiate with you about any objections they have to your plan.

- **The confirmation hearing** is the hearing at which the bankruptcy judge approves or rejects your proposed repayment plan. Often, the trustee indicates to the judge whether or not the plan seems feasible, and the judge defers to the trustee's opinion. The judge may ask a few questions, however. Your creditors may raise many objections—including that you've gotten farther behind on your mortgage, car payment, or other secured debts since filing your bankruptcy papers, or that your plan isn't feasible, wasn't proposed in good faith, or discriminates against certain creditors. The judge will rule on these objections and may require you to change your repayment plan. Courts commonly hold the confirmation hearing immediately after the meeting of the creditors.

- **A valuation hearing** may be requested by a creditor (or you) to determine the value of an item of collateral. This frequently comes up when you claim that the collateral (such as a car) is worth less than you owe and you want to pay only its value through your plan. If you or a creditor request a valuation hearing, your confirmation hearing will be postponed or the court will hold the valuation hearing immediately before the confirmation hearing.

- **A relief from stay hearing** may be requested by a creditor who wants to pursue collection efforts against you. This could come up, for example, if you fall farther behind on your mortgage or car payments after you file your bankruptcy papers and your proposed plan doesn't provide for repayment of the additional arrearage.

- **The discharge hearing** takes place at the end of your case. Few courts require you to come to court for a discharge hearing. You'll probably just receive a letter from the court letting you know that your case is over and that any balance remaining on your dischargeable debts has been discharged. ■

3

Adding Up Your Secured and Unsecured Debts

Converting from Chapter 7 bankruptcy. If you originally filed for Chapter 7 bankruptcy and are now converting your case to Chapter 13 bankruptcy, you need only to file a Chapter 13 plan. Skip ahead to Ch. 7, *Writing Your Chapter 13 Bankruptcy Plan*.

If you think you want to file for Chapter 13 bankruptcy, you need to add up your debts and classify them as "secured" or "unsecured." This is important, because to qualify for Chapter 13 bankruptcy, your secured debts cannot exceed $922,975, and your unsecured debts cannot exceed $307,675. These limits increase every three years. (If your debts are over the limit, you may still qualify for Chapter 13 bankruptcy with a little effort. See Sections A4 and B2, below.)

This chapter explains how to classify your debts (it's easier than it may sound) and contains worksheets to help you add them up.

If you clearly qualify. If you are pretty certain that your secured debts don't come close to $922,975 and your unsecured debts are way below $307,675, you can skip ahead to Ch. 4, *Calculating Your Disposable Income*.

A. Secured Debts

A secured debt is linked to a specific item of property, called collateral, that guarantees payment of the debt. If you don't pay, the creditor is entitled to take the collateral. For example, mortgages and car loans are secured debts.

Use Worksheets 2 and 3, below, to add up your secured debts. Keep in mind that there are two kinds of secured debts: those you agree to, such as a mortgage, and those created without your consent, such as a lien against your property recorded by the IRS because you haven't paid your taxes.

---

1. Liens You Agree To: Security Interests

If you voluntarily pledge property as collateral—that is, as a guarantee that you will pay a debt—the lien on your property is called a security interest. If you signed a security agreement, it may well have given the creditor the right to take the property (the collateral) if you miss a payment.

Here are some common examples of security interests:

- **Mortgages** (called deeds of trust in some states), which are loans to buy or refinance a house or other real estate. The real estate is collateral for the loan. If you fail to pay, the lender can foreclose.

- **Home equity loans** (second mortgages) from banks or finance companies, such as loans to do work on your house. The house is collateral for the loan. If you fail to pay, the lender can foreclose.

- **Loans for cars, boats, tractors, motorcycles, or RVs.** Here, the vehicle is the collateral. If you fail to pay, the lender can repossess it.

- **Store charges with a security agreement.** Almost all store purchases on credit cards are unsecured. Some stores, however, notably Sears, print on the credit card slip or other receipt that "Sears retains a security interest in all hard goods (durable goods) purchased" or make customers sign security agreements when they use their store charge card. For example, if you buy a major appliance on credit, the store may require you to sign a security agreement in which you agree that the item purchased is collateral for your repayment. If you don't pay back the loan, the seller can take the property. (In Vermont, a bankruptcy court has ruled that store charges are unsecured, not secured, under Vermont state law. *In re Oszajca*, 199 B.R. 103 (D. Vt. 1996).)

- **Personal loans from banks, credit unions, or finance companies.** Often you must pledge valuable personal property, such as a paid-off motor vehicle, as collateral.

To add up your voluntary security interests, fill in the first two columns of Worksheet 2. (The other columns are explained later.) A sample is shown below; a blank tear-out is in Appendix 2.

As you fill in the worksheets, keep in mind the following:

- **Joint debts.** List 100% of all debts you incurred with someone else—such as a spouse, non-marital partner, parent, or child.
- **Disputed debts.** List all debts claimed by creditors, even if you don't think you owe them or disagree about the amount. If the exact amount of a debt hasn't yet been determined, use the amount the creditor claims you owe.

Contesting Disputed Debts in Chapter 13 Bankruptcy

When you fill out your Chapter 13 bankruptcy papers, you must list all disputed debts. But this doesn't mean you admit to owing them. In fact, one great feature of Chapter 13 bankruptcy is that you can use your bankruptcy case to contest the validity of any debt. For example, let's say the IRS claims you owe $100,000 in back taxes. You agree you owe something, but nowhere near that amount—more like $15,000. After you file your Chapter 13 case, you file papers with the bankruptcy court to establish whether and how much you owe the IRS. This eliminates the need for you to use Tax Court or another forum outside of bankruptcy to resolve the problem.

Contesting the validity of a debt in Chapter 13 bankruptcy is beyond the scope of this book and normally requires help from a lawyer.

Column 1: Description of debt/name of creditor. In the first column, enter your secured debts in the appropriate categories. If a debt does not fall into a category on the form, list it under Other. For instance, you may have given a lawyer a security interest in any money you may recover in a lawsuit against a person who injured you.

Column 2: Total outstanding balance. Enter the total amount you owe on each debt. You can find out the total by calling the lender. If you are uncertain about the amount, put your best estimate and a question mark.

➡️ **Doing some work now will save you time later.** Once you've filled out Columns 1 and 2, you can skip ahead to Section 2 to calculate the amount of your nonconsensual liens. But if you want to speed up the process of completing your bankruptcy forms, fill out Columns 3, 4, and 5 now.

Column 3: Amount of regular monthly payment. Enter the amount of your regular monthly payment for each debt.

Column 4: Total amount of arrears. Multiply the amount of your regular monthly payment by the number of months you are behind. Add to that any late fees, attorney fees, and collection costs assessed by the lender. Enter the total in Column 4.

Column 5: Present value of collateral. In this column, enter the current value of the property that secures the debt. For purposes of completing the worksheet, use your best estimates. When you're ready to fill out and file your bankruptcy papers, you may need to come up with more precise figures.

2. Liens Created Without Your Consent: Nonconsensual Liens

A creditor can, in some circumstances, get a lien on your property without your consent. These liens are termed nonconsensual liens. In theory, a nonconsensual lien gives the creditor a right to force the sale of the property in order to get paid. In practice, however, few creditors force a sale of property, because so much time and expense are involved. Instead, they wait until you sell or refinance the property—when the lien must be paid off to give the new owner clear title to the property.

Worksheet 2: Secured Debts With Voluntary Security Interests

1 Description of debt/ name of creditor	2 Total outstanding balance	3 Regular monthly payment	4 Total amount of arrears	5 Present value of collateral
Mortgages and home equity loans				
Home Bank Mortgage	177,516	1,236	12,360	210,000
West Bank Home Equity Loan	14,000	1,000	13,000	210,000
Motor vehicle loans				
GMAC	9,171	405	405	8,500
Personal loans				
Department store charges **with security agreements**				
Sears—new washer and dryer	850	30	300	600
Other				
Martha Kwok, attorney —interest in outcome of lawsuit (lien on house)	unknown	—	—	210,000

Total $ __201,537__

There are three major types of nonconsensual liens:

- **Judicial liens.** A judicial lien can be imposed on your property only after somebody sues you and wins a money judgment against you. In most states, the judgment creditor then must record (file) the judgment with the county or state; the recorded judgment creates the lien on your real estate in that county or state. In a few states, a judgment entered against you by a court automatically creates a lien on the real estate you own in that county—that is, the judgment creditor doesn't have to record the judgment to get the lien.

- **Statutory liens.** Some liens are created automatically by law. For example, in most states when you hire someone to work on your house, the worker or supplier of materials automatically gets a mechanic's lien (also called a materialman's lien) on the house if you don't pay. So does a homeowners' association, in some states, if you don't pay your dues or special assessments.

- **Tax liens.** Federal, state, and local governments have the authority to impose liens on your property if you owe delinquent taxes. If you owe money to the IRS or other taxing authority, the debt is secured *only* if the taxing authority has recorded a lien against your property (and you still own the property) or has issued a notice of tax lien and the equity in your home or retirement plan is sufficient to cover the amount of the debt. If there is no lien, no lien notice, or insufficient equity, your tax debt is unsecured and should be included on Worksheet 4.

Use Worksheet 3 to add up these debts. A sample is shown below; a blank tear-out copy is in Appendix 2.

Column 1: Description of debt/name of creditor. List your nonconsensual lienholders in the appropriate categories.

Column 2: Amount of debt. Enter the total amount of each debt. If you are uncertain, put your best estimate and a question mark.

Filling out the rest of Worksheet 3 will let you determine whether any of your debts are "undersecured." An undersecured debt is partially secured (and so goes on this worksheet) and partially unsecured (and so goes on Worksheet 4, too).

Column 3: Property affected by lien. Identify the property affected by each lien. If you are like most people, this is your house—but not always. Let's look at this by type of lien.

- **Judicial liens.** In every state a judicial lien affects real estate you own in the county where the lien is recorded or the judgment is entered. In most states, a judicial lien does not affect your personal property.

  However, in the following states, a judicial lien also affects your personal property in the county:
  - Alabama
  - Connecticut
  - Florida
  - Georgia
  - Maine
  - Massachusetts
  - Mississippi
  - New Hampshire, and
  - Rhode Island.

  But that's not the end of it. A judgment creditor can also file the judgment with the state motor vehicles department, imposing a lien on any car, truck, motorcycle, or other motor vehicle you own. You may not know about this lien until the creditor files a claim with the bankruptcy court describing its interest as secured (this is covered in Ch. 9, *After You File Your Case*) or you check with the motor vehicles department.

- **Statutory liens.** Statutory liens affect your real estate.

- **Tax liens.** A lien recorded by a local government for unpaid property tax affects your real estate. Similarly, if your state taxing authority sends you a bill and you don't contest or pay it, the state can record a tax lien against your real estate in that state. And if you don't pay an IRS bill, the IRS can record a Notice of Federal Tax Lien at your county land records office or your Secretary of State's office, which lien attaches to all of your property.

Column 4: Present value of property. In this column, enter the current value of the property listed in Column 3. For purposes of completing the worksheet, use your best estimates. When you're ready to fill out and file your bankruptcy papers, you may need to come up with more precise figures.

To determine whether any of the debts are undersecured, subtract the amount of the debt (Column 2) from the present value of the collateral (Column 4).

3 / 6   CHAPTER 13 BANKRUPTCY: REPAY YOUR DEBTS

Worksheet 3: Secured Debts Created Without Your Consent

1 Description of debt/ name of creditor	2 Amount of debt	3 Property affected by lien	4 Present value of property
Judicial liens			
Columbia Community Hospital	26,000	House	210,000
Dr. Anton Gurnev	16,000	House	210,000
Statutory liens			
Tax liens			
IRS	17,990	House	210,000

Total $ 59,990

EXAMPLE: Your car is worth $7,500 but a creditor has filed a lien with the motor vehicle department for $10,000. The debt is undersecured by $2,500.

A debt may also be undersecured if you have many liens all secured by the same property (Column 3), and the total of those liens (some may be on Worksheet 2 and some may be on Worksheet 3) exceeds the present value of the property. In that situation, the creditors who filed their liens the latest are the ones whose debts are undersecured.

EXAMPLE: Your house is worth $210,000. You still owe $177,000 on your mortgage (which is listed in Worksheet 2). In the same year, you took out a $14,000 home equity loan (in March), the IRS recorded a Notice of Federal Tax Lien for nearly $18,000 (in June), and two judgment creditors recorded judgment liens for $42,000 against your house (in July). The home equity loan and IRS's lien are secured. The judgment creditors' liens, however, are undersecured.

If all or any portion of a debt on this worksheet is undersecured, erase the undersecured amount from Column 2 and enter it on Worksheet 4, Unsecured Debts.

NOTE: Mortgages Receive Special Treatment. Mortgages secured by your residence cannot be split into secured and unsecured portions. A special Chapter 13 rule singles out mortgages for this special protection.

However, there is an exception to this exception. If the mortgage is completely unsecured, that is, no equity is available to protect any part of it, then it does not qualify for special protection. In such a case, the entire mortgage amount will be treated as an unsecured claim.

If you have a completely unsecured second mortgage (or home equity loan), courts in most parts of the United States will allow you to "strip off" the mortgage entirely, upon the completion of your Chapter 13 plan, whether or not you paid any of the debt in your plan. (To see the relevant court cases, go to *In re Zimmer*, 313 F.3d 1220 (9th Cir. 2002); *In re Lane*, 280 F.3d 663 (6th Cir. 2002); *In re Pond*, 252 F.3d 122 (2d Cir. 2001); *In re Tanner*, 217 F.3d 1357 (11th Cir. 2000); *In re Mann*, 249 B.R. 831 (B.A.P. 1st Cir. 2000);

In re Bartee, 212 F.3d 277 (5th Cir. 2000); and *In re McDonald*, 205 F.3d 606 (3d Cir. 2000).)

The bottom line is: if you have multiple mortgages on a home that has declined in value, you may be able to completely eliminate one or more of the junior mortgages. Contact a Chapter 13 bankruptcy lawyer who is experienced in the procedures followed in your district. (The required procedure varies from jurisdiction to jurisdiction.)

3. Total Up Your Secured Debts

Add together the totals from Worksheet 2, Column 2 (Total outstanding balance), and Worksheet 3, Column 2 (Total amount of debt). The figure must be under $922,975 for you to qualify for Chapter 13 bankruptcy.

4. Turning Secured Debts Into Unsecured Ones: Lien Avoidance

In certain limited circumstances, you can ask the bankruptcy court to eliminate (avoid) liens on certain property. This procedure, called lien avoidance, turns the debt into an unsecured one. This can help you in two situations:

- Your secured debts are over the $922,975 limit.
- If in your Chapter 13 plan you will propose repaying less than 100% of your unsecured debts, you can bring down the total amount you will pay through your plan.

Although it may sound complicated, lien avoidance is a routine procedure. You request lien avoidance by typing and filing a document called a "motion" with the bankruptcy court. Complete instructions for preparing and filing a motion to avoid a lien are in Ch. 9, *After You File Your Case*, Section K. Liens that can be avoided are described here.

a. Security Interests

A security interest (remember—that's a secured debt you agree to) can be avoided only if it meets the criteria listed below.

1. The lien must be the result of a loan which you obtained by pledging property you already own as collateral. This is called a "nonpossessory nonpurchase-money security interest."

That's sounds complicated, but it makes sense when you break it down:

- "Nonpossessory" means the creditor does not physically keep the collateral you've pledged as collateral. You keep it in your possession; the creditor only retains a lien on it. (In contrast, if you leave your property at a pawn shop to get a loan, that is a possessory security interest—for which this lien avoidance procedure is not available.)
- "Nonpurchase money" means that the money loaned was not the money used to purchase the collateral.
- "Security interest" means the lien was created by a voluntary agreement between you and the creditor.

The most common examples of nonpossessory nonpurchase-money security interests are home equity loans and personal loans where a car is pledged as collateral. Unfortunately, as explained in criterion #3, below, these two most common types of collateral are not included in the list of eligible property. Consequently, the situations in which you can use this procedure, as a practical matter, are quite limited.

2. The property you pledged must be "exempt." To see whether the property is exempt, look at Appendix 1.

3. The collateral you pledged must be any of the following property:
   - household furnishings, household goods, clothing, appliances, books, musical instruments, or jewelry that are primarily for your personal, family, or household use
   - health aids professionally prescribed for you or a dependent
   - animals or crops held primarily for your personal, family or household use—but only the first $5,000 of the lien can be avoided, or
   - implements, professional books, or tools used in a trade (yours or a dependent's)—but only the first $5,000 of the lien can be avoided.

A security interest cannot be removed from real estate or from a motor vehicle unless the vehicle is a tool of your trade. Generally, a motor vehicle is not considered a tool of trade unless you use it as an integral part of your business—for example, if you do door-to-door sales

Special Rules for Avoiding Judicial Liens

Bankruptcy rules place additional limits on avoiding judicial liens on real estate or which arose from a divorce.

Real estate. When you file for bankruptcy, something called your homestead exemption protects some or all of your equity in your residence. Your equity is the amount by which the value of the property exceeds the total of any mortgages and other consensual liens on the property.

EXAMPLE: Zoe and Bud own a $100,000 house with an $80,000 mortgage; their equity is $20,000. The homestead exemption in their state is $30,000. Although a creditor has recorded a $200,000 judgment (judicial) lien against Zoe and Bud's home, their equity is fully protected because it is less than the homestead exemption amount. This means that if the creditor forced a sale of the house, Zoe and Bud would be entitled to their homestead exemption before the creditor with the $200,000 judgment would be entitled to any money.

If no equity remains after the consensual liens and homestead exemption are deducted, you can entirely eliminate (avoid) the judicial liens on the property.

EXAMPLE: Zoe and Bud could eliminate the entire $200,000 lien because the consensual lien (the $80,00 mortgage) plus the homestead exemption ($30,000) together total more than the value of their property. After the lien is gone, the debt is unsecured and treated like all other unsecured, dischargeable debts in Chapter 13.

Divorce. Because the law places a high priority on protecting the interests of children and former spouses, bankruptcy law prohibits you from avoiding a judicial lien that secures a debt to your ex-spouse or children for alimony or child support. But in some divorces, it's not always clear if a lien is for support or is just to pay marital bills. In the latter case, the lien may be avoided.

Worksheet 4: Unsecured Debts

1 Description of debt/ name of creditor	2 Total outstanding balance	3 Regular monthly payment	4 Total amount of arrears
Student loans			
Department of Education	18,140	600	18,140
Unsecured consolidation loans			
Unsecured personal loans			
Swamp Bank	4,000	275	1,110
Medical (doctors', dentists', and hospital) bills			
Lawyers' and accountants' bills			
Credit and charge cards			
American Express	6,841	6,841	6,841
Swamp Bank	9,111	30	180
Discover	4,400	35	210
Department store and gasoline credit cards			
Macy's	3,204	30	180
Chevron	289	—	289
J.C. Penney's	1,517	15	90

Worksheet 4: Unsecured Debts (continued)

1 Description of debt/ name of creditor	2 Total outstanding balance	3 Regular monthly payment	4 Total amount of arrears
Alimony or child support arrears			
Back rent			
Unpaid utility bills (gas, electric, water, phone, cable, garbage)			
Bell Phone Company	737	—	737
Tax debts (no lien recorded on undersecured portion)			
Other			

Total $ __48,239__

If your unsecured debts add up to more than $307,675 you cannot file for Chapter 13 bankruptcy.

or delivery work. It is not considered a tool of trade if you simply use it to get to and from your workplace, even if you have no other means of commuting.

b. Nonconsensual Liens

A nonconsensual lien (remember—that's a secured debt you didn't agree to) can be avoided only if it meets two criteria:

1. The lien must be a judicial lien, which can be removed from *any* exempt property, including real estate and cars.

2. You must be able to claim the property as exempt.

If you determine that a lien can be avoided, erase the debt from this worksheet and enter it on Worksheet 4, Unsecured Debts.

B. Unsecured Debts

An unsecured debt is any debt for which you haven't pledged collateral and for which the creditor has not filed a lien against you. If the debt is unsecured, the creditor is not entitled to repossess or seize any of your property if you don't pay.

Most debts are unsecured. Some of the common ones are:

- credit and charge card (Visa, MasterCard, American Express, Discover, and the like), purchases, and cash advances
- department store credit card purchases, unless the store "retains a security interest" in the items you buy or requires you to sign a security agreement (see Section A1, above)
- gasoline company credit card purchases
- back rent
- medical bills
- alimony and child support
- student loans
- utility bills
- loans from friends or relatives, unless you signed a promissory note secured by some property you own
- health club dues
- lawyer's and accountants' bills
- church or synagogue dues, and
- union dues.

1. Adding Up Your Unsecured Debts

Use Worksheet 4 to record your unsecured debts. A sample is shown below; a blank tear-out copy is in Appendix 2.

You must list all your debts if you want them to be discharged. However, you may skip some listed debts when you total up your debts to figure out if you qualify for Chapter 13 bankruptcy.

For example, you should list—but not include in your debt total—debts for which you don't yet know the exact amount you owe. An example would be where you are sued by someone who suffered injuries in an auto accident where you were at fault, but the court has not yet decided how much you have to pay.

Likewise, you must list—but not include in your debt total—debts that depend upon the occurrence of a future event, that may never occur. An example would be where you cosigned a loan, won't be liable to pay it unless the principal debtor defaults, and the principal debtor is current on the payments. Another example would be where you are sued for breaching a contract; you'll incur a debt for breaching the contract only if you lose the lawsuit.

If your liability for a debt, or the amount of the debt, depends on the outcome of a lawsuit, file your Chapter 13 bankruptcy papers before the case ends (or even begins). If your liability isn't settled, it won't be counted toward the $307,675 unsecured debt limit. Once you file your Chapter 13 bankruptcy papers, the lawsuit is automatically stopped. Remember though, if the amount of a debt has been determined and you dispute the debt, you still must list the entire amount until you successfully contest it.

List all debts on the bankruptcy forms. If you file for bankruptcy before your liability is determined, you might assume it's okay to leave the debt off your bankruptcy papers. Don't. If you don't list the debt, you won't be able to eliminate it in your Chapter 13 case and you might even have your case dismissed. So be sure to list it—even if the other party has only threatened to sue you—and note that the amount is "not yet determined."

Column 1: Description of debt/name of creditor. List your debts in the appropriate categories. If a debt does not fall into a category—such as a debt to your child care provider or a judicial lien that is undersecured—list it under Other.

Column 2: Total outstanding balance. Enter the total amount you owe on each debt. Find out the total by looking at your most recent bill or calling the lender. If you are uncertain, put your best estimate and a question mark. When you've listed all debts, enter the total for Column 2.

Doing some work now will save you time later. Once you figure out the total amount of your unsecured debts, you can skip ahead to Ch. 4. If you want to speed up the process of completing your bankruptcy papers, you can fill out Columns 3 and 4.

Column 3: Regular monthly payment. Enter the amount of your regular monthly payment for each debt or the monthly minimum for your credit and charge (including department store and gasoline company) cards. If there is no monthly minimum payment, leave this column blank.

Column 4: Total amount of arrears. Multiply the amount of your regular or minimum monthly payment by the number of months you are behind. If you are not required to make monthly payments, use the amount from Column 2, the total outstanding balance. Add any late fees, attorney fees, and collection costs assessed by the lender. If the lender has declared you to be in default, enter the entire amount. Enter the total in Column 4.

2. Turning Unsecured Debts Into Secured Ones

If your debts are over the unsecured limit, but you're not at the secured limit, you can move some debts from the unsecured category to the secured category. All you have to do is voluntarily give a creditor a security interest in an unsecured debt. You can do this by pledging an item of your property, such as your house or car, as collateral to guarantee repayment of the debt. By making the debt secured, however, you will have to repay it in full in your Chapter 13 case. ■

4

Calculating Your Disposable Income

When you submit your Chapter 13 repayment plan to the bankruptcy court, you must show that 1) you have enough "disposable income" to propose a repayment plan that meets all bankruptcy law requirements, and 2) that you are going to dedicate all of your "disposable income" to paying your creditors for at least three years. (11 U.S.C. § 1325(b).)

For purposes of Chapter 13 bankruptcy, your disposable income is everything you earn, less reasonably necessary expenses for:

- supporting yourself and your dependents, and
- continuing, preserving, and operating any business you run.

This chapter shows you how to calculate your monthly income and what the bankruptcy court will consider reasonably necessary expenses. When you file your court papers, your creditors, the bankruptcy trustee, and the bankruptcy court will look to see that you are maximizing your income and minimizing your expenses in order to get your disposable income as high as possible. If you are not, the trustee or your unsecured creditors may object to your Chapter 13 plan, on the ground that you are not making your best effort to repay your debts. (See Ch. 9, *After You File Your Case.*)

A. What You Earn

Your bankruptcy papers must include the total amount of your income, and must identify one or more regular sources of income which you will use to pay your debts.

1. Total Up Your Income

The first step in determining your disposable income is to total up your income from all sources. You can use Worksheet 5: Your Total Monthly Income; a tear-out copy is in Appendix 2.

If you're married and living with your spouse, include information for both spouses whether or not you are filing jointly. If you are married but separated and filing alone, enter information for only you.

Column 1: Source of income. In Part A, list the jobs for which you receive a salary or wages. In Part B, list all self-employment for which you receive income,

including farm income and sales commissions. In Part C, list any other sources of income. Here are some examples of other kinds of income.

- **Bonus pay.** List all regular bonuses you receive, such as an annual $500 end-of-year bonus.
- **Dividends and interest.** List all sources of dividends or interest—for example, bank accounts, security deposits, or stocks.
- **Alimony or child support.** Enter the type of support you receive for yourself (alimony, spousal support, or maintenance) or on behalf of your children (child support).
- **Pension or retirement income.** List the source of any pension, annuity, IRA, Keogh, or other retirement payments you receive.
- **Other public assistance.** Enter the types of any public benefits, such as SSI, public assistance, disability payments, veterans' benefits, unemployment compensation, workers' compensation or any other government benefit, which you receive.
- **Other.** Identify any other sources of income, such as a tax refund you received within the past year or anticipate receiving within the next year, or payments you receive from friends or relatives. If, within the past 12 months, you received any one-time lump sum payment (such as the proceeds from an insurance policy or from the sale of a valuable asset), don't list it as income. (You should, however, include it in your bankruptcy papers as an asset. See Ch. 6, *Completing the Bankruptcy Forms.*)

Column 2: Amount of each payment. For each source of income you listed in Parts A and B of Column 1, enter the amount you receive each pay period. If you don't receive the same amount each period, average the last 12. Then enter your mandatory deductions for each pay period. Again, enter an average of the last 12 months if these amounts vary. For the income you listed in Part A, you probably need to get out a pay stub to see how much is deducted from your paycheck. Subtract the deductions and enter your net income in the Subtotal blank in Column 2.

In Part C, enter the amount of each payment for each source of income.

Column 3: Period covered by each payment. For each source of income, enter the period covered by each payment—such as weekly, twice monthly (24

Worksheet 5: Your Total Monthly Income

1 Source of Income	2 Amount of each payment	3 Period covered by each payment	4 Amount per month
A. Wages or Salary			
Job 1: _Medical Technician_			
Gross pay, including overtime	$ 1,250	semimonthly	
Subtract:			
Federal taxes	141		
State taxes	40		
Social Security (FICA)	96		
Union dues	60		
Insurance payments			
Child support wage withholding			
Other mandatory deductions (specify): _city tax_	13		
Subtotal	$ 900		1,800
Job 2: _P/T Teacher_			
Gross pay, including overtime	$ 2,001	monthly	
Subtract:			
Federal taxes	153		
State taxes	296		
Social Security (FICA)	89		
Union dues			
Insurance payments			
Child support wage withholding			
Other mandatory deductions (specify): _city tax_	20		
Subtotal	$ 1,443		1,443
Job 3: _____			
Gross pay, including overtime	$		
Subtract:			
Federal taxes			
State taxes			
Social Security (FICA)			
Union dues			
Insurance payments			
Child support wage withholding			
Other mandatory deductions (specify):			
Subtotal	$		

Worksheet 5: Your Total Monthly Income (continued)

1 Source of Income	2 Amount of each payment	3 Period covered by each payment	4 Amount per month
B. Self-Employment Income			
Job 1:			
Pay	$		
Subtract:			
Federal taxes			
State taxes			
Self-employment taxes			
Other mandatory deductions (specify):			
Subtotal	$		
Job 2:			
Pay	$		
Subtract:			
Federal taxes			
State taxes			
Self-employment taxes			
Other mandatory deductions (specify):			
Subtotal	$		
C. Other Sources			
Bonuses _Christmas_	600	yearly	50
Dividends and interest _money market_	12	monthly	12
Rent, lease, or license income			
Royalties			
Note or trust income			
Alimony or child support you receive _cs_	360	monthly	360
Pension or retirement income			
Social Security			
Other public assistance			
Other (specify):			
Other (specify):			
Other (specify):			
Total monthly income			$ 3,665

times a year), every other week (26 times a year), monthly, quarterly (common for royalties), or annually (common for farm income).

Column 4: Amount per month. Multiply or divide the subtotals (or amounts in Part C) in Column 2 to determine the monthly amount. For example, if you are paid twice a month, multiply the Column 2 amount by two. If you are paid every other week, multiply the amount by 26 (for the annual amount) and divide by 12. (The shortcut is to multiply by 2.167.)

When you are done, total up Column 4. This is your total monthly income.

2. What Income Will Fund the Plan

Although you must include all sources of income when figuring out your monthly disposable income, be aware that you may not be able to use all of these sources of income to fund your Chapter 13 plan. You will probably have no problem if you plan to use salary or wage income to fund your plan. Other types of income, however, may cause a problem if the court thinks they are not reliable enough. And there are special problems using government benefits and some pension payments.

a. Irregular or Fluctuating Income

Here is how a judge may rule if you propose to fund your plan with irregular or fluctuating income:

- **Receipts from a business.** You may have to provide the bankruptcy court with documents showing a history of regular draws that resemble income—such as $750 per week for a year. The court may not let you use receipts from a business to fund your plan if it appears that you simply draw money for personal purposes whenever necessary. Also, because you will need to show that your income is stable, the bankruptcy court may not approve a plan that relies on income from a recently started business.
- **Income from irregular or seasonal work.** If you receive a fairly steady amount of money over the course of a year—even if your work is irregular or seasonal and your pay is not the same from one month to the next—the court will probably approve your Chapter 13 plan. If your primary source of income is completely unpredictable—for example, you work through a temp agency—you may have problems getting your plan approved by the bankruptcy court.
- **Sales and other commissions.** As long as you can show the bankruptcy court that you receive commissions fairly regularly, you should not have any problem using those commissions to fund your Chapter 13 plan.
- **Rent, lease, or license receipts, royalties, and note or trust income.** As long as the payments are regular and likely to continue, you should not have any trouble using this income to fund your plan. If you get royalties for a product where sales have been steadily decreasing, the court probably won't approve your plan. Note or trust income, in particular, is often used to fund Chapter 13 plans because it is regular, predictable, and likely to continue.
- **Alimony or child support.** Alone, these may not be enough to fund your plan, but they can be a component. If your support is apt to go down any time in the next 36 months—for example, your son is 17 and child support will end when he turns 18—the court will probably not let you use the support to fund your plan or will require that you identify another source of income to make up the difference.
- **Payments from relatives or friends.** Many people are supported by grown children who help out or live at home and pay rent, or receive payments from a nonmarital partner or a generous relative. Because there is rarely any legal obligation to make these payments, the difficulty in using this money to fund a Chapter 13 plan is convincing the bankruptcy court that the payments will continue. If you file for bankruptcy without your spouse, but your spouse supports you, the bankruptcy court will probably not let you apply the support toward your plan payments.
- **Proceeds from selling property.** Like many people, you may want to fund your Chapter 13 plan by selling property. But if you propose to fund your plan wholly by selling assets, virtually every court will deny confirmation of your plan, although the court will probably let you supplement payments under the plan with the sales

proceeds after your plan is confirmed. A rare court will let you fund your plan with the proceeds of the sale of property, but only if you demonstrate the likelihood of the sale (such as a house being aggressively marketed, having an offer on it, or the sale is already in escrow), and that it will provide enough money to fund the plan (such as the sale of a house with substantial equity in it). The court may also require you to outline your fallback plan in case a sale does not materialize.

- **Bonuses.** Bonuses will rarely be enough to fund an entire Chapter 13 plan, but the bankruptcy court may require that you make supplemental payments into your plan during the months in which you receive bonuses or vacation pay. Or, you may be able to use this money to make up missed payments on a secured debt ("cure a default") and use your other income to make the regular payments under your plan.
- **Dividends and interest.** This may be another good source of income to cure a default, but will rarely be enough to fund a plan.

b. Pension or Retirement Income

There are two potential limitations on using pension income to fund a Chapter 13 plan. First, bankruptcy courts sometimes order whoever pays you money—your employer, for example—to deduct a certain amount from your check and send it to the bankruptcy trustee. This is called an income deduction order. Many pension plans, however, prohibit the administrator from paying proceeds to anyone other than the beneficiary. The bankruptcy court might not let you use your pension payments to fund the plan if the pension plan administrator won't obey an income deduction order.

Second, one court has held that payments from a pension plan that meets the requirements of the federal Employee Retirement Income Security Act (ERISA) cannot be used to fund a Chapter 13 plan, because you have only limited access to the money. (*McLean v. Central States, Southeast & Southwest Areas Pension Fund*, 762 F.2d 1204 (4th Cir. 1985).) But other courts disagree with that opinion. See *In re Taylor*, 212 F.2d 395 (8th Cir. 2000) *Cert. denied* 531 U.S. 1010.

c. Government Benefits

Social Security could present a problem if it's the only source of income for your Chapter 13 plan. The Social Security Act prohibits the Social Security Administration from paying benefits to anyone other than the designated recipient. Therefore, the Social Security Administration will not comply if the bankruptcy court orders it to pay your benefits directly to the court. One court has taken this to mean that Social Security payments do not constitute regular income to fund a Chapter 13 plan. (*In re Buren*, 725 F.2d 1080 (6th Cir. 1984).) But other courts disagree (see *In re Hagel*, 184 B.R. 793 (9th Cir. BAP 1995)).

Other government entities that pay you benefits may also refuse to comply with an income deduction order. In addition, if you'll be using disability or workers' compensation benefits, the bankruptcy court will be concerned with the duration of the benefits, especially if you won't be able to go back to work when they end. Similarly, unemployment benefits last only 26 weeks, and you'll have to prove another source of income after they end. You could probably use strike funds to initially fund your plan because once the strike is over, you are likely to go back to work.

B. What You Spend

Your disposable income is your income minus your reasonably necessary expenses. These expenses include what it costs you to:

- support yourself and your dependents, and
- continue, preserve, and operate any business you run.

When you file your bankruptcy papers, you will include a list of all your monthly expenses. Your creditors, the bankruptcy trustee, and the judge will scrutinize the list. The most common objection raised by creditors is that a debtor's expenses are not reasonably necessary. The court will not be looking to reject your expenses just for the sake of a rejection, but a judge who sees inflated or unreasonable expenses will reject your repayment plan. Rejection of your plan isn't the end of your case. You can submit a modified plan or agree to a modification of your plan during the confirmation hearing, where the judge approves or rejects your plan.

Record your monthly expenditures on Worksheet 6: Your Total Monthly Expenses; a tear-out copy is in Appendix 2. You will use this information when you fill out your bankruptcy forms.

What's Reasonable?

When it comes to expenses, what is considered reasonable varies from debtor to debtor, court to court, and even region to region. In general, expenses for luxury items or services (such as a gardener) will not be allowed. If an expense seems particularly high, the court will look to see if you can achieve the same goal by spending less—the court will let you live adequately, not high on the hog. For example, if you are making $550 per month payments on a Cadillac, the court will probably allow $300 per month toward a Chevrolet or other less expensive car, freeing another $250 per month of disposable income. Courts also tend to disallow as expenses any voluntary payments to retirement plans, unless the debtor is approaching retirement age or is financially challenged. (See *In re Behlke*, 358 F.3d 429 (6th Cir. Ohio 2004).)

But some courts *will* allow a seemingly extravagant expense if all other expenses are reasonable. And some might allow an expense that isn't, strictly speaking, necessary, if it furthers a valid goal—such as sending your children to private school. Probably most judges will let you buy the daily newspaper (courts like the public to be informed) but won't let you keep a ballet or opera subscription. (Don't worry, you can go to an occasional movie.)

Helpful resources. *Cost of Living Schedules.* The federal government publishes these schedules, which you can find on the Internet or at the public library, for different regions of the country. The IRS publishes "National Standards for Allowable Living Standards," and "Housing and Utilities Allowable Living Expenses." The schedules can help you figure out if your food and shelter costs are above average for where you live. The trustee will have these schedules; you will have to provide justification if your expenses are way out of line.

Chapter 13 Bankruptcy, by Keith M. Lundin (Bankruptcy Press, Inc.). This clearly-written book contains several examples of what courts have ruled as reasonable and unreasonable expenses. Chapter 5, Sections 33 through 41, discusses disposable income; Section 36 specifically looks at expenses reasonably necessary for support. This book is written for attorneys, and you will probably have to go to a law library to find it. (Ch. 12, *Help Beyond the Book*, explains how to find a law library you can use.)

Here are some guidelines for completing Worksheet 6.

A. Your residence. If your rent or mortgage payment is unusually high for your area, the court might suggest that you move in order to bring this expense down, if alternate housing is easily available. If you will make your mortgage payment through your Chapter 13 repayment plan because you are behind a few months, don't list your payments here.

If your estimates of maintenance and upkeep are high, you may have to provide the court with documentation for past years' expenses. Obviously, the court will want you to maintain your home's condition, but will want you to do so as inexpensively as is reasonable.

B. Utilities. List your monthly utility expenses. Be sure to take a monthly average of gas, heating fuel, and electricity if your bills vary month to month. Some courts might refuse high phone bills—for example, if you call a parent or child in a distant city every day. A court might also reject the expense of cable TV, so this may be a service you'll have to drop. Or the court might let you keep basic cable, but not allow expenses for premium channels.

C. Food. To determine whether or not your figure is reasonable, the court will most likely compare it to the federal cost of living figure for your area. (See "What's Reasonable?" above.) If your expenses are higher than average, be ready to explain them—for example, because a family member needs a special diet. The court is not going to allow much—if anything—for eating out beyond an occasional family dinner at McDonald's.

D. Personal effects. Certainly, the court will let you buy toiletries and drug store items and will even permit a monthly haircut. But the court will probably reject an expense of $80 per month to get your hair done, knowing that many discount places charge about $15.

E. Clothing. You are not expected to go naked or wear only hand-me-downs. You can buy clothes and even pay to have the clothing cleaned. But extravagant or frequent purchases won't be allowed. A court might reject a high amount or suggest that you buy used clothing for your still-growing children. To get an idea of how much you spend now, total up the clothing purchases you have receipts or credit card statements for, or that are in your check register.

F. Medical. The court will want you to maintain your medical insurance coverage, so it will allow the expense of medical insurance for you and your dependents. Don't list payments for bills from medical providers and hospitals for services you've already received. The court will probably want you to pay those through your Chapter 13 plan—that is, out of your disposable income. The court might let you include 100% of the bill as part of your monthly expenses if you need ongoing medical care and the provider won't provide it unless you pay your bill in full—if this is your situation, you can include the expense on this worksheet. The court may also reject expenses for mental health therapy and instead suggest that you visit a free or low-cost county mental health facility.

G. Transportation. The court will let you pay a reasonable amount to get to and from work. But if a less expensive alternative exists—for example, taking the bus instead of driving—the court may allow only enough to pay the lesser expense. As a practical matter, such a decision would mean that you wouldn't be allowed to deduct car expenses from your monthly income in determining your disposable income. It does not mean that the court would seize your car keys or prohibit you from driving your car to work. If the court objects completely to you having a car, the court might disallow monthly lease or purchase payments. This is highly unlikely, although if your payments are very high, the court might allow only a portion and suggest that you trade the car in for a less expensive model. The court will also allow expenses for vehicle insurance, maintenance, and registration, if the court thinks it's necessary for you to have a car.

H. Dependents. You are permitted to claim expenses for the support of your dependents, including your children. These expenses include child care, clothes,

books, an occasional movie, and the like. The court may reject allowances for your children unless they're just some pocket change. Also, courts are reluctant to let you send your children to private school if it means your creditors won't be paid. You may be able to convince the court of the need for private school, however, if the public schools in your area are quite bad or dangerous, you want your children to receive religious education, or your child has special educational needs. If your child is in college, a court may not let you deduct tuition at an expensive private university, but may let you count the payments for a state college.

I. Your or your spouse's education. If either you or your spouse is currently in school, list your expenses here. The court may reject a portion of these expenses if you or your spouse could be working and increasing the family's income.

J. Miscellaneous personal expenses. Often, these are the expenses that your creditors, the trustee, and the court scrutinize the most. Some courts do not think you should be allowed any expenses for entertainment, to participate in any hobbies that cost money, or to buy gifts for friends or relatives. As with all expenses, the key to getting these expenses approved is their reasonableness. You can't include in your budget money to see Broadway shows, maintain a sailing hobby, keep a subscription to an expensive journal, or renew your country club membership. You can probably budget to go out to or rent an occasional movie or go bowling, get your local newspaper, keep your membership at the local Y, and take care of your pet.

K. Charitable contributions. Due to a 1998 amendment to the bankruptcy code, you can include donations to charity, in an amount not to exceed 15% of your income, as part of your expenses. (11 U.S.C. § 1325(b).) The code defines charity as including both religious and nonreligious organizations. Some courts have expressed hostility to this provision and have disallowed certain charitable contributions—even though the code seems to clearly allow them.

L. Insurance. The court generally will let you maintain your disability or life insurance, especially if your health is compromised and you may need the disability insurance, or if you have young children or other dependents who would need the life insurance money if you died. If you have a whole life insurance policy, you may be told to convert it into a term policy, which has much lower premiums.

Worksheet 6: Your Total Monthly Expenses

1 Expenses	2 Amount per month	1 Expenses	2 Amount per month
A. Your residence		Maintenance	75
Rent or mortgage	950	Registration	15
Second mortgage or home equity loan	150	**H. Dependents**	
Homeowners' association fee		Child care	250
Property taxes	50	Allowances	
Homeowners' or renters' insurance		Clothes	
Maintenance and upkeep	100	Tuition	
B. Utilities		School books	
Telephone	70	**I. Your or your spouse's education**	
Gas, heating fuel, electricity	35	(Do not include student loan payment)	
Water and sewer	35	Tuition	
Garbage	40	Books and fees	
Cable	20	**J. Miscellaneous personal expenses**	
C. Food		Entertainment	20
At home	400	Recreation/hobbies	
Restaurants	80	Newspapers and magazines	12
D. Personal effects		Books	
Toiletries	50	Gifts	10
Drugstore items	30	Memberships	10
Personal grooming (haircuts)	30	Pet supplies/veterinarian	10
Other		**K. Charitable contributions**	25
E. Clothing		**L. Insurance**	
Purchases	40	(Do not include health, home, or motor vehicle insurance)	
Laundry/dry cleaning	15	Disability	
F. Medical		Life	35
Medical or health insurance		Other	
Dental insurance	15	**M. Support payments**	
Deductibles and copayments	60	Alimony, maintenance, or spousal support	
Doctor		Child support	
Dentist		Support of other dependents not living at home	
Eye doctor		**N. Regular business expenses**	
Medicines/prescriptions		**O. Other**	
Hospital		(Do not include back income taxes or	
Therapist		unsecured installment debts, such as	
G. Transportation		student loan, personal loan, or credit	
Car payment	208	card accounts. These debts will be	
Gasoline	30	paid through your plan.)	
Tolls and parking	30		
Auto insurance	100	**Total monthly expenses**	$ 3,000

Worksheet 7: Your Disposable Income

1. **Total Monthly Income** (from Worksheet 5) $ _____3,665_____

2. Subtract Total Monthly Expenses (from Worksheet 6)   – _____3,000_____

3. **Total Monthly Disposable Income** $ _____665_____

Total Amount Proposed to Pay Unsecured Creditors

Typical Chapter 13 repayment plan: $\dfrac{665}{\text{Line 3}}$ x   36 months   = $ _____23,940_____

Extended Chapter 13 repayment plan: $\dfrac{665}{\text{Line 3}}$ x   60 months   = $ _____39,900_____

M. Support payments. You must continue making court-ordered child support and alimony payments during your Chapter 13 bankruptcy case; the court will not reject these payments. If you voluntarily support others, however, the court will not allow any unreasonable expenses for people you are not obligated to support. The court may allow expenses to support an elderly parent, but probably won't let you deduct expenses for a roommate, nonmarital partner, nonmarital partner's child, adult child, or stepchild.

N. Regular business expenses. If you own or run a business, include your monthly necessary business expenses. You will have to prepare a separate statement of income and expenses for the operation of your business and attach it to your bankruptcy papers when you file them. This book doesn't tell you how to do that; however, anyone with a financial background, such as a banker, accountant, bookkeeper, or tax preparer, can help you draft one.

O. Other. List any additional expenses here, other than payments you are making on back income taxes and on unsecured installment debts such as student loans, credit card accounts, and personal loans. Don't include back taxes and unsecured installment debts because these debts are paid out of your disposable income through your Chapter 13 plan. Be ready to justify to the court the reasonableness of any expenses you do list.

C. What's Left—Your Disposable Income

To repeat: your disposable income is the money you pay into your Chapter 13 plan.

To calculate your disposable income, use Worksheet 7, above. Begin with the Total Monthly Income figure at the bottom of Worksheet 5. Subtract from it the Total Monthly Expenses figure in the bottom of Worksheet 6. The difference is your total monthly disposable income—the amount you have to fund your Chapter 13 plan.

Next, multiply your total monthly disposable income by 36, the number of months in a typical Chapter 13 plan. This will give you the total amount you will propose to pay your creditors.

This amount must equal or exceed the amount you calculated in Worksheet 1 in Ch. 2, *An Overview of Chapter 13 Bankruptcy*, Section B. If it doesn't, the bankruptcy court will not approve your plan. You may have to ask the court to extend your plan up to 60 months (the maximum allowed) or cut back your expenses in order to increase your disposable income. ■

Calculating the Value of Your Nonexempt Property

In bankruptcy, the property you own falls into one of two categories: exempt or nonexempt. If you were to file for Chapter 7 bankruptcy, exempt property is what you would get to keep—under no circumstances could the bankruptcy trustee take it away from you. Nonexempt property, on the other hand, would be what the bankruptcy trustee could take and sell to pay off your unsecured creditors.

When you file for Chapter 13 bankruptcy, you do not give up any property to the bankruptcy trustee. But the difference between exempt and nonexempt property is still important, for two reasons:

1. When you file for Chapter 13 bankruptcy, you must list all your property and specify precisely which property you claim as exempt.

2. In Chapter 13 bankruptcy, you must pay your unsecured creditors at least as much as they would have gotten if you had filed for Chapter 7 bankruptcy. This means that you must figure out the current value of your nonexempt property, and make sure that your repayment plan provides that your unsecured creditors will receive at least that amount over the life of your plan. (11 U.S.C. § 1325(a)(4).)

Using Worksheet 8 in this chapter, you can create an inventory of your property and total up the nonexempt portion.

If you originally filed for Chapter 7 bankruptcy and are now converting your case to Chapter 13 bankruptcy, much of the information you need for Worksheet 8 is already on your bankruptcy papers.

A. Identifying Your Property

The property you own on the day you file for bankruptcy is called your "bankruptcy estate." With very few exceptions (discussed below), property you acquire after you file for bankruptcy isn't included in your bankruptcy estate.

⚠ **It's not always obvious what you own.** When you file for bankruptcy, special rules determine what is considered yours and what you must report to the bankruptcy court. For example, property you've recently given away may still be considered yours. And not everything you might think you own is part of your bankruptcy

estate—for example, a pension you are entitled to receive at retirement, but over which you have no or limited control now, is not part of your bankruptcy estate.

Before you start filling in Worksheet 8: Your Exempt and Nonexempt Property, read this section to make sure you understand what's yours, legally. A checklist of common types of property precedes the worksheet; it may help you.

1. Property You Own and Possess

The property that you own and possess—for example, a car, real estate, clothing, books, TV, stereo system, furniture, tools, boat, artworks, or stock certificates—is included in your bankruptcy estate.

Property you control but which belongs to someone else is not part of your bankruptcy estate, because you don't have the right to sell it or give it away.

EXAMPLE 1: A parent establishes a trust for her child and names you as trustee to manage the money in the trust until the child's 18th birthday. You possess and control the money, but it's solely for the child's benefit and cannot be used for your own purposes. It isn't part of your bankruptcy estate.

EXAMPLE 2: Your sister has gone to Zimbabwe for an indefinite period and has loaned you her TV while she's gone. Although you might have use of the set for years to come, you don't own it. It isn't part of your bankruptcy estate.

2. Property You Own But Don't Possess

You can own something even if you don't have physical possession of it. For instance, you may own a share of your vacation cabin in the mountains, but never go there yourself. Or you may own furniture or a car that someone else is using. Other examples include a deposit held by your stockbroker, a security deposit held by your landlord or a utility company, or a distant business you've invested money in.

3. Property You Are Entitled to Receive

Property that you have a legal right to receive but haven't yet received when you file for bankruptcy is included in your bankruptcy estate. The most common examples are:

- wages you have earned but have not yet been paid, and
- a tax refund that is legally due you but which you haven't yet received.

Here are some other examples:

- vacation or termination pay you earned before filing for bankruptcy
- property you've inherited, but not yet received, from someone who has died (if you're a beneficiary in the will or revocable trust of someone who is still alive, you're not yet entitled to receive the property, because the will or trust document could be changed)
- proceeds of an insurance policy, if the death, injury, or other event that gives rise to payment has occurred; for example, if you were the beneficiary of your father's life insurance policy, and your father has died but you haven't received your money yet, the amount you're entitled to is part of your bankruptcy estate
- compensation you're legally entitled to receive for an injury, even if the amount hasn't yet been determined; if you have a valid claim against someone who injured you, you have a legal right to be compensated, even though the amount you're entitled to hasn't been determined in a lawsuit or agreement. Don't try to put an amount in your worksheet or bankruptcy papers; instead, just list your claim. The trustee may pursue the case on your behalf if the trustee thinks it will result in money for your creditors.
- money owed you for goods or services you've provided (accounts receivable); even if you're pretty certain you won't be paid, that money is considered part of your bankruptcy estate, and you must list the amount you are owed
- income generated by property in your bankruptcy estate before you filed for bankruptcy, but which you haven't received; this includes, for example, rent from commercial or residential real estate, royalties from copyrights or patents, and dividends earned on stocks.

ERISA-Qualified Retirement Plans

If you own a retirement plan that is covered by the federal law called ERISA (Employee Retirement Income Security Act), it is not considered part of your bankruptcy estate. The reason is somewhat complex, involving both ERISA law and bankruptcy law. (11 U.S.C. § 541 (c)(2); *Patterson v. Shumate*, 504 U.S. 753 (1992).) Essentially, the retirement plan is not considered property of the estate because you have limited access to the money. To find out whether or not your retirement plan is covered by ERISA, call the benefits coordinator on your job or the pension plan administrator.

If your retirement plan is not covered by ERISA, it is still exempt if:

- you use your state exemption system, and
- the retirement plan is listed in your state exemption system or the federal nonbankruptcy exemption list.

If your retirement plan isn't ERISA-qualified or specifically listed in your state exemption system, don't give up yet. Many courts have ruled that certain non-ERISA retirement accounts are exempt under state or federal law. For example, bankruptcy courts in many states have held that Individual Retirement Accounts (IRAs) are exempt.

The U.S. Supreme Court will rule in 2005 on whether IRAs are exempt under the federal bankruptcy exemptions. (The case is *Rousey v. Janeway*, which is on appeal from an 8th Circuit opinion saying that IRAs do not get federal exemption status. Meanwhile, the 2nd, 5th, 6th, and 9th Circuit Courts of Appeal have all gone the other way and ruled that IRAs are exempt. A majority of states protect IRAs and Roth IRAs under their state exemption laws, but a few states do not.

If it looks like you might lose your retirement plan in bankruptcy, see a lawyer before filing.

4. Property You've Recently Given Away

Property given away or repossessed shortly before you file for bankruptcy may still be considered part of your bankruptcy estate, and the trustee has legal authority to take it back.

On this worksheet, list:

- all property you gave away or transferred to an insider (friend, relative, corporation you own, or business partner) for less than fair market value during the year prior to your bankruptcy filing date
- payments made to an insider creditor during the year immediately preceding your bankruptcy filing date, and
- payments exceeding a total of $600 made to a regular creditor during the three-month period immediately preceding your bankruptcy filing date.

Don't unload property. Because you must pay your creditors at least the value of your nonexempt property, you may be tempted to give away some of that property to friends or relatives before you file, and then not list the items in your bankruptcy papers. This is both dishonest and foolhardy. If the bankruptcy court finds out, it will dismiss your case and probably bar you from filing for 180 days.

5. Proceeds From Property of the Bankruptcy Estate

If property of your bankruptcy estate earns income or otherwise produces money after you file for bankruptcy, this money is also part of your bankruptcy estate. This includes income you earn from personal services performed after you file for bankruptcy to the extent that the income is needed to fund your repayment plan. Your spouse's income from personal services is also part of the bankruptcy estate, even if your spouse is not filing for bankruptcy with you.

6. Property You Own With Your Spouse (If You Are Filing Alone)

If you're married but filing alone, your state's law determines which property is part of your bankruptcy estate and which isn't. The chart below summarizes the rules for various kinds of marital property ownership. Read the rest of this section to determine which kind of property you own.

a. Community Property States

Most states west of the Rocky Mountains and in the Southwest use a Spanish-based system of marital property ownership called "community property":

Alaska	Louisiana	Texas
Arizona	Nevada	Washington
California	New Mexico	Wisconsin
Idaho		

In community property states, as a general rule, all property either spouse earns during the marriage is community property, owned jointly by both spouses. Gifts and inheritances received specifically by one spouse, and property owned by one spouse before the marriage or acquired after permanent separation, are not community property.

If you're married and file for bankruptcy, all the community property you and your spouse own is considered part of *your* bankruptcy estate, even if your spouse doesn't file. (11 U.S.C. § 541(a)(2).)

This is true even if the community property might not be divided 50-50 if you were to divorce. For example, in some community property states, if one spouse made a contribution of separate property toward the purchase of a community asset, that spouse is entitled to be reimbursed for the down payment at divorce. But if the other spouse files for bankruptcy alone, then the entire community asset—including the portion the first spouse would be reimbursed—will have to be listed on the bankruptcy papers.

EXAMPLE: Paul and Sonya live in California, a community property state. Sonya contributed $20,000 of her separate property toward the purchase of their house. All the rest of the money used to pay for the house is from community funds, and the house is considered community property. If Paul and Sonya were to divorce and split the house proceeds, Sonya would be entitled to $20,000 more than Paul as reimbursement for her down payment. But they aren't divorced, and Paul files for bankruptcy without Sonya. Their house is worth $250,000. Paul must list that entire value on his bankruptcy papers—that is, he can't subtract the $20,000 Sonya would be entitled to if they divorced.

Marital Property Included in Your Bankruptcy Estate	
For property co-owned as:	**List your ownership share as:**
Joint Tenancy	**50% of value**
Community Property	**100% of value** Community property is responsible for all debts incurred by either spouse.
Tenancy by the Entirety	**0% to 100% of value** If you own property as tenancy by the entirety, the property may or may not be included in the bankruptcy estate, depending on the laws of where the property is located. • In many states, if the bankruptcy petition lists no joint marital debts, then the bankruptcy estate must exclude all tenancy by the entirety property. (See, for example, *In re Sinnreich*, 391 F.3d 1295 (11th Cir. 2004) applying Florida law.) • However, at least one court (in Rhode Island) has held that a husband must list his share of the value of all entireties property as 100%. (See *In re Ryan*, 282 B.R. 742, (D. R.I. 2002).) • Still other courts invoke a complex formula—involving the life expectancy of each spouse—to arrive at unusual ownership percentages such as 46.5%. (See, *In re Pletz*, 221 F.3d 1114; *In re Basher*, 291 B.R. 357 (E.D. Pa. 2003.) Given the uncertainty in this area of law, it is probably best to list your ownership share as 50% on your worksheet and forms but with a note explaining to the trustee that you could not sell your share for that amount because your marriage owns it as tenancy by the entirety. This will notify the trustee and your creditors which items of property you own in this manner. When it comes time to list "exemptions" you will claim this property as exempt on your bankruptcy forms if your state allows such an exemption. (See the exemption chart for your state in Appendix 1.)

If you file alone, your separate property is also part of your bankruptcy estate. Your spouse's separate property isn't.

EXAMPLE: Paul owns an airplane as his separate property (he owned it before he married Sonya), and Sonya came to the marriage owning a grand piano. Because only Paul is filing for bankruptcy, Paul's airplane is part of his bankruptcy estate, but Sonya's piano isn't.

If you are not sure what is community property and what isn't, you may need to do some research into your state's property laws. (See Ch. 12, *Help Beyond the Book*, for tips on doing legal research.)

b. Common Law Property States

Most states east of the Rocky Mountains use a marital property system based on English "common law." In these states (all states other than those listed in Subsection a, above), when only one spouse files for bankruptcy, the bankruptcy estate includes:

- that spouse's separate property, and
- half of the couple's jointly owned property unless it is owned as tenancy by the entirety (see Subsection c).

The general rules of property ownership in these states are as follows:

- Property that has only one spouse's name on a title certificate (car, house, stocks), even if bought with joint funds, belongs to that spouse separately.
- Property that was purchased, received as a gift, or inherited jointly for the use of both spouses is jointly owned, unless a title slip has only one spouse's name on it (which means it belongs to that spouse separately, even if both spouses use it).
- Property that one spouse buys with separate funds or receives as a gift or inheritance for that spouse's separate use is that spouse's separate property (again, unless a title certificate shows differently).

c. Special Rules for Property Owned as Tenancy by the Entirety

In about half of all common law property states—primarily in the Midwest and East Coast—real estate can be owned by married couples as a "tenancy by the entirety." This means that the property belongs to the marriage, rather than to one spouse or another. Some states also allow it for personal property, such as joint bank accounts. (See, for example, *In re McNeilly*, 249 B.R. 576 (1st Cir. BAP, 2000) (joint account with Vermont bank).)

In the states listed here, property owned in this manner enjoys unique and rather complex protections from creditors. (Some other states recognize this form of ownership, but do little to protect it.)

    East: Delaware, Maryland, Massachusetts, North Carolina, Pennsylvania, Rhode Island, Vermont, Virginia

Midwest: Illinois, Indiana, Michigan, Missouri, Ohio

    South: Florida, North Carolina, Tennessee

    West: Hawaii, Wyoming.

The key thing to understand is that, if you're filing separately and have numerous debts in your name alone, having tenancy-by-the-entirety property helps you. That's because your tenancy-by-the-entirety property cannot, in the states above, be reached by creditors to pay your individual, nonjoint debts. However, this is an extremely complex area of the law, so if you're in this situation you'd be wise to hire a bankruptcy attorney.

How to tell if you own property in this manner.

In most of the states listed above, any property owned jointly by a married couple is presumed to be owned as a tenancy by the entirety unless the title document specifies otherwise. Documents for property held as tenancy by the entirety often follow the owners' names with the phrase "as husband and wife," which serves as a red flag to creditors that the property is held as tenancy by the entirety.

How tenancy by the entirety ownership protects property from creditors

Long ago, British lawyers invented "Tenancy by the Entirety" as a way of protecting family assets from being squandered by a free-spending spouse. Unlike other forms of joint ownership, tenancy by the entirety ownership means that the *married couple* owns the property but the *individual* spouses do not—at least not while both spouses are alive and married to each other.

Each spouse owns certain rights to the property, including the right to prevent the other spouse from selling or giving away any part of it. As long as the marriage is intact, neither spouse, acting alone, can sell or transfer any part of the property without the participation of the other spouse. Nor can either spouse, acting alone, pledge the property as collateral for a loan.

Extending this logic, laws in the states listed above prohibit creditors with claims against an individual spouse from filing a lien against property held as tenancy by the entirety property, or forcing its partition and sale.

Under federal bankruptcy law, a state's protection against creditors also blocks the bankruptcy trustee from going after tenancy by the entirety property—but only if the bankruptcy petition lists no joint claims against the couple. That is, all claims in the bankruptcy filing must be against a spouse in his or her name alone. If there are joint debts listed in the bankruptcy papers, then the trustee can go after property held as tenancy by the entirety, unless some other exemption (for example, a homestead exemption) protects the property.

In Virginia, this protection persists even if the couple files jointly, as long as none of their nonmortgage debts are joint debts. See *In re Bunker,* 312 F.3d 145 (4th Cir. 2002). In many states, however, this protection is lost whenever spouses file jointly. See, for example, *In the Matter of Steury,* 94 B.R. 553, 556 (Bankr. N.D. Ind. 1988).

How to determine the value of your share of tenancy by the entirety property

Because you can't independently sell your share of property owned as tenancy by the entirety, it is difficult to place an exact value on your current "share." Yet the bankruptcy forms require you to come up with such a value. How to do this is a question that has vexed courts, and many different answers have resulted.

- In many states, if the bankruptcy petition lists no joint marital debts, then the bankruptcy estate must exclude all tenancy by the entirety property. (See, for example, *In re Sinnreich,* 391 F.3d 1295 (11th Cir. 2004) applying Florida law.)
- However, at least one court (in Rhode Island) has held that a husband must list his share of the value of all entireties property as 100%.
- Still other courts invoke a complex formula—involving the life expectancy of each spouse—to arrive at unusual ownership percentages such as 46.5%. (*In re Pletz,* 221 F.3d 1114 (9th Cir. 2000).)

Given the uncertainty in this area of law, on your worksheet and forms it is probably best to list your ownership share as 50%, but with a note explaining to the trustee that you could not sell your share for that amount because your marriage owns it as tenancy by the entirety. This will notify the trustee and your creditors which items of property you own in this manner. When it comes time to list "exemptions" you will claim this property as exempt if your state allows it. (See the exemption chart for your state in Appendix 1.)

More information

For a remarkably clear explanation of tenancy by entirety law, read the U.S. Supreme Court case of *United States v. Craft,* 535 U.S. 274 (2002). Note however, that the issue in the *Craft* case involved tax law, and courts have not extended its ruling to bankruptcy cases. See *In re Sinnreich,* 391 F.3d 1295 (11th Cir. 2004) and cases cited in that opinion. See Ch. 12 for more information on doing legal research and finding a bankruptcy lawyer if you need one.

Worksheet 8 Checklist

Column 1: Your Property

1. Real Estate
- ☐ Residence
- ☐ Condominium or co-op apartment
- ☐ Mobile home
- ☐ Mobile home park space
- ☐ Rental property
- ☐ Vacation home or cabin
- ☐ Business property
- ☐ Undeveloped land
- ☐ Farmland
- ☐ Boat/marina dock space
- ☐ Burial site
- ☐ Airplane hangar

2. Cash on hand
- ☐ In your home
- ☐ In your wallet
- ☐ Under your mattress

3. Deposits of money
- ☐ Bank account
- ☐ Brokerage account (with stockbroker)
- ☐ Certificates of deposit (CDs)
- ☐ Credit union deposit
- ☐ Escrow account
- ☐ Money market account
- ☐ Money in a safe deposit box
- ☐ Savings and loan deposit

4. Security deposits
- ☐ Electric
- ☐ Gas
- ☐ Heating oil
- ☐ Prepaid rent
- ☐ Security deposit on rental unit
- ☐ Rented furniture or equipment
- ☐ Telephone
- ☐ Water

5. Household goods, supplies, and furnishings
- ☐ Antiques
- ☐ Appliances
- ☐ Carpentry tools
- ☐ China and crystal
- ☐ Clocks
- ☐ Dishes
- ☐ Food (total value)
- ☐ Furniture
- ☐ Gardening tools
- ☐ Home computer (for personal use)
- ☐ Lamps
- ☐ Lawn mower or tractor
- ☐ Microwave oven
- ☐ Radios
- ☐ Rugs
- ☐ Sewing machine
- ☐ Silverware and utensils
- ☐ Small appliances
- ☐ Snow blower
- ☐ Stereo system
- ☐ Telephones and answering machines
- ☐ Televisions
- ☐ Vacuum cleaner
- ☐ Video equipment (VCR, Camcorder)

6. Books, pictures, and other art objects, stamp, coin, and other collections
- ☐ Art prints
- ☐ Bibles
- ☐ Books
- ☐ Coins
- ☐ Collectibles (such as political buttons, baseball cards)
- ☐ Compact discs, records, and tapes
- ☐ Family portraits
- ☐ Figurines
- ☐ Original art works
- ☐ Photographs
- ☐ Stamps
- ☐ Videotapes and DVDs

7. Apparel
- ☐ Clothing
- ☐ Furs

8. Jewelry
- ☐ Engagement and wedding ring
- ☐ Gems
- ☐ Precious metals
- ☐ Watches

9. Firearms, sports equipment, and other hobby equipment
- ☐ Board games
- ☐ Bicycles
- ☐ Camera equipment
- ☐ Electronic musical equipment
- ☐ Exercise machine
- ☐ Fishing gear
- ☐ Guns (rifles, pistols, shotguns, muskets)
- ☐ Model or remote cars or planes
- ☐ Musical instruments
- ☐ Scuba diving equipment
- ☐ Ski equipment
- ☐ Other sports equipment
- ☐ Other weapons (swords and knives)

10. Interests in insurance policies
- ☐ Credit insurance
- ☐ Disability insurance
- ☐ Health insurance
- ☐ Homeowners' or renters' insurance
- ☐ Term life insurance
- ☐ Whole or universal life insurance

11. Annuities

12. Pension or profit-sharing plans
- ☐ IRA
- ☐ Keogh
- ☐ Pension or retirement plan
- ☐ 401(k) account

13. Stocks and interests in incorporated and unincorporated companies

14. Interests in partnerships
- ☐ Limited partnership interest
- ☐ General partnership interest

15. Government and corporate bonds and other investment instruments
- ☐ Corporate bonds
- ☐ Deeds of trust
- ☐ Mortgages you own
- ☐ Municipal bonds
- ☐ Promissory notes
- ☐ U.S. savings bonds

16. Accounts receivable
- ☐ Accounts receivable from business
- ☐ Commissions already earned

17. Family support
- ☐ Alimony (spousal support, maintenance) due under court order
- ☐ Child support payments due under court order
- ☐ Payments due under divorce property settlement

18. Other debts owed you where the amount owed is known and definite
- ☐ Disability benefits due
- ☐ Disability insurance due
- ☐ Judgments obtained against third parties you haven't yet collected
- ☐ Sick pay
- ☐ Social Security benefits due
- ☐ Tax refund due under returns already filed
- ☐ Vacation pay earned
- ☐ Wages due
- ☐ Workers' compensation due

19. Powers exercisable for your benefit other than those listed under real estate
- ☐ Right to receive, at some future time, cash, stock, or other personal property placed in an irrevocable trust
- ☐ Current payments of interest or principal from a trust
- ☐ General power of appointment over personal property

20. Interests due to another person's death
- ☐ Property you are entitled to receive as a beneficiary of a living trust, if the trustor has died
- ☐ Expected proceeds from a life insurance policy if the insured has died
- ☐ Inheritance from an existing estate in probate (the owner has died and the court is overseeing the distribution of the property) even if the final amount is not yet known
- ☐ Inheritance under a will that is contingent upon one or more events occurring, but only if the will writer has died

21. All other contingent claims and claims where the amount owed you is not known, including tax refunds, counterclaims, and rights to setoff claims (claims you think you have against a person, government, or corporation, but haven't yet sued on—remember, you do not need to list the amount of your claim now; just list the claim itself)
- ☐ Claims against a corporation, government entity or individual
- ☐ Potential tax refund, if return not yet filed

22. Patents, copyrights, and other intellectual property
- ☐ Copyrights
- ☐ Patents
- ☐ Trade secrets
- ☐ Trademarks
- ☐ Tradenames

23. Licenses, franchises, and other general intangibles
- ☐ Building permits
- ☐ Cooperative association holdings
- ☐ Exclusive licenses
- ☐ Liquor licenses
- ☐ Nonexclusive licenses
- ☐ Patent licenses
- ☐ Professional licenses

24. Automobiles and other vehicles
- ☐ Car
- ☐ Mini-bike or motor scooter
- ☐ Mobile or motor home if on wheels
- ☐ Motorcycle
- ☐ Recreational vehicle (RV)
- ☐ Trailer
- ☐ Truck
- ☐ Van

25. Boats, motors, and accessories
- ☐ Boat (canoe, kayak, rowboat, shell, sailboat, pontoon boat, yacht, etc.)
- ☐ Boat radar, radio, or telephone
- ☐ Outboard motor

26. Aircraft and accessories
- ☐ Aircraft radar, radio, or other accessories
- ☐ Aircraft

27. Office equipment, furnishings, and supplies
- ☐ Art work in your office
- ☐ Computers, software, modems, printers (for business use)
- ☐ Copier
- ☐ Fax machine
- ☐ Furniture
- ☐ Rugs
- ☐ Supplies
- ☐ Telephones
- ☐ Typewriters

28. Machinery, fixtures, equipment, and supplies used in business
- ☐ Military uniforms and accouterments
- ☐ Tools of your trade

29. Business inventory

30. Livestock, poultry, and other animals
- ☐ Birds
- ☐ Cats
- ☐ Dogs
- ☐ Fish and aquarium equipment
- ☐ Horses
- ☐ Other pets
- ☐ Livestock and poultry

31. Crops—growing or harvested

32. Farming equipment and implements

33. Farm supplies, chemicals, and feed

34. Other personal property of any kind
- ☐ Church pew
- ☐ Health aids (for example, wheelchair, crutches)
- ☐ Portable spa or hot tub
- ☐ Season tickets
- ☐ Country club or golf club membership

Worksheet 8: Your Exempt and Nonexempt Property

1 Your property	2 Value of property (actual dollar or garage sale value)	3 Your ownership share (%, $)	4 Amount of liens	5 Amount of your equity	6 Exempt? If not, enter nonexempt amount
1. Real estate					
House	390,000	100%, 390,000	475,000	0	0
2. Cash on hand					
(state source, such as wages, public benefits, etc.)					
Wages	120	100%, 120	0	120	120
3. Deposits of money					
(state source, such as wages, public benefits, etc.)					
Checking account—wages	3,000	100%, 3,000	0	3,000	3,000
4. Security deposits					
Phone company	75	100%, 75	0	75	75
5. Household goods, supplies, and furnishings					
Major appliances	2,500	100%, 2,500	0	2,500	0
Furniture	1,000	100%, 1,000	0	1,000	800
Kitchen goods, bedding	500	100%, 500	0	500	500
6. Books, pictures, art objects; stamp, coin, and other collections					
Books	2,250	100%, 2,250	0	2,250	750
Photos	20	100%, 20	0	20	0

Worksheet 8: Your Exempt and Nonexempt Property (continued)

1 Your property	2 Value of property (actual dollar or garage sale value)	3 Your ownership share (%, $)	4 Amount of liens	5 Amount of your equity	6 Exempt? If not, enter nonexempt amount
7. Apparel					
Clothing	1,500	100%, 1,500	0	1,500	0
8. Jewelry					
Diamond brooch (antique)	3,000	100%, 3,000	0	3,000	3,000
Wedding/engagement rings	1,000	100%, 1,000	0	1,000	0
9. Firearms, sports equipment, and other hobby equipment					
Skis	1,500	100%, 1,500	0	1,500	1,500
10. Interests in insurance policies					
Life insurance (cash value)	4,331	100%, 4,331	4,000	331	331
11. Annuities					
Annuity contract	8,007	100%, 8,007	0	8,007	0
12. Pension or profit-sharing plans (do not include ERISA-qualified pensions; see Chapter 5, Section A3)					
13. Stocks and interests in incorporated and unincorporated companies					

Worksheet 8: Your Exempt and Nonexempt Property (continued)

1 Your property	2 Value of property (actual dollar or garage sale value)	3 Your ownership share (%, $)	4 Amount of liens	5 Amount of your equity	6 Exempt? If not, enter nonexempt amount
14. Interests in partnerships					
15. Government and corporate bonds and other investment instruments					
Seattle city bond	500	100%, 500	0	500	500
16. Accounts receivable					
17. Family support					
18. Other debts owed you where the amount owed is known and definite					
Judgment against former landlord for security deposit	600	100%, 600	0	600	600
19. Powers exercisable for your benefit other than those listed under real estate					
20. Interests due to another person's death					

Worksheet 8: Your Exempt and Nonexempt Property (continued)

Your property	Value of property (actual dollar or garage sale value)	Your ownership share (%, $)	Amount of liens	Amount of your equity	Exempt? If not, enter nonexempt amount
1	**2**	**3**	**4**	**5**	**6**
21. All other contingent claims and claims where the amount owed you is not known					
22. Patents, copyrights, and other intellectual property					
23. Licenses, franchises, and other general intangibles					
24. Automobiles and other vehicles					
1996 Saturn	11,700	100%, 11,700	9,500	2,200	0
1965 Mustang	20,000	25%, 5,000	0	1,000	4,700
25. Boats, motors, and accessories					
26. Aircraft and accessories					
27. Office equipment, furnishings, and supplies					
28. Machinery, fixtures, equipment, and supplies used in business					

Worksheet 8: Your Exempt and Nonexempt Property (continued)

1 Your property	2 Value of property (actual dollar or garage sale value)	3 Your ownership share (%, $)	4 Amount of liens	5 Amount of your equity	6 Exempt? If not, enter nonexempt amount
29. Business inventory					
30. Livestock, poultry, and other animals					
Dog	300	100%, 300	0	300	300
31. Crops					
32. Farming equipment and implements					
33. Farm supplies, chemicals, and feed					
34. Other personal property					
Mariners Season Tickets	1,800	50%, 900	0	900	900

Subtotal	17,076
Wildcard Exemption	− 1,000
Total Value of Nonexempt Property	16,076

This is the minimum amount you will have to pay your unsecured creditors through your Chapter 13 plan.

B. Listing Your Exempt and Nonexempt Property

When you've completed Column 1 of Worksheet 8, you will have a complete inventory of your exempt and non-exempt property. (Ignore the other columns for now. Instructions for completing them are in Section C, below.)

List everything you own worth $50 or more. Lump together low-valued items, such as kitchen utensils. The checklist preceding the sample worksheet should help you think of items. A blank tear-out copy of the worksheet is in Appendix 2.

If you're married, enter all property owned by you or your spouse, and indicate (in parentheses next to the listed item) whether the property is owned by husband (H), wife (W), or jointly (J).

If you are married and filing alone, read Section A6, above, to figure out which property to include on the worksheet.

For cash on hand and deposits of money, state the source of each, such as wages or salary, public benefits, insurance policy proceeds, or the proceeds from the sale of an item of property. You may be able to exempt a portion of that money if you can show it came from an exempt source, such as public benefits.

C. Determining the Value of Your Nonexempt Property

Remember that when you file for Chapter 13 bankruptcy, you must pay your unsecured creditors at least as much as they would have gotten if you had filed for Chapter 7 bankruptcy—that is, the amount your nonexempt property is worth. This means that before you can propose a repayment plan, you must figure out the current value of your nonexempt property. Completing Columns 2–6 of Worksheet 8 will help you make that determination.

All your property may be exempt! In many states the exemptions available to people filing bankruptcy are so liberal that there is no nonexempt property. So, if you're lucky enough to live in one of these states, don't think you've done something wrong.

1. Value of Your Property (Column 2)

In Column 2, enter a value for each item of property listed in Column 1. Estimate if you don't know the exact amount. As long as your estimates are reasonable, no one—not the bankruptcy judge, the bankruptcy trustee, or your creditors—is likely to object. Trustees have years of experience and a pretty good sense of what things are worth. On your bankruptcy papers, you can briefly explain any uncertainties.

If you own an item jointly with someone who is not filing for bankruptcy with you (such as a nonmarital partner, parent, child, sibling, or nonfiling spouse), put the value of the entire asset, not just your share, here. In Column 3 you will enter your share. Also, if you still owe money on an item of property, put the entire value here. In Column 4 you'll list how much you still owe.

Fluctuating Values

The court will want to know the value of your property as of the date you file your bankruptcy papers. But the value of some property changes over time. Depending on the economy and the type of property, the value can fluctuate a lot, even in a short period of time. If you plan to file your papers within a few weeks, don't worry about changes in value. If you don't file your papers for several months, however, you probably should review your figures for any changes.

Here are some suggestions for valuing specific items:

- **Real estate.** For purposes of the worksheet, use your best estimate. When it comes time to transfer this information to your bankruptcy papers, you may have to do some work to determine a more precise figure. With a house, for example, you will need an estimate of its market value from a local real estate agent or appraiser. If you own another type of real estate—such as land used to grow crops—you will have to put the amount it would bring in at a forced sale. As a general rule, your estimate must be close to real market conditions to stand up in court.

- **Cars.** Start with the low *Kelley Blue Book* price. (You can find this book at the public library or online at www.kbb.com.) If the car needs substantial repairs, reduce the value by the amount they would cost. If the car's worth is below the *Blue Book* value, be prepared to show why. (A letter from a mechanic should be enough.) An alternative source of used car values can be found at www.edmunds.com.

- **Older goods.** Estimate their market value—that is, what you could sell the items for at a garage sale or through a classified ad. Want ads in a local flea market or penny-saver newspaper are a good place to look for prices. If the item isn't listed, begin with the price you paid and then deduct about 20% for each year you've owned the item. For example, if you bought a camera for $400 three years ago, subtract $80 for the first year (down to $320), $64 for the second year (down to $256) and $51 for the third year (down to $205).

- **Insurance.** For unmatured whole life and universal life insurance policies, put the accrued loan value; call your insurance agent for this figure. Don't put the amount of benefits the policy will pay, unless you're the beneficiary of an insurance policy and the insured person has died. Other kinds of insurance—term life, disability, renter's, homeowner's, etc.—have a loan value of zero.

- **Stocks and bonds.** If you have a mutual fund or brokerage account, use the value from your latest statement. You can look up a specific stock's current value in a newspaper business section. If you can't find the listing, call your broker and ask. If the stock isn't traded publicly, you will have to ask an officer of the corporation for the value assigned at the most recent shareholder meeting.

- **Jewelry, antiques, and other collectibles.** Any valuable jewelry or collection should be appraised before you file your bankruptcy papers. For now, if you think you can give a fairly accurate estimate, put it down.

2. Your Ownership Share (Column 3)

In Column 3, enter two amounts:
- the percentage of your ownership interest in the property listed in Column 1, and
- the dollar value of your ownership interest in the property listed in Column 1.

EXAMPLE: You and your brother jointly bought a music synthesizer worth $10,000. Your ownership share is one-half, worth $5,000. List both the percentage (50%) and the dollar amount ($5,000) in Column 3.

 If you're married. If you're filing jointly with your spouse, put your combined share here. If you're filing alone, read Section A6, above, to determine how to list your ownership share.

3. Amount of Liens (Column 4)

In Column 4, put the total amount of all legal claims (liens) against the property. Even if you own only part of the property, enter the full amount of the liens.

EXAMPLE: You own a house. You owe $63,000 on your first mortgage, the IRS has recorded a lien for a $17,000 tax debt, and a hospital sued you, got a judgment, and recorded a lien for an $11,000 bill you owe. The total amount of all liens on your house is $91,000.

The amount of the liens may exceed the property's value. That means that there is no nonexempt value to include in the calculation of how much you must pay your unsecured creditors.

A complete list of liens—and information on matching a lien to the property it secures—is in Worksheets 2 and 3 in Ch. 3, *Adding Up Your Secured and Unsecured Debts*, Section A.

4. Amount of Your Equity (Column 5)

Your equity is the amount you would get to keep if you sold the property.

If you own the property alone (or if you and your spouse own it and you live in a community property state or you are filing jointly), calculate your equity by subtracting the amount in Column 4 from the property's total value (Column 2). Put this amount in Column 5. If you get a negative number, enter "0."

EXAMPLE: The liens on your house total $91,000. Your house is worth $105,000. The amount of your equity is $14,000.

If you are married, filing singly, live in a common law property state, and own the property with your spouse or you own the property with someone other than your spouse with whom you're filing for bankruptcy, calculating your equity is a little more complex. Only your property—not a co-owner's—is used to calculate how much you must pay your unsecured creditors in bankruptcy.

1. **All liens on the property are from jointly incurred debts.** Subtract the amount of the liens from the total value of the property, and multiply the result by your ownership share.
2. **All liens on the property are from debts you incurred alone.** Subtract the amount of the liens from the total value of your share of the property.
3. **The property has liens from both jointly and solely incurred debts.** Subtract the amount of the jointly incurred liens from the total value of the property, and multiply the result by your ownership share. Then subtract the amount of the solely incurred liens.

EXAMPLE: You co-own your $220,000 house with your nonmarital partner. You and your partner owe your mortgage lender $160,000. In addition, the IRS has filed a Notice of Federal Tax Lien against your house for a tax bill of $25,000 owed by you alone. You figure the amount of your equity as follows:

- Subtract the $160,000 joint mortgage lien from the $220,000 value, leaving $60,000. Multiply by your ownership share, 50%. The result is $30,000.
- Subtract the $25,000 IRS lien owed solely by you from the $30,000. Your equity in the house is $5,000, which is what you list in Column 5.

5. Is the Property Exempt? (Column 6)

In Chapter 13 bankruptcy, you don't have to turn over any property to the bankruptcy trustee, but you need to tell the court what property you think is legally exempt. That's because the payments you make in Chapter 13 bankruptcy must, at a minimum, be equal to the value of your nonexempt property.

a. An Overview of Exemptions

Each state has its own list of what items of property are exempt in bankruptcy. Many states exempt, for instance, all health aids, ordinary household furniture, and clothing.

Other kinds of property are exempt up to a limit. For instance, cars are often exempt up to a certain amount—usually between $1,200 and $2,500. An exemption limit means that any equity above the limit is considered nonexempt. So if your car is worth $3,500 and your state's motor vehicle exemption is $1,200, you can claim only $1,200 of the equity as exempt. The other $2,300 is part of the nonexempt total—the minimum amount your unsecured creditors must receive in your Chapter 13 case.

In addition to specific exemptions, many states (as well as the federal exemption system) offer what's known as a wildcard exemption. Wildcard exemptions provide a value that can be applied to any type of property. For instance, if the state provides a wildcard exemption of $1,000, you could apply this wildcard to exempt a $500 pool table and a $500 jet ski, neither of which would be specifically exempt under the state or federal exemption systems.

b. Determining Which of Your Property Is Exempt

To determine which of your property is exempt, carefully follow the steps below.

Keep in mind that the more property that is exempt, the less you will have to pay your unsecured creditors. As you go through the lists of exempt property, give yourself the benefit of the doubt. If it appears that a particular exemption covers all or part of a property item, claim it. If the trustee challenges you and asks the court to rule on the matter, you can decide then whether or not to fight.

Step 1: Choose an exemption system.

If you live in one of the states listed below, you must choose between two sets of exemptions. If your state isn't listed, skip to Step 2.

Arkansas	Michigan	Rhode Island
California	Minnesota	Texas
Connecticut	New Hampshire	Vermont
District of Columbia	New Jersey	Washington
Hawaii	New Mexico	Wisconsin
Massachusetts	Pennsylvania	

In all of these states (except California), you must choose between your state's exemptions and a list of federal bankruptcy exemptions. You can't mix and match, however—if you pick your state's exemption system, you may use only its exemptions, and the same goes if you pick the federal bankruptcy system. If you and your spouse jointly file for bankruptcy, both of you must select the same system.

Special rules for Californians. Californians must choose between two different systems enacted by the state, not a state system and the federal system. As you read the discussion below, substitute "California System 1" for "your state exemptions" and "California System 2" for "the federal exemptions."

Look in Appendix 1 for:
- your state's exemptions plus the federal *non-bankruptcy* exemptions—these are mostly federal pension benefits which all debtors who use state exemptions are entitled to select from (they are at the very end of Appendix 1), and
- the federal bankruptcy exemptions list (it appears after all the state lists but before the federal *non-bankruptcy* exemptions).

Compare the federal bankruptcy exemptions list to your state's list plus the federal *nonbankruptcy* exemptions to see how each treats valuable items, such as your home and car.

You may be able to "double" exemptions. The federal bankruptcy exemptions allow married couples filing jointly to each claim a full set of exemptions. This is called "doubling." Many state exemption systems do not allow doubling or do not allow doubling for certain types of property, such as the homestead exemption (which exempts equity in your residence). In some states, the legislature has expressly allowed or prohibited doubling. In others, the courts have allowed or prohibited doubling. In still others, neither the courts nor the legislature has addressed the issue. If that is the case, doubling is probably allowed. If you are doubling an exemption in one piece of property (like a house or a car), title to the property must be in both spouses' names. And just because a state allows you to double one exemption does not mean you can double all exemptions.

In Appendix 1, we've noted whether a court or state legislature has expressly allowed or prohibited doubling. If the chart doesn't say, it is probably safe to double. However, keep in mind that this area of the law changes rapidly—legislation or court decisions regarding doubling issued after the publication date of this book will not be reflected in the chart.

- **Your home.** If the equity in your home is your major asset, your choice may be dictated by the "homestead" exemption alone. Compare your state's homestead exemption to the $17,425 federal exemption. In several states (Alaska, Arizona, Arkansas, California System 1, Colorado, Connecticut, District of Columbia, Florida, Hawaii, Idaho, Iowa, Kansas, Louisiana, Maine, Massachusetts, Minnesota, Mississippi, Montana, Nevada, New Hampshire, New Mexico, North Dakota, Oklahoma, Oregon, Rhode Island, South Dakota, Texas, Utah, Vermont, Washington, West Virginia, and Wisconsin), the homestead exemption is $20,000 or more. In these states, you can exempt more equity in your home if you choose the state exemption system. In other states, such as Michigan, New Jersey, and Pennsylvania, the state homestead exemption is $17,425 or less. In these states, you can exempt more equity in your home if you choose the federal exemption system.

  In California System 2, you can exempt up to $18,675. And if you don't own real estate, you can apply this System 2 homestead to property of any type (System 2 also offers an additional $1,000 exemption as a wildcard).

⚠ Immediate change to homestead exemption in bankruptcy bill. The bankruptcy bill now heading toward passage would immediately limit the homestead exemption to $125,000 in real estate for people who moved to their current state within the past 1,215 days (three years and four months). This change won't affect most people; most states' homestead exemptions aren't that high, anyway. But be aware of the change if you moved within the 1,215-day period to Arkansas, California, the District of Columbia, Florida, Iowa, Kansas, Louisiana, Massachusetts, Minnesota, Nevada, Oklahoma, Rhode Island, South Dakota, or Texas; and have more than $125,000 in equity in real estate. Check for more information about the new law at Nolo's website (www.nolo.com).

- **Other valuable property.** If the equity in your home isn't a factor in your decision, identify the most valuable items you own. Look at the federal bankruptcy exemptions and your state and the federal *nonbankruptcy* exemptions. Which list helps you bring down the value of your nonexempt property?

  EXAMPLE: Andy lives in New Mexico, a state that offers both the regular state exemptions and the federal exemptions. Andy rents a home and has $20,000 worth of equity in a customized van. The New Mexico state vehicle exemption is $4,000. In addition, the New Mexico state exemptions provide a "wildcard" exemption of $2,500. Because Andy has $13,500 worth of unprotected equity under the New Mexico state exemptions, he would have to repay his unsecured creditors at least that much money under his Chapter 13 plan. However, if Andy uses the federal exemptions, he will be able to use the $2,775 vehicle exemption and the federal wildcard exemption of $9,650 for a total of $12,425. This would leave him $7,575 of nonexempt equity in the van, a far smaller amount to repay under this Chapter 13 plan.

- **Your pension.** If your pension is covered by the federal law called ERISA, remember that it isn't considered part of your bankruptcy estate and

has no effect on the value of your nonexempt property.

If your pension is not covered by ERISA, it is exempt only if you use your state's exemptions and the pension is covered by either your state exemption list or the federal *nonbankruptcy* exemption list. See "ERISA-Qualified Retirement Plans" in Section A3, above.

Step 2: Decide which items you listed on Worksheet 8 are exempt under the exemption system you're using.

In evaluating whether or not your cash on hand and deposits of money are exempt, look to the source of the money, such as welfare benefits, insurance proceeds, or wages.

Efficiency Suggestion: While you're determining which of your property is exempt, write down in Column 6 the laws that authorize each exemption. (These are listed in Appendix 1.) You will need this information when you fill out Schedule C of your bankruptcy papers.

Step 3: If you are using your state exemptions, decide which items you listed on Worksheet 8 are exempt under the federal *nonbankruptcy* exemptions.

If you use your state exemptions (this includes all Californians), you may also select from a list of federal nonbankruptcy exemptions. These are mostly military and other federal benefits, as well as 75% of wages you have earned but have not yet been paid. You cannot, however, combine your exemptions if the federal nonbankruptcy exemptions duplicate your state's exemptions.

EXAMPLE: You're using your state's exemptions. Both your state and the federal *nonbankruptcy* exemptions let you exempt 75% of unpaid wages owed you. You cannot combine the exemptions to claim 100% of your wages; 75% is all you can exempt.

Step 4: Determine the value of all nonexempt items.

Look at each nonexempt property value. If an item (or group of items) is completely exempt, put "0" in Column 6.

If an item (or group of items) is exempt to a certain amount (for example, household goods to $4,000), total up the value of all items that fall into the category, using the values in Column 5. From that, subtract the total amount of the exemption. What is left is the non-exempt value. Enter that in Column 6.

EXAMPLE: Desmond's state exempts several categories of items, including books, clothing, appliances, household goods, and furnishings to a total of $2,500. His rare book collection is worth $4,000 and his clothing $500 and his household goods and furnishings another $1,500, for a total value of $6,000. He can exempt only $2,500 worth of his books, clothing, appliances, household goods, and furnishings. He enters the nonexempt amount—$3,500—in Column 6.

If an item (or group of items) is not exempt at all, copy the amount from Column 5 to Column 6.

6. The Minimum Amount You Must Pay in Chapter 13 Bankruptcy

Once you've filled in Columns 1–6 for all items, total up Column 6. This is the value of your nonexempt property. If the exemption system you're using has a wildcard exemption, subtract that amount from the total. The total amount goes on Worksheet 1 from Ch. 2, on which you calculate the minimum amount you must pay your unsecured creditors. ■

Completing the Bankruptcy Forms

Now that you've added up your secured and unsecured debts, calculated your disposable income, and calculated the value of your nonexempt property, you are ready to fill out your bankruptcy papers.

This chapter shows you how to fill out all of the forms for a Chapter 13 bankruptcy case, except your Chapter 13 repayment plan. (How to write your plan is covered in Ch. 7, *Writing Your Chapter 13 Bankruptcy Plan*.) For the most part, filling out the forms in this chapter is simple—it's just a matter of putting the right information in the right blanks. If you completed the worksheets in the earlier chapters, you've already done much of the work.

➡ **Emergency filing.** Most people file all their bankruptcy forms at once, but you don't have to. If you need to stop a foreclosure or have another emergency, you can file the two-page Voluntary Petition, together with a form called a Matrix, which lists the name, address, and zip code of each of your creditors. The automatic stay, which stops collection efforts against you—including a foreclosure—will then go into effect. You will have 15 days to file the rest of the forms, including your Chapter 13 plan. (Bankruptcy Rules 1007(c), 3015(b).) See Ch. 8, *Filing Your Bankruptcy Papers*, Section C, for instructions.

A. Finding the Right Bankruptcy Court

Because bankruptcy is a creature of federal, not state, law, you must file for bankruptcy in a special federal bankruptcy court. There are federal bankruptcy courts all over the country. You need to find the right one to file in.

The federal court system divides the country into judicial districts. Every state has at least one judicial district; most states have more. Normally, you file in the bankruptcy court for the federal judicial district where you've lived during the greater part of the previous 180 days—probably in the nearest sizable city.

EXAMPLE: For the past two months, you've lived in San Luis Obispo, which is in California's central judicial district. Before that you lived in Santa Rosa, in California's northern judicial district. Because

during the past six months you lived longer in the northern district than the central, you should file in the bankruptcy court in the northern district. If it's too inconvenient to file there, you could wait another month, when you would qualify to file in the central district court.

If you own or run a business and are including in your bankruptcy papers business debts for which you are personally liable, you have another option. You can file in the district where your principal place of business has been located during the previous 180 days, or where the business's principal assets were located during that period.

To find a bankruptcy court in your state, check the government listings in your white pages ("United States, Courts"), call directory assistance, ask your local librarian, or visit the court directory link at www.bankruptcydata.com. If you live in a state with more than one district, call the court in the closest city and ask whether that district includes your county or zip code.

B. Before You Begin: Get Some Information From the Court

Although bankruptcy courts operate similarly throughout the country, every bankruptcy court has its own requirements for filing bankruptcy papers. If your papers don't meet these local requirements, the court clerk may reject them. So before you begin preparing your papers, contact your bankruptcy court to find out its requirements. You'll save yourself a lot of trouble—and probably impress the court clerk with your conscientiousness.

The sample letter below outlines what you need to find out from the court. A tear-out copy is in Appendix 2. When you send it, include a large, self-addressed envelope. Call the court and ask whether you need to affix return postage; many, but not all, courts mail without charge. Especially in urban areas, you may get no response to a letter. If you don't hear back within a reasonable time, visit the court and get the information in person. The information might also be on the Internet. (See www.bankruptcydata.com) Most courts post local forms and rules online.

Letter to Bankruptcy Court

Sandra Smith
432 Oak Street
Cincinnati, Ohio 45219
(123) 456-7890

July 2, 20XX

United States Bankruptcy Court
Atrium Two, Room 800
221 East Fourth Street
Cincinnati, OH 45202

TO THE COURT CLERK:

Please send me the following materials or information:
- A copy of all local forms published by this court for filing a Chapter 13 bankruptcy, such as:
  - ☐ Chapter 13 bankruptcy cover sheet
  - ☐ Chapter 13 plan
  - ☐ worksheet showing the Chapter 13 plan calculation
  - ☐ summary of the Chapter 13 plan
  - ☐ separate creditor mailing list (matrix)
  - ☐ income deduction order and information on when to submit it
  - ☐ business report for debtor engaged in business
  - ☐ proof of claim (in case I must file claim on behalf of a creditor).
- Copies of all local rules applicable in a Chapter 13 case—rules for the judicial district, this bankruptcy court, and any applicable division.
- A copy of the court's calendar.
- The number of copies or sets of all forms I must file.
- The order in which forms should be submitted.

I have additional questions:
1. Is the filing fee still $155? Is the administrative fee still $39?
2. Can I make my plan payments with a personal check? If not, can I use cash or am I limited to cashier's checks and money orders?
3. Is there more than one division for this bankruptcy court? If so, in which division should I file?
4. Must I submit a mailing matrix?
5. Must I submit an income deduction order?
6. Should I two-hole punch my papers or is that done by the court?

I've enclosed a self-addressed envelope for your reply. Thank you.

Sincerely,

Sandra Smith
Sandra Smith

1. Fees

Currently, the court charges a $155 filing fee and a $39 administrative fee for filing a Chapter 13 bankruptcy case. Fees change, however, so verify the amounts with the court.

You must eventually pay the fees regardless of your income. You can, however, ask the court for permission to pay the combined $194 filing fee in installments. (Instructions for making this request are in Ch. 8, *Filing Your Bankruptcy Papers*, Section B.) You can pay in up to four installments over four months. You can't pay an attorney or typing service until you've fully paid your fees—the court is entitled to its money first.

2. Forms

This book contains all the official, fill-in-the-blanks bankruptcy forms. You can also download these forms from www.uscourts.gov/bankform/index.html. In addition to the official forms, which must be filed in every bankruptcy court, your local bankruptcy court may require you to file one or two forms that it has developed. Often, these forms ask for a summary of information you provide on the official forms.

There is no official fill-in-the-blanks form for the Chapter 13 repayment plan. (Ch. 7, *Writing Your Chapter 13 Bankruptcy Plan*, provides detailed instructions on how to write a plan.) Several bankruptcy courts, however, have developed their own form, which they require debtors to use.

You can get all local forms from your local bankruptcy court, a local stationery store, or, possibly, from the court's website. We can't, of course, include all local forms in this book, or tell you how to complete them. Most, however, are self-explanatory.

3. Local Court Rules

Bankruptcy courts must adhere to the local rules established for their federal judicial district, as described in Section A, above. In addition, most bankruptcy courts publish local rules that govern the court's procedures. To add further bureaucracy, in courts with multiple divisions, each division may develop its own set of local rules.

In general, local rules—whether set by your judicial district, bankruptcy court, or local division—seldom apply to Chapter 13 bankruptcy cases. Instead, they primarily concern Chapter 11 business bankruptcies and contested matters that rarely come up in Chapter 13 cases. But occasionally, a rule does affect a Chapter 13 bankruptcy. For example, in New Mexico, if you are married but filing alone, you must file a statement listing your spouse's name, address, and Social Security number. You must also certify that your papers include your nonfiling spouse's community income, expenses, debts, and assets.

You can get your local rules from the bankruptcy court (possibly on its website)—but be prepared to comb through reams of material to find the one or two rules that might apply in your case. Having the rules on hand will help you, however, if the court clerk, trustee, or bankruptcy judge refers you to a certain rule to follow when filing a form or making a request to the court.

One local practice set by your court is the dates and times the court schedules hearings. You can find out this information by requesting a copy of the court's calendar.

4. Number of Copies

Before filing your papers, be sure you know how many copies your court requires. Many courts require that you file the original and as many as four additional copies of each form.

Courts that have switched to electronic filing (for attorneys only) will probably want only the original and one copy. The clerk will retain the original for scanning into the court's database and return the copy to you for your records.

Most courts prefer that your forms be filed in a particular order. Most bankruptcy court clerks will have a sample available at the desk that shows the preferred order. If you are unable to get this information by other means, visit the court and request a viewing of their sample filing.

C. What Forms to File

You must file the forms listed below. Despite the length of this list, completing your bankruptcy forms will not be as hard as it looks. This is especially true if you completed the Worksheets in Chs. 2, 3, 4, and 5; most of the information you need for these forms you can transfer directly from the worksheets.

Bankruptcy Forms Checklist

- ☐ Form 1—Voluntary Petition
- ☐ Form 6, which consists of:
  - ☐ Schedule A—Real Property
  - ☐ Schedule B—Personal Property
  - ☐ Schedule C—Property Claimed as Exempt
  - ☐ Schedule D—Creditors Holding Secured Claims
  - ☐ Schedule E—Creditors Holding Unsecured Priority Claims
  - ☐ Schedule F—Creditors Holding Unsecured Nonpriority Claims
  - ☐ Schedule G—Executory Contracts and Unexpired Leases
  - ☐ Schedule H—Codebtors
  - ☐ Schedule I—Current Income
  - ☐ Schedule J—Current Expenditures
  - ☐ Summary of Schedules A through J
  - ☐ Declaration Concerning Debtor's Schedules (in which you declare under penalty of perjury that the information you put in the schedules is true and correct)
- ☐ Form 7—Statement of Financial Affairs (in which you provide information about your economic affairs during the past several years)
- ☐ Form 21—Statement of Social Security Number
- ☐ Mailing Matrix (on which you list your creditors and their addresses)
- ☐ Required local forms.

Note: Forms 2, 4, and 5 aren't on the list because they aren't used in Chapter 13 voluntary bankruptcy filings; Form 3 is an Application to Pay the Filing Fee in Installments.

Using Nolo Forms

The content and numbering of the official bankruptcy forms are determined by the Bankruptcy Rules, a set of rules issued by the United States Supreme Court. Private publishers are free to modify the format of official forms, as long as each form asks the same questions in the same order.

Courts are required by law to accept all forms that:
- contain the questions and answers prescribed by the official forms
- are printed on one side only, and
- have adequate top margins.

The forms in this book meet all official Bankruptcy Rule requirements. If the court clerk tries to reject any of these forms—perhaps because the clerk is used to seeing forms published by a different company, with its own unique format—politely remind the clerk of the rules. (Bankruptcy Rules 5005, 9009, and 9029.)

If you are still having a problem, download the forms from the official court website at www.uscourts.gov/bankform.

Should Married Couples File Jointly or Not?

As a general rule, married debtors will want to file jointly. But if one spouse separately owes all or most of the debts, that spouse may want to file singly.

For example, if Tom and Joan are married, and Tom brought a lot of debts to the marriage while Joan has squeaky clean credit, it may make sense for Tom to file separately. At least one court has ruled that a married couple can, as a practical matter, extend a Chapter 13 plan past the five-year limit by each spouse filing singly. *In re Nahat,* 315 B.R. 368 (N.D. Tex. 2004). In that case the husband filed a three-year plan and the wife filed a five-year plan, extending the total amount of time the couple was in Chapter 13 to seven years. If you are married but one or both of you are thinking of filing singly, consult a bankruptcy attorney before doing so.

Bankruptcy courts are not, at this time, recognizing same-sex marriages or domestic partnerships. People in these relationships must file for bankruptcy on their own.

D. Tips for Filling In the Forms

Here are some tips to make filling in your forms easier and the whole bankruptcy process smoother.

Use your worksheets. If you completed the worksheets in Chs. 2, 3, 4, and 5, you've already done a lot of the work. It will save you lots of time if you refer to them. If you skipped those chapters, refer to Worksheet 7 (Ch. 5) for help in identifying what property you should list in your bankruptcy forms.

Use the samples. A sample completed form accompanies each form's instructions. Refer to it while you fill in your bankruptcy papers. Bear in mind, though, that these are examples only. Even if you live in Arizona, the same state as our fictional bankruptcy filers, your completed forms will look very different.

Photocopy the forms before you start. You can't tear out and file the forms in Appendix 2 because they are slightly smaller than regulation size, due to bookbinding requirements. Good photocopies of the forms on 8½" by 11" paper will work fine, however. Make at least two photocopies of all the forms in the appendix. Make the photocopies single-sided, even if, to save space, we've printed them double-sided in the appendix. Keep the originals (from Appendix 2) so you can make additional copies if you need them. Or, download and print the forms from the Federal Judiciary's website at www.uscourts.gov/bankform.

Start with drafts. First, fill in the forms in pencil, so you can make corrections along the way. Prepare final forms to file with the court only after you've double-checked your drafts.

Type your final forms. Although you are not required to type your forms, many courts prefer that they be typed, and the court clerk is likely to be friendlier if you show up with neatly typed forms. If you don't have a typewriter, many libraries have typewriters available to the public free or for a small rental fee. Or you can hire a bankruptcy petition preparer to type your forms with the information you provide. (See Ch. 12, *Help Beyond the Book*.)

Be ridiculously thorough. Always err on the side of giving too much information rather than too little. If you leave information off the forms, the bankruptcy trustee or court may become suspicious of your motives, and you may be in for rough sledding. If you leave creditors off the forms, these creditors won't be bound by your plan and can come after you for payment—hardly the result you want. Also, you are signing the papers under penalty of perjury and some bankruptcy judges will dismiss your case if you omit a creditor (perhaps because you don't want that creditor to know about your bankruptcy) simply because you didn't tell the complete truth. Finally, if you don't accurately describe your recent property transactions, the court may refuse to approve your Chapter 13 repayment plan.

Answer every question. Most questions have a box to check if your answer is "none." If a question doesn't have a "none" box and the question doesn't apply to you, type in "N/A" for "not applicable." This will let the trustee know that you didn't overlook it. If the question has a number of blanks, put "N/A" in only the first blank if it is obvious that it applies to the other blanks as well. If it's not clear, put "N/A" in every blank.

Don't worry about repetition. Sometimes different forms, or different questions on the same form, ask for the same or overlapping information. Don't worry about providing the same information multiple times—too much information is never a sin in bankruptcy court.

Explain uncertainties. If you can't figure out which category on a form to use for a debt or item of property, list the debt or item in what you think is the appropriate place and briefly note next to your entry that you're

Sample Continuation Page

In re: Joshua and Alice Milton, Debtors.

Form 7, Statement of Financial Affairs

Continuation Page 1

11. Closed Financial Accounts: Bank of Iowa, 150 Broadway, Cedar Rapids, IA 52407; Savings Account No. 1-23-567-890, final balance of $3,446.18; closed September 11, 20xx.

---

uncertain. The important thing is to disclose the information somewhere. The bankruptcy trustee will sort it out, if necessary.

Be scrupulously honest. You must swear, under penalty of perjury, that you've been truthful on your bankruptcy forms. If you are not scrupulously honest, the court will probably dismiss your bankruptcy case—and you could even be prosecuted for perjury if it's evident that you deliberately lied.

If you run out of room, use continuation pages. The space for entering information is sometimes skimpy, especially if you're filing jointly. Most of the forms come with preformatted continuation pages if you need more room. But if there is no continuation form, you can easily prepare one yourself, using a piece of regular white 8½" by 11" paper. (A sample is shown above.) On the official form, put "see continuation page" next to the question you're working on and then enter the additional information on the continuation page. Label the continuation pages with your name, the form name, and "Continuation Page 1," "Continuation Page 2," and so on. Be sure to attach all continuation pages to the appropriate forms when you file your bankruptcy papers.

Get help if you need it. If your situation is very complicated, you're unsure about how to complete a form, or you run into trouble when you go to file your papers, consult a bankruptcy attorney or do some legal research before proceeding. (See Ch. 12, *Help Beyond the Book.*)

Getting Help From the Trustee Before You File

In some small districts, where there is only one trustee, the Chapter 13 bankruptcy trustee may be willing to help you complete your bankruptcy forms or answer some basic questions. To contact the trustee before you file, call the bankruptcy court clerk. Explain that you are planning to file a Chapter 13 bankruptcy case and that you have a question for the trustee. The clerk should give you the trustee's name and phone number. (11 U.S.C. § 1302 (b)(4).)

E. Form 1—Voluntary Petition

Filing your Voluntary Petition gets your bankruptcy started and puts the automatic stay into effect, stopping creditors from trying to collect from you. A sample Voluntary Petition and line-by-line instructions follow.

First Page

Court Name. At the top of the first page, fill in the first two blanks with the name of the judicial district you're filing in, such as the "Central District of California." If your state has only one district, type XXXXXX in the first blank. If your state divides its districts into divisions, type the division after the state name, such as "Northern District of Ohio, Eastern Division." (Sections

(Official Form 1) (12/03)

FORM B1	**United States Bankruptcy Court**	**Voluntary Petition**
XXXXXX	**District of** Arizona, Tucson Division	

Name of Debtor (if individual, enter Last, First, Middle): Herchoo, Martin P.	Name of Joint Debtor (Spouse) (Last, First, Middle): Herchoo, Ellen G.
All Other Names used by the Debtor in the last 6 years (include married, maiden, and trade names): N/A	All Other Names used by the Joint Debtor in the last 6 years (include married, maiden, and trade names): Gomacho, Ellen A.
Last four digits of Soc. Sec. No./Complete EIN or other Tax I.D. No. (if more than one, state all): 7890	Last four digits of Soc. Sec.No./Complete EIN or other Tax I.D. No. (if more than one, state all): 3210
Street Address of Debtor (No. & Street, City, State & Zip Code): 19068 Cactus Drive Tucson, AZ 85700	Street Address of Joint Debtor (No. & Street, City, State & Zip Code): 19068 Cactus Drive Tucson, AZ 85700
County of Residence or of the Principal Place of Business: Pima	County of Residence or of the Principal Place of Business: Pima
Mailing Address of Debtor (if different from street address): N/A	Mailing Address of Joint Debtor (if different from street address): N/A

Location of Principal Assets of Business Debtor (if different from street address above): N/A

Information Regarding the Debtor (Check the Applicable Boxes)

Venue (Check any applicable box)

☒ Debtor has been domiciled or has had a residence, principal place of business, or principal assets in this District for 180 days immediately preceding the date of this petition or for a longer part of such 180 days than in any other District.

☐ There is a bankruptcy case concerning debtor's affiliate, general partner, or partnership pending in this District.

Type of Debtor (Check all boxes that apply)		**Chapter or Section of Bankruptcy Code Under Which** **the Petition is Filed** (Check one box)
☒ Individual(s) ☐ Railroad ☐ Corporation ☐ Stockbroker ☐ Partnership ☐ Commodity Broker ☐ Other_____ ☐ Clearing Bank		☐ Chapter 7 ☐ Chapter 11 ☒ Chapter 13 ☐ Chapter 9 ☐ Chapter 12 ☐ Sec. 304 - Case ancillary to foreign proceeding
Nature of Debts (Check one box) ☒ Consumer/Non-Business ☐ Business		**Filing Fee** (Check one box) ☒ Full Filing Fee attached
Chapter 11 Small Business (Check all boxes that apply) ☐ Debtor is a small business as defined in 11 U.S.C. § 101 N/A ☐ Debtor is and elects to be considered a small business under 11 U.S.C. § 1121(e) (Optional)		☐ Filing Fee to be paid in installments (Applicable to individuals only) Must attach signed application for the court's consideration certifying that the debtor is unable to pay fee except in installments. Rule 1006(b). See Official Form No. 3.

Statistical/Administrative Information (Estimates only)

☒ Debtor estimates that funds will be available for distribution to unsecured creditors.

☐ Debtor estimates that, after any exempt property is excluded and administrative expenses paid, there will be no funds available for distribution to unsecured creditors.

THIS SPACE IS FOR COURT USE ONLY

Estimated Number of Creditors	1-15	16-49	50-99	100-199	200-999	1000-over
	☒	☐	☐	☐	☐	☐

Estimated Assets	$0 to $50,000	$50,001 to $100,000	$100,001 to $500,000	$500,001 to $1 million	$1,000,001 to $10 million	$10,000,001 to $50 million	$50,000,001 to $100 million	More than $100 million
	☐	☐	☒	☐	☐	☐	☐	☐

Estimated Debts	$0 to $50,000	$50,001 to $100,000	$100,001 to $500,000	$500,001 to $1 million	$1,000,001 to $10 million	$10,000,001 to $50 million	$50,000,001 to $100 million	More than $100 million
	☐	☐	☒	☐	☐	☐	☐	☐

A and B, above, explain how to find out what district and division to file in.)

Name of Debtor. Enter your full name, last name first. Use the form of your name that you use on your checks, driver's license, and other formal documents.

Name of Joint Debtor (Spouse). If you are married and filing jointly with your spouse, put your spouse's name, last name first, in the "joint debtor" box. Again, use the name that appears on formal documents. If you're filing alone, type "N/A" anywhere in the box.

All Other Names. If you have been known by any other name in the last six years, list it here. If you've operated a business as an individual proprietor during the previous six years, include your trade name (fictitious or assumed business name preceded by "dba" for doing business as). You don't need to include minor variations in spelling or form. For instance, if your name is John Lewis Odegard, don't put down that you're sometimes known as J.L. But if you've used the pseudonym J.L. Smith, list it. If you're uncertain, list the name if you think you may have used it with a creditor. It can't hurt. The purpose of this box is to make sure that when your creditors receive notice of your bankruptcy filing, they'll know who you are. Do the same for your spouse (in the box to the right) if you are filing jointly. If you're filing alone, type "N/A" anywhere in the box to the right.

Soc. Sec./Tax I.D. No. Enter the last four digits of your Social Security number. If you have a taxpayer I.D. number, enter the last four digits of it as well. Do the same for your spouse (in the box to the right) if you are filing jointly. If you're filing alone, type "N/A" anywhere in the box to the right.

Street Address of Debtor. Enter your current street address. Even if you get all of your mail at a post office box, list the address of your personal residence. Do the same for your spouse—in the box to the right—if you are filing jointly, even if it is the same.

County of Residence. Enter the county of your residence. Do the same for your spouse—in the box to the right—if you are filing jointly. Otherwise, type "N/A" in the box.

Mailing Address of Debtor. Enter your mailing address if it is different from your street address. If it isn't, put "N/A." Do the same for your spouse—in the box to the right—if you are filing jointly, even if it is the same.

Location of Principal Assets of Business Debtor. If you—or your spouse if you are filing jointly—have been self-employed or operated a business as a sole proprietor within the last two years, you'll be considered a "business debtor." This means you will have to provide additional information on Form 7 (Section G, below). If your business has assets—such as machines or inventory—list their primary location here. If they are all located at your home or mailing address, enter that address. If you haven't operated a business in the last two years, type "N/A."

Venue. Check the first box. This is where you explain why you're filing in this particular bankruptcy court. (See Section A, above.)

Type of Debtor. Check the first box, "Individual(s)," even if you have been self-employed or operated a sole proprietorship during the previous two years. The other boxes are for people filing different kinds of bankruptcy cases.

Nature of Debt(s). Check "Consumer/Non-Business" if you aren't in business and haven't been for the previous two years, or if most of your debts are owed personally, not by your business. If, however, the bulk of your indebtedness arises from your business, check "Business." If you are in doubt, check "Business."

Chapter 11 Small Business. Type "N/A" anywhere in the box.

Chapter or Section of Bankruptcy Code Under Which the Petition Is Filed. Check "Chapter 13."

Filing Fee. If you will attach the entire $194 fee, check the first box. If you plan to ask the court for permission to pay the filing fee ($155) in installments, check the second box. (Instructions are in Ch. 8, *Filing Your Bankruptcy Papers*, Section B.)

Statistical/Administrative Information. Here you estimate information about your debts and assets. If you completed the worksheets in Chs. 2, 3, 4, and 5, you may be able to fill in these sections now. If you didn't complete those worksheets, wait until you've completed the other forms before providing this information. But remember to come back and check the appropriate boxes before filing.

If you plan to make an emergency filing (Ch. 8, *Filing Your Bankruptcy Papers*, Section C) use the worksheets to arrive at your best estimates.

Second Page

Name of Debtor(s). Enter your name and your spouse's, if you are filing jointly.

Prior Bankruptcy Case Filed Within Last 6 Years. If you haven't filed a bankruptcy case within the previous six years, type "N/A" in the boxes. If you—or your spouse, if you're filing jointly—have filed recently, enter the requested information. You can still file for Chapter 13 bankruptcy unless within the previous 180 days the court dismissed your bankruptcy case for willfully failing to follow a court order, or if you voluntarily dismissed your case after a creditor asked the court to remove the automatic stay.

Pending Bankruptcy Case Filed by Any Spouse, Partner or Affiliate of This Debtor. If your spouse has a bankruptcy case pending anywhere in the country, enter the requested information. The term affiliate refers to a related business under a corporate structure, and partner refers to a business partnership. Neither entity is eligible to file for Chapter 13 bankruptcy. If this doesn't apply, type "N/A" in the boxes.

Signatures of Debtors (Individual/Joint). You—and your spouse, if you are filing jointly—must sign where indicated. If you are filing singly, type "N/A" on the joint debtor signature line. Include your telephone number and date.

Signature of Debtor (Corporation/Partnership). Type "N/A" on the first line.

Signature of Attorney. Type "N/A" on the first line.

Exhibit B. Type "N/A" on the first line.

Exhibit C. Check the "No" box unless you have property that you think might be harmful to public health and safety. If you think you might have such property, complete Exhibit C in Appendix 2.

Signature of Non-Attorney Petition Preparer. If a nonattorney bankruptcy petition preparer typed your forms, have that person complete this section. Otherwise, type "N/A" anywhere on the first line.

F. Form 6—Schedules

"Form 6" refers to a whole series of forms, called schedules, that provide the trustee and court with a picture of your current financial situation. Most of the information needed for these schedules was asked for in the worksheets which—we hope—you completed earlier. Completed sample forms and instructions are shown below.

1. Schedule A—Real Property

Here you list all the real property (real estate) you own as of the date you'll file the petition. Even if you don't own any real estate, you still must complete the top of this form.

If you filled in Worksheet 8: Your Exempt and Non-exempt Property, in Ch. 5, get it out. Much of the information you listed in the first section goes on Schedule A. If you didn't fill out the worksheet, go back to Ch. 5 for help on what to include here.

Note on Leases and Timeshares. All leases should be listed on Schedule G, not Schedule A. So if you hold a timeshare lease in a vacation cabin or property, lease a boat dock or underground portions of real estate for mineral or oil exploration, or otherwise lease or rent real estate of any description, don't list it on Schedule A. (See Section 7, below.) There is one exception: if you have an interest in a timeshare that is secured (you'll have to look at your timeshare agreement), list that interest here, not on Schedule G. You are really buying a part of that timeshare, not merely leasing it.

A completed sample of Schedule A and line-by-line instructions follow.

In re. Type your name and, if you're filing jointly, the name of your spouse.

Case No. If you made an emergency filing, fill in the case number already assigned by the court. Otherwise, leave this blank.

Description and Location of Property. List the type of property—for example, house, farm, or unimproved lot—and street address of every piece of real property you own. You don't need to include the legal description (the description on the deed) of the property.

 If you don't own real estate. Type "N/A" anywhere in the first column and move on to Schedule B.

Nature of Debtor's Interest in Property. In this column, you need to give the legal term for the nature of the interest you, your spouse, or you and your spouse together have in the real estate. The vast majority of

(Official Form 1) (12/03)   FORM B1, Page 2

Voluntary Petition *(This page must be completed and filed in every case)*	Name of Debtor(s): Herchoo, Martin & Ellen	

Prior Bankruptcy Case Filed Within Last 6 Years (If more than one, attach additional sheet)		
Location Where Filed: N/A	Case Number:	Date Filed:

Pending Bankruptcy Case Filed by any Spouse, Partner or Affiliate of this Debtor (If more than one, attach additional sheet)		
Name of Debtor: N/A	Case Number:	Date Filed:
District:	Relationship:	Judge:

Signatures

Signature(s) of Debtor(s) (Individual/Joint)

I declare under penalty of perjury that the information provided in this petition is true and correct.
[If petitioner is an individual whose debts are primarily consumer debts and has chosen to file under chapter 7] I am aware that I may proceed under chapter 7, 11, 12 or 13 of title 11, United States Code, understand the relief available under each such chapter, and choose to proceed under chapter 7.
I request relief in accordance with the chapter of title 11, United States Code, specified in this petition.

X   *Martin Herchoo*
Signature of Debtor

X   *Ellen Herchoo*
Signature of Joint Debtor
    (520) 555-9394
Telephone Number (If not represented by attorney)
    2/25/xx
Date

Signature of Attorney

X   N/A
Signature of Attorney for Debtor(s)

_____
Printed Name of Attorney for Debtor(s)

_____
Firm Name

_____
Address

_____
Telephone Number

_____
Date

Signature of Debtor (Corporation/Partnership)

I declare under penalty of perjury that the information provided in this petition is true and correct, and that I have been authorized to file this petition on behalf of the debtor.

The debtor requests relief in accordance with the chapter of title 11, United States Code, specified in this petition.

X   N/A
Signature of Authorized Individual

_____
Printed Name of Authorized Individual

_____
Title of Authorized Individual

_____
Date

N/A   **Exhibit A**
(To be completed if debtor is required to file periodic reports (e.g., forms 10K and 10Q) with the Securities and Exchange Commission pursuant to Section 13 or 15(d) of the Securities Exchange Act of 1934 and is requesting relief under chapter 11)

☐   Exhibit A is attached and made a part of this petition.

Exhibit B
N/A   (To be completed if debtor is an individual whose debts are primarily consumer debts)
I, the attorney for the petitioner named in the foregoing petition, declare that I have informed the petitioner that [he or she] may proceed under chapter 7, 11, 12, or 13 of title 11, United States Code, and have explained the relief available under each such chapter.

X _____
Signature of Attorney for Debtor(s)   Date

Exhibit C
Does the debtor own or have possession of any property that poses or is alleged to pose a threat of imminent and identifiable harm to public health or safety?
☐   Yes, and Exhibit C is attached and made a part of this petition.
☒   No

Signature of Non-Attorney Petition Preparer

I certify that I am a bankruptcy petition preparer as defined in 11 U.S.C. § 110, that I prepared this document for compensation, and that I have provided the debtor with a copy of this document.
        N/A
_____
Printed Name of Bankruptcy Petition Preparer

_____
Social Security Number (Required by 11 U.S.C. § 110)

_____
Address

Names and Social Security numbers of all other individuals who prepared or assisted in preparing this document:

If more than one person prepared this document, attach additional sheets conforming to the appropriate official form for each person.

X _____

Signature of Bankruptcy Petition Preparer

_____
Date

A bankruptcy petition preparer's failure to comply with the provisions of title 11 and the Federal Rules of Bankruptcy Procedure may result in fines or imprisonment or both 11 U.S.C. §110; 18 U.S.C. §156.

FORM B6A
(6/90)

In re ___Herchoo, Martin & Ellen___,   Case No._____
　　　　　　　　　Debtor   (If known)

SCHEDULE A—REAL PROPERTY

Except as directed below, list all real property in which the debtor has any legal, equitable, or future interest, including all property owned as a co-tenant, community property, or in which the debtor has a life estate. Include any property in which the debtor holds rights and powers exercisable for the debtor's own benefit. If the debtor is married, state whether husband, wife, or both own the property by placing an "H," "W," "J," or "C" in the column labeled "Husband, Wife, Joint, or Community." If the debtor holds no interest in real property, write "None" under "Description and Location of Property."

Do not include interests in executory contracts and unexpired leases on this schedule. List them in Schedule G—Executory Contracts and Unexpired Leases.

If an entity claims to have a lien or hold a secured interest in any property, state the amount of the secured claim. See Schedule D. If no entity claims to hold a secured interest in the property, write "None" in the column labeled "Amount of Secured Claim."

If the debtor is an individual or if a joint petition is filed, state the amount of any exception claimed in the property only in Schedule C—Property Claimed as Exempt.

DESCRIPTION AND LOCATION OF PROPERTY	NATURE OF DEBTOR'S INTEREST IN PROPERTY	HUSBAND, WIFE, JOINT, OR COMMUNITY	CURRENT MARKET VALUE OF DEBTOR'S INTEREST IN PROPERTY WITHOUT DEDUCTING ANY SECURED CLAIM OR EXEMPTION	AMOUNT OF SECURED CLAIM
Home located at 19068 Cactus Drive Tucson, AZ 85700	Fee Simple	C	$275,000	$239,715 mortgage $16,080 home equity loan $1,215 judgment lien

Total ➡ $ $275,000

(Report also on Summary of Schedules.)

people own property in "fee simple"—an ancient legal term that means simply that you own the property outright. Even if the property has a mortgage or other liens on it, as long as you have the right to sell the house, leave it to your heirs, and make alterations to it, your ownership is fee simple. A fee simple interest may be owned by one person or by several people jointly. Normally, if you are listed on the deed as an owner—even if you own the property with someone else as joint tenants, tenants in common, or tenants by the entirety—the ownership interest is fee simple.

You should also mention the form of marital ownership if it is a kind that may affect the rights of creditors.

EXAMPLE: "Fee simple, held by the debtor(s) as tenants by the entirety."

Other kinds of ownership are much rarer, and much more complicated—and often involve property you don't even think of yourself as owning. But that property, too, must be listed. Several of these kinds of ownership are listed below. If this material makes your head spin, don't worry about it. Identify all property you own, think you own, or might own in Column 1 and leave Column 2 blank. After you file for bankruptcy, the trustee can help you sort it out.

- **Life estate.** This is your right to possess and use property only during your lifetime. You can't sell the property, give it away, or leave it to someone when you die. Instead, when you die, the property passes to whomever was named in the document (trust, deed, or will) that created your life estate. This type of ownership is usually created when the owner of a piece of real estate wants his surviving spouse to live on the property for her life, but then have the property pass to his children. The surviving spouse has a life estate. Surviving spouses who are beneficiaries of A-B or marital bypass trusts have life estates.
- **Future interest.** This is your right to own property sometime in the future. A common future interest is owned by a person who—under the terms of a deed, will, or trust—will own the property at some point in the future. But until the person who signed the will or living trust dies, you have no future ownership interest in the property because the person making the will or living trust can easily amend the document to cut you out.
- **Lienholder.** If you are the holder of a mortgage, deed of trust, judgment lien, or mechanic's lien on real estate, you have an ownership interest in the real estate. Put "lienholder" in Column 2.
- **Easement holder.** If you are the holder of a right to travel on or otherwise use property owned by someone else, you have an easement.
- **Power of appointment.** If you have a legal right, given to you in a will or transfer of property, to sell a specified piece of someone's property, put "power of appointment" in Column 2.
- **Beneficial ownership under a real estate contract.** If you have signed a binding real estate contract, but don't yet own the property, you have a "beneficial interest"—that is, the right to own the property once the formalities are completed.

Husband, Wife, Joint, or Community. If you're not married, put "N/A." If you are married—whether or not you are filing with your spouse—indicate whether the real estate is owned:

- by the husband (H)
- by the wife (W)
- jointly by husband and wife in a common law property state (J) or
- jointly by husband and wife as community property (C)—a form of joint ownership that applies to property acquired by couples living in Arizona, California, Idaho, Louisiana, Nevada, New Mexico, Texas, Washington, or Wisconsin. California also includes in this category any real property acquired by a couple in another state that they own when they move to California.

Current Market Value of Debtor's Interest in Property Without Deducting Any Secured Claim or Exemption. Enter the current fair market value of your real estate ownership interest. With a house, you will need an estimate of its market value from a local real estate agent or appraiser. If you own another type of real estate—such as land used to grow crops—you will have to put the amount it would bring in at a forced sale. Don't figure in homestead exemptions or any mortgages or other liens on the property.

If you own the property with someone else who is not filing for bankruptcy, put only your ownership share in this column. For example, if you and your brother own a home as joint tenants (you each own 50%), split the current market value in half.

See Ch. 5, Section A6, for information on how to list your share of property owned as tenancy by the entirety.

If your interest is intangible—for example, you are a beneficiary of real estate held in trust that won't be distributed for many years—provide an estimate, explaining why you can't be more precise.

Total. Add the amounts in the fourth column and enter the total in the box at the bottom of the column.

Amount of Secured Claim. Here is where you list mortgages and other debts secured by the property. If there is no secured claim of any type on the real estate, enter "None." If there is, enter separately the amount of each outstanding mortgage, deed of trust, home equity loan, or lien (judgment lien, mechanic's lien, materialmen's lien, tax lien, or the like) that is claimed against the property.

If you don't know the balance on your mortgage, deed of trust, or home equity loan, call the lender. To find out the values of liens, visit the land records office in your county and look up the parcel in the records; the clerk can show you how. Or you can order a title search through a real estate attorney or title insurance company. If you own several pieces of real estate and there is one lien on file against all the real estate, list the full amount of the lien for each separate property item. Don't worry if, taken together, the value of the liens on property is higher than the value of the property; it's quite common.

How you itemize liens in this schedule won't affect how your property or the liens will be treated in bankruptcy. The idea here is to notify the trustee of all possible liens that may affect your real estate.

If you can't find the amounts and you can't afford to pay for a title search, identify the lien and state "amount unknown."

2. Schedule B—Personal Property

Here you must list and value all of your personal property—that is, everything except real estate. Include all property—whether or not it is security for a debt or

is exempt. If you didn't fill in Worksheet 8, turn to Ch. 5, *Calculating the Value of Your Nonexempt Property*, for explanations and suggestions about property for each of the schedule's categories.

Be scrupulously honest and ridiculously thorough. Don't make the common mistake of thinking that listing your property isn't important because you don't have to turn any property over to the trustee in Chapter 13 bankruptcy. The trustee may review your papers to determine whether or not your unsecured creditors will be receiving at least the value of the nonexempt property. If you omit property—deliberately or accidentally—and the court discovers your omission, the court will not confirm your Chapter 13 plan. Worse, it may dismiss your case.

A completed sample and line-by-line instructions follow. If you need more room, attach a continuation sheet. (See Section D, above.)

In re and **Case No.** Follow the instructions for Schedule A.

Type of Property. The form lists general categories of personal property. You can leave this column as is.

None. If you don't own property that fits in a category listed in the first column, enter an "X" in this column next to the category.

Description and Location of Property. List specific items that fall in each general category. See the checklist preceding Worksheet 8 (Ch. 5, *Calculating the Value of Your Nonexempt Property*) for some prompts on property to list here. Separately list all items worth $50 or more. Combine small items into larger categories whenever reasonable. For example, you don't need to list every spatula, colander, garlic press, and ice cream scoop; instead, put "kitchen utensils." If you list numerous items in one category (as is likely for household goods and furnishings), you may need to attach a continuation sheet.

Most of your personal property is probably at your residence. If so, write a sentence at the top of the form or column to that effect: "All property is located at my/our residence unless otherwise noted." Indicate specifically when the facts are different. If someone else holds property for you (for example, you loaned your aunt your color TV), put that person's name and address in this column.

FORM B6B
(10/89)

In re _____ Herchoo, Martin & Ellen _____ ,   Case No._____
                              Debtor   (If known)

SCHEDULE B—PERSONAL PROPERTY

Except as directed below, list all personal property of the debtor of whatever kind. If the debtor has no property in one or more of the categories, place an "X" in the appropriate position in the column labeled "None." If additional space is needed in any category, attach a separate sheet properly identified with the case name, case number, and the number of the category. If the debtor is married, state whether husband, wife, or both own the property by placing an "H," "W," "J," or "C" in the column labeled "Husband, Wife, Joint, or Community." If the debtor is an individual or a joint petition is filed, state the amount of any exemptions claimed only in Schedule C—Property Claimed as Exempt.

Do not include interests in executory contracts and unexpired leases on this schedule. List them in Schedule G—Executory Contracts and Unexpired Leases.

If the property is being held for the debtor by someone else, state that person's name and address under "Description and Location of Property."

TYPE OF PROPERTY	NONE	* All property is located at our residence unless otherwise noted. DESCRIPTION AND LOCATION OF PROPERTY	HUSBAND, WIFE, JOINT, OR COMMUNITY	CURRENT MARKET VALUE OF DEBTOR'S INTEREST IN PROPERTY, WITHOUT DEDUCTING ANY SECURED CLAIM OR EXEMPTION
1. Cash on hand.		Cash from wages	C	300
2. Checking, savings or other financial accounts, certificates of deposit, or shares in banks, savings and loan, thrift, building and loan, and homestead associations, or credit unions, brokerage houses, or cooperatives.		Account #743-011-6281193 (checking) Pima County Bank, 1700 Truman Blvd., Tucson, AZ 85700 (wages)	C	500
		Account #9918736249 (money market) Sputter Investment House, P.O. Box E, Hackensack, NJ 07000 (wages)	C	300
3. Security deposits with public utilities, telephone companies, landlords, and others.	X			
4. Household goods and furnishings, including audio, video, and computer equipment.		Refrigerator	C	300
		Stove	C	250
		Dishwasher	C	250
		Microwave	C	200
		Kitchen table/chairs	C	300
		Stereo system	C	600
		2 TVs & VCR	C	450
		Living room couch, 2 chairs, coffee table	C	475
		2 beds with bedding	C	300
		2 dressers	C	125
		2 desks (1 specially designed)	C	1,000
		10 bookcases	C	500
		Mac computer & printer	C	2,000
		Washer/Dryer	C	400
		Minor appliances	C	100
		Barbecue	C	50
		Children's toys	C	60
		Kitchen utensils, gadgets, etc.	C	50

FORM B6B-cont.
(10/89)

In re ___Herchoo, Martin & Ellen___ ,   Case No._____
Debtor   (If known)

SCHEDULE B—PERSONAL PROPERTY
(Continuation Sheet)

TYPE OF PROPERTY	NONE	DESCRIPTION AND LOCATION OF PROPERTY	HUSBAND, WIFE, JOINT, OR COMMUNITY	CURRENT MARKET VALUE OF DEBTOR'S INTEREST IN PROPERTY, WITHOUT DEDUCTING ANY SECURED CLAIM OR EXEMPTION
5. Books, pictures and other art objects, antiques, stamp, coin, record, tape, compact disc, and other collections or collectibles.		Books Lithographs Record/tape/CD Collection	C C C	250 150 300
6. Wearing apparel.		Clothing	C	500
7. Furs and jewelry.		Wedding & engagement rings Watches Earrings	C C C	1,000 200 100
8. Firearms and sports, photographic, and other hobby equipment.		Camera, lenses, tripod Ice skates	W C	600 150
9. Interests in insurance policies. Name insurance company of each policy and itemize surrender or refund value of each.		Life insurance policy, Lively Ins Co., 120 Manhattan Street, NY, NY 10000 Policy #631171-41 Life insurance policy, Lifetime Co., 52 Mitchell Ave., Hartford, CT 06400. Policy #71WY5919-1160	C C	4,000 2,000
10. Annuities. Itemize and name each issuer.	X			
11. Interests in IRA, ERISA, Keogh, or other pension or profit sharing plans. Itemize.		ERISA Qualified Pension Plan Teachers Fund, 1000 Wallace Way, Phoenix, AZ 85700. Policy #X145900-1730 IRA at Pima County Bank, 1700 Truman Blvd., Tucson, AZ 85700. Account #743-011-6287491	 H/C W/C	0 18,900 8,633
12. Stock and interests in incorporated and unincorporated businesses. Itemize.	X			
13. Interests in partnerships or joint ventures. Itemize.	X			

FORM B6B-cont.
(10/89)

In re ___Herchoo, Martin & Ellen_____,   Case No._____
              Debtor   (If known)

SCHEDULE B—PERSONAL PROPERTY
(Continuation Sheet)

TYPE OF PROPERTY	NONE	DESCRIPTION AND LOCATION OF PROPERTY	HUSBAND, WIFE, JOINT, OR COMMUNITY	CURRENT MARKET VALUE OF DEBTOR'S INTEREST IN PROPERTY, WITHOUT DEDUCTING ANY SECURED CLAIM OR EXEMPTION
14. Government and corporate bonds and other negotiable and non-negotiable instruments.	X			
15. Accounts receivable.	X			
16. Alimony, maintenance, sup-port, and property settlements to which the debtor is or may be entitled. Give particulars.	X			
17. Other liquidated debts owing debtor including tax refunds. Give particulars.		First quarter 20xx royalty payment due Martin	H/C	6,911
18. Equitable or future interest, life estates, and rights or powers exercisable for the benefit of the debtor other than those listed in Schedule of Real Property.	X			
19. Contingent and noncontin-gent interests in estate of a decedent, death benefit plan, life insurance policy, or trust.	X			
20. Other contingent and unliqui-dated claims of every nature, including tax refunds, counterclaims of the debtor, and rights to setoff claims. Give estimated value of each.	X			
21. Patents, copyrights, and other intellectual property. Give particulars.		Martin holds a copyright in several high school and junior college level math textbooks, some published before marriage, others during	H/C	unknown
22. Licenses, franchises, and other general intangibles. Give particulars.	X			

FORM B6B-cont.
(10/89)

In re ____Herchoo, Martin & Ellen_____,   Case No._____
                        Debtor   (If known)

SCHEDULE B—PERSONAL PROPERTY
(Continuation Sheet)

TYPE OF PROPERTY	NONE	DESCRIPTION AND LOCATION OF PROPERTY	HUSBAND, WIFE, JOINT, OR COMMUNITY	CURRENT MARKET VALUE OF DEBTOR'S INTEREST IN PROPERTY, WITHOUT DEDUCTING ANY SECURED CLAIM OR EXEMPTION
23. Automobiles, trucks, trailers, and other vehicles and accessories.		20xx Nissan Maxima 19xx Ford Taurus	C W	7,400 1,000
24. Boats, motors, and accessories.	X			
25. Aircraft and accessories.	X			
26. Office equipment, furnishings, and supplies.	X			
27. Machinery, fixtures, equipment, and supplies used in business.	X			
28. Inventory.	X			
29. Animals.		2 Horses	C	1,000
30. Crops—growing or harvested. Give particulars.	X			
31. Farming equipment and implements.	X			
32. Farm supplies, chemicals, and feed.	X			
33. Other personal property of any kind not already listed, such as season tickets. Itemize.	X			
			Total ➡	$ 61,604

____0____ continuation sheets attached

(Include amounts from any continuation sheets attached. Report total also on Summary of Schedules.)

Here are further instructions for answering some of the questions:

Question 1: Include all cash you have on the date you file the petition.

Questions 1 and 2: Explain the source of any cash on hand or money in financial accounts—for example, from wages, Social Security payments, or child support. This will help later as you decide whether any of this money qualifies as exempt property.

Question 11: Although ERISA-qualified pension plans are not part of the bankruptcy estate, list them here anyway and write: "This is an ERISA-qualified pension plan which is not part of the bankruptcy estate." In the Current Market Value column, enter $0.

Category 16: List all child support or alimony arrears—that is, money that should have been paid to you but hasn't been. Specify the dates the payments were due and missed, such as "$250 monthly child support payments for June, July, August, and September 20xx."

Category 17: List all money owed to you and not yet paid other than child support and alimony. If you've obtained a court judgment against someone but haven't been paid, list it here. State the defendant's name, the date of the judgment, the court that issued the judgment, the amount of the judgment, and the kind of case (such as car accident). It's important that you identify any legal claims you think you may have against a person or entity. Otherwise, once your plan is confirmed, you may have given up your right to pursue these claims during or after your Chapter 13 bankruptcy, if the court finds that your omission of the claims was deliberate. See *De Leon v. Comcar Industries, Inc.*, 321 F.3d 1289 (C.A. Fla. 2003).

Category 19: If you have inherited money and want to keep it out of your bankruptcy estate, many states give you an absolute right to disclaim the inheritance. For example, if you are one of several siblings who have inherited property from a deceased parent, you could disclaim your share (assuming your state allows it) and have it go to the other siblings instead of to your unsecured creditors. If you have the right to disclaim under your state's law, the inheritance should not be considered part of your bankruptcy estate. However, the better practice is to list the inheritance here with a notation that you have disclaimed it.

Category 21: State what the patent, copyright, trademark, or the like is for. Give the number assigned by the issuing agency and length of time the patent, copyright, trademark, or the like will last.

Category 22: List all licenses and franchises, what they cover, the length of time remaining, who they are with, and whether or not you can transfer them to someone else.

Questions 23-25: Include the make, model, and year of each item.

Category 30: For your crops, state whether or not they've been harvested, whether or not they've been sold, and if so to whom and for how much, the amount of any loan you've taken out against them, and whether or not they are insured.

Husband, Wife, Joint, or Community. If you're not married, put "N/A" at the top of the column.

If you are married and own all or most of your personal property jointly with your spouse, put one of the following statements on the top or bottom of the form:

- **If you live in a community property state:** "All property is owned jointly as community property unless otherwise indicated." Then note when a particular item is owned by only H or W.

- **If you live in any other state:** If you own joint property as tenancy by the entirety say "All property is jointly owned as tenancy by the entirety unless otherwise indicated." Otherwise say "All property is jointly owned unless otherwise indicated."

If you are married and own many items separately, for each item specify ownership by:

- husband (H)
- wife (W)
- jointly by husband and wife (J), or
- jointly by husband and wife in a community property state (C).

For more information on ownership of property by married couples, see Ch. 5, *Calculating the Value of Your Nonexempt Property*, Sections A5 and A6.

Current Market Value of Debtor's Interest in Property, Without Deducting Any Secured Claim or Exemption. You can take the information requested here from column 3 of Worksheet 8. Put the current market value of your share of the property, without regard to any secured interests or exemptions. For example, if you own a car worth $6,000, still owe $4,000 on the car note, and your state's motor vehicle exemption is $1,200, put down $6,000 for the market value of the car.

Total. Add the amounts in this column and put the total in the box at the bottom of the last page. If you used any continuation pages in addition to the pre-printed form, remember to attach those pages and include the amounts from them in the total.

3. Schedule C—Property Claimed as Exempt

When you work on this form, you'll need to refer frequently to several other documents. Have in front of you:

- Worksheet 8 (from Ch. 5)
- your drafts of Schedules A and B
- the list of state or federal bankruptcy exemptions you'll be using (from Appendix 1), and
- if you're using your state's exemptions, the additional *nonbankruptcy* federal exemptions (from Appendix 1).

Set out below are a sample completed Schedule C and line-by-line instructions.

In re and **Case No.** Follow the instructions for Schedule A.

Debtor elects the exemptions to which the debtor is entitled under: If you're using the federal exemptions, check the top box. If you're using your state exemptions (this includes all Californians), check the lower box.

The following instructions cover one column at a time. The easiest way to proceed is to list one exempt item and complete all columns for that item before moving on to the next exempt item.

Description of Property. In this column, you list the property, both real and personal, you claim is exempt under bankruptcy law. In completing this schedule, be sure to use the same descriptions you used Schedule A and Schedule B.

⚠️ **If your state has a wildcard exemption.** In Ch. 5, when you completed Worksheet 8, you simply subtracted the amount of the wildcard exemption from the total amount of your nonexempt property. Now you must identify property, up to the value of your wildcard exemption, that you couldn't otherwise exempt. You can do this by adding the wildcard exemption to an item of

property only partially exempt, or by exempting an item which otherwise isn't exempt at all.

EXAMPLE: Kentucky doesn't exempt family heirlooms, but does provide a wildcard exemption of $1,000 for any property. Loretta has three antiques, each worth $300, that she wants to keep. She applies the $1,000 wildcard exemption to these items, which makes them exempt. She can use the remaining $100 on any other property she chooses.

Specify Law Providing Each Exemption. For every item, you must list the specific law that allows you to claim the item as exempt. You can find citations to the specific laws that create exemptions in the state and federal exemption lists in Appendix 1.

You can simplify this process by typing, on the top of the form, the name of the statutes you are using. The name is noted at the top of the exemption list you use. For example, you might type "All law references are to the Florida Statutes Annotated unless otherwise noted."

For each item of property, enter the citation (number) of the specific law that creates the exemption, as set out on the exemption list. If you use any reference other than one found in your state statutes, such as federal *nonbankruptcy* exemptions or a court case, list the entire reference for the exempt item.

Value of Claimed Exemption. List the full exemption amount allowed. The amount allowed is listed in Appendix 1.

 Bankruptcy rules allow married couples to double all exemptions unless state law expressly prohibits it. That means that each of you can claim the entire amount of each exemption, if you are filing jointly. If your state's chart in Appendix 1 doesn't say that your state forbids doubling, it is probably safe to double. If you are married and doubling your exemptions, put a note to this effect on the form. (See sample Schedule C.)

FORM B6C
(6/90)

In re ___Herchoo, Martin & Ellen_____,   Case No._____
                    Debtor   (If known)

SCHEDULE C—PROPERTY CLAIMED AS EXEMPT

Debtor elects the exemptions to which debtor is entitled under:

(Check one box)

☐ 11 U.S.C. § 522(b)(1):   Exemptions provided in 11 U.S.C. § 522(d). **Note: These exemptions are available only in certain states.**

X 11 U.S.C. § 522(b)(2):   Exemptions available under applicable nonbankruptcy federal laws, state or local law where the debtor's domicile has been located for the 180 days immediately preceding the filing of the petition, or for a longer portion of the 180-day period than in any other place, and the debtor's interest as a tenant by the entirety or joint tenant to the extent the interest is exempt from process under applicable nonbankruptcy law.

DESCRIPTION OF PROPERTY	SPECIFY LAW PROVIDING EACH EXEMPTION	VALUE OF CLAIMED EXEMPTION	CURRENT MARKET VALUE OF PROPERTY WITHOUT DEDUCTING EXEMPTIONS
Real Property Home located at 19068 Cactus Drive, Tucson, AZ 85700	33-1101	17,990	275,000
Financial accounts Account #743-011-6281193 (checking). Pima County Bank, 1700 Truman Blvd., Tucson, AZ 85700	33-1126(A)(7)	300	300
Household goods			
Refrigerator	33-1123	300	300
Stove	33-1123	250	250
Dishwasher	33-1123	250	250
Microwave	33-1123	200	200
Kitchen table/chairs	33-1123	300	300
Stereo System	33-1123	600	600
2 TVs & VCR	33-1123	450	450
Living room couch, 2 chairs, coffee table	33-1123	475	475
2 beds with bedding	33-1123	300	300
2 dressers	33-1123	125	125
2 desks (1 specially designed)	33-1123	1,000	1,000
10 bookcases	33-1123	500	500
Mac computer & printer	33-1123	2,000	2,000
Washer/dryer	33-1123	400	400
Minor appliances	33-1123	100	100
Barbecue	33-1123	50	50
Children's toys	33-1123	60	50
Kitchen utensils, gadgets, etc.	33-1123	50	50
Books, pictures, etc.			
Books	33-1125	250	250
Lithograph	33-1127	150	150

Because we are married, we each claim a full set of exemptions to the extent permitted by law. All references are to the Arizona Revised Statutes unless otherwise noted.

In re <u>Herchoo, Martin & Ellen</u>

SCHEDULE C—PROPERTY CLAIMED AS EXEMPT
(Continuation Sheet)

DESCRIPTION OF PROPERTY	SPECIFY LAW PROVIDING EACH EXEMPTION	VALUE OF CLAIMED EXEMPTION	CURRENT MARKET VALUE OF PROPERTY WITHOUT DEDUCTING EXEMPTIONS
<u>Apparel</u> Clothing	33-1125	500	500
<u>Furs & jewelry</u> Wedding & engagement rings	33-1125	1,000	1,000
Watches	33-1125	200	200
<u>Insurance</u> Life insurance policy with Lively Insurance Co., 120 Manhattan St., NY, NY 10000 #631171-41	20-1131(D)	4,000	4,000
Life insurance policy with Lifetime Co., 52 Mitchell Ave., Hartford, CT 06400. #71 WY5919-1160	33-1126(A)(5)	2,000	2,000
<u>Pensions</u> Teacher's Fund, 1000 Wallace Way, Phoenix, AZ Policy #X145900-1730	38-762	18,900	18,900
IRA at Pima County Bank, 1700 Truman Blvd., Tucson, AZ 85700. #743-011-6287491	<u>In re Herrscher</u>, 121 B.R. 29 (D. Ariz. 1990)	8,633	8,633
<u>Automobiles</u> 19XX Ford Taurus	33-1125	1,000	1,000
<u>Animals</u> 2 Horses	33-1125	1,000	1,000

WARNING: Do Not Limit Exemption Amounts to Claimed Value

If the amount allowed is greater than the current value of the object, common practice is to list an amount equal to the current value, but not more than that amount.

In some districts, it is risky to follow this custom. If a creditor challenges your valuation, and successfully gets the valuation increased, some courts have held that the debtor is stuck with the claimed exemption amount—now less than full value—so the property is no longer fully exempt.

Most courts, however, are reasonable enough to assume, if a debtor is claiming an exempt amount identical to the claimed value, that the debtor is in effect claiming the item as completely exempt.

Nevertheless, to leave nothing to chance, it's a good idea to add a general note to the bottom of the form that states that:

"Unless specifically stated otherwise, the debtors claim 100% of their interest in each item listed in this schedule as exempt."

Of course, do not include this statement for a wildcard exemption that you are splitting among several items by using specific exemption amounts for each item.

If you are using part or all of a wildcard exemption in addition to a regular exemption, list both amounts. For example, if the regular exemption for an item of furniture is $200, and you plan to exempt it to $500 using $300 from your state's wildcard exemption, list $200 across from the citation for the regular exemption, and the $300 across from the citation for the wildcard exemption (or across from the term "wildcard").

Current Market Value of Property Without Deducting Exemption. Enter the fair market value of your ownership interest in the item you are claiming as exempt. For most items, the amount should be the same as you listed on Schedules A and B. However, if you listed the item as part of a group in Schedule B, list it separately here and assign it a separate fair market value.

4. Schedule D—Creditors Holding Secured Claims

In this schedule, you list all creditors who hold claims secured by your property. This includes:

- lenders who hold a mortgage or deed of trust on your real estate
- creditors who have won lawsuits against you and recorded judgment liens against your property
- lawyers to whom you have granted a security interest in the outcome of a lawsuit, so that the collection of their fees would be postponed (the expected court judgment is the collateral)
- contractors who have filed mechanics' or materialmen's liens on your real estate
- taxing authorities, such as the IRS, that have filed tax liens against your property or issued a notice of tax lien, but only if the equity in your property covers the amount of the debt
- creditors with either a purchase money or nonpurchase money security agreement (for definitions, see Ch. 3, *Adding Up Your Secured and Unsecured Debts*, Section A), and
- all parties who are trying to collect a secured debt, such as collection agencies and attorneys.

Line-by-line instructions and a completed sample of Schedule D follow. Worksheets 1, 2, and 3 from Ch. 3, *Adding Up Your Secured and Unsecured Debts*, may be of help here.

In re and **Case No.** Follow the instructions for Schedule A.

☐ **Check this box if debtor has no creditors holding secured claims to report on this Schedule D.** Check the box at the bottom of Schedule D's instructions if you have no secured creditors. If you have no secured creditors, you can go on to Schedule E.

Creditor's Name and Mailing Address Including Zip Code. Here you list all secured creditors, preferably in alphabetical order. For each, fill in the account number, if you know it, the name and the complete mailing address, including zip code (call the creditor or the post office and get it if you don't have it).

Note: Bankruptcy filings are a matter of public record. To protect your privacy, the law only requires that you list the last four digits of any account numbers. However, if you feel comfortable doing so, you can list the entire account number.

Should You List a Rent-to-Own Contract as Secured Debt?

If you are renting an item under a contract that says you will own it when the final payment is paid, you may have a choice on how to classify it. If your state law allows it, you may want to consider treating it as a "credit sale with property subject to a security interest" and list the debt as a secured debt on Schedule D. Treating a contract in this manner gives you certain rights, including the right to retain the property by paying the amount that the property is currently worth, rather than the full contract amount. (See Ch. 7 *Writing Your Chapter 13 Bankruptcy Plan*, Section I2.)

If you cannot classify the contract as a credit sale, you will have to treat the obligation as a lease or unexpired contract and decide whether you want to keep making payments on it. If you decide to stop making monthly payments before the contract is finished, the creditor has a right to take the property from you—even if the sum total of the rent you've already paid far exceeds the property's current value.

For more on this subject, see the instructions for Schedule G, in Section F7 below.

Credit Card Debts

Most credit card debts, whether the card is issued by a bank, gasoline company, or department store, are unsecured and should be listed on Schedule F. Some department stores, however, claim to retain a security interest in all durable goods such as appliances and electronics bought using the store credit card. (A bankruptcy court in Vermont, however, has ruled that Sears charge debts are unsecured under state law. *In re Oszajca*, 199 B.R. 103 (D. Vt. 1996).) Also, if you were issued a bank or store credit card as part of a plan to restore your credit, you may have had to post property or cash as collateral for debts incurred on the card. If either of these exceptions applies to you, list the credit card debt on Schedule D.

If you have more than one secured creditor for a given debt, list the original creditor first and then immediately list the other creditors. For example, if you've been sued or hounded by a collection agency, list the information for the attorney or collection agency after the original creditor.

If, after typing up your final papers, you discover that you've missed a few creditors, don't retype the papers to preserve perfect alphabetical order. Simply add the creditors at the end. If your creditors don't all fit on the first page of Schedule D, make as many copies of the preprinted continuation page as you need to fit them all.

Codebtor. If someone else (other than a spouse if you are filing jointly) can be legally forced to pay your debt to a listed secured creditor, enter an "X" in this column and list the codebtor in the creditor column of this schedule.

The most common codebtors are:

* cosigners
* guarantors (people who guarantee payment of a loan)
* ex-spouses with whom you jointly incurred debts before divorcing
* joint owners of real estate or other property, if a lien was filed against the property
* coparties in a lawsuit, if a judgment lien has been recorded against both coparties
* nonfiling spouses in a community property state (most debts incurred by a nonfiling spouse during marriage are considered community debts, which means both spouse are equally liable for them), and
* nonfiling spouses in states other than community property states, for debts incurred by the filing spouse for necessities such as food, shelter, clothing, and utilities.

Husband, Wife, Joint, or Community. Follow the instructions for Schedule A. Take special care in listing which debts are owed jointly versus debts that are in your name alone. Note that this schedule is asking for who is liable for the debt, not who owns the property that secures it. It is possible to have debts owed by you alone that are secured by jointly owned property. This can be extremely important if you are married and filing alone, as explained in Chapter 5, Section A6.

Date Claim Was Incurred, Nature of Lien, and Description and Market Value of Property Subject to Lien. This column calls for a lot of information about each secured debt. Let's take the elements one at a time.

Date Claim Was Incurred. Enter the date the secured claim was incurred. For most claims, this is the date you signed the security agreement or mortgage. If you didn't sign a security agreement with the creditor, the date is most likely the date a contractor, judgment creditor, or taxing authority recorded a lien against your property. If you listed two or more creditors on the same secured claim (such as the lender and a collection agency), put the same date for both.

Nature of Lien. Here are the possibilities:

- **Purchase-money security interest**—if the debt was incurred to purchase the property, as with a mortgage or car note. The security interest must have been "perfected" (filed or recorded with the appropriate agency) within ten days of being created to be valid. (*Fidelity Financial Services v. Fink*, 522 U.S. 211 (1998); 11 U.S.C. § 547 (e)(2)(A).)

- **Nonpossessory nonpurchase-money security interest**—if the debt was incurred for a purpose other than buying the collateral, as with refinanced home loans, home equity loans, or loans from finance companies.

- **Possessory nonpurchase-money security interest**—if you own property that has been pledged to a pawnshop.

- **Judgment lien**—if the creditor sued you, obtained a court judgment, and recorded a lien against your property.

- **Tax lien**—if a taxing authority recorded a lien against your property.

- **Child support lien**—if you owe child support and your child's other parent has recorded a lien against your property.

- **Mechanics' or materialmen's liens**—if someone performed work on real property, a vehicle, or other property, wasn't paid, and recorded a lien.

If you don't know what kind of lien you are dealing with, put "Don't know nature of lien" after the date. The bankruptcy trustee will help you figure it out later.

See Ch. 3, *Adding Up Your Secured and Unsecured Debts*, Section A, for complete definitions of the different types of liens.

Description of Property. Describe each item of real estate and personal property that is collateral for the secured debt listed in the first column. Use the same description you used on Schedule A for real estate, or Schedule B for personal property. If a creditor's lien covers several items of property, list all items affected by the lien.

Market Value of Property. The amount you put here must be consistent with what you put on Schedule A or B. If you co-own the property, list only your ownership interest as you did on Schedules A and B. If you put only the total value of a group of items on Schedule B, you must now get more specific. For instance, if a department store has a secured claim against your washing machine, and you listed your "washer/dryer set" on Schedule B, now you must provide the washer's specific market value. This may be on Worksheet 8; if it isn't, see the instructions for the "Current Market Value" of Schedule B.

Contingent, Unliquidated, Disputed. Indicate whether the creditor's secured claim is contingent, unliquidated, or disputed. Check all categories that apply. If you're uncertain of which to choose, check the one that seems closest. If none applies, leave them blank. Briefly, these terms mean:

Contingent. The claim depends on some event that hasn't yet occurred and may never occur. For example, if you cosigned a secured loan, you won't be liable unless the principal debtor defaults. Your liability as cosigner is contingent upon the default.

Unliquidated. This means that a debt may exist, but the exact amount hasn't been determined. For example, say you've sued someone for injuries you suffered in an auto accident, but the case isn't over. Your lawyer has taken the case under a contingency fee agreement—she'll get a third of the recovery if you win, and nothing if you lose—and has a security interest in the final recovery amount. The debt to the lawyer is unliquidated, because you don't know how much, if anything, you'll win.

Disputed. A claim is disputed if you and the creditor do not agree about the existence or amount of the debt. For instance, the IRS says you owe $10,000 and has put a lien on your property, and you say you owe $500. Remember that you can use bankruptcy court to contest the validity of any debt you dispute.

Amount of Claim Without Deducting Value of Collateral. For each secured creditor, put the amount it would

Form B6D
(12/03)

In re ___Herchoo, Martin & Ellen_____,   Case No. _____
                 Debtor   (If known)

SCHEDULE D - CREDITORS HOLDING SECURED CLAIMS

State the name, mailing address, including zip code and last four digits of any account number of all entities holding claims secured by property of the debtor as of the date of filing of the petition. The complete account number of any account the debtor has with the creditor is useful to the trustee and the creditor and may be provided if the debtor chooses to do so. List creditors holding all types of secured interests such as judgment liens, garnishments, statutory liens, mortgages, deeds of trust, and other security interests. List creditors in alphabetical order to the extent practicable. If all secured creditors will not fit on this page, use the continuation sheet provided.

If any entity other than a spouse in a joint case may be jointly liable on a claim, place an "X" in the column labeled "Codebtor," include the entity on the appropriate schedule of creditors, and complete Schedule H - Codebtors. If a joint petition is filed, state whether husband, wife, both of them, or the marital community may be liable on each claim by placing an "H," "W," "J," or "C" in the column labeled "Husband, Wife, Joint, or Community."

If the claim is contingent, place an "X" in the column labeled "Contingent." If the claim is unliquidated, place an "X" in the column labeled "Unliquidated." If the claim is disputed, place an "X" in the column labeled "Disputed." (You may need to place an "X" in more than one of these three columns.)

Report the total of all claims listed on this schedule in the box labeled "Total" on the last sheet of the completed schedule. Report this total also on the Summary of Schedules.

☐   Check this box if debtor has no creditors holding secured claims to report on this Schedule D.

CREDITOR'S NAME, MAILING ADDRESS INCLUDING ZIP CODE, AND ACCOUNT NUMBER (See instructions above.)	CODEBTOR	HUSBAND, WIFE, JOINT, OR COMMUNITY	DATE CLAIM WAS INCURRED, NATURE OF LIEN, AND DESCRIPTION AND MARKET VALUE OF PROPERTY SUBJECT TO LIEN	CONTINGENT	UNLIQUIDATED	DISPUTED	AMOUNT OF CLAIM WITHOUT DEDUCTING VALUE OF COLLATERAL	UNSECURED PORTION, IF ANY
ACCOUNT NO. XX-1149-20811 Big Home Loan Bank 232 Desert Way Tucson, AZ 85700		C	11/03; purchase money secured debt; mortgage on home VALUE $ 275,000				239,715	0
ACCOUNT NO. XX-1149-63114 Big Home Loan Bank 232 Desert Way Tucson, AZ 85700		C	3/03; nonpurchase-money secured debt, home equity loan VALUE $ 275,000				16,080	0
ACCOUNT NO. VR00M396 Car Finance Co. P.O. Box 1183 San Ramon, CA 94000		C	6/03; purchase-money secured debt, car loan (19xx Nissan Maxima) VALUE $ 7,400				8,250	850
ACCOUNT NO. SCC 157381 Ken Williams 17 North Rippington St. Tucson, AZ 85700		C	6/03; judgment lien on real property in Pima county VALUE $ 275,000				1,215	1,215 (We will file Motion to Avoid Lien)

___0___ continuation sheets attached

Subtotal ▸ • $ 265,260
(Total of this page)

Total ▸ • $ 265,260
(Use only on last page)

(Report total also on Summary of Schedules)

take to pay off the secured claim, regardless of what the property is worth. The lender can tell you the amount if you call and ask for the "payoff amount."

EXAMPLE: Your original loan was for $13,000 plus $7,000 in interest (for $20,000 total). You've made enough payments so that $10,000 in principal will cancel the debt; you would put $10,000 in the column. In some cases, the amount of secured claim may be more than the market value of the property.

If you have more than one creditor for a given secured claim (for example, the lender and a collection agency), list the amount of the debt only for the lender and put ditto marks (") for each subsequent creditor.

Subtotal/Total. Total the amounts in the Amount of Claim column for each page. Do not include the amounts represented by the ditto marks if you listed multiple creditors for a single debt. On the final page of Schedule D, which may be the first page or a pre-printed continuation page, enter the total of all secured claims.

Unsecured Portion, If Any. If your share of the market value of the collateral is equal to or greater than the amount of the claim, enter "0," meaning that the creditor's claim is fully secured. If the market value of the collateral is less than the amount of the claim(s) listed, enter the difference here. If you will file a motion with the court to eliminate the lien, note that here.

EXAMPLE: If the market value of your car is $5,000 but you still owe $6,000 on your car loan, enter $1,000 in this column ($6,000 – $5,000). This is the amount of the loan that is unsecured by the collateral (your car).

If you list an amount in this column for a creditor, do not list this amount again on Schedule F (where you will list all other creditors with unsecured claims). Otherwise, this unsecured amount will be listed twice.

5. Schedule E—Creditors Holding Unsecured Priority Claims

Schedule E identifies certain "priority" creditors who must be paid in full under your plan.

Set out below are a sample completed Schedule E and line-by-line instructions.

In re and **Case No.** Follow the instructions for Schedule A.

☐ **Check this box if debtor has no creditors holding unsecured priority claims to report on this Schedule E.** The most common priority claims are unsecured income tax debts and past-due alimony or child support. There are several other categories of priority debts, however. Before deciding whether or not you can check this box, examine each of the following categories.

☐ **Extensions of credit in an involuntary case.** Don't check this box. You are filing a voluntary, not an involuntary, Chapter 13 case.

☐ **Wages, salaries, and commissions.** If you owe a current or former employee of your business wages, vacation pay, or sick leave which was earned within 90 days before you file for bankruptcy or within 90 days of the date you ceased your business, check this box. If you owe money to an independent contractor who did work for you which was earned within 90 days before you file for bankruptcy or within 90 days of the date you ceased your business, you may have to check this box—but only if in the 12 months before you file for bankruptcy, this independent contractor earned at least 75% of his or her total independent contractor receipts from you. In either case, only the first $4,650 you owe (per employee or independent contractor) is a priority debt.

☐ **Contributions to employee benefit plans.** Check this box only if you owe contributions to an employee benefit fund for services rendered by an employee of your business within 180 days before you file your petition or within 180 days of the date you ceased your business.

☐ **Certain farmers and fishermen.** Check this box only if you operated a grain storage facility and owe money to a grain producer, or if you operated a fish produce or storage facility and owe money to a U.S. fisherman for fish or fish products. In either case, only the first $4,650 you owe (per grain producer or fisherman) is a priority debt.

☐ **Deposits by individuals.** If you took deposit money from people who planned to purchase, lease, or rent goods or services from you, which you never delivered, you may owe a priority debt. For the debt to qualify as a priority, the goods or services would have had to

Form B6E
(04/04)

In re ___Herchoo, Martin & Ellen___   Case No._____
                 Debtor   (if known)

SCHEDULE E - CREDITORS HOLDING UNSECURED PRIORITY CLAIMS

A complete list of claims entitled to priority, listed separately by type of priority, is to be set forth on the sheets provided. Only holders of unsecured claims entitled to priority should be listed in this schedule. In the boxes provided on the attached sheets, state the name, mailing address, including zip code, and last four digits of the account number, if any, of all entities holding priority claims against the debtor or the property of the debtor, as of the date of the filing of the petition. The complete account number of any account the debtor has with the creditor is useful to the trustee and the creditor and may be provided if the debtor chooses to do so.

If any entity other than a spouse in a joint case may be jointly liable on a claim, place an "X" in the column labeled "Codebtor," include the entity on the appropriate schedule of creditors, and complete Schedule H-Codebtors. If a joint petition is filed, state whether husband, wife, both of them or the marital community may be liable on each claim by placing an "H,""W,""J," or "C" in the column labeled "Husband, Wife, Joint, or Community."

If the claim is contingent, place an "X" in the column labeled "Contingent." If the claim is unliquidated, place an "X" in the column labeled "Unliquidated." If the claim is disputed, place an "X" in the column labeled "Disputed." (You may need to place an "X" in more than one of these three columns.)

Report the total of claims listed on each sheet in the box labeled "Subtotal" on each sheet. Report the total of all claims listed on this Schedule E in the box labeled "Total" on the last sheet of the completed schedule. Repeat this total also on the Summary of Schedules.

☐ Check this box if debtor has no creditors holding unsecured priority claims to report on this Schedule E.

TYPES OF PRIORITY CLAIMS (Check the appropriate box(es) below if claims in that category are listed on the attached sheets)

☐ **Extensions of credit in an involuntary case**

Claims arising in the ordinary course of the debtor's business or financial affairs after the commencement of the case but before the earlier of the appointment of a trustee or the order for relief. 11 U.S.C. § 507(a)(2).

☐ **Wages, salaries, and commissions**

Wages, salaries, and commissions, including vacation, severance, and sick leave pay owing to employees and commissions owing to qualifying independent sales representatives up to $4,925* per person earned within 90 days immediately preceding the filing of the original petition, or the cessation of business, whichever occurred first, to the extent provided in 11 U.S.C. § 507(a)(3).

☐ **Contributions to employee benefit plans**

Money owed to employee benefit plans for services rendered within 180 days immediately preceding the filing of the original petition, or the cessation of business, whichever occurred first, to the extent provided in 11 U.S.C. § 507(a)(4).

☐ **Certain farmers and fishermen**

Claims of certain farmers and fishermen, up to $4,925* per farmer or fisherman, against the debtor, as provided in 11 U.S.C. § 507(a)(5).

☐ **Deposits by individuals**

Claims of individuals up to $2,225* for deposits for the purchase, lease, or rental of property or services for personal, family, or household use, that were not delivered or provided. 11 U.S.C. § 507(a)(6).

Form B6E
(04/04)

In re   <u>Herchoo, Martin & Ellen</u> ,   Case No._____
               Debtor   (if known)

☐ **Alimony, Maintenance, or Support**

Claims of a spouse, former spouse, or child of the debtor for alimony, maintenance, or support, to the extent provided in 11 U.S.C. § 507(a)(7).

☒ **Taxes and Certain Other Debts Owed to Governmental Units**

Taxes, customs duties, and penalties owing to federal, state, and local governmental units as set forth in 11 U.S.C. § 507(a)(8).

☐ **Commitments to Maintain the Capital of an Insured Depository Institution**

Claims based on commitments to the FDIC, RTC, Director of the Office of Thrift Supervision, Comptroller of the Currency, or Board of Governors of the Federal Reserve System, or their predecessors or successors, to maintain the capital of an insured depository institution. 11 U.S.C. § 507 (a)(9).

* Amounts are subject to adjustment on April 1, 2007, and every three years thereafter with respect to cases commenced on or after the date of adjustment.

<u> 1</u> continuation sheets attached

Form B6E - Cont.
(04/04)

In re ___Herchoo, Martin & Ellen_____,   Case No. _____
               Debtor   **(If known)**

SCHEDULE E - CREDITORS HOLDING UNSECURED PRIORITY CLAIMS
(Continuation Sheet)

_____Taxes_____
TYPE OF PRIORITY

CREDITOR'S NAME, MAILING ADDRESS INCLUDING ZIP CODE, AND ACCOUNT NUMBER (See instructions.)	CODEBTOR	HUSBAND, WIFE, JOINT, OR COMMUNITY	DATE CLAIM WAS INCURRED AND CONSIDERATION FOR CLAIM	CONTINGENT	UNLIQUIDATED	DISPUTED	AMOUNT OF CLAIM	AMOUNT ENTITLED TO PRIORITY
ACCOUNT NO. 123-456-7890 IRS Fresno, CA 93776		C	April 15, 19xx, 19xy, 20xx Tax Liability				33,762	33,762
ACCOUNT NO.								
ACCOUNT NO.								
ACCOUNT NO.								
ACCOUNT NO.								

Sheet no. _1_ of _1_ sheets attached to Schedule of Creditors Holding Priority Claims

                      Subtotal▶ $ 33,762
               (Total of this page)
                          Total▶ $ 33,762
(Use only on last page of the completed Schedule E.)
(Report total also on Summary of Schedules)

have been put to personal, family, or household use. Only the first $2,100 owed (per person) is a priority debt.

☐ **Alimony, maintenance, or support.** Check this box if you are behind on your payments to a spouse, former spouse, child, the court, your welfare department, or anyone else for alimony or child support.

☐ **Taxes and certain other debts owed to governmental units.** Check this box if you owe unsecured back taxes or any other debts to the government, such as fines imposed for driving under the influence of drugs or alcohol. As explained in Ch. 7, Section G, *Writing Your Chapter 13 Bankruptcy Plan*, not all tax debts are unsecured priority claims. If the IRS has issued a notice of federal tax lien and the equity in your property fully covers the amount of your tax debt, your debt is a secured debt. It should be on Schedule D, not on this schedule. If the IRS has sent you a bill or assessed taxes against you, but has not issued a notice of lien, the debt goes on this schedule, even if you dispute the amount. If your audit is still going on, however, you generally don't have to list the debt as it hasn't yet been determined.

☐ **Commitments to Maintain the Capital of an Insured Depository Institution.** Don't check this box. It's for business bankruptcies.

If you checked none of the priority debt boxes, go back and check the first box on the form, showing you have no unsecured priority claims to report.

If you checked any of the priority debt boxes, make as many photocopies of the Schedule E continuation sheet as the number of priority debts you checked. You will need to complete a separate sheet for each type of debt. Here is how to complete a continuation page for each type of debt.

In re and **Case No.** Follow the instructions for Schedule A.

Type of Priority. Enter one of the types of priority you checked on page 1 of this schedule.

Creditor's Name and Mailing Address, Including Zip Code. List the name and complete mailing address (including zip code) of each priority creditor, as well as the account number if you know it.

Note: The law only requires that you list the last four digits of account numbers, to protect your privacy, since your bankruptcy petition is a matter of public record. But if you feel comfortable doing so list the entire number.

You may have more than one priority creditor for a given debt. For example, if you've been sued or hounded by a collection agency, list the attorney or collection agency in addition to the lender.

Codebtor. If someone else can be legally forced to pay your debt to a listed priority creditor, enter an "X" in this column and list the codebtor in the creditor column of this schedule. Common codebtors are listed in the instructions for Schedule D.

Husband, Wife, Joint, or Community. Follow the instructions for Schedule A.

Date Claim Was Incurred and Consideration for Claim. State the date you incurred the debt—this may be a specific date or a period of time. Also briefly state what the debt is for. For example, "goods purchased," "hours worked for me," or "deposit for my services." With wages, salaries, commissions, contributions to employee benefit plans, money owed farmers and fisherman, deposits by individuals, and child support or alimony, put the approximate time over which you failed to make the payments unless you can identify one or two specific dates. With taxes and other debts to the government, note the most recent date you received notice that you owe money or the date any unfiled tax returns were due.

Contingent, Unliquidated, Disputed. Follow the instructions for Schedule D.

Total Amount of Claim. For the priority debt other than taxes, put the amount it would take to pay off the debt in full, even if it's more than the amount considered a priority. For taxes, if part of your tax debt is secured and included on Schedule D, list only the amount that is unsecured (and therefore a priority). If the amount isn't determined, write "not yet determined" in this column.

Subtotal/Total. Total the amounts in the Total Amount of Claim column on each page. If you use continuation pages for additional priority debts, enter the total of all priority debts on the final page. If the amount of any debt has not yet been determined, put the total of all the other debts. At the bottom of the first page, fill in the number of continuation pages you are attaching.

Amount Entitled to Priority. If the priority claim is larger than the maximum permitted (for example, you owe $5,000 in wages to a former employee), put the maximum ($4,300) here. If the claim is less than the maximum, put the amount you entered in the Total Amount of Claim column.

6. Schedule F—Creditors Holding Unsecured Nonpriority Claims

In this schedule, list all creditors you didn't list in Schedules D or E. For purposes of completing Schedule F, it doesn't matter that the debt might be nondischargeable (that is, it won't be wiped out at the end of your bankruptcy case), such as back child support or a student loan. It also doesn't matter if you believe that you don't owe the debt. It's essential that you list every creditor to whom you owe, or possibly owe, money. You might be able to copy most of this information from Worksheet 4, Unsecured Debts (Ch. 3), if you filled it out.

Below are a sample completed Schedule F and line-by-line instructions. Use as many preprinted continuation pages as you need.

In re and **Case No.** Follow the instructions for Schedule A.

☐ **Check this box if debtor has no creditors holding unsecured nonpriority claims to report on this Schedule F.** Check this box if you have no other unsecured debts beyond those you listed on Schedule E. For example, if you are filing for Chapter 13 bankruptcy to get current on your mortgage or to pay off your fully secured tax debt, and you have no other creditors, you would check this box. But read the instructions, and "Easy-to-Overlook Creditors," below, before checking this box.

Creditor's Name and Mailing Address, Including Zip Code. List, preferably in alphabetical order, the name and complete mailing address of each unsecured creditor currently owed or who is trying to collect the debt, as well as the account number if you know it.

Note: To protect your privacy, the law requires that you list only the last four digits of any account numbers, since bankruptcy filings are a matter of public record. However, if you feel comfortable doing so, list the entire account number.

If you have more than one unsecured creditor for a given debt, list the original creditor first and then immediately list the other creditors. For example, if you've been sued or hounded by a collection agency, list the attorney or collection agency in addition to the original creditor. (But you don't have to list a collection agency that had the debt a while back and has ceased collection efforts.)

Easy-to-Overlook Creditors

One debt may involve several different creditors. Remember to include:

- your ex-spouse, if you are obligated under a divorce decree or settlement agreement to pay joint debts, turn any property over to your ex, or make payments as a result of your property division
- anyone who cosigned a promissory note, loan application, or the like for you
- any holder of a loan or promissory note that you cosigned for someone else
- anybody to whom the debt has been assigned or sold and any other person (such as a bill collector or attorney) trying to collect the debt, and
- anyone who may sue you because of a car accident, business dispute, or the like.

When you are typing your final papers, if you get to the end and discover that you left a creditor off, don't redo the whole list in search of perfect alphabetical order. Just add the creditors at the end.

Codebtor. If someone else can be legally forced to pay your debt to a listed unsecured creditor, enter an "X" in this column and list the codebtor in the creditor column of this schedule. The instructions for Schedule D list common codebtors.

Husband, Wife, Joint, or Community. Follow the instructions for Schedule A.

Date Claim Was Incurred and Consideration for Claim. If Claim is Subject to Setoff So State. Specify when the debt was incurred. It may be one date or a period of time. With credit card debts, put the approximate time over which you ran up the charges unless the unpaid charges were made on one or two specific dates. If there is more than one creditor for a single debt, list the same date for each creditor.

Then state what the debt was for. You can be general ("clothes" or "household furnishings") or specific ("refrigerator" or "teeth capping").

If you are entitled to a setoff against the debt—that is, the creditor owes you some money, too—list the

Form B6F (12/03)

In re _____ Herchoo, Martin & Ellen _____ ,   Case No. _____

                          Debtor   (If known)

SCHEDULE F- CREDITORS HOLDING UNSECURED NONPRIORITY CLAIMS

State the name, mailing address, including zip code, and last four digits of any account number, of all entities holding unsecured claims without priority against the debtor or the property of the debtor, as of the date of filing of the petition. The complete account number of any account the debtor has with the creditor is useful to the trustee and the creditor and may be provided if the debtor chooses to do so. Do not include claims listed in Schedules D and E. If all creditors will not fit on this page, use the continuation sheet provided.

If any entity other than a spouse in a joint case may be jointly liable on a claim, place an "X" in the column labeled "Codebtor," include the entity on the appropriate schedule of creditors, and complete Schedule H - Codebtors. If a joint petition is filed, state whether husband, wife, both of them, or the marital community maybe liable on each claim by placing an "H," "W," "J," or "C" in the column labeled "Husband, Wife, Joint, or Community."

If the claim is contingent, place an "X" in the column labeled "Contingent." If the claim is unliquidated, place an "X" in the column labeled "Unliquidated." If the claim is disputed, place an "X" in the column labeled "Disputed." (You may need to place an "X" in more than one of these three columns.)

Report total of all claims listed on this schedule in the box labeled "Total" on the last sheet of the completed schedule. Report this total also on the Summary of Schedules.

☐   Check this box if debtor has no creditors holding unsecured claims to report on this Schedule F.

CREDITOR'S NAME, MAILING ADDRESS INCLUDING ZIP CODE, AND ACCOUNT NUMBER (See instructions, above.)	CODEBTOR	HUSBAND, WIFE, JOINT, OR COMMUNITY	DATE CLAIM WAS INCURRED AND CONSIDERATION FOR CLAIM. IF CLAIM IS SUBJECT TO SETOFF, SO STATE.	CONTINGENT	UNLIQUIDATED	DISPUTED	AMOUNT OF CLAIM WITHOUT DEDUCTING VALUE OF COLLATERAL
ACCOUNT NO. 4931 802 1171A City Savings Visa P.O. Box 110110 Indianapolis, IN 46000		C	4/xx–12/xx, credit card charges				12,789
ACCOUNT NO. Miles Murayama, Esq. Jones, Jones,& Murayama 19 Whitehall Ave. Tucson, AZ 85700		C	"				"
ACCOUNT NO. 6968371142 River Bank 11 River Road Sacramento, CA 95000	X	C	12/xx; personal consolidation loan				3,918
ACCOUNT NO. 							

____ 1 continuation sheets attached

Subtotal • • $

Total • • $ 16,707

(Report also on Summary of Schedules)   N/A

Form B6F - Cont.
(12/03)

In re   Herchoo, Martin & Ellen   ,   Case No. _____

_____

Debtor   **(If known)**

SCHEDULE F - CREDITORS HOLDING UNSECURED NONPRIORITY CLAIMS
(Continuation Sheet)

CREDITOR'S NAME, MAILING ADDRESS INCLUDING ZIP CODE, AND ACCOUNT NUMBER	CODEBTOR	HUSBAND, WIFE, JOINT, OR COMMUNITY	DATE CLAIM WAS INCURRED AND CONSIDERATION FOR CLAIM. IF CLAIM IS SUBJECT TO SETOFF, SO STATE.	CONTINGENT	UNLIQUIDATED	DISPUTED	AMOUNT OF CLAIM WITHOUT DEDUCTING VALUE OF COLLATERAL
ACCOUNT NO. 5564113211 Rural Bank MasterCard P.O. Box 2105 Chicago, IL 60600		C	6/xx–12/xx; credit card charges				6,452
ACCOUNT NO. Patricia Washington, Esq. Washington & Lincoln Legal Plaza, Suite 1 Chicago, IL 60600		C	"				"
ACCOUNT NO. 31-6294-81172 Sweeter's Bank 937 Main Street Tucson, AZ 85700	X	C	1/xx; personal loan to pay for dental work				1,411
ACCOUNT NO.							
ACCOUNT NO.							

Sheet no. _1_ of _1_ sheets attached to Schedule of
Creditors Holding Unsecured Nonpriority Claims

Subtotal • • $ 7,863

(Total of this page)

Total • • $ 24,570

(Use only on last page of the completed Schedule E.)

(Report total also on Summary of Schedules)

amount and briefly state why you think you are entitled to a setoff.

Contingent, Unliquidated, Disputed. Follow the instructions for Schedule D.

Amount of Claim. List the amount of the debt claimed by the creditor, even if you dispute the amount. That way, it will all be wiped out if it's discharged at the end of your bankruptcy case. If there's more than one creditor for a single debt, put the debt amount across from the original creditor and put ditto marks (") across from each subsequent creditor you list. Be as precise as possible when stating the amount. If you must approximate, write "approx." after the amount.

Subtotal/Total. Total the amounts in the last column for this page. Do not include the amounts represented by the ditto marks if you listed multiple creditors for a single debt. On the final page (which may be the first page or a preprinted continuation page), enter the total of all unsecured claims. On the first page, in the bottom left corner, note the number of continuation pages you are attaching.

7. Schedule G—Executory Contracts and Unexpired Leases

In this form, you list every executory contract or unexpired lease that you're a party to. "Executory" means the contract is still in force—that is, both parties are still obligated to perform important acts under it. Similarly, "unexpired" means that the contract or lease period hasn't run out—that is, it is still in effect.

If you are delinquent in payments that were due under a contract or lease, list the delinquency as a debt on Schedule D, E, or F, not here. The purpose of this schedule is to identify your existing obligations. As a part of your Chapter 13 plan, you will state whether you want to continue the lease or contract, or end your obligation.

Common examples of executory contracts and unexpired leases are:

- residential leases or rental agreements
- business leases or rental agreements
- car leases
- service contracts
- business contracts

- time-share contracts or leases
- "rent-to-own" contracts for household property
- contracts of sale for real estate
- copyright or patent license agreements
- leases of real estate (surface and underground) for the purpose of harvesting timber, minerals, or oil
- future homeowners' association fee requirements
- agreements for boat docking privileges, and
- insurance contract policies.

A sample completed Schedule G is shown below.

Rent-to-Own Contracts: Leases or Security Agreements?

Rent-to-own contracts are one of the most common forms of predatory lending, and one of the most damaging for debtors.

Take, for example, the case of a Pennsylvania debtor who had already paid $1,400 worth of monthly payments in a rent-to-own contract for a used refrigerator. The final payment on the contract was still a way off when the debtor filed for Chapter 13. The creditor asked the court for permission to repossess the refrigerator if the debtor didn't continue to make payments under the rent-to-own contract. The debtor argued that the creditor had already received far more than the refrigerator was worth, and therefore was not entitled to receive more. The court ruled for the creditor, granting it permission to repossess the refrigerator despite the fact that the debtor had already paid the creditor $1,400 for it. The creditor could repossess because, under the rent-to-own agreement, the debtor had no ownership right until the final payment was made. (*In re Rembert*, 293 B.R. 664, (Bankr. M.D. Pa., 2003.)

This result may seem shocking, but Pennsylvania is one of several states that have laws requiring this result.

In the absence of such a state law, many courts still treat such contracts as a credit sale of property subject to a security interest. (See, for example, *In re Crummie*, 194 B.R. 230 (Bankr. N.D. Cal. 1996.) If the contract qualifies as a credit sale agreement with a security interest, you would list the debt on Schedule D.

B6G
(10/89)

In re ___Herchoo, Martin & Ellen_____ ,   Case No._____
                        Debtor   (if known)

SCHEDULE G - EXECUTORY CONTRACTS AND UNEXPIRED LEASES

  Describe all executory contracts of any nature and all unexpired leases of real or personal property. Include any timeshare interests.
  State nature of debtor's interest in contract, i.e., "Purchaser," "Agent," etc. State whether debtor is the lessor or lessee of a lease.
  Provide the names and complete mailing addresses of all other parties to each lease or contract described.

  NOTE: A party listed on this schedule will not receive notice of the filing of this case unless the party is also scheduled in the appropriate schedule of creditors.

☐ Check this box if debtor has no executory contracts or unexpired leases.

NAME AND MAILING ADDRESS, INCLUDING ZIP CODE, OF OTHER PARTIES TO LEASE OR CONTRACT.	DESCRIPTION OF CONTRACT OR LEASE AND NATURE OF DEBTOR'S INTEREST. STATE WHETHER LEASE IS FOR NONRESIDENTIAL REAL PROPERTY. STATE CONTRACT NUMBER OF ANY GOVERNMENT CONTRACT.
Summer Vacations Co. P.O. Box 1811 53 West Waterway Blvd. Cape Cod, MA 01000 Manager: Darcy Perkpoint	Leased Timeshare; agreement signed 7/xx; 25-year lease with 22 years remaining

Below are line-by-line instructions for Schedule G.

In re and **Case No.** Follow the instructions for Schedule A.

☐ **Check this box if debtor has no executory contracts or unexpired leases.** Check this box if it applies and go on to Schedule H; otherwise, complete the form.

Name and Mailing Address, Including Zip Code, of Other Parties to Lease or Contract. Provide the name and full address (including zip code) of each party— other than yourself—to each lease or contract. These parties are either people who signed agreements or the companies for whom these people work. If you're unsure about whom to list, include the person who signed an agreement, any company whose name appears on the agreement, and anybody who might have an interest in having the contract or lease enforced. If you still aren't sure, put "don't know."

Description of Contract or Lease and Nature of Debtor's Interest. State Whether Lease Is for Nonresidential Real Property. State Contract Number of any Government Contract. For each lease or contract, give:

- a description of the basic type (for instance, residential lease, commercial lease, car lease, business obligation, copyright license)
- the date the contract or lease was signed
- the date the contract is to expire (if any)
- a summary of each party's rights and obligations under the lease or contract, and
- the contract number, if the contract is with any government body.

8. Schedule H—Codebtors

In Schedules D, E, and F, you identified those debts for which you have codebtors—usually, a cosigner, guarantor, ex-spouse, nonfiling spouse, or nonmarital partner. You must also list those codebtors here.

As long as your Chapter 13 case is pending, collection efforts against your codebtors must cease. The creditor can't go after the codebtor unless at the end of your Chapter 13 bankruptcy case, the court discharges (wipes out) a balance on the debt. Most Chapter 13 debtors avoid this by paying in full their debts with codebtors.

Below are a sample completed Schedule H and line-by-line instructions.

In re and **Case No.** Follow the instructions for Schedule A.

☐ **Check this box if debtor has no codebtors.** Check this box if it applies; otherwise, complete the form.

Name and Address of Codebtor. List the name and complete address (including zip code) of each codebtor. If the codebtor is a nonfiling spouse, put all names by which that person was known during the previous six years.

Name and Address of Creditor. List the name and address of each creditor (as listed on Schedule D, E, or F) to which each codebtor is indebted.

EXAMPLE: Tom Martin cosigned three different loans —with three different banks—for Mabel Green, who is now filing for Chapter 13 bankruptcy. In the first column, Mabel lists Tom Martin as a codebtor. In the second, Mabel lists each of the three banks.

If you are married and filing alone. If you live in a community property state, your spouse may be a codebtor for most of the debts you listed in Schedules D, E, and F. This is because in these states, most debts incurred by one spouse are owed by both spouses. In this event, just list your spouse as a codebtor; and in the second column, simply write "all creditors listed in Schedules D, E, and F, except:" and then list any creditors whom you owe solely.

9. Schedule I—Current Income of Individual Debtor(s)

Worksheet 5 in Ch. 4, designed to calculate your income, contains all the information you need to complete Schedule I.

Below is a sample completed Schedule I, and line-by-line instructions. If you're married and filing jointly, you must fill in information for both spouses. If you are married but filing alone, you must still fill in the information for both spouses unless you and your spouse are separated.

In re and **Case No.** Follow the instructions for Schedule A.

Debtor's Marital Status. Enter your marital status. Your choices are single, married, separated (you aren't living with your spouse and plan never to again), widowed, or divorced. You are divorced only if you have received a final judgment of divorce from a court.

B6H
(6/90)

In re ___Herchoo, Martin & Ellen_____ ,   Case No. _____
                    Debtor   (if known)

SCHEDULE H - CODEBTORS

    Provide the information requested concerning any person or entity, other than a spouse in a joint case, that is also liable on any debts listed by debtor in the schedules of creditors. Include all guarantors and co-signers. In community property states, a married debtor not filing a joint case should report the name and address of the nondebtor spouse on this schedule. Include all names used by the nondebtor spouse during the six years immediately preceding the commencement of this case.

☐ Check this box if debtor has no codebtors.

NAME AND ADDRESS OF CODEBTOR	NAME AND ADDRESS OF CREDITOR
Maria Montumba 63 "C" Street Sacramento, CA 95000	River Bank 11 River Road Sacramento, CA 95000 Sweeter's Bank 937 Main Street Tucson, AZ 85700

Dependents of Debtor and Spouse. List the ages and relationships of all persons who receive at least half of their support from you and your spouse. This may include your children, your spouse's children, your parents, other relatives, and domestic partners. It does not include your spouse, unless you are filing alone. Do not list their names.

Employment. Provide the requested employment information. If you have more than one employer, enter "See continuation sheet" just below the box containing the employment information and then complete a continuation sheet. If you are retired, unemployed, or disabled, put that.

Income. Enter your estimated monthly gross income from regular employment, before any payroll deductions are taken. In the second blank, put your estimated monthly overtime pay. Add them together and enter the subtotal in the third blank.

If you are self-employed or an independent contractor, use the blank below labeled "Regular income from operation of business or profession or farm." Also, attach a sheet of paper. Call it "Attachment to Schedule I" and include your name (and spouse's name if you're filing jointly) and a separate statement of income and expenses for the operation of your business. Anyone with a financial background (such as a banker, accountant, bookkeeper, or tax preparer) can help you draft one.

Payroll Deductions. In the four blanks, enter the deductions taken from your gross salary. The deductions listed are the most common ones, but you may have others to report. Other possible deductions are state disability taxes, wages withheld or garnished for child support, credit union loan payments, or perhaps payments on a student loan or a car.

Subtotal of Payroll Deductions. Add your payroll deductions and enter the subtotal.

Total Net Monthly Take Home Pay. Subtract your payroll deductions subtotal from your income subtotal.

Regular income from operation of business or profession or farm. If you are self-employed or operate a sole proprietorship, enter your monthly income from that source here. If it's been fairly steady for at least one calendar year, divide the amount you entered on your most recent tax return (IRS Form 1040 Schedule C) by 12 for a monthly amount. If your income hasn't been steady for at least one calendar year, enter the average

net income from your business or profession for the past three months. In either case you must attach a statement of your income. Use your most recent filed IRS Schedule C.

Income from real property. Enter your monthly income from real estate rentals, leases, or licenses (such as mineral exploration, oil, and the like).

Interest and dividends. Enter the average estimated monthly interest you receive from bank or security deposits and other investments, such as stocks.

Alimony, maintenance or support payments payable to the debtor for the debtor's use or that of dependents listed above. Enter the average monthly amount you receive for your support (alimony, spousal support, or maintenance) or that of your children (child support).

Social Security or other government assistance. Enter the total monthly amount you receive in Social Security, TNAF, SSI, public assistance, disability payments, veterans' benefits, unemployment compensation, workers' compensation, or any other government benefit. If you receive food stamps, include their monthly value. Specify the source of the benefits.

Pension or retirement income. Enter the total monthly amount of all pension, annuity, IRA, Keogh, or other retirement benefits you currently receive.

Other monthly income. Specify any other income (such as royalty payments or payments from a trust) you receive on a regular basis and enter the monthly amount here. You may have to divide by 3, 6, or 12 if you receive the payments quarterly, semiannually, or annually.

Total Monthly Income. Add all additional income to the Total Net Monthly Take Home Pay amount and enter the grand total in the box.

Total Combined Monthly Income. If you are married, add your total income to your spouse's total income and enter the result here.

Your Total Monthly Income (or Total Combined Monthly Income if you are filing jointly) should be the same figure as your Total Monthly Income on Worksheet 5.

Describe any increase or decrease of more than 10% in any of the above categories anticipated to occur within the year following the filing of this document. Identify any changes in your pay or other income—in excess of 10%—that you expect in the coming year. This information could be crucial in getting your

Form B6I
(12/03)

In re ___Herchoo, Martin & Ellen_____ ,   Case No._____
             Debtor   **(if known)**

SCHEDULE I - CURRENT INCOME OF INDIVIDUAL DEBTOR(S)

The column labeled "Spouse" must be completed in all cases filed by joint debtors and by a married debtor in a chapter 12 or 13 case whether or not a joint petition is filed, unless the spouses are separated and a joint petition is not filed.

Debtor's Marital Status: Married	DEPENDENTS OF DEBTOR AND SPOUSE		
	RELATIONSHIP son		AGE 12

Employment:	**DEBTOR**	**SPOUSE**
Occupation	Teacher/Writer	Lab Technician
Name of Employer	Tucson High School & Community College	Pima County Hospital
How long employed	16 years / 1 year	3 months
Address of Employer	37 Wichita Path	4000 Carpenter Drive
	Tucson, AZ 85700	Tucson, AZ 85700

		DEBTOR	SPOUSE
Income: (Estimate of average monthly income)			
Current monthly gross wages, salary, and commissions (pro rate if not paid monthly.)		$ 4,000	$ 2,000
Estimated monthly overtime		$ 0	$ 0
SUBTOTAL		$ 4,000	$ 2,000
LESS PAYROLL DEDUCTIONS			
a. Payroll taxes and social security		$ 800	$ 400
b. Insurance		$ 250	$ 0
c. Union dues		$ 50	$ 0
d. Other (Specify: _____)		$ 0	$ 0
SUBTOTAL OF PAYROLL DEDUCTIONS		$ 1,100	$ 400
TOTAL NET MONTHLY TAKE HOME PAY		$ 2,900	$ 1,600
Regular income from operation of business or profession or farm (attach detailed statement)		$ 0	$ 0
Income from real property		$ 0	$ 0
Interest and dividends		$ 0	$ 0
Alimony, maintenance or support payments payable to the debtor for the debtor's use or that of dependents listed above.		$ 0	$ 0
Social security or other government assistance (Specify) _____		$ 0	$ 0
Pension or retirement income		$ 0	$ 0
Other monthly income		$ 0	$ 0
(Specify) Royalties from math textbooks _____		$ 1,600	$ 0
		$	$
TOTAL MONTHLY INCOME		$ 4,510	$ 1,600

TOTAL COMBINED MONTHLY INCOME $ 6,110   (Report also on Summary of Schedules)

Describe any increase or decrease of more than 10% in any of the above categories anticipated to occur within the year following the filing of this document:

Ellen currently works 30 hours/week, and is in a probation period. At six months, her income should go up (we're not sure how much) and she hopes to go up to 40 hours some time in the coming year.

Chapter 13 plan approved by the court. If your income is apt to go down, you'll need to show where you will make up the difference in order to make your Chapter 13 plan payments. If your income is likely to go up, the court will probably schedule an increase in your Chapter 13 plan payments.

10. Schedule J—Current Expenditures of Individual Debtor(s)

Worksheets 6 and 7 in Ch. 4, designed to calculate your expenses and disposable income, contain all the information you need to complete Schedule J.

Below is a sample completed Schedule J, and line-by-line instructions. If you're married and filing jointly, you must fill in information for both spouses. If you are married but filing alone, only fill in the information for yourself.

In re and **Case No.** Follow the instructions for Schedule A.

☐ **Check this box if a joint petition is filed and debtor's spouse maintains a separate household. Complete a separate schedule of expenditures labeled "Spouse."** If you and your spouse are jointly filing for bankruptcy, but maintain separate households (for example, you've recently separated), check this box and make sure that you each fill out a separate Schedule J.

Expenditures. For each listed item, fill in your monthly expenses. If you make some payments biweekly, quarterly, semiannually, or annually, prorate them to show your monthly payment. Here are some pointers:

- Do not list payroll deductions that you listed on Schedule I.
- Include payments you make for your dependents' expenses, as long as those expenses are reasonable and necessary for their support.
- **Utilities—Other:** This includes garbage and cable TV service.
- **Installment payments—Other:** Write "credit card accounts" on one line and enter your total monthly payments for them. Put the average amount you actually pay, even if it's less than it should be. On the other line put "loans" (except auto loans) and enter your total payments.

Total Monthly Expenses. Total up all your expenses. Your Total Monthly Expenses should be the same figure as your Total Monthly Expenses on Worksheet 6.

For Chapter 12 and Chapter 13 Debtors Only. Enter your Total Monthly Income (or Total Combined Monthly Income if you are filing jointly) from Schedule I in blank A. Enter the Total Monthly Expenses from just above in blank B. Subtract the difference and enter it in blank C. (This should match your Total Monthly Disposable Income amount from Worksheet 7.)

Blank D asks for the amount you are proposing to pay your creditors during your Chapter 13 case. You probably won't be able to fill this in until after you write your plan in Ch. 7. For now, you can put a checkmark on the form next to blank D as a reminder that you must return to this question after you write your plan.

Once your plan is written. If you proposed in your Chapter 13 repayment plan to pay your unsecured creditors less than 100% of what you owe, then enter the number you put in blank C—that is, your entire disposable income for the length of your plan. If you proposed to pay your unsecured creditors 100% of what you owe, then enter the amount you intend to pay each month to pay off your creditors over 36 months or however many months you want your plan to last.

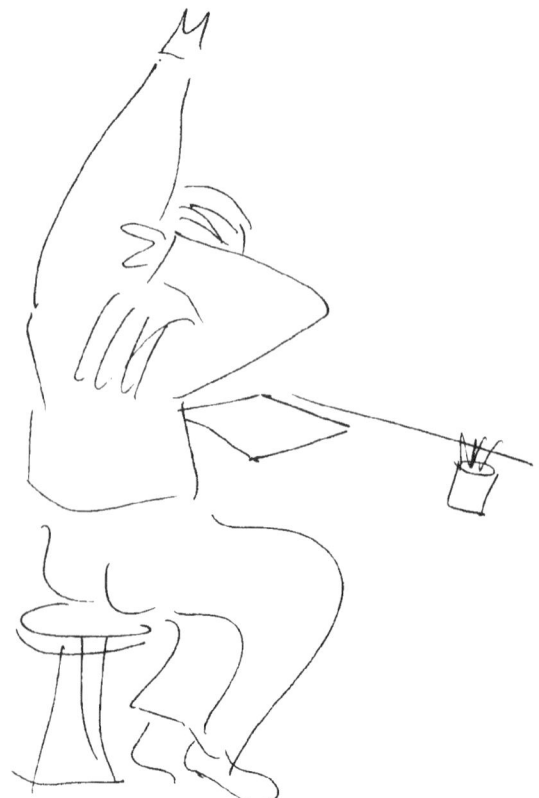

Form B6J
6/90

In re ___Herchoo, Martin & Ellen_____,   Case No._____
                              Debtor   (If known)

SCHEDULE J—CURRENT EXPENDITURES OF INDIVIDUAL DEBTOR(S)

Complete this schedule by estimating the average monthly expenses of the debtor and the debtor's family. Pro rate any payments made bi-weekly, quarterly, semi-annually, or annually to show monthly rate.

☐ Check this box if a joint petition is filed and debtor's spouse maintains a separate household. Complete a separate schedule of expenditures labeled "Spouse."

Rent or home mortgage payment (include lot rented for mobile home)	$ 2,160
Are real estate taxes included? Yes X No _____	
Is property insurance included? Yes X No _____	
Utilities: Electricity and heating fuel	$ 75
Water and sewer	$ 65
Telephone	$ 50
Other ___garbage, cable___	$ 40
Home maintenance (repairs and upkeep)	$ 150
Food	$ 600
Clothing	$ 50
Laundry and dry cleaning	$ 15
Medical and dental expenses	$ 50
Transportation (not including car payments)	$ 60
Recreation, clubs and entertainment, newspapers, magazines, etc.	$ 20
Charitable contributions	$ 20
Insurance (not deducted from wages or included in home mortgage payments)	
Homeowner's or renter's	$ 0
Life	$ 125
Health	$ 0
Auto	$ 60
Other ___Disability___	$ 80
Taxes (not deducted from wages or included in home mortgage payments)	
(Specify: _____)	$ _____
Installment payments: (In Chapter 12 and 13 cases, do not list payments to be included in the plan)	
Auto	$ 355
Other ___Home equity loan___	$ 335
Other _____	$ 0
Alimony, maintenance, and support paid to others	$ 0
Payments for support of additional dependents not living at your home	$ 0
Regular expenses from operation of business, profession, or farm (attach detailed statement)	$ 0
Other _____	$ 0
TOTAL MONTHLY EXPENSES (Report also on Summary of Schedules)	$ 4,310

[FOR CHAPTER 12 AND CHAPTER 13 DEBTORS ONLY]
Provide the information requested below, including whether plan payments are to be made bi-weekly, monthly, annually, or at some other regular interval.

A. Total projected monthly income	$ 6,110
B. Total projected monthly expenses	$ 4,310
C. Excess income (A minus B)	$ 1,800
D. Total amount to be paid into plan each ___month___	$ 1,800
(interval)	

11. Summary of Schedules

This form helps the bankruptcy trustee and judge get a quick look at your bankruptcy filing. Below is a completed Summary and line-by-line instructions follow it.

Court Name. Copy this information from Form 1—Voluntary Petition.

In re and **Case No.** Follow the instructions for Schedule A.

Name of Schedule. This column just lists the schedules you've filled out. Don't add anything.

Attached (Yes/No). You should have completed all of the schedules, so type "Yes" in this column for each schedule.

Number of Sheets. Enter the number of pages you completed for each schedule. Remember to count continuation pages. Enter the total at the bottom of the column.

Amounts Scheduled. For each column—Assets, Liabilities, and Other—copy the totals from Schedules A, B, D, E, F, I, and J and enter them where indicated. Add up the amounts in the Assets and Liabilities columns and enter their totals at the bottom.

Now, go back and fill in the statistical/administrative information on page 1 of Form 1—Voluntary Petition.

12. Declaration Concerning Debtor's Schedules

In this form, you are required to swear that everything you have said on your schedules is true and correct. Deliberate lying (perjury) is a major sin in bankruptcy. It could cost you your bankruptcy discharge, a fine of up to $500,000, and up to five years in prison.

Below is a completed Declaration and instructions.

In re and **Case No.** Follow the instructions for Schedule A.

Declaration Under Penalty of Perjury by Individual Debtor. Enter the total number of pages in your schedules (the number on the Summary plus one for the summary itself). Enter the date and sign the form. If you are filing jointly, be sure that your spouse signs and dates the form.

Certification and Signature of Non-Attorney Bankruptcy Petition Preparer. If a BPP typed your forms, have that person complete this section. Otherwise, type "N/A" anywhere in the box.

Declaration Under Penalty of Perjury on Behalf of Corporation or Partnership. Enter "N/A" anywhere in this blank.

United States Bankruptcy Court

_____ XXXXX _____ District of __Arizona, Tucson Division__

In re __Herchoo, Martin P. & Ellen_____ , Case No._____
Debtor (If known)

SUMMARY OF SCHEDULES

Indicate as to each schedule whether that schedule is attached and state the number of pages in each. Report the totals from Schedules A, B, D, E, F, I and J in the boxes provided. Add the amounts from Schedules A and B to determine the total amount of the debtor's assets. Add the amounts from Schedules D, E and F to determine the total amount of the debtor's liabilities.

NAME OF SCHEDULE		ATTACHED (YES/NO)	NUMBER OF SHEETS	AMOUNTS SCHEDULED		
				ASSETS	LIABILITIES	OTHER
A	Real Property	Yes	1	$ 275,000		
B	Personal Property	Yes	4	$ 61,604		
C	Property Claimed as Exempt	Yes	2			
D	Creditors Holding Secured Claims	Yes	1		$ 265,260	
E	Creditors Holding Unsecured Priority Claims	Yes	2		$ 33,762	
F	Creditors Holding Unsecured Nonpriority Claims	Yes	2		$ 24,570	
G	Executory Contracts and Unexpired Leases	Yes	1			
H	Codebtors	Yes	1			
I	Current Income of Individual Debtor(s)	Yes	1			$ 6,110
J	Current Expenditures of Individual Debtor(s)	Yes	1			$ 4,310
	Total Number of Sheets of All Schedules ➡		16			
	Total Assets ➡			$ 336,604		
	Total Liabilities ➡				$ 323,592	

Official Form 6-Cont.
(12/03)

In re ___Herchoo, Martin & Ellen_____ ,   Case No. _____
                    Debtor   (If known)

DECLARATION CONCERNING DEBTOR'S SCHEDULES

DECLARATION UNDER PENALTY OF PERJURY BY INDIVIDUAL DEBTOR

I declare under penalty of perjury that I have read the foregoing summary and schedules, consisting of _____ 17 _____

sheets, and that they are true and correct to the best of my knowledge, information, and belief.   *(Total shown on summary page plus 1.)*

Date ____2/25/xx_____   Signature: ____*Martin Herchoo*_____
                                                                                                Debtor

Date ____2/25/xx_____   Signature: ____*Ellen Herchoo*_____
                                                                                        (Joint Debtor, if any)

                                                                          [If joint case, both spouses must sign.]

- -

CERTIFICATION AND SIGNATURE OF NON-ATTORNEY BANKRUPTCY PETITION PREPARER (See 11 U.S.C. § 110)

I certify that I am a bankruptcy petition preparer as defined in 11 U.S.C. § 110, that I prepared this document for compensation, and that I have provided the debtor with a copy of this document.

_____N/A_____   _____
Printed or Typed Name of Bankruptcy Petition Preparer   Social Security No.
                                                                                                (Required by 11 U.S.C. § 110(c).)

_____

_____
Address

Names and Social Security numbers of all other individuals who prepared or assisted in preparing this document:

If more than one person prepared this document, attach additional signed sheets conforming to the appropriate Official Form for each person.

X _____   _____
Signature of Bankruptcy Petition Preparer   Date

A bankruptcy petition preparer's failure to comply with the provisions of title 11 and the Federal Rules of Bankruptcy Procedure may result in fines or imprisonment or both. 11 U.S.C. § 110; 18 U.S.C. § 156.

- -

DECLARATION UNDER PENALTY OF PERJURY ON BEHALF OF A CORPORATION OR PARTNERSHIP

I, the _____N/A_____ [the president or other officer or an authorized agent of the corporation or a member or an authorized agent of the partnership] of the _____ [corporation or partnership] named as debtor in this case, declare under penalty of perjury that I have read the foregoing summary and schedules, consisting of _____ sheets, and that they are true and correct to the best of my knowledge, information, and belief.   *(Total shown on summary page plus 1.)*

Date _____   Signature: _____

                                                            _____
                                                            [Print or type name of individual signing on behalf of debtor.]

[An individual signing on behalf of a partnership or corporation must indicate position or relationship to debtor.]

Penalty for making a false statement or concealing property: Fine of up to $500,000 or imprisonment for up to 5 years or both. 18 U.S.C. §§ 152 and 3571.

G. Form 7—Statement of Financial Affairs

Congratulations—you're almost through. For most people, the Statement of Financial Affairs is the last form to fill in before writing the repayment plan (Ch. 7). This form gives information about your recent financial transactions, such as payments to creditors, sales, or other transfers of property and gifts. The questions on the form are, for the most part, self-explanatory. Spouses filing jointly combine their answers and complete only one form.

If you have no information for a particular item, check the "None" box. If you fail to answer a question and don't check "None," you will have to amend your papers—that is, file a corrected form—after you file. Add continuation sheets if necessary. Be sure the information you put on this form matches the information you put on other forms asking the same questions.

A completed Statement of Financial Affairs and instructions for questions that are not self-explanatory follow.

Court name. Copy this information from Form 1—Voluntary Petition.

In re and **Case No.** Follow the instructions for Schedule A.

1. Income from employment or operation of business. Enter your gross income so far this calendar year and for the two prior calendar years. This means the total income before taxes and other payroll deductions or business expenses are removed.

2. Income other than from employment or operation of business. Include interest, dividends, royalties, workers' compensation, other government benefits, and all other money you have received from sources other than your job or business during the last two years. Provide the source of each amount, the dates received, and the reason you received the money, so that the trustee can verify it.

3. Payments to creditors. Here you list payments you've recently made to creditors. There are two kinds of creditors—regular and insiders. An insider—defined on the first page of the Statement of Financial Affairs —is essentially a relative or close business associate. All other creditors are regular creditors.

a. **List any payment over $600 made to a regular creditor,** if the payment was made:

- to repay a loan, installment purchase, or other debt
- during the 90 days before you file your bankruptcy petition.

b. **List any payment made to an insider creditor,** if the payment was made within one year before you file your bankruptcy petition. Include alimony and child support payments.

The purpose of these questions is to discover if you have "preferred" any creditor over others. The trustee can demand that the creditor turn over the amount of any payment listed here to the court, so the trustee can use the money to pay your other unsecured creditors. This rarely happens in Chapter 13 bankruptcy, however, unless you propose to pay your unsecured creditors very little (such as 10%) or nothing.

4. Suits, executions, garnishments and attachments.

a. Include all court actions that you are currently involved in or which you were involved in during one year before filing. Court actions include personal injury cases, small claims court lawsuits, contract disputes, divorces, paternity suits, support or custody modification actions, criminal prosecutions, and the like. For each case, include:

- **Caption of the suit and case number.** The caption is the case title (such as *John Jones v. Ginny Jones*). The case number is assigned by the court clerk and appears on the first page of any court-filed paper.
- **Nature of the proceeding.** A phrase, or even a one-word description, is sufficient. For example, "suit by debtor for damage to debtor's car caused by accident" or "divorce."
- **Court and location.** This information is on any court paper you received or prepared.
- **Status or disposition.** State whether the case is awaiting trial, is pending a decision, is on appeal, or has ended.

b. If, at any time during the year before you file for bankruptcy, your wages, real estate, or personal property were taken from you under the authority of a court order to pay a debt, enter the requested information. If you don't know the exact date, put "on or about" the approximate date.

5. Repossessions, foreclosures and returns. If, at any time during the year before you file for bankruptcy, a creditor repossessed or foreclosed on property you had bought and were making payments on, or had pledged as collateral for a loan, give the requested information. For instance, if your car, boat, or video equipment was repossessed because you defaulted on your payments, describe it here. Also, if you voluntarily returned property to a creditor because you couldn't keep up the payments, enter that here.

6. Assignments and receiverships.

a. If, at any time during the 120 days (four months) before you file for bankruptcy, you assigned (legally transferred) your right to receive benefits or property to a creditor to pay a debt, list it here. Examples include voluntarily assigning a percentage of your wages to a creditor for several months or assigning a portion of a personal injury award to an attorney. (Involuntarily turning your wages or property over to someone else is a garnishment or attachment—Item 4—not an assignment.) The assignee is the person to whom the assignment was made, such as the creditor or attorney. The terms of the assignment should be given briefly—for example, "wages assigned to Snorkle's Department Store to satisfy debt of $500."

b. Identify all of your property that has been in the hands of a court-appointed receiver, custodian, or other official during the year before you file for bankruptcy. If you've made child support payments directly to a court, and the court in turn paid your child's other parent, list those payments here.

7. Gifts. Provide the requested information about gifts you've made in the past year. The bankruptcy court and trustee want this information to make sure you haven't improperly unloaded any property before filing for bankruptcy so you wouldn't have to pay much to your unsecured creditors. List all charitable donations over $100 and gifts to family members over $200.

You don't have to list gifts to family members that are "ordinary and usual," but there is no easy way to identify such gifts. The best test is whether someone outside of the family might think the gift was unusual under the circumstances. If so, list it. Forgiving a loan is also a gift, as is charging interest substantially below the market rate. Other gifts include giving a car or pre-paid trip to a business associate.

8. Losses. Provide the requested information about recent financial losses.

9. Payments related to debt counseling or bankruptcy. If you paid an improperly high fee to an attorney, bankruptcy petition preparer, debt consultant, or debt consolidator, the trustee may try to get some of it back if you are not proposing to pay much to your unsecured creditors. Be sure to list all payments someone else made on your behalf (such as your mother helping you out by paying your attorney's bill) as well as payments you made directly.

10. Other transfers. List all real estate and personal property that you've sold or used as collateral for a secured debt during the last year. Some examples are selling or abandoning (junking) a car, pledging your house as security (collateral) for a loan, granting an easement on real estate, or trading property.

Don't include any gifts you listed in Item 7. Also, don't list property you parted with as a regular part of your business or financial affairs. For example, if you operate a mail order book business, don't list the books you sold during the past year. Similarly, don't put down payments for regular goods and services, such as your phone bill, utilities, or rent.

11. Closed financial accounts. Provide information for each account in your name or for your benefit that was closed during the past year or transferred to someone else.

12. Safe deposit boxes. Provide information for each safe deposit box you've had within the past year.

13. Setoffs. A setoff is when a creditor, often a bank, uses money in a customer's account to pay a debt owed to the creditor by that customer. Here, list any setoffs your creditors have made during the last 90 days.

14. Property held for another person. Describe all property you've borrowed, or are storing or holding in trust for someone. Examples are funds in an irrevocable trust controlled by you and property you're holding as executor or administrator of an estate.

15. Prior addresses. If you have moved within the two years before you file for bankruptcy, list all of your residences within those two years.

16. Spouses and former spouses. If you lived in a community property state within six years prior to filing for bankruptcy, list the name of your spouse and of any former spouses who lived with you in the community property state.

Form 7
(12/03)

FORM 7. STATEMENT OF FINANCIAL AFFAIRS

UNITED STATES BANKRUPTCY COURT

_____Northern_____ **DISTRICT OF** __Arizona, Eastern Division__

In re: ____Herchoo, Martin and Ellen____,   Case No. _____
              (Name)   (if known)
                    Debtor

STATEMENT OF FINANCIAL AFFAIRS

This statement is to be completed by every debtor. Spouses filing a joint petition may file a single statement on which the information for both spouses is combined. If the case is filed under chapter 12 or chapter 13, a married debtor must furnish information for both spouses whether or not a joint petition is filed, unless the spouses are separated and a joint petition is not filed. An individual debtor engaged in business as a sole proprietor, partner, family farmer, or self-employed professional, should provide the information requested on this statement concerning all such activities as well as the individual's personal affairs.

Questions 1 - 18 are to be completed by all debtors. Debtors that are or have been in business, as defined below, also must complete Questions 19 - 25. **If the answer to an applicable question is "None," mark the box labeled "None."** If additional space is needed for the answer to any question, use and attach a separate sheet properly identified with the case name, case number (if known), and the number of the question.

DEFINITIONS

"In business." A debtor is "in business" for the purpose of this form if the debtor is a corporation or partnership. An individual debtor is "in business" for the purpose of this form if the debtor is or has been, within the six years immediately preceding the filing of this bankruptcy case, any of the following: an officer, director, managing executive, or owner of 5 percent or more of the voting or equity securities of a corporation; a partner, other than a limited partner, of a partnership; a sole proprietor or self-employed.

"Insider." The term "insider" includes but is not limited to: relatives of the debtor; general partners of the debtor and their relatives; corporations of which the debtor is an officer, director, or person in control; officers, directors, and any owner of 5 percent or more of the voting or equity securities of a corporate debtor and their relatives; affiliates of the debtor and insiders of such affiliates; any managing agent of the debtor. 11 U.S.C. § 101.

---

1.   **Income from employment or operation of business**

None
☐

State the gross amount of income the debtor has received from employment, trade, or profession, or from operation of the debtor's business from the beginning of this calendar year to the date this case was commenced. State also the gross amounts received during the **two years** immediately preceding this calendar year. (A debtor that maintains, or has maintained, financial records on the basis of a fiscal rather than a calendar year may report fiscal year income. Identify the beginning and ending dates of the debtor's fiscal year.) If a joint petition is filed, state income for each spouse separately. (Married debtors filing under chapter 12 or chapter 13 must state income of both spouses whether or not a joint petition is filed, unless the spouses are separated and a joint petition is not filed.)

AMOUNT	SOURCE (if more than one)
$24,000	Husband (1/1/xx–7/3/xx)
$12,000	Wife (1/1/xx–7/3/xx)
$48,000	Husband (20xy)
$24,000	Wife (20xy)
$48,000	Husband (20xz)
$24,000	Wife (20xz)

2

2. Income other than from employment or operation of business

None ☐

State the amount of income received by the debtor other than from employment, trade, profession, or operation of the debtor's business during the **two years** immediately preceding the commencement of this case. Give particulars. If a joint petition is filed, state income for each spouse separately. (Married debtors filing under chapter 12 or chapter 13 must state income for each spouse whether or not a joint petition is filed, unless the spouses are separated and a joint petition is not filed.)

AMOUNT	SOURCE
$38,000	Husband: Royalties from math textbooks 20xx–20xy)

3. Payments to creditors

None ☐

a. List all payments on loans, installment purchases of goods or services, and other debts, aggregating more than $600 to any creditor, made within **90 days** immediately preceding the commencement of this case. (Married debtors filing under chapter 12 or chapter 13 must include payments by either or both spouses whether or not a joint petition is filed, unless the spouses are separated and a joint petition is not filed.)

NAME AND ADDRESS OF CREDITOR	DATES OF PAYMENTS	AMOUNT PAID	AMOUNT STILL OWING
Summer Vacations Co. P.O. Box 1811 53 W. Waterway Blvd. Cape Cod, MA 01000	5/17/xx	$750	$8,800

None ☒

b. List all payments made within **one year** immediately preceding the commencement of this case to or for the benefit of creditors who are or were insiders. (Married debtors filing under chapter 12 or chapter 13 must include payments by either or both spouses whether or not a joint petition is filed, unless the spouses are separated and a joint petition is not filed.)

NAME AND ADDRESS OF CREDITOR AND RELATIONSHIP TO DEBTOR	DATE OF PAYMENT	AMOUNT PAID	AMOUNT STILL OWING

4. Suits and administrative proceedings, executions, garnishments and attachments

None ☐

a. List all suits and administrative proceedings to which the debtor is or was a party within **one year** immediately preceding the filing of this bankruptcy case. (Married debtors filing under chapter 12 or chapter 13 must include information concerning either or both spouses whether or not a joint petition is filed, unless the spouses are separated and a joint petition is not filed.)

CAPTION OF SUIT AND CASE NUMBER	NATURE OF PROCEEDING	COURT OR AGENCY AND LOCATION	STATUS OR DISPOSITION
City Savings v. Ellen Herchoo, #01-8080 (W)	Suit for money judgment	Maricopa County Court Phoenix, AZ	open

3

None
☒

b. Describe all property that has been attached, garnished or seized under any legal or equitable process within **one year** immediately preceding the commencement of this case. (Married debtors filing under chapter 12 or chapter 13 must include information concerning property of either or both spouses whether or not a joint petition is filed, unless the spouses are separated and a joint petition is not filed.)

NAME AND ADDRESS OF PERSON FOR WHOSE BENEFIT PROPERTY WAS SEIZED	DATE OF SEIZURE	DESCRIPTION AND VALUE OF PROPERTY

5. Repossessions, foreclosures and returns

None
☒

List all property that has been repossessed by a creditor, sold at a foreclosure sale, transferred through a deed in lieu of foreclosure or returned to the seller, within **one year** immediately preceding the commencement of this case. (Married debtors filing under chapter 12 or chapter 13 must include information concerning property of either or both spouses whether or not a joint petition is filed, unless the spouses are separated and a joint petition is not filed.)

NAME AND ADDRESS OF CREDITOR OR SELLER	DATE OF REPOSSESSION, FORECLOSURE SALE, TRANSFER OR RETURN	DESCRIPTION AND VALUE OF PROPERTY

6. Assignments and receiverships

None
☒

a. Describe any assignment of property for the benefit of creditors made within **120 days** immediately preceding the commencement of this case. (Married debtors filing under chapter 12 or chapter 13 must include any assignment by either or both spouses whether or not a joint petition is filed, unless the spouses are separated and a joint petition is not filed.)

NAME AND ADDRESS OF ASSIGNEE	DATE OF ASSIGNMENT	TERMS OF ASSIGNMENT OR SETTLEMENT

None
☒

b. List all property which has been in the hands of a custodian, receiver, or court-appointed official within **one year** immediately preceding the commencement of this case. (Married debtors filing under chapter 12 or chapter 13 must include information concerning property of either or both spouses whether or not a joint petition is filed, unless the spouses are separated and a joint petition is not filed.)

NAME AND ADDRESS OF CUSTODIAN	NAME AND LOCATION OF COURT CASE TITLE & NUMBER	DATE OF ORDER	DESCRIPTION AND VALUE OF PROPERTY

4

7. Gifts

None
☒

List all gifts or charitable contributions made within **one year** immediately preceding the commencement of this case except ordinary and usual gifts to family members aggregating less than $200 in value per individual family member and charitable contributions aggregating less than $100 per recipient. (Married debtors filing under chapter 12 or chapter 13 must include gifts or contributions by either or both spouses whether or not a joint petition is filed, unless the spouses are separated and a joint petition is not filed.)

NAME AND ADDRESS OF PERSON OR ORGANIZATION	RELATIONSHIP TO DEBTOR, IF ANY	DATE OF GIFT	DESCRIPTION AND VALUE OF GIFT

8. Losses

None
☐

List all losses from fire, theft, other casualty or gambling within **one year** immediately preceding the commencement of this case **or since the commencement of this case**. (Married debtors filing under chapter 12 or chapter 13 must include losses by either or both spouses whether or not a joint petition is filed, unless the spouses are separated and a joint petition is not filed.)

DESCRIPTION AND VALUE OF PROPERTY	DESCRIPTION OF CIRCUMSTANCES AND, IF LOSS WAS COVERED IN WHOLE OR IN PART BY INSURANCE, GIVE PARTICULARS	DATE OF LOSS
Mountain bike; $800	Son's bicycle was stolen. Insurance covered replacement. We purchased new bike on 6/20/xx	4/20/xx

9. Payments related to debt counseling or bankruptcy

None
☐

List all payments made or property transferred by or on behalf of the debtor to any persons, including attorneys, for consultation concerning debt consolidation, relief under the bankruptcy law or preparation of a petition in bankruptcy within **one year** immediately preceding the commencement of this case.

NAME AND ADDRESS OF PAYEE	DATE OF PAYMENT, NAME OF PAYOR IF OTHER THAN DEBTOR	AMOUNT OF MONEY OR DESCRIPTION AND VALUE OF PROPERTY
John White, Esq. 21 Main St. Tucson, AZ 85700	6/17/xy	(J) $500 for consultation and form preparation

10. Other transfers

None
☒

List all other property, other than property transferred in the ordinary course of the business or financial affairs of the debtor, transferred either absolutely or as security within **one year** immediately preceding the commencement of this case. (Married debtors filing under chapter 12 or chapter 13 must include transfers by either or both spouses whether or not a joint petition is filed, unless the spouses are separated and a joint petition is not filed.)

NAME AND ADDRESS OF TRANSFEREE, RELATIONSHIP TO DEBTOR	DATE	DESCRIBE PROPERTY TRANSFERRED AND VALUE RECEIVED

5

11. Closed financial accounts

None
☐

List all financial accounts and instruments held in the name of the debtor or for the benefit of the debtor which were closed, sold, or otherwise transferred within **one year** immediately preceding the commencement of this case. Include checking, savings, or other financial accounts, certificates of deposit, or other instruments; shares and share accounts held in banks, credit unions, pension funds, cooperatives, associations, brokerage houses and other financial institutions. (Married debtors filing under chapter 12 or chapter 13 must include information concerning accounts or instruments held by or for either or both spouses whether or not a joint petition is filed, unless the spouses are separated and a joint petition is not filed.)

NAME AND ADDRESS OF INSTITUTION	TYPE OF ACCOUNT, LAST FOUR DIGITS OF ACCOUNT NUMBER, AND AMOUNT OF FINAL BALANCE	AMOUNT AND DATE OF SALE OR CLOSING
Tucson Savings 1818 Desert Avenue Tucson, Arizona	(H) Checking Account #058-118061 final balance $345	5/14/xx

12. Safe deposit boxes

None
☒

List each safe deposit or other box or depository in which the debtor has or had securities, cash, or other valuables within **one year** immediately preceding the commencement of this case. (Married debtors filing under chapter 12 or chapter 13 must include boxes or depositories of either or both spouses whether or not a joint petition is filed, unless the spouses are separated and a joint petition is not filed.)

NAME AND ADDRESS OF BANK OR OTHER DEPOSITORY	NAMES AND ADDRESSES OF THOSE WITH ACCESS TO BOX OR DEPOSITORY	DESCRIPTION OF CONTENTS	DATE OF TRANSFER OR SURRENDER, IF ANY

13. Setoffs

None
☒

List all setoffs made by any creditor, including a bank, against a debt or deposit of the debtor within **90 days** preceding the commencement of this case. (Married debtors filing under chapter 12 or chapter 13 must include information concerning either or both spouses whether or not a joint petition is filed, unless the spouses are separated and a joint petition is not filed.)

NAME AND ADDRESS OF CREDITOR	DATE OF SETOFF	AMOUNT OF SETOFF

14. Property held for another person

None
☐

List all property owned by another person that the debtor holds or controls.

NAME AND ADDRESS OF OWNER	DESCRIPTION AND VALUE OF PROPERTY	LOCATION OF PROPERTY
2004 Lakeshore Dr. Lakeport, CA 95453	19xx Ford Pickup 4X4 $2,500	

15. Prior address of debtor

6

None ☒   If the debtor has moved within the **two years** immediately preceding the commencement of this case, list all premises which the debtor occupied during that period and vacated prior to the commencement of this case. If a joint petition is filed, report also any separate address of either spouse.

ADDRESS   NAME USED   DATES OF OCCUPANCY

16. Spouses and Former Spouses

None ☒   If the debtor resides or resided in a community property state, commonwealth, or territory (including Alaska, Arizona, California, Idaho, Louisiana, Nevada, New Mexico, Puerto Rico, Texas, Washington, or Wisconsin) within the **six-year period** immediately preceding the commencement of the case, identify the name of the debtor's spouse and of any former spouse who resides or resided with the debtor in the community property state.

NAME

17. Environmental Information.

For the purpose of this question, the following definitions apply:

"Environmental Law" means any federal, state, or local statute or regulation regulating pollution, contamination, releases of hazardous or toxic substances, wastes or material into the air, land, soil, surface water, groundwater, or other medium, including, but not limited to, statutes or regulations regulating the cleanup of these substances, wastes, or material.

"Site" means any location, facility, or property as defined under any Environmental Law, whether or not presently or formerly owned or operated by the debtor, including, but not limited to, disposal sites.

"Hazardous Material" means anything defined as a hazardous waste, hazardous substance, toxic substance, hazardous material, pollutant, or contaminant or similar term under an Environmental Law

None ☒   a. List the name and address of every site for which the debtor has received notice in writing by a governmental unit that it may be liable or potentially liable under or in violation of an Environmental Law. Indicate the governmental unit, the date of the notice, and, if known, the Environmental Law:

SITE NAME   NAME AND ADDRESS   DATE OF   ENVIRONMENTAL
AND ADDRESS   OF GOVERNMENTAL UNIT   NOTICE   LAW

None ☒   b. List the name and address of every site for which the debtor provided notice to a governmental unit of a release of Hazardous Material. Indicate the governmental unit to which the notice was sent and the date of the notice.

SITE NAME   NAME AND ADDRESS   DATE OF   ENVIRONMENTAL
AND ADDRESS   OF GOVERNMENTAL UNIT   NOTICE   LAW

7

None
☒

c. List all judicial or administrative proceedings, including settlements or orders, under any Environmental Law with respect to which the debtor is or was a party. Indicate the name and address of the governmental unit that is or was a party to the proceeding, and the docket number.

NAME AND ADDRESS OF GOVERNMENTAL UNIT	DOCKET NUMBER	STATUS OR DISPOSITION

---

18 . Nature, location and name of business

None
☒

a. If the debtor is an individual, list the names, addresses, taxpayer identification numbers, nature of the businesses, and beginning and ending dates of all businesses in which the debtor was an officer, director, partner, or managing executive of a corporation, partnership, sole proprietorship, or was a self-employed professional within the **six years** immediately preceding the commencement of this case, or in which the debtor owned 5 percent or more of the voting or equity securities within the **six years** immediately preceding the commencement of this case.

If the debtor is a partnership, list the names, addresses, taxpayer identification numbers, nature of the businesses, and beginning and ending dates of all businesses in which the debtor was a partner or owned 5 percent or more of the voting or equity securities, within the **six years** immediately preceding the commencement of this case.

If the debtor is a corporation, list the names, addresses, taxpayer identification numbers, nature of the businesses, and beginning and ending dates of all businesses in which the debtor was a partner or owned 5 percent or more of the voting or equity securities within the **six years** immediately preceding the commencement of this case.

NAME	TAXPAYER I.D. NO. (EIN)	ADDRESS	NATURE OF BUSINESS	BEGINNING AND ENDING DATES

None
☒

b. Identify any business listed in response to subdivision a., above, that is "single asset real estate" as defined in 11 U.S.C. § 101.

NAME	ADDRESS

The following questions are to be completed by every debtor that is a corporation or partnership and by any individual debtor who is or has been, within the **six years** immediately preceding the commencement of this case, any of the following: an officer, director, managing executive, or owner of more than 5 percent of the voting or equity securities of a corporation; a partner, other than a limited partner, of a partnership; a sole proprietor or otherwise self-employed.

*(An individual or joint debtor should complete this portion of the statement **only** if the debtor is or has been in business, as defined above, within the six years immediately preceding the commencement of this case. A debtor who has not been in business within those six years should go directly to the signature page.)*

8

19. Books, records and financial statements

None ☒   a.   List all bookkeepers and accountants who within the **two years** immediately preceding the filing of this bankruptcy case kept or supervised the keeping of books of account and records of the debtor.

NAME AND ADDRESS   DATES SERVICES RENDERED

None ☒   b.   List all firms or individuals who within the **two years** immediately preceding the filing of this bankruptcy case have audited the books of account and records, or prepared a financial statement of the debtor.

NAME   ADDRESS   DATES SERVICES RENDERED

None ☒   c.   List all firms or individuals who at the time of the commencement of this case were in possession of the books of account and records of the debtor. If any of the books of account and records are not available, explain.

NAME   ADDRESS

None ☒   d.   List all financial institutions, creditors and other parties, including mercantile and trade agencies, to whom a financial statement was issued within the **two years** immediately preceding the commencement of this case by the debtor.

NAME AND ADDRESS   DATE ISSUED

20. Inventories

None ☒   a.   List the dates of the last two inventories taken of your property, the name of the person who supervised the taking of each inventory, and the dollar amount and basis of each inventory.

DATE OF INVENTORY   INVENTORY SUPERVISOR   DOLLAR AMOUNT OF INVENTORY
                                                      (Specify cost, market or other basis)

None ☒   b.   List the name and address of the person having possession of the records of each of the two inventories reported in a., above.

DATE OF INVENTORY   NAME AND ADDRESSES OF CUSTODIAN
                                                        OF INVENTORY RECORDS

9

21 . Current Partners, Officers, Directors and Shareholders

None
☒
a. If the debtor is a partnership, list the nature and percentage of partnership interest of each member of the partnership.

    NAME AND ADDRESS   NATURE OF INTEREST   PERCENTAGE OF INTEREST

None
☒
b. If the debtor is a corporation, list all officers and directors of the corporation, and each stockholder who directly or indirectly owns, controls, or holds 5 percent or more of the voting or equity securities of the corporation.

                                               NATURE AND PERCENTAGE
    NAME AND ADDRESS   TITLE   OF STOCK OWNERSHIP

22 . Former partners, officers, directors and shareholders

None
☒
a. If the debtor is a partnership, list each member who withdrew from the partnership within **one year** immediately preceding the commencement of this case.

    NAME   ADDRESS   DATE OF WITHDRAWAL

None
☒
b. If the debtor is a corporation, list all officers, or directors whose relationship with the corporation terminated within **one year** immediately preceding the commencement of this case.

    NAME AND ADDRESS   TITLE   DATE OF TERMINATION

23 . Withdrawals from a partnership or distributions by a corporation

None
☒
If the debtor is a partnership or corporation, list all withdrawals or distributions credited or given to an insider, including compensation in any form, bonuses, loans, stock redemptions, options exercised and any other perquisite during **one year** immediately preceding the commencement of this case.

NAME & ADDRESS OF RECIPIENT, RELATIONSHIP TO DEBTOR	DATE AND PURPOSE OF WITHDRAWAL	AMOUNT OF MONEY OR DESCRIPTION AND VALUE OF PROPERTY

10

24. Tax Consolidation Group.

None

If the debtor is a corporation, list the name and federal taxpayer identification number of the parent corporation of any consolidated group for tax purposes of which the debtor has been a member at any time within the **six-year period** immediately preceding the commencement of the case.

NAME OF PARENT CORPORATION   TAXPAYER IDENTIFICATION NUMBER (EIN)

---

25. Pension Funds.

None

If the debtor is not an individual, list the name and federal taxpayer identification number of any pension fund to which the debtor, as an employer, has been responsible for contributing at any time within the **six-year period** immediately preceding the commencement of the case.

NAME OF PENSION FUND   TAXPAYER IDENTIFICATION NUMBER (EIN)

---

* * * * * *

11

[If completed by an individual or individual and spouse]

I declare under penalty of perjury that I have read the answers contained in the foregoing statement of financial affairs and any attachments thereto and that they are true and correct.

Date _July 3, 20xx_____   Signature _*Martin Herchoo*_____
                                                    of Debtor

Date _July 3, 20xx_____   Signature_ *Ellen Herchoo*_____
                                                    of Joint Debtor
                                                    (if any)

_____

[If completed on behalf of a partnership or corporation]

I, declare under penalty of perjury that I have read the answers contained in the foregoing statement of financial affairs and any attachments thereto and that they are true and correct to the best of my knowledge, information and belief.

Date _____   Signature _____

                                                                 _____
                                                                 Print Name and Title

[An individual signing on behalf of a partnership or corporation must indicate position or relationship to debtor.]

_____ continuation sheets attached

Penalty for making a false statement: Fine of up to $500,000 or imprisonment for up to 5 years, or both. 18 U.S.C. § 152 and 3571

CERTIFICATION AND SIGNATURE OF NON-ATTORNEY BANKRUPTCY PETITION PREPARER (See 11 U.S.C. § 110)

I certify that I am a bankruptcy petition preparer as defined in 11 U.S.C. § 110, that I prepared this document for compensation, and that I have provided the debtor with a copy of this document.   N/A

_____   _____
Printed or Typed Name of Bankruptcy Petition Preparer   Social Security No.
                                                                                    (Required by 11 U.S.C. § 110(c).)

_____

Address

Names and Social Security numbers of all other individuals who prepared or assisted in preparing this document:

If more than one person prepared this document, attach additional signed sheets conforming to the appropriate Official Form for each person.

X _____   _____
Signature of Bankruptcy Petition Preparer   Date

A bankruptcy petition preparer's failure to comply with the provisions of title 11 and the Federal Rules of Bankruptcy Procedure may result in fines or imprisonment or both. 18 U.S.C. § 156.

17. Environmental information. This is self-explanatory. Read the questions carefully and provide the requested information.

18. Nature, location and name of business. Provide the information requested in question "a." If the majority of your business income for any one business comes from renting, leasing, or otherwise operating a single piece of real property (other than an apartment building with less than four units), include your business name and the address of the property in "b."

➡ **Shortcut for nonbusiness debtors.** Only debtors who have operated a profession or business, or who have been otherwise self-employed, any time during the six years before filing for bankruptcy, must complete questions 19–25. If you have not operated a business, put an X in the remaining "None" boxes, type "N/A" right before question 19, and go to the signature page.

19. Books, records and financial statements.

a. Identify every person other than yourself who was involved in the accounting of your business during the previous two years. Usually this means a bookkeeper or accountant. If you were the only person involved in your business's accounting, check "None."

b. If your books weren't audited by a firm or individual during the past two years, check "None." Otherwise, fill in the requested information.

c. Usually, you, your bookkeeper, accountant, ex-business associate, or possibly an ex-mate will have business records. If any are missing, explain; the more the loss of your records was beyond your control, the better off you'll be.

d. You may have prepared a financial statement if you applied to a bank for a loan or line of credit for your business or in your own name. If you're self-employed and applied for a personal loan to purchase a car or house, you probably submitted a financial statement as evidence of your ability to repay. Financial statements include:

- balance sheet (compares assets with liabilities)
- profit and loss statement (compares income with expenses)
- financial statement (provides an overall financial description of a business).

20. Inventories. If your business doesn't have an inventory because it's a service business, check "None." If your business does deal in products, but you were primarily the middle person or original manufacturer, put "no inventory required" or "materials purchased for each order as needed." If you have an inventory, fill in the information requested in items "a" and "b."

21. Current partners, officers, directors and shareholders. Check "None" for "a" and "b."

22. Former partners, officers, directors and shareholders. Check "None" for "a" and "b."

23. Withdrawals from a partnership or distributions by a corporation. Check "None."

24. Tax consolidation group. Check "None."

25. Pension funds. Check "None."

If completed by an individual or individual and spouse. Sign and date this section. If you're filing jointly, be sure your spouse dates and signs it as well.

If completed on behalf of a partnership or corporation. Type "N/A."

Certification and Signature of Non-Attorney Bankruptcy Petition Preparer. If a BPP typed your forms, have that person complete this section. Otherwise, type "N/A" anywhere in the box.

Be sure to insert the number of continuation pages, if any, you attached.

H. Mailing Matrix

When you file your bankruptcy forms, you may need to include something called a "Mailing Matrix." The Mailing Matrix is a blank page divided into approximately 30 boxes. You type in the names and addresses of your creditors. The trustee photocopies the page to create mailing labels and mail notice of your bankruptcy filing to your creditors.

Some courts don't require a Mailing Matrix, while other courts have their own forms. (This is one of the questions you should ask the court clerk before you fill out your papers.) If you need to provide a Matrix, but your court doesn't have its own, you can use the form in Appendix 2. Here's how to fill it out:

Step 1: On a separate piece of paper, make a list of all your creditors, in alphabetical order. You can copy them off of Schedules D, E, F, and H. Be sure to include cosigners and joint debtors. If you and your spouse jointly incurred a debt and are filing jointly, however, don't include your spouse. Also include collection agencies or attorneys, if you've been sued. And if you're seeking to discharge marital debts you assumed during a divorce, include both your ex-spouse and the creditors.

Step 2: Make several copies of the Mailing Matrix form.

Step 3: In the top left-hand box on the sheet you designate as the first page of your Mailing Matrix, enter your name and address. Then enter the names and addresses of each creditor, one per box and in alphabetical order (or in the order required by your local bankruptcy court). Use as many sheets as you need.

I. Form 21—Statement of Social Security Number

To protect your privacy, federal bankruptcy forms changed in December 2003 and now require only the last four digits of your Social Security number. However, the trustee and creditors still need access to your full, nine-digit Social Security. Form 21 serves this purpose.

J. Income Deduction Order

Your bankruptcy court might require you to draft and submit an Income Deduction Order with the rest of your Chapter 13 bankruptcy papers. (You can ask the court clerk if you must prepare one when you send your letter requesting local forms and information.)

An Income Deduction Order is an order from the bankruptcy court sent to your employer. It requires the employer to automatically deduct from your wages your Chapter 13 monthly payment and send that money to the bankruptcy court.

Below is a sample Income Deduction Order. To complete your own, type up the sample—filling in the information requested in italics. Some courts have their own forms; if yours does, use it. Leave blank any information you don't yet know.

UNITED STATES BANKRUPTCY COURT

_[Name of district]_____ DISTRICT OF _____ _[Your state]_____

In re _____)

[Set forth here all names including)
married, maiden, and trade names used)
by debtor within last 6 years.])

Debtor(s)) Case No. _[leave this blank]_____

Address _____)

)

_____) Chapter 13

)

Employer's Tax Identification (EIN) No(s). [if any]:)

_____)

Last four digits of Social Security No(s): _____)

INCOME DEDUCTION ORDER

TO: [Name of Employer
    Address
    City, State, Zip Code]
    Attention: Payroll Department

_____[Name of debtor employed by this employer]_____, (Debtor), whose Social Security number is

_____[your or your spouses's Social Security number]_____, has filed a Petition under Chapter 13 of

the Bankruptcy Code with this Court, and a proposed plan for paying his/her debts.

_____[Name of trustee]_____ has been appointed Standing Chapter 13 Trustee by the U.S.

Trustee and has accepted the appointment.

Section 1325(b) of the Bankruptcy Code authorizes this Court to order an entity from whom Debtor

receives income to pay all or any part of that income to the Standing Trustee.

IT IS THEREFORE ORDERED that until you receive further order from this Court or from the Standing

Trustee that you withhold from the wages payable to the Debtor, the sum of $ ____[monthly plan amount]____

each month, beginning with the date of this Order. You are further Ordered to pay the money withheld to the

Standing Trustee, at the address shown below, in convenient installments at least once a month, the first payment to be paid within one month from the date below. Each successive monthly installment must be paid to the Standing Trustee on or before the last day of each month thereafter.

Dated: _____   _____
                                    U.S. Bankruptcy Judge

Order prepared by:
[Your name
Your street address
Your city, state, zip
Your telephone number]

Copy mailed to:

[Trustee's name]
Standing Chapter 13 Trustee
[Trustee's street address
Trustee's city, state, zip
Trustee's telephone number]

[Name of Employer
Employer's street address
Employer's city, state, zip
Employer's telephone number]

Writing Your Chapter 13 Bankruptcy Plan

Your Chapter 13 bankruptcy plan is the key to your whole bankruptcy case. It's the document in which you tell the court exactly how you plan to repay your debts: the total amount you intend to pay to each creditor, how much you can pay each month, and how many months you need to pay.

This chapter shows you how to put together your plan, using the information on the sample bankruptcy forms in Ch. 6.

Because your Chapter 13 plan is such an important part of your bankruptcy case, you may be anxious about writing one. To make matters worse, if you've seen any Chapter 13 plan forms, they may have put you off with their legal jargon and their requests for information you don't have or understand. *Don't worry.* Writing a Chapter 13 plan is not that difficult. The plan is usually only one or two pages. This chapter will tell you everything you must include in your plan, and it includes sample filled-in forms. Looking at them as you go along may make things clearer.

Do your best in writing your plan. If you don't know what information should go in a certain blank, leave it empty or venture a guess.

Before you file, you can ask the trustee to go over your plan and help you fill in the gaps (See Ch. 6, *Completing the Bankruptcy Forms*, Section D, for tips on working with the trustee before you file.) Or, you can hire a lawyer to review your plan—or to write it for you. (See Ch. 12, *Help Beyond the Book.*)

If you submit a plan with a number of mistakes, that's okay too. The trustee will help you sort it all out. You have an absolute right to file a modified plan with the bankruptcy court any time before your confirmation hearing; most Chapter 13 debtors submit at least one modified plan. In most courts, you do have to notify all of your creditors when you modify your plan, however.

A. Chapter 13 Plan Forms

There is no official Chapter 13 plan form that all bankruptcy courts use. About a third of all courts, however, have developed their own forms. If your court has its own Chapter 13 plan form, use the information in this chapter to complete it. (You may already know if your court has its own form; see Ch. 6, *Completing the Bankruptcy Forms*, Section B.)

If your court doesn't have its own plan form or you haven't been able to figure out if your court has its own plan form, you have three choices:

- **Visit the law library.** See if it has *Chapter 13 Practice Guide*, by Keith M. Lundin (Wiley Law Publications). This two-volume loose-leaf book contains the "required, preferred or sample" plan form for every bankruptcy court in the nation. It's organized first by state, then by district, and even further by division.

- **Use other plans from your court as models.** In some bankruptcy districts where there is no court-generated form, many of the local attorneys submit similar-looking Chapter 13 plans. If you'd like to create a plan that might be familiar to your court, ask the court clerk for a court file that contains a completed and approved Chapter 13 plan. (Court files are a matter of public record.) If the clerk won't help you, ask for the Chapter 13 trustee's phone number. Call the trustee and make the same request.

- **Use one of the forms in this book.** Appendix 2 contains Chapter 13 plan forms from three different bankruptcy courts. You can photocopy and use any of these forms. If you do, the bankruptcy judge or trustee may be unfamiliar with the format or (pleasantly) surprised to see such a complete Chapter 13 plan from a do-it-yourselfer. If you are asked how you developed your Chapter 13 plan, just explain that you used forms from other courts (found in this Nolo publication) as models.

If you will create your own form from scratch, or need more room than is provided on one of the forms in Appendix 2, just use plain white paper, 8½" x 11". No matter what source you use to create your plan, be sure to type your final draft.

Checklist of Chapter 13 Plan Elements

Most Chapter 13 plans must tell the court how you propose to pay:

- ☐ The trustee's fee
- ☐ Priority tax debts
- ☐ Other priority debts
- ☐ Nondischargeable unsecured debts (some courts don't ask for this)
- ☐ Dischargeable unsecured debts
- ☐ Postconfirmation debts (optional).

In addition, your plan must specify:

- ☐ How long your plan will last (usually three years)
- ☐ How often you'll make payments (usually monthly)
- ☐ How you'll deal with your contracts and leases (some courts don't ask for this)
- ☐ Whether you'll be making any direct payments to creditors—that is, outside of your plan
- ☐ The order in which creditors will be paid (optional).

B. How Long Your Plan Will Last

One of the first things you state in your plan is how long you want it to last. The bankruptcy code does not specify precisely how long a Chapter 13 plan must last. (11 U.S.C. § 1322(c).) Most debtors, however, propose three-year repayment plans. If you want a longer or shorter plan, you will need the permission of the bankruptcy court. (Additional information on the length of the plan is in Ch. 2, *An Overview of Chapter 13 Bankruptcy*, Section C, and Ch. 4, *Calculating Your Disposable Income*, Section C.)

1. Fewer Than Three Years

If you have enough disposable income to pay off all of your unsecured debts (this includes your priority debts) in less than three years, you can propose a shorter plan. Otherwise, you'll have to make payments for at least three years. The bankruptcy code requires that you dedicate your disposable income to your plan for a minimum of three years unless you can pay off your debts sooner.

2. Longer Than Three Years

The bankruptcy court might approve a plan that lasts more than three years, but under no circumstances can the court approve a plan that lasts more than five years. Here are some situations in which you might want to request a longer-term plan:

- **To pay off a secured debt.** Section I, below, explains how to handle secured debts (other than mortgages) in your plan. One way is to reduce your debt to the value of your collateral and pay it off through your plan. For example, if you owe $9,000 on your car but it's only worth $4,500, you could keep your car through Chapter 13 bankruptcy by paying $4,500 through your plan. If you can't afford to pay it off in three years, you can propose a longer plan.

- **To meet any payment percentage required by the court.** In some courts, the judge will not approve your plan unless you propose paying your unsecured creditors a significant portion of what you owe them, usually at least 70%. To meet that goal, these courts will readily approve a plan up to five years.

  In other courts, the judge will approve plans that propose paying unsecured creditors nothing at all or as little as 5% of what you owe. These courts usually won't approve a plan lasting more than three years if the sole reason is to pay unsecured creditors more. These courts reason that if you dedicate your disposable income for three years, that's all the bankruptcy law requires, even if your unsecured creditors receive very little.

- **To avoid objections from unsecured creditors who must wait to get paid.** When you start making plan payments, the trustee will pay your secured creditors and priority creditors before your general unsecured creditors. If your plan pays very little to your unsecured creditors, they may object to a three-year plan and try to force you into a longer plan so they can get paid more. The courts will often accommodate such creditors' requests. For example, if you have mortgage arrears (a secured debt) and a tax debt (a priority debt) that will take you 28 months to pay, your unsecured creditors would receive money for only the last eight months of a three-year plan. But if your plan lasted four years, these same creditors would be paid for 20 months.

- **To repay your nondischargeable debts.** If you have an unsecured nonpriority, nondischargeable debt, such as a student loan or child support delinquency, most bankruptcy courts will approve a plan that lasts more than three years so you can pay off the debt. If, however, you propose a plan that will pay 100% on such a debt, you may have to pay 100% on your other unsecured debts, too. (See Section J, below.)

C. Your Payment Schedule

Somewhere near the top of your plan, you'll need to say how often you want to make your plan payments to the trustee. Most Chapter 13 bankruptcy debtors make plan payments once a month. If you are paid more often or less often, however, you can pay the trustee on your schedule, such as:

- weekly
- every other week
- twice a month (such as on the 1st and 16th)
- quarterly (this might be convenient if you receive royalties, quarterly dividends, or quarterly payments from a trust)
- semiannually (some publishers and producers pay royalties only twice a year; farmers often sell crops only twice yearly)
- annually (usually in the case of farmer who is paid once a year for crops), or
- seasonally (if you're a construction worker, you may not be able to make payments in winter; a teacher may make small payments, or none at all, during the summer).

If you propose making quarterly, semiannual, or annual payments to the trustee, the payments will have to be large. You will also need to show the bankruptcy court, at the confirmation hearing, evidence of your past income (copies of your income tax returns for the past three to five years), which the court will use as an indication of your future income. The court might especially be inclined to approve your plan if you offer to make small monthly payments in between the larger quarterly, semiannual, or annual payments.

D. The Order in Which Creditors Will Be Paid

Most trustees pay creditors in the order in which they appear on the Chapter 13 repayment plan. You are not required to follow that order. But if you want your creditors paid in a different order, you'll have to specify how in your Chapter 13 plan.

You must pay the trustee's fee and support arrears before paying other debts. If you have mortgage arrears, and a tax debt, your lender and the taxing authority will each want to be paid next. In fact, your mortgage lender will probably object to your plan if it doesn't provide for payment of your mortgage arrears before your tax debts.

Below is the order in which most debtors ask the trustee to pay their creditors. If this isn't the order on your plan form, or you want to change this order, specify the changes you want in the "Other Provisions" or "Special Provisions" section of your plan. (See Section M, below.)

1. **Administrative claims.** The bulk of your first few payments will go toward your filing fee if you ask the court for permission to pay it in installments. In addition, the trustee's fee will come off the top of all of your payments. The bankruptcy code states that the filing fee and trustee's fee must be paid before your debts are. (11 U.S.C. § 1326(b).) Administrative claims include any fees that you owe to a bankruptcy lawyer or other lawyer who delivers nonbankruptcy services to you during the course of your Chapter 13 case (for instance, a lawyer handling your divorce) and therefore must also be paid before other debts. (See *In re Powell,* 314 B.R. 567 (N.D. Texas 2004).

2. **Support arrears.** These are priority debts, which you may not want paid until after your secured debt defaults are paid. But public policy dictates that child support and alimony arrears be paid as soon as possible in Chapter 13 bankruptcy.

3. **Mortgage defaults.** If your loan was obtained before October 22, 1994 you'll probably want these claims paid early because you must pay interest on them. (See Section H2, below.)

4. **Other secured debt defaults.** Again, these claims should be paid early because you must pay interest on them.

5. **Priority debts.** The IRS and other priority creditors are entitled to be paid before your unsecured creditors. (Paying priority creditors is covered in Sections F and G, below.)

6. **Unsecured creditors.** They are usually paid last. But you may have to specify how you want unsecured creditors paid. (See Section J, below.)

E. Reducing the Trustee's Fee

Remember—the trustee is entitled to keep 3% to 10% of every payment you make, and most trustees take the full 10%. So for every $100 you pay your creditors, you actually have to pay the trustee either $110 or $111.11. (Trustees use different formulas to calculate their fees; they are explained in Ch. 2, *An Overview of Chapter 13 Bankruptcy*, Section F.)

Here are some ways to reduce the trustee's fee:

- If you are current on your mortgage, propose making your mortgage payments directly to your lender—that is, "outside of the plan." (See Section L, below.) The trustee doesn't get a cut of the payments you make directly.

- If you are not current on your mortgage—that is, you will use your Chapter 13 plan to make up the missed payments and get back on track—you can ask the trustee at the creditors' meeting (explained in Ch. 9, *After You File Your Case*, Section E) to waive the portion of the fee that is based on your regular mortgage payment. The trustee might be willing, if making the monthly payments will be really tight for you.

- If you will propose selling a valuable asset to make certain payments, you should also propose disbursing the money yourself. Otherwise, up to 10% of the proceeds will go to the trustee, not your creditors.

F. The Order in Which Priority Debts Will Be Paid

Many plans ask you to identify "priority" creditors. You listed them on Schedule E—Creditors Holding Unsecured Priority Claims. Other plans simply state that the trustee will pay all priority creditors in full;

presumably, the trustee will get the information from Schedule E.

The trustee will pay priority debts in the order listed below unless you request otherwise in your plan.

1. Administrative costs and fees paid to the bankruptcy court, including filing and administrative fees, and the trustee's fee.

2. Attorney's fees, if you hire an attorney for help with your Chapter 13 case.

3. Wages, salaries, and commissions earned by people who worked for you within 90 days before you filed for bankruptcy, up to $4,300.

4. Contributions you owe to an employee benefit fund for services rendered by an employee of your business.

5. Deposits you took from individuals who intended to purchase, lease, or rent goods or services which you never delivered, up to $1,950.

6. Claims of certain people who produce grain or run fisheries, up to $4,300.

7. Alimony and child support you owe to an ex-spouse and children from former relationships.

8. Tax debts. (Figuring out the priority portion of your tax debt is covered in Section G, below.)

The only reason you might change this order is if a creditor threatens to object to your plan unless you agree to pay that creditor earlier. You might as well go along with a creditor who decides to be a squeaky wheel this way. Because these priority creditors are paid in full (and without interest), the order in which they are paid doesn't really matter.

G. Paying Back Taxes

In your plan, you must provide for payment of your back taxes, interest, and penalties. Unlike your other debts, your tax debts may fall into one, two, or even three different categories on your Chapter 13 plan. Pay close attention to the rules.

1. Categorizing Your Federal Income Tax Debt

If you have a federal income tax debt, how you handle it in your plan depends on what category it falls into: dischargeable, secured, or priority. (See "Classifying Your Tax Debt," below.)

Classifying Your Tax Debt

If...	Your tax debt is...
All of the following are true: • the tax year for which you owe taxes ended more than three years before the date you plan to file your bankruptcy case • you properly filed your tax return (if the IRS filed a Substitute for Return for you, it doesn't count unless you agreed and signed the substitute return for the year in question at least two years before filing for bankruptcy) • the IRS has not assessed the taxes against you within 240 days before you plan to file your bankruptcy case, and • the IRS has not recorded a Notice of Federal Tax Lien with your county land records office.	**Dischargeable,** meaning you can completely eliminate your income tax debt, and the interest and penalties associated with it. If your bankruptcy court approves Chapter 13 plans in which unsecured creditors receive nothing or very little, you can eliminate your dischargeable tax debt without paying very much. You'll pay a small amount through your plan, and at the end of your case the balance will be wiped out. (See Section J, below.) If, however, your bankruptcy court requires you to pay a higher percentage of unsecured debts, you might be better off filing for Chapter 7 bankruptcy. (This is explained in Ch. 1, *Should You File for Chapter 13 Bankruptcy?*)
• The IRS has recorded a Notice of Federal Tax Lien.	**Secured,** meaning you may be able to discharge your personal liability in bankruptcy, but the lien remains. If you don't pay off the entire debt during your case, the IRS can seize property you owned before filing to cover the rest. Practically speaking, the IRS looks to collect from real estate and retirement plans.
Your tax debt is not dischargeable or secured.	**Priority,** which means that it must be paid in full in your Chapter 13 plan.
Your tax debt is not dischargeable or secured. The IRS has recorded a Notice of Federal Tax Lien, but your property (again, real estate or retirement plan) won't cover what you owe the IRS.	**Undersecured** (if you have no seizable assets) or partially undersecured (if you have some). The undersecured portion is dischargeable if the first three conditions listed above for dischargeable taxes are met.

2. Interest

The majority of bankruptcy courts have ruled that "interest follows the tax." This means that if your income tax debt is dischargeable, so is the interest on that debt. And if your tax debt is secured or a priority debt, so is the interest you owe on it. However, if you complete the payments under the plan, then the interest on the priority debt will be discharged.

3. Penalties

Penalties are treated a little differently than is interest.
   A penalty is dischargeable if:
   • the event giving rise to the penalty (such as your failure to file a return or to file it on time) occurred over three years before you file for bankruptcy, or
   • the tax is dischargeable.
   Income tax penalties are considered a priority only if you are fined because the IRS suffered a monetary loss. This is rarely, if ever, the case.

4. Dealing With Tax Debts in Your Repayment Plan

How you deal with your tax debts in your repayment plan will depend on how those debts are classified. Here are the three ways tax debts are classified and how to deal with them in your plan.
   • If a portion of your IRS debt is *unsecured* and *nonpriority* (see "Classifying Your Tax Debt," above), that portion is treated like any other unsecured debt. Through your plan, you will pay a percentage of the debt without interest. Upon completion of the plan, the rest of the debt will be discharged.
   • If a portion of your IRS debt is an *unsecured priority debt*, you must pay it in full through your repayment plan. During the plan, interest accrues but you don't have to pay it. If you complete the plan, the interest is discharged. If you do not complete the plan, you will be responsible for interest as well as any unpaid principal balance.
   • If a portion of your IRS debt is *secured*, you must pay it in full with interest.

IRS proof of claim. The IRS will submit a proof of claim that identifies the portions of your tax debt that it believes are secured, unsecured, and priority. Unfortunately this proof of claim may arrive after your confirmation hearing. If your plan has been confirmed and the IRS sees your tax debt differently than it is treated in your confirmed plan, you may need to amend the plan. If this happens, get help from a bankruptcy lawyer.

5. Other Tax Debts

State income tax debts are usually handled the same way federal income taxes are.

Help from a lawyer. If you have a substantial state income tax debt, speak to a bankruptcy attorney before you file to find out if any special state rules apply.

All other tax debts—including payroll taxes, excise taxes, and property taxes—are priority debts. (If your county has filed a lien against your property for your failure to pay your property taxes, however, the debt is secured, not a priority.)

H. Paying Mortgage Arrears

If you're like a lot of people, you're filing for Chapter 13 bankruptcy because you've gotten behind on your mortgage and are afraid of losing the house. In general, Chapter 13 bankruptcy lets you get back on track with a mortgage.

If your mortgage is current. If you are not behind on your mortgage, you can skip this section. The bankruptcy court will probably let you continue making your regular mortgage payments directly to your lender. (See Section L, below.)

If you are behind on your mortgage, you most likely have two choices: either give the house back to the lender or pay the overdue amount in your plan. In a small number of cases, you may have a third or fourth option: to reduce your obligation under the mortgage to the current value of your house or to eliminate some liens on the property. Each of these options is discussed below.

1. Give the House Back

If you just can't deal with your mortgage any longer, you can simply give your house back to the lender, who will then sell it at a foreclosure sale. The lender cannot refuse to take the house back.

If the sale nets the lender enough money to pay off your debt, you're home free—the debt is gone. If there is any excess (which is highly unlikely), you are entitled to it.

If, however, the market value of the house has fallen and the sale brings in less than what you owe, or there are additional liens on the house, the difference is called a deficiency balance. You treat it like any other dischargeable unsecured debt. (See Section J, below.) In a few states, however, even if the sale brings in less than you owe, the sale wipes out your obligation completely—that is, there is no deficiency balance.

If you want to give your house back to the lender rather than get current on your mortgage, state that in your plan. In the section of your Chapter 13 plan labeled "Special Provisions" or "Other Provisions," write "I am behind on my house mortgage. I want to surrender the collateral rather than cure the default."

2. Make Up Missed Payments and Reinstate the Loan

If you want to keep your house, you must make up your missed payments, reinstate the loan, and keep making the payments under the original contract. This is called, in Chapter 13 parlance, "curing the default."

In the section of your plan labeled "Home Mortgage" or something similar, you must provide information about your mortgage loan, including some or all of the following:

- the name of the mortgage company
- the total amount you are behind (called arrears), plus late fees, attorney fees, and collection costs
- the rate of interest you propose to pay on the arrears (if the mortgage loan was signed before October 22, 1994; see Subsection b, below)
- the months you missed your payments
- how many months you propose to take to pay the arrears, and
- the amount of your regular monthly payment. (While you pay off the past-due amount, you also make the regular payments called for under your original agreement.)

Bankruptcy rules require that your mortgage arrears be paid through your plan within a "reasonable time." Virtually every court has a rule (written or unwritten) limiting you to a specific number of months—anywhere from six to 60. Most courts want the mortgage made current within a year. For example, in your plan you might state that you want the trustee to apply all of your first seven months' payments to your mortgage arrears.

If Your Lender Has Started Foreclosure Proceedings

If your lender has started to foreclose against you, your right to cure the default depends on how far along the foreclosure proceeding is. If the lender has accelerated the loan (declared the entire balance due), or has gone to court and obtained a foreclosure judgment, you usually can still cure the default. Some courts let lenders proceed with foreclosure if you don't cure the default at the same moment you file for bankruptcy. The reasoning is that a plan proposal or its confirmation isn't a cure and that only the cure stops a foreclosure. Of course, your lender may be happy to stop the foreclosure when you file the plan.

If the foreclosure sale has already occurred, you cannot cure the default through Chapter 13 bankruptcy. This is true even if your state law gives you a "redemption right," which lets you buy back the house from the person who bought it at the foreclosure sale as long as a new deed hasn't yet been recorded. (11 U.S.C. § 1322(c)(1).)

Help from a lawyer. If your house has been sold at foreclosure, see a lawyer before filing for Chapter 13 bankruptcy.

a. Curing a Balloon Payment Default

For loans signed on or after October 22, 1994 you can cure the default even if the final mortgage payment (in your original contract) is due before the final payment in your Chapter 13 plan. (11 U.S.C. § 1322(c)(2).) This change in the law was intended to help people cure a default on a balloon payment.

> EXAMPLE: When Ed bought his house, he took out a 30-year first mortgage from a bank and borrowed the rest (in the form of a second mortgage) from the seller. The second mortgage required Ed to make monthly payments of $200 for 24 months and then pay a balance (balloon) of $12,000. Ed made the 24 monthly payments, but he defaulted on the balloon. He can use Chapter 13 bankruptcy to pay it off over time.

This law also helps people who are in arrears with only a few months or years left on their mortgage (very few people who file for Chapter 13 bankruptcy).

b. Paying Interest on Mortgage Arrears

If your mortgage loan was signed on or after October 22, 1994 you do not have to pay interest on the arrears. (11 U.S.C. § 1322(e).)

If, however, you propose to cure a default on a mortgage loan signed before that date, you must pay interest on the arrears. (*Rake v. Wade,* 508 U.S. 464 (1993).) This is tantamount to paying interest on interest, because each mortgage payment already includes interest. (Presumably, that's why Congress eliminated the interest requirement in the 1994 legislation.)

No law prescribes the exact interest rate you must pay. Most bankruptcy judges require you to pay your mortgage rate; others allow you to pay the current market interest rate.

Most plan forms don't have a blank for mortgage arrears interest. If your court's form doesn't have a blank, your best bet is to leave the interest figure off. If the lender doesn't object, you won't have to pay it. If the lender does object, you can amend your plan and add it to the "Special Provisions" or "Other Provisions" section.

3. Reduce the Note to the Current Value of the House

Although the Bankruptcy Code generally prohibits debtors from modifying the terms of their mortgage in Chapter 13 bankruptcy, a growing number of courts allow debtors to get around this restriction. If your court allows it, you can reduce the secured portion of your debt to the value of the house and treat the difference as a general unsecured debt.

Modification is not a realistic option for most people, however, for two reasons:

• To get the court to approve a modification, you must show that at least a part of the loan is secured by something other than your residence and the land it is sitting on. (11 U.S.C. § 1322(b)(2).)

• If the court allows the modification, you will have to pay the present value of your house in full *during* your plan—just three to five years.

Modification could help you if you still have a lot to pay on your mortgage and your property has dropped substantially in value.

> **Help from a lawyer.** Modifying your mortgage as a part of your Chapter 13 bankruptcy case is beyond the scope of this book. Consult a bankruptcy attorney.

To figure out whether you might qualify for a modification, look at your mortgage agreement to see if anything besides your residence is collateral for your mortgage loan. Here are some possibilities:

• **Multiunit property.** If you live in one unit (your primary residence), but your loan was for the purchase of a multiunit building, the court may allow modification because the mortgage is secured by units other than your residence.

• **An adjacent lot or other buildings on the premises.** The other property is especially likely to be considered not a part of your residence if it produces income—for example, farmland.

• **A mobile home you live in, but which is considered personal property.** If you have a mobile home on the property and it is part (or all) of the collateral for the mortgage loan, it isn't considered your residence if your state law defines mobile homes as personal property, not real estate. The court may reject this argument if the mobile home is permanently attached to the land.

- **Fixtures, rents, royalties, mineral rights, insurance proceeds, escrow accounts, equipment, and appliances.** The court might reject your request if the other security interest (such as an empty escrow account) has no value.
- **Credit, life, or other insurance.**
- **The residence and personal property.** Some creditors, such as consolidation lenders, take a security interest in appliances, furniture, and other personal property. In this situation, the mortgage loan is not secured solely by the residence.

- **Two loans from the same lender for the residence and something else.** You might have a mortgage and car loan from the same lender, and clauses in both agreements declare house and car collateral for both loans. In this situation, the security for your mortgage is the house and the car, not just your house.

In addition, the court might permit modification if the value has dropped so significantly that your mortgage debt is totally unsecured.

4. Eliminate or Reduce Liens on the Property

As explained in Ch. 3, *Adding Up Your Secured and Unsecured Debts*, Section A4, you may be able to eliminate or reduce some liens on your real estate.

If You Have More Than One Mortgage

If you have more than one mortgage on your home, and your home has declined in value, one or more of those mortgages may be "completely unsecured." Such mortgages can be "stripped off" (eliminated) in a Chapter 13 bankruptcy in most—but not all—parts of the United States.

First, you need to make sure that the mortgage you're hoping to strip is "completely unsecured." To meet this definition, all superior mortgages must add up to more than your house is worth, leaving no equity to secure the second (or third or subsequent) mortgage. Do not include your exemption amount in this calculation (unlike calculations involved in avoiding judicial liens, described in Chapter 3, Section A4).

Once you show that your mortgage (or home equity loan) is a completely unsecured second, courts in most jurisdictions will allow you to "strip off" the mortgage upon the completion of your plan. This is true whether or not you paid any of the debt in your

plan. (For the relevant court cases, see *In re Zimmer*, 313 F.3d 1220 (9th Cir. 2002); *In re Lane*, 280 F.3d 663 (6th Cir. 2002); *In re Pond*, 252 F.3d 122 (2d Cir. 2001); *In re Tanner*, 217 F.3d 1357 (11th Cir. 2000); *In re Mann*, 249 B.R. 831 (B.A.P. 1st Cir. 2000); *In re Bartee*, 212 F.3d 277 (5th Cir. 2000); and *In re McDonald*, 205 F.3d 606 (3d Cir. 2000).)

If you think you might have a completely unsecured mortgage, contact an experienced Chapter 13 bankruptcy lawyer—and one who practices in your district. The required procedure may vary from jurisdiction to jurisdiction. (For a discussion of procedural requirements in various districts see *In re Robert*, 313 B.R. 545 (Bkrtcy. N.D. N.Y. 2004); *In re Millspaugh*, 302 B.R. 90 (Bkrtcy. D. Idaho 2003). These cases say this can be done with a simple valuation motion under Rule 3012, but some other jurisdictions require more complex procedures.)

I. Paying Other Secured Debts

One of the most alluring features of Chapter 13 bankruptcy is that it offers many ways of dealing with secured debts. Secured debts, remember, are those for which you pledged a particular item of property as collateral (such as a car loan) or where the creditor has recorded a lien against you. (Mortgage arrears are handled differently from all other secured debts in Chapter 13 bankruptcy; see Section H, above.)

The options for dealing with nonmortgage secured debts are described below. In your plan, you must state what option you've chosen for every secured debt. Here are your choices:

- Surrender the property to the secured creditor.
- Pay, through your plan, the amount of the debt or the current value of the property, whichever is less.
- Make up the missed payments and reinstate the loan.
- Eliminate or reduce liens on the property.
- Sell the property.
- File a Chapter 7 bankruptcy before you file a Chapter 13 bankruptcy.

1. Surrender the Property

You can always simply give the collateral to the secured creditor after you file for bankruptcy. The creditor will sell the property at a repossession sale. The creditor cannot refuse to accept the collateral.

If the sale nets the creditor enough money to pay off your debt, you're home free—the debt is gone. If there is any excess (which is highly unlikely), you are entitled to it.

If, however, the sale brings in less than what you owe, the difference is called a deficiency balance. You treat it like any other dischargeable unsecured debt—pay off some or all of it through your plan, and have the rest wiped out at the end of your case. (See Section J, below.) In the states listed below, however, even if the sale brings in less than you owe, surrendering the property wipes out your obligation completely—that is, there is no deficiency balance.

Offering to surrender the property is a good strategy in three situations:

- If, under your state's law, you will not be liable for any deficiency balance.
- The creditor wants the property because it is still worth a lot, and in exchange, will not require you to pay the deficiency balance, if any.
- The creditor doesn't want the property because it has depreciated in value. If you propose to surrender the collateral, the creditor may offer to let you keep it and pay the debt at a low interest rate. (You must pay interest on secured debts in your Chapter 13 plan. Negotiating the interest rate is discussed in Section 2b, below.)

If you want to surrender the property, indicate it in the "Other Provisions" or "Special Provisions" section of your plan. You can simply put something like, "We want to return the washer and dryer set to Sears."

It is possible to surrender collateral even if you don't have it. For instance, if a married couple separates and the nonfiling spouse has the collateral, the filing spouse can surrender his or her interest in the collateral without having to deal with the nonfiling spouse. (See *In re Anderson*, 316 B.R. 321 (W.D. Arkansas 2004).

2. Pay the Amount of the Debt or the Current Value of the Property

If you want to keep an item of collateral, you can propose, in your plan, to pay either the amount you owe the creditor or the current value of the property, whichever is less. No matter which amount you propose to pay, you can pay it off over time—that is, through your Chapter 13 plan.

Most people choose to pay the creditor the value of the property. This option is widely known as a "cramdown." That's because if you've had the secured property for a while, it's probably gone down in value to the point that you owe more than it's worth. If you decide on this course, here is what you must do:

- You must repay this entire amount during your plan. If you can't pay off the debt within 36 months, you can propose a plan to last up to 60 months.
- In the plan, where you list the amount of the secured claim, put down the current value of the property, not the amount you owe on the original

States That Don't Impose Deficiency Balances on Personal Property		
State	**Code Section**	**When Deficiency Balance Prohibited**
Alabama	Ala. Code § 5-19-13	If you paid $1,000 or less for the collateral.
Arizona	Ariz. Rev. Stat. § 44-5501	If you paid $1,000 or less for the collateral.
California	Cal. Civil Code § 1812.5	If you bought goods on installment.
	Cal. Health & Safety Code § 18038.7	On a mobile home, manufactured home, commercial coach, truck camper, or floating home.
Colorado	Colo. Rev. Stat. § 4-9-503	On a mobile home or trailer unless you have vacated or donated the property or the lender has a court judgment.
	Colo. Rev. Stat. § 5-5-103	If you paid $3,000 or less for the collateral.
Connecticut	Conn. Gen. Stat. § 36a-785(f),(g)	All repossession sales except for cars or boats with a cash price over $2,000.
District of Columbia	D.C. Code Ann. § 28-3812(e)	If you paid $2,000 or less for the collateral.
Florida	Fla. Stat. Ann. § 516.31(3)	If you paid $2,000 or less for the collateral.
Idaho	Idaho Code § 28-45-103(3)	If you paid $1,000 or less for the collateral.
Indiana	Ind. Code Ann. § 24-4.5-5-103 and 750 Ind. Admin. Code § 1-1-1	If you paid $3,300 or less for the collateral.
Kansas	Kan. Stat. Ann. § 16a-5-103	If you paid $1,000 or less for the collateral.
Louisiana	La. Rev. Stat. Ann. § 13:4108.2	If the seller does not get an appraisal before the sale, unless you have agreed in writing to a sale without an appraisal.
Maine	Me. Rev. Stat. Ann. tit. 9-A § 5-103	If you paid $2,800 or less for the collateral.
Maryland	Md. Com. Law § 12-626	If you paid $2,000 or less for the collateral.
Massachusetts	Mass. Gen. Laws ch. 255, § 13J(e)	If unpaid balance is under $2,000.
Minnesota	Minn. Stat. Ann. § 325G.22	If amount financed was $5,700 or less.
Missouri	Mo. Rev. Stat. § 408.556	If amount financed was $500 or less.
Nebraska	Neb. Rev. Stat. § 45-184	If unpaid balance is $3,000 or less.
Oklahoma	14A Okla. Stat. Ann. § 5-103	If you paid $3,800 or less for the collateral.
South Carolina	S.C. Code Ann. § 37-5-103	If you paid $4,200 or less for the collateral.
Utah	Utah Code Ann. § 70C-7-101	If you paid $3,000 or less for the collateral.
West Virginia	W. Va. Code Ann. § 46A-2-119	If unpaid balance is $1,000 or less.
Wisconsin	Wis. Stat. § 425.209	If unpaid balance is $1,000 or less.
Wyoming	Wyo. Stat. Ann. § 40-14-503	If you paid $1,000 or less for the collateral.

debt. (You and the creditor must agree on this amount; see Subsection a, below.)

- In the plan, you must specify the interest rate you will pay. (Determining the interest rate is covered in Subsection b, below.)
- In the plan, you must agree that the creditor's security interest—the lien on the property—will remain until you have paid the secured claim. Some plans include this language. If yours does not, you'll have to list the collateral in the "Secured Debts" section of your plan. If you don't, the creditor may object to your plan, in which case the court won't approve it.
- The creditor will probably insist that you sign a document in which you agree to maintain insurance on the property and otherwise take good care of it. This is called providing "adequate protection." You must do this in case you can't finish your Chapter 13 plan and later want to give the property back to the creditor.

a.   Determining the Current Value of the Property

You and the creditor must agree on the current value. But first, you must agree on what is meant by "current." Most debtors and creditors agree to use the value of the property on the date of the hearing where the judge confirms or denies the plan. If the property needs to be appraised, you could use the date of the appraisal. A few debtors and creditors agree to use the value of the property as of the date the debtor filed the bankruptcy petition. For most property, it doesn't really matter.

Then comes the important part: agreeing on the value of the property, which is the amount you'll have to pay the creditor. Debtors and creditors disagree on the method to use to determine the value. Debtors want the figure as low as possible: the value if they were forced to sell at a yard sale. Creditors want the figure as high as possible: the replacement value—that is, the amount it would cost a debtor to buy a comparable item.

In 1997, the U.S. Supreme court ruled that, in this situation (that is, a Chapter 13 cramdown) the creditor is entitled to receive the replacement value—the amount it would cost a debtor to obtain property of like age and condition. See *Associates Commercial*

Corporation v. Rash, 520 U.S. 953 (1997). Since this decision was handed down, courts have limited it to apply only to Chapter 13 cramdowns. In other situations (for example, in Chapter 7 redemption cases) the secured creditor is entitled only to the wholesale value of the property.

Though the court ruled that a creditor is entitled to replacement value in this situation, it also mentioned numerous factors a debtor could use to establish a lower replacement value than might otherwise be expected: For example, the replacement value of a used car is not simply the retail used car price for that make and model. The retail used car price may reflect the added value of warranties, reconditioning, or storage that the dealer has done. Your car, presumably, has none of these features, so an exact replacement would be worth less than the going retail used car price, to that extent.

Finally, *Rash* emphasized that it's relevant to look at what purchasing opportunities are actually available to the debtor for replacing the item. That is, a debtor who does not have access to the wholesale market cannot claim a wholesale price as replacement value. Debtors must cite prices in the retail market that is available to them. However, since most everyone has access to eBay and other discount avenues for direct purchasing of used items from other owners—outside of traditional wholesale/retail channels—debtors may be able to establish a replacement value that is not much higher than the yard sale value.

Negotiations regarding the value of the collateral usually take place informally. You can begin the process by calling the creditor before you file your plan to see if you can agree on an amount. If you can't, just include a value in your Chapter 13 plan; if the creditor disagrees, the creditor will have to take the next step.

If the creditor disagrees with your chosen value, the creditor will probably file a paper scheduling a "valuation hearing" before the bankruptcy judge. This hearing will probably be held just before your confirmation hearing. Asking for a valuation hearing will prevent the trustee from using your value if you and the creditor can't reach an agreement informally.

At the same time the creditor files the paper (you'll get a copy), the creditor will contact you (or your attorney) and try to reach an agreement. Sometimes negotiations take place over the telephone. Often, you actually negotiate the value at the meeting of the creditors, which takes place before the confirmation and valuation hearings.

If you can't reach an agreement, the judge will establish the value at the valuation hearing. If you have reached an agreement by then, the court will review the amount, if the creditor requested a valuation hearing. Only in rare instances would a court reject the value agreed to by you and the creditor and set the value on its own.

Some courts have adopted hard and fast rules for recently purchased goods. For instance, in one recent case the court adopted a rule that goods purchased in the previous 90 days are worth the same as the purchase price. (See *In re Spraggins*, 316 B.R. 317 (E.D. Wis. 2004).)

b. Determining the Interest Rate

Until recently, the question of how to set an interest rate for secured claims other than mortgages was hotly debated, with various bankruptcy courts issuing inconsistent rulings. However, in 2004 the U.S. Supreme Court settled the matter and announced a formula for Chapter 13 cases. (Till v. SCS Credit Corporation, 541 U.S. 465 (2004).) The Court said the rate should be the national prime rate, adjusted upward slightly for the additional risk of lending to a bankrupt debtor. In that case, that risk was deemed to be 1.5% over prime. Lower courts have generally approved adjustments in the range of 1%-3% over prime.

The bankruptcy court in your district may already have a rate stated on its standard Chapter 13 plan form. If your court has not set an interest rate, you and your creditor will have to negotiate a rate or ask the court to decide, using the formula announced by the Supreme Court.

c. When Is the Lien Extinguished?

When a debtor proposes to pay the creditor the value of the property under the Chapter 13 plan, the question arises, when is the lien is actually extinguished?

There are three possible answers:

- As soon as the secured claim amount is fully paid, but before the plan is complete. (See, for examples, *In re Campbell*, 180 B.R. 686 (M.D.

Fla. 1985); *In re Murray-Hudson*, 147 B.R. 960 (Bankr. N.D. Cal. 1992); *In re Shorter*, 237 B.R. 443 (Bankr. N.D. Ill. 1999).) This is best for debtors, because it eliminates the lien even if the Chapter 13 plan is never finished.
- Not until the entire Chapter 13 plan is completed.
- Not until the debtor receives the final discharge. (See, for example, *In re Archie*, 240 B.R. 425, 426-27.) This is worse for debtors because it means that if you don't complete your Chapter 13 plan, the creditors lien will spring back to life even though you paid the full value of the property.

The trustee will know the local custom in your court. Make sure your plan specifies that the lien is extinguished as soon as the amount is paid, so that the lien will not spring back into existence if the case is dismissed prematurely or converted to Chapter 7. Here is a sample clause: "The holder of any allowed secured claim provided for by the plan shall retain a lien securing such claim until the amount for which the claim is allowed as secured is paid in full."

Note that some courts ignore such a clause and hold that, despite such language in a plan, the lien is not eliminated unless the debtor completes the entire Chapter 13 plan. (See, for example, *In re McPherson*, 230 B.R. 99 (Bankr. E.D. Ky. 1999).)

Be sure to talk with the trustee so that you have a full understanding of what the court in your district allows.

3. Make Up Missed Payments and Reinstate the Loan ("Cure the Default")

If you want to keep a particular item of secured property, you can make up your missed payments, reinstate the loan, and make the payments under the original contract. This is called, in Chapter 13 parlance, "curing the default."

You can cure the default and reinstate the loan only if the final payment in your original contract is due after the final payment in your Chapter 13 plan will be made. (Note, this is different than the rule for home mortgages. See Section H2a, above.) For example, you could cure a default on a car loan if your car note has 40 monthly payments left on it and you are proposing a standard 36-month Chapter 13 plan.

This strategy makes sense in three situations:

- The property is worth as much as or more than you owe. If the property is worth less than the debt, you are better off paying only the value of the property. (See Section 2, above.)
- The property is worth less than you owe, but it would take you more than 60 months (the maximum length of a Chapter 13 plan) to pay it off.

EXAMPLE: You have eight years left on your boat loan; although the boat has decreased in value, it is worth only slightly less than what you still owe. In addition, your Chapter 13 plan payments are being used mostly to pay off a large tax bill. You cannot afford to also pay the value of your boat in only five years. You could afford to keep the boat if you paid off the rest of the loan in the remaining eight years.

- The interest rate in the original contract is much lower than the interest rate the lender will agree to now. If you reduced your debt to the current value of the property, but would end up paying more overall because you would have to pay a higher interest rate, you are better off curing the default.

EXAMPLE: Laurel bought professional photography equipment for $14,500, to be paid over two years at 6.25%. She still owes $12,000 and the equipment is now worth $10,500. She is tempted to pay that amount through her plan, but interest rates have jumped and she'll have to pay at least 10.75% on the balance. Laurel would need the full three years of her plan to pay the $10,500. At 10.75%, she'll pay more than if she cures the default and pays off the $12,000.

4. Eliminate or Reduce Liens on the Property

You can ask the court to eliminate or reduce ("avoid") liens on certain types of property. Unlike the option discussed in Section 2, above—which can be used on any property and any debt—this procedure, which is called lien avoidance, applies only to certain property considered "exempt" under bankruptcy law. (11 U.S.C. § 522(f).)

Lien avoidance costs nothing, involves only a moderate amount of paperwork, and allows you to keep—or even sell—your property without paying anything. It is the best and most powerful tool for getting rid of liens. But it has several important restrictions, which are described in Ch. 3, *Adding Up Your Secured and Unsecured Debts*, Section A.

How much a lien is reduced depends on the value of the property and the limits, if any, on the amount of the exemption. Here are the rules:

- If the property is entirely exempt or worth less than the legal exemption limit, the court will eliminate the entire lien. You'll get to keep the property without paying the creditor anything.
- If the property is worth more than the exemption limit, the lien is not entirely eliminated. It is reduced to the difference between the exemption limit and either the property's value or the amount of the debt, whichever is less.

EXAMPLE: A creditor has a $500 lien on Harold's guitar, which is worth $300. In Harold's state, a guitar is exempt only to $200. He could get the lien reduced to $100. The other $400 of the lien is eliminated (avoided).

If you want to avoid a lien on your secured property, you must state that in your Chapter 13 plan. In the section of your plan labeled "Special Provisions" or "Other Provisions," write "I will file a motion to avoid the [*specify either judicial lien or nonpossessory non-purchase money security interest*] from my [*identify the collateral*]." The actual procedure for asking the court to avoid the lien is in Ch. 9, *After You File Your Case*, Section H.

5. Sell the Property

You can propose, in the "Special Provisions" or "Other Provisions" section of your plan, to sell secured property to get cash to pay the secured creditor. But this option isn't usually a good one. First, few bankruptcy courts will let you sell secured property. Second, you would want to do it only if the sale would bring in more than you owe the creditor—that is, the property has increased in value since you acquired it. But most secured property, such as cars, household goods, and furniture, goes down in value over time, not up.

6. File a Chapter 7 Bankruptcy Before You File a Chapter 13 Bankruptcy

The last option is to put your Chapter 13 bankruptcy on hold for a while and file for Chapter 7 bankruptcy first. This is sometimes called a "Chapter 20" bankruptcy.

The reason to add this layer of complexity to your bankruptcy is that in Chapter 7 bankruptcy, you can wipe out most unsecured debts and eliminate your personal liability on a secured debt. Then, as soon as your Chapter 7 bankruptcy is over (the typical case lasts four to six months), you can immediately file a Chapter 13 bankruptcy to pay off your nondischargeable debts and the liens that remain on your property. In your Chapter 13 bankruptcy, you would use one of the options discussed just above.

This strategy makes good sense if you have little or no nonexempt property and a lot of dischargeable unsecured debts which you could wipe out in Chapter 7 bankruptcy. If your debts are mostly secured, priority, or nondischargeable and would have to be paid in full, however, don't bother filing a Chapter 7 bankruptcy first because Chapter 7 bankruptcy won't eliminate enough of your debts to justify filing.

J. Paying Your Unsecured Creditors

In Chapter 13 bankruptcy, unsecured debts are handled less formally than are secured debts and priority debts. After all, most people file a Chapter 13 bankruptcy case to take care of secured debts and priority debts. Their unsecured creditors generally get only whatever money is left over.

The information that follows on unsecured debts is long. But you may not have to read all—or even any—of it. Before going on, look at the sections of your plan form which deal with unsecured creditors. If your plan simply asks you list the name of each creditor and the amount you owe, copy that information from Schedule F—Creditors Holding Unsecured Nonpriority Claims—which you completed in Ch. 6. Then go on to Section K. The trustee will pay your secured and priority debts first and give the leftovers to your unsecured creditors. The trustee will pay them equal amounts. If you have five unsecured creditors and pay $525 into your plan every month, each creditor will get $105 a month from the time that your secured or priority debts have been paid until the end of your case, no matter how much they are owed.

Keep reading this section, however, if:

- Your plan form requires more information—for example, you must label the type of plan you are submitting.
- You want to pay a greater percentage of some unsecured debts than others.
- You have secured debts and your plan form asks you to specify how much each secured creditor will receive every month.
- You want to include a provision in your plan for paying postpetition debts—that is, the bills you default on after your plan is confirmed.
- Your court requires you to add a certain percentage to payments your unsecured creditors receive.

1. How Unsecured Creditors Will Be Paid

Some Chapter 13 plan forms require that you label the plan as either a "pro tanto" or a "fixed percentage" plan. Other plans require you to specify how the trustee should pay your unsecured creditors, but don't require a label.

In a typical Chapter 13 bankruptcy case, your first several payments (perhaps even the first year of payments) or the bulk of each early payment is used to pay your priority and secured debts (your mortgage and tax arrears, for example). Later payments, or a small portion of the early ones, are divided among your unsecured creditors.

a.   Pro Tanto Plans

In a pro tanto (Latin for "for so long") plan, you pay X dollars for Y months without specifying in your plan how much your unsecured creditors will receive. All you do is specify the order in which you want your priority and secured creditors paid. What's left goes to your unsecured creditors.

Pro tanto plans are easy to administer, so bankruptcy trustees like them. Unsecured creditors sometimes object to pro tanto plans at the confirmation hearing, however, because they simply receive what's left over, not a specified amount of money.

b.   Fixed Percentage Plans

In a fixed percentage plan, you pay your unsecured creditors a set percentage of what you owe them. (The three sample plans in Section M are fixed percentage plans.) Some fixed percentage plans provide for payment of 100% of unsecured debts, others less. A fixed percentage plan is completed when your unsecured creditors have received the percentage stated in the plan, not a specific number of months. For example, you might anticipate that it will take 43 months to pay your unsecured creditors 17% of what they are owed. If any creditor fails to file a claim with the trustee requesting to be paid (creditors must file claims to get paid), the trustee won't pay that creditor and you'll be done with your plan in fewer than 43 months.

There are four types of fixed percentage plans: base, greater than, pro rata, and per capita. Bankruptcy trustees are least likely to object to base and greater than plans. Trustees favor them because they let the bankruptcy court confirm your plan before the deadline for filing creditor's claims has passed. Pro rata and per capital plans don't. (How this works is explained in Ch. 9, *After You File Your Case*.)

Another reason trustees like base and greater than plans is that they have found that debtors do a good job of estimating the amount owed on their unsecured debts and therefore propose realistic plans.

Here is how the four kinds of plans work.

- **Base plan.** In a base plan, you calculate the total amount you must pay on all claims—secured, priority, and unsecured—over the life of your case. When you have paid the amount you initially calculated, your bankruptcy case is over. It is similar to a pro tanto plan, except that in a pro tanto plan, you specify how much you will pay each month for a set number of months. In a base plan, you pay a set amount of money no matter how long it takes—if you're short a few months, your plan will have to be extended to make up the difference. If you pay extra during some months, your plan will end sooner than you might have originally thought.

- **Greater than plan.** In a greater than plan, you first estimate the amount you owe your unsecured creditors. You then propose paying your unsecured creditors a set amount or a set percentage, whichever is greater.

  EXAMPLE: In your plan, you state that you will pay a "base of $5,700 or 75% of unsecured claims, whichever is greater." You believe that you owe $7,600 in unsecured debts. After your Chapter 13 plan is approved, an unsecured creditor you forgot about files a claim for $1,200. Your total unsecured debts are $8,800, not the $7,600 you originally believed. To satisfy your greater than plan, you must pay 75% of $8,800, or $6,600 not 75% of $7,600. The court can just extend the plan until you've paid a minimum.

- **Pro rata plan.** In a pro rata plan, creditors with small claims receive a smaller percentage of your monthly payment than do creditors with large claims. Each creditor is paid a percentage equal to the percentage its claim is compared to your total unsecured debts. In your plan, you state the actual dollar amount that each creditor will receive each month.

EXAMPLE: You plan to pay the trustee $110 each month ($10 for the trustee's fee) with $100 of it to be divided among your three unsecured creditors. You owe these creditors $500, $1,000, and $1,500 respectively. Each month, the trustee will pay the first creditor $17 ($^1/_6$ of the $100), the second one $33 ($^1/_3$ of the $100), and the third one $50 ($^1/_2$ of the $100).

- **Per capita plan.** In a per capita plan, your creditors split the monthly payment equally. So in the above example, each creditor would receive $33 (actually, one would get $34 because trustees don't pay out change). This means that smaller claims are paid more quickly than the larger ones. Some trustees prefer this kind of plan because it's easy to administer. Many creditors, however, consider per capita plans unfair, and may object at the confirmation hearing. Their reason is that if you dismiss your case or convert it to Chapter 7 bankruptcy (which happens in the majority of Chapter 13 cases), the creditors with smaller debts will have unfairly benefited.

2. Classifying Unsecured Creditors

Some plans require that you specify, in the section labeled "Unsecured Creditors," who gets paid in full and who gets less. The simplest way to handle it is to propose paying all your existing unsecured creditors the same percentage. This method is allowed even if some creditors have nondischargeable debts (which you must eventually pay back completely) and some have dischargeable debts (which you need pay only a portion of). But if you choose this option and pay less than 100%, you will owe a balance on your nondischargeable debts at the end of your case. (See Subsection b, below.)

Your other option is to create classes of unsecured creditors, specifying what percentage each class will receive. Some plan forms ask, in the section labeled "Separate Class of Unsecured Creditors" or "Special Classes" (or "Other Provisions" or "Special Provisions" if your plan has no specific section) for the following:

- a description of the class (these are described in Subsections a and b, below)
- the total amount owed to the class of creditors
- the creditors who fall into the class.

The court must approve your classifications for them to take effect, and you cannot unfairly discriminate against any specific creditor. Any creditor who feels your classifications are unfair will object to your Chapter 13 plan. The rest of this section discusses how you may want to classify creditors.

a. Dischargeable Debts

Even though you are not required to repay dischargeable debts in full in bankruptcy, you may want to pay back 100% of some or all of them. Not all courts permit separate classifications in order to pay these debts in full, however. Here is how the court is likely to rule if you create a separate class for one or more dischargeable debts:

- **Your codebtors.** Courts sometimes allow a separate classification of debts with codebtors so that you can repay the debt in full. A court is especially likely to permit it if you must maintain a working relationship with your codebtor (such as a business partner), or if your codebtor can't pay the debt because of illness or disability.
- **Creditors with whom you have an ongoing relationship.** The court may permit a separate class if you or a family member has an ongoing medical problem and needs continued treatment from the practitioner you want to pay. Your other creditors may object, however, and demand that you provide proof that the medical care cannot be provided by a different practitioner. Or, if you want to make up past-due rent and it would be difficult for you to find a new place to live, a court might allow your landlord to be put in a separate class.
- **Debts to business creditors.** The court will probably allow this separate class to be repaid in full if the creditor provides you with insurance coverage or materials essential to run your business.
- **Debts based on their amounts.** Many bankruptcy courts allow you to classify unsecured debts based on their amounts, especially if you have no nonexempt property. For instance, you could create two classes: one to pay 100% of debts of $1,000 and less and another to pay 10% of debts over $1,000. Unsecured creditors rarely object to this kind of classification, because at least they are getting something through your plan.

- **Postpetition debts.** You may want to create a class of "postpetition debts," or new debts you incur after your plan is approved. If you don't create such a class now, you'll have to pay any postpetition debts out of your income (what you're not paying into your plan).

  To pay them through your plan, state the following in the section labeled "Special Class of Unsecured Creditors" or something similar: "separate class of postpetition debts to be repaid at 100%, with interest." You can include the class now—when you write your plan—or you can file a written request (motion) with the bankruptcy court to modify your plan later on. (See Ch. 10, *After Your Plan Is Approved*, Section C.)

b. Nondischargeable Debts

A nondischargeable debt is an unsecured debt that must be repaid in full. If you don't pay it in full in your Chapter 13 bankruptcy case, you will owe a balance after your case is over. You may want to create a separate class of nondischargeable debts so you can pay them in full while paying a smaller percentage to other unsecured creditors.

This practice, however, is rarely permitted, because it means other unsecured creditors get less of the pie. Probably the best way to deal with most nondischargeable debts is to pay them with your general class of unsecured creditors. If the creditor insists that you acknowledge that you will owe a balance at the end of your Chapter 13 case, add a sentence to the "Other Provisions" or "Special Provisions" section stating as much. Here's an example:

> "I will pay my unsecured creditors, including the Department of Education, 38% through my plan. I agree that I will owe the balance to the Department of Education at the end of my case."

To keep the creditor from adding on the interest abated during your bankruptcy case when it's over, you can file a second Chapter 13 case at the close of the first case to pay off the balance, Alternatively, you might propose paying all unsecured debts the same percentage for 36 months and then paying only the nondischargeable debts during months 37–60.

For detailed information on determining whether or not debts are dischargeable, see Ch. 2, *An Overview of Chapter 13 Bankruptcy*, Section D.

Here is how courts are likely to rule if you want to separately classify common kinds of nondischargeable debts:

Student loans. Bankruptcy courts have little sympathy for debtors who want to eliminate a student loan at the expense of their other creditors. Only a few bankruptcy courts will let you create a separate class of student loans to repay them in full.

You may have another option for dealing with a nondischargeable student loan. In some courts, you can treat it like a long-term secured debt—that is, pay back the arrears through your plan (cure the default), and then make payments during and after your plan. (See Section I, above.)

Intoxicated driving debts. Bankruptcy courts have even less sympathy for debtors who want to eliminate a debt resulting from the death of, or personal injury to, someone because you drove while intoxicated by alcohol or drugs, while your other creditors get less. You probably will not be able to create a separate class.

However, the court may approve of a separate classification for fines resulting from a drunk driving conviction if there is a good reason for the classification, such as the need to have one's driving privileges restored in order to continue working. *In re Gallipo*, 282 B.R. 917 (E.D. Wash. 2002).

Restitution or criminal fine. Don't look to the bankruptcy court for help in separately classifying a criminal fine or a debt for restitution included in a sentence you received while you pay your other creditors less. You probably will not be able to create a separate class.

 You can sometimes ask for discharge of a supposedly nondischageable debt. If you think you can convince the court to rule that a particular nondischargeable debt is in fact dischargeable given the facts of your case, you can file a complaint asking the court to make that determination. For instance, a student loan can be discharged if the court finds that a hardship exists. Because of the length of the normal Chapter 13 case, and the possibility of your economic situation improving, the court may be reluctant to rule on the hardship issue until you near completion of your plan. (See *In re Bender*, 368 F.3d. 846 (8th Cir. 2004). On the other hand, some courts may be willing to rule on the hardship issue prior to your plan confirmation if your ability to propose a confirmable plan depends on the resolution of that issue.

3. Compensation on Payments

Because your unsecured creditors will be paid through your plan over several years, they will actually receive less than they're entitled to because the payments you make years from now will be made with inflated dollars, worth less than they are now.

To see that your unsecured creditors aren't short-changed, some bankruptcy courts require you to increase your overall payments by a percentage established by the court. It's based on the current interest rate in your area; you can find out by calling the trustee. Although this is in essence an interest charge, courts never call it that—the law says that in Chapter 13 bankruptcy, unsecured creditors aren't entitled to interest.

Few, if any, plan forms ask you to include this unofficial interest payment in your calculations. But if you don't calculate it in, your unsecured creditors may object. You can leave it off your plan to begin with; if the trustee or a creditor objects, you can add it to your plan before the confirmation hearing.

K. Dealing With Contracts and Leases

In the "Special Provisions" or "Other Provisions" section of your Chapter 13 bankruptcy plan, you must tell the court what you plan to do with any executory contracts and unexpired leases. (You listed these on Schedule G, in Ch. 6, *Completing the Bankruptcy Forms*.) Type in one of the following three choices:

- "I will reject the contract or lease." In this case, your obligation under the agreement ends.
- "I will assume the contract or lease." In this case, your obligation under the agreement continues.
- "I will assign the contract or lease." In this case, your obligation under the agreement is transferred to someone else.

Here are some issues to keep in mind as you make your choices:

- In most courts, if you do not specifically reject, assume, or assign a nonresidential lease within 60 days of filing the case, the lease is considered rejected, and you must surrender the leased property. (11 U.S.C. § 365(d)(4).)
- If you have defaulted on a lease or contract—for example, you owe back rent—but you still have some rights under the agreement, you can continue it by paying the arrears through your plan (curing the default) and making payments through the plan. (See Section I, above.)
- If you have defaulted on a lease or contract in a nonmonetary way—for example, you breached a residential lease clause prohibiting pets—you can use the time that the Chapter 13 bankruptcy automatic stay gives you to get into compliance. So while the landlord is barred from proceeding with an eviction, you could find a home for the animal and continue payments on your lease.
- If you decide to continue (assume) a lease or contract, there may be consequences as well:
  - If, after your plan is confirmed, you change your mind and reject the agreement, you must compensate the creditor in full for any loss resulting from the rejection—such as the costs the landlord incurs in rerenting your apartment.
  - If your lease has a purchase option, and your right to exercise that option arises during your Chapter 13 case, you cannot postpone that option until after your bankruptcy case ends. Your only option is to proceed as specified in the agreement.

L. Making Payments Directly to Creditors

You can propose, in your Chapter 13 plan, to pay certain debts directly—that is, not through the bankruptcy court. The main reason to do that is to reduce the trustee's fee you must pay. (See Section E, above.)

Bankruptcy courts and trustees frown on direct payments for several reasons:

- **They reduce the trustee's fee.**
- **They may reduce your ability to make the payments under your plan.** The failure rate for Chapter 13 bankruptcy cases is much higher when debtors make direct payments than when they don't. This is because when funds are tight, debtors tend to make the direct payments before paying the trustee.
- **You may be creating an unfair classification.** Creditors paid through the plan may object that the creditors who are paid directly are being treated more favorably.

Many trustees, however, allow debtors to make limited payments outside the plan. The most common payments allowed are:

- **Regular mortgage payments if you are not in default.** If, however, you are in default and intend to pay the arrears through your plan, you may be required to make your regular mortgage payments through the plan, too.
- **Regular car purchase or lease payments if you are not in default.**
- **Payments to a creditor with whom you have an ongoing relationship.** For example, you may want to pay a doctor outside the plan, so you or a family member can continue to receive treatment.

M. Sample Plans

Even if you've breezed through the instructions in this chapter, you may still feel a little intimidated when it's time to sit down and write your own plan. Keep in mind that your plan doesn't have to be flawless when you first submit it. To help you, here are three sample Chapter 13 plans, using the forms in Appendix 2. Your plan, obviously, won't be the same as any of them—but it may make things easier if you see how some debtors fill in all the blanks.

The hypothetical debtors who completed these plan forms are Martin and Ellen Herchoo, the same debtors who completed the forms in Ch. 6. A summary of their debts appears below.

The Herchoos propose paying their disposable income—$1,800 a month—into their plan to pay these debts. Their secured debt arrearages and priority debts, which must be paid in full, plus the unsecured debts for which they have cosigners and want to pay back in full, total $51,343. Their trustee charges a fee of 10%; that amounts to $5,134, meaning they must pay at least $56,477. The Herchoos calculate that by paying $1,800 a month, it will take a little over 31 months to pay the $56,477.

Take Advantage of Rising Home Values

A growing trend, made possible by the nearly nationwide phenomenon of quickly rising home values, is for debtors to borrow against the increased value of their exempt homestead equity (increases that occurred postconfirmation of the plan)—then pay off their remaining Chapter 13 plan obligations with a single check. It's not a complete fresh start but it's easier than seeing the Chapter 13 plan to completion.

However, to make such a strategy work, you must overcome some hurdles. In many districts, if the borrowing will necessitate modifying your Chapter 13 plan, the trustee may demand that your ability to pay be reassessed. If you're starting to look more solvent, the trustee may require you to pay 100% of the allowed unsecured claims. (For a sampling of the relevant court cases on this, compare *In re Tran*, 309 B.R. 330 (9th Cir. B.A.P. (Cal.) 2004); *In re Guentert*, 206 B.R. 958, 961 (Bankr. W.D. Mo. 1997) (motion to make lump -sum payment is motion to modify); and *In re Easley*, 205 B.R. 334, 335 (Bankr. M.D. Fla. 1996) (motion to complete payments is motion to modify), with *In re Bergolla*, 232 B.R. 515, 516 (Bankr. S.D.

Fla. 1999) (motion to make lump-sum payment does not warrant modification); and *In re Smith*, 237 B.R. 621, 623 (Bankr. E.D. Tex. 1999) (rejecting secured creditor's attempt to construe lump-sum payment as motion to modify).)

Debtors can avoid this "pay 100%" problem by structuring their Chapter 13 plan properly at the outset, so that repayment won't trigger a need for modification of the original plan. A well-structured plan will provide for all of the following:

1. The debtor's home must be excluded from the bankruptcy estate. (A debtor cannot pledge estate property without the court's permission.)
2. The plan must allow the debtor to incur postconfirmation debt without the court's permission.
3. The debtor must make mortgage payments outside the plan.

If you think there's a chance that this kind of strategy might benefit you, find an experienced bankruptcy professional to help you structure your plan in a way that keeps your options open.

Summary of Debts:
Martin and Ellen Herchoo

Debt		Type	Comments
Mortgage arrears		Secured	They are in arrears five months at $2,160 per month.
Interest on arrears	1,080		They must pay 10% interest on arrears.
Car loan arrears	372	Secured	They are in arrears one month; figure includes interest. They will propose paying the balance of this loan directly —$355 per month.
IRS		Priority	
Bank personal loan	3,918	Unsecured	This loan has a cosigner; they propose paying it back in full.
Bank personal loan	1,411	Unsecured	This loan has a cosigner; they propose paying it back in full.
Leased timeshare	8,880	Unsecured	They will reject this lease, making the debt unsecured.
Visa		Unsecured	
MasterCard	6,452	Unsecured	
Court judgment	1,215	Unsecured	They will file a motion to avoid a judicial lien on the house, making the debt unsecured.
Home equity loan	—	Secured	This debt is not in default; they will propose to pay it directly—$335 per month.

To keep the trustee's fees down, the Herchoos decide to propose paying their regular monthly mortgage and car loan payments directly to the creditors instead of through their plan. However, as we have emphasized, the normal rule is that you must make regular payments on a secured debt through the plan if your plan also proposes to cure arrearages in those payments. This means that the trustee will very likely reject the

Herchoos' plan, at least as to the mortgage payment provision. The trustee might allow the car payment to be made directly since the Herchoos are only one month in default.

If the trustee or court insist that the Herchoos amend their plan to bring the mortgage payments under its umbrella, this will have serious consequences for the overall plan. That's because the trustee will now collect 10% on the mortgage payments, or an additional $216 per month. For the Herchoos to pay this off without a new source of income, they'll have to either amend the plan to last for a longer time period or propose to pay a smaller percentage of the unsecured debts.

Their other debts total $29,336. They don't know how much of these debts their court will require them to repay. So they calculate how many additional months it will take them to pay a small percentage (26%), about half, and 100% of these debts.

Here are the results:

Additional Months to Repay Debt

		36 months		40 months		49 months
Amount paid each month	x	1,800	x	1,800	x	1,800
Total amount paid	=	64,800	=	72,000	=	88,200
Amount paid on secured, priority, and cosigned debts	–	$ 56,477	–	$ 56,477	–	$ 56,477
Total left for unsecured debts	=	8,323	=	15,523	=	31,723
Less 10% for trustee	–	832	–	1,552	–	3,172
Total paid to unsecured creditors	=	$ 7,491	=	$13,971	=	$28,551
Percentage repaid on unsecured debts		26%		48%		97%*

*To repay their unsecured debts in full, they'd make a smaller payment in the 50th month.

The plan forms, below, will give you an idea of what a plan looks like, but keep in mind that even if you have similar debts, your plan will look very different.

26% PLAN

(ATTORNEY NAME:) _____ not applicable _____
(ADDRESS:) _____
(CITY:) _____ (STATE:) _____
(ZIP:) _____
(PHONE NUMBER:) (____) _____
(BAR NUMBER:) _Debtors Pro Se_____

DEBTORS: _Martin and Ellen Herchoo_____   CASE NO.: _____

DEBTORS PRELIMINARY CHAPTER 13 PLAN

DATE OF PLAN _2/23/xx_____   FIRST PAYMENT DUE TO TRUSTEE __3/25/xx_____

INCOME $ _6,110_____ TRUSTEE PAYMENTS $ _1,800____ FOR _36_ MONTHS   PLAN BASE AMOUNT $ _____

EXPENSES $ _4,310_____ $ _____ FOR ____ MONTHS   UNSECURED % _26___

SURPLUS $ _1,800_____ $ _____ FOR ____ MONTHS

ADMINISTRATIVE   NOTICING FEES: # _____ + 3 X 3 X .79 = $ _____
                  ATTORNEY FEES: TOTAL _____ THRU PLAN _____

HOME MORTGAGE   Regular payments beginning _3/1/xx__ to be paid direct. Arrearages to be paid by Trustee as follows:

	ARREARS	THRU	%	TERM	PAYMENT
1ST LIEN _Big Home Loan Bank_____	$ _10,800_	_____	10	6 mos	$ _1,800_
2ND LIEN _____	$ _____	_____	___	_____	$ _____

SECURED CREDITORS	COLLATERAL	CLAIM	VALUE	%	TERM	PAYMENT
1. Car Finance Co._____	20xx Nissan_____	$ _372_	$ _7,400_	8	1 mo.	$ _372_
2. _____	_____	$ _____	$ _____	___	_____	$ _____
3. _____	_____	$ _____	$ _____	___	_____	$ _____
4. _____	_____	$ _____	$ _____	___	_____	$ _____
5. _____	_____	$ _____	$ _____	___	_____	$ _____

ANY DEFICIENCY WILL AUTOMATICALLY BE "SPLIT" AND INCLUDED IN UNSECURED.

PRIORITY CREDITORS	TYPE	DISPUTED AMOUNT	CLAIM	TERM	PAYMENT
1. IRS _____	tax	$ _____	$ _33,762_____	19 mos.	$ _1,800_
2. _____	_____	$ _____	$ _____	_____	$ _____

SPECIAL CLASS		BASIS	AMOUNT	TERM	PAYMENT
1. River Bank_____	codebtor_____	_____	$ _3,918_	2+ mos.	$ _1,800_
2. Sweeter's Bank_	codebtor_____	_____	$ _1,411_	1 mo.	$ _1,411_

UNSECURED CREDITORS	CLAIM		CREDITORS	CLAIM		CREDITORS	CLAIM
1. Summer Vacations Co.	$ _8,880_	6.	_____	$ _____	11.	_____	$ _____
2. Visa_____	$ _12,789_	7.	_____	$ _____	12.	_____	$ _____
3. MasterCard_____	$ _6,452_	8.	_____	$ _____	13.	_____	$ _____
4. Ken Williams_____	$ _1,215_	9.	_____	$ _____	14.	_____	$ _____
5. _____	$ _____	10.	_____	$ _____	15.	_____	$ _____

TOTAL UNSECURED AND DEFICIENCIES $ _29,336_____

☒ CHECK HERE IF ADDITIONAL INFORMATION APPEARS ON REVERSE SIDE (EXECUTORY CONTRACTS? MISCELLANEOUS?)

CERTIFICATE OF SERVICE

I certify that a copy of the above and foregoing "Debtor's Preliminary Chapter 13 Plan" and an "Authorization for Preconfirmation Disbursement" was by me on this _25th__ day _February_____ of 20_xx_ served on the trustee and all creditors listed on the original matrix and any amended matrix filed in this case by United States First Class mail.

Martin Herchoo   Ellen Herchoo
Attorney for Debtor or Pro Se Debtor

SPECIAL PROVISIONS:

(Balloon, proceeds of sale,

recovery on lawsuit, etc.)

1. We reject our leased time share with Summer Vacations Co. _____

2. We will file a Motion to avoid Ken Williams's judicial lien against our house. _____

3. We propose making our regular house and car payments, and our home equity loan payments ($335/month), outside

    the plan. _____

ADDITIONAL CREDITORS:

HOME MORTGAGE:

	ARREARS	THRU	%	TERM	PAYMENT
3RD LIEN _____	$ _____	_____	___	_____	$ _____
4TH LIEN _____	$ _____	_____	___	_____	$ _____

SECURED CREDITORS	COLLATERAL	CLAIM	VALUE	%	TERM	PAYMENT
6. _____	_____	$ _____	$ _____	___	_____	$ _____
7. _____	_____	$ _____	$ _____	___	_____	$ _____
8. _____	_____	$ _____	$ _____	___	_____	$ _____
9. _____	_____	$ _____	$ _____	___	_____	$ _____
10. _____	_____	$ _____	$ _____	___	_____	$ _____

PRIORITY CREDITORS	DISPUTED AMOUNT	CLAIM	TERM	PAYMENT
3. _____	$ _____	$ _____	_____	$ _____
4. _____	$ _____	$ _____	_____	$ _____

SPECIAL CLASS	BASIS	AMOUNT	TERM	PAYMENT
3. _____	_____	$ _____	_____	$ _____
4. _____	_____	$ _____	_____	$ _____

UNSECURED CREDITORS	CLAIM	CREDITORS	CLAIM	CREDITORS	CLAIM
_____	$ _____	_____	$ _____	_____	$ _____
_____	$ _____	_____	$ _____	_____	$ _____
_____	$ _____	_____	$ _____	_____	$ _____
_____	$ _____	_____	$ _____	_____	$ _____

48% PLAN

DEBTOR(S) _____Martin and Ellen Herchoo_____   CASE NO. _____

CHAPTER 13 PLAN OR SUMMARY

I. The projected disposable income of the debtor(s) is submitted to the supervision and control of the Trustee and the Debtor(s) shall pay to the Trustee the sum of:

$ _1,800_____   ☐ Weekly   ☐ Biweekly   ☐ Semimonthly   ☒ Monthly

☒ Direct Payment   ☐ Payroll Deduction on Wages of: _____   ☐ Debtor   ☐ Spouse

Length of plan is approximately __40_____ months, and total debt to be paid through plan is approximately $_70,445_____.

II. From the payments so received the Trustee shall make disbursements as follows:

A. PRIORITY payments described in 11 U.S.C. § 507 in full in deferred cash payments.

B. The holder of each allowed SECURED claim shall retain the lien securing such claim until a discharge is granted and such claim shall be paid in full with interest at a rate of ___10____% per annum in deferred cash payments as follows:

1. Mortgage Debts:

Name of Mortgage company	Home-stead Yes/No	Total amount of debt	Arrears to be paid by Trustee	Months included in arrearage amount	Postpetition payments to begin Month/Year (Direct to creditor)	–OR– Amount of regular mortgage to be paid by Trustee
Big Home Loan Bank	yes	239,715	10,800	10/xx–2/xx	3/xx	

2. Other Secured Debts:

				If Applicable**	
Name of creditor	Total amount of debt	Debtor's value	Description of collateral	Interest factor	Debtor's Fixed Payments
Car Finance Co.	8,250		20xx Nissan		355

C. The Debtor(s) will make direct payments as follows:

Name of creditor	Total of debt	Description of collateral	Reason for direct payment
Car Finance Co.	8,250	20xx Nissan	only one month in arrears
Big Home Loan Bank	16,080	home	not in default (335/mo)

D. Special provisions. Explanation:

1. We reject our leased homeshare with Summer Vacations Co.

2. We will file a Motion to Avoid Ken Williams's judicial lien against our house.

3. Please pay 100% on unsecured debts with codebtors: Personal loan from River Bank; Personal loan from Sweeter's Bank.

☒ This is an original plan.

☐ This is an amended plan replacing plan dated _____ .

☒ This plan proposes to pay unsecured creditors __48__ %.

☒ Insurance on vehicle: ☒ Proof of Insurance attached, OR:

☐ Insurance through Trustee requested

Dated: __2/23/xx_____   *Martin Herchoo*
                                    Signature of Debtor

Dated: __2/23/xx_____   *Ellen Herchoo*
                                    Signature of Debtor

100% PLAN

CHAPTER 13 PLAN

In Re: Martin and Ellen Herchoo

Debtor
In a joint case,
debtor means debtors in this plan.

Dated: 2/23/xx

Case No. _____

1. PAYMENTS BY DEBTOR —

   a. As of this date of this plan, the debtor has paid the trustee $ __0__ .

   b. After the date of this plan, the debtor will pay the trustee $ _1,800_ per _month_ for _49_ months, beginning within 30 days after the filing of this plan for a total of $ _88,200_ .

   c. The debtor will also pay the trustee _$1,203 in the 50th month_ _____

   d. The debtor will pay the trustee a total of $ _89,403_ [line 1(a) + line 1(b) + line 1(c)].

2. PAYMENTS BY TRUSTEE — The trustee will make payments only to creditors for which proofs of claim have been filed, make payments monthly as available, and collect the trustee's percentage fee of 10% for a total of $ _8,940_ [line 1 (d) x .10] or such lesser percentage as may be fixed by the Attorney General. For purposes of this plan, month one (1) is the month following the month in which the debtor makes the debtor's first payment. Unless ordered otherwise, the trustee will not make any payments until the plan is confirmed. Payments will accumulate and be paid following confirmation.

3. PRIORITY CLAIMS — The trustee shall pay in full all claims entitled to priority under § 507, including the following. The amounts listed are estimates only. The trustee will pay the amounts actually allowed.

Creditor	Estimated Claim	Monthly Payment	Beginning in Month #	Number of Payments	TOTAL PAYMENTS
a. Attorney Fees	$ _____	$ _____	_____	_____	$ _____
b. Internal Revenue Service	$ _33,762_	$ _1,800_	_7_	_19_	$ _33,762_
c. State Dept. of Revenue	$ _____	$ _____	_____	_____	$ _____
d. _____	$ _____	$ _____	_____	_____	$ _____
e. TOTAL					$ _33,762_

4. LONG-TERM SECURED CLAIMS NOT IN DEFAULT — The following creditors have secured claims. Payments are current and the debtor will continue to make all payments which come due after the date the petition was filed directly to the creditors. The creditors will retain their liens.

   a. _Home equity loan through Big Home Loan Bank ($335 a month)_

   b. _____

5. HOME MORTGAGES IN DEFAULT [§ 1322 (b)(5)] — The trustee will cure defaults (plus interest at the rate of 8 per cent per annum) on claims secured only by a security interest in real property that is the debtor's principal residence as follows. The debtor will maintain the regular payments which come due after the date the petition was filed. The creditors will retain their liens. The amounts of default are estimates only. The trustee will pay the actual amounts of default.

Creditor	Amount of Default	Monthly Payment	Beginning in Month #	Number of Payments	TOTAL PAYMENTS
a. Big Home Loan Bank	$ _10,800_	$ _2,160_	$ _1_	$ _6_	$ _10,800_
b. _____	$ _____	$ _____	$ _____	$ _____	$ _____
c. _____	$ _____	$ _____	$ _____	$ _____	$ _____
d. TOTAL					$ _10,800_

Chapter 13 Plan   **Page 2**

6. OTHER LONG-TERM SECURED CLAIMS IN DEFAULT [§ 1322 (b)(5)] — The trustee will cure defaults (plus interest at the rate of 8 per cent per annum) on other claims as follows and the debtor will maintain the regular payments which come due after the date the petition was filed. The creditors will retain their liens. The amounts of default are estimates only. The trustee will pay the actual amounts of default.

	Creditor	Amount of Default	Monthly Payment	Beginning in Month #	Number of Payments	TOTAL PAYMENTS
a.	Car Finance Co.	$ 372	$ 355	7	1	$ 372
b.		$	$			$
c.		$	$			$
d.	TOTAL					$ 372

7. OTHER SECURED CLAIMS [§ 1325 (a)(5)] — The trustee will make payments to the following secured creditors having a value as of confirmation equal to the allowed amount of the creditor's secured claim using a discount rate of 8 percent. The creditor's allowed secured claim shall be the creditor's allowed claim or the value of the creditor's interest in the debtor's property, whichever is less. The creditors shall retain their liens. NOTE: NOTWITHSTANDING A CREDITOR'S PROOF OF CLAIM FILED BEFORE OR AFTER CONFIRMATION, THE AMOUNT LISTED IN THIS PARAGRAPH AS A CREDITOR'S SECURED CLAIM BINDS THE CREDITOR PURSUANT TO 11 U.S.C. § 1327 AND CONFIRMATION OF THE PLAN WILL BE CONSIDERED A DETERMINATION OF THE CREDITOR'S ALLOWED SECURED CLAIM UNDER 11 U.S.C. § 506 (a).

	Creditor	Claim Amount	Secured Claim	Monthly Payment	Beginning in Month #	Number of Payments	TOTAL PAYMENTS
a.		$	$	$			$
b.		$	$	$			$
c.		$	$	$			$
d.	TOTAL						$ 0

8. SEPARATE CLASS OF UNSECURED CREDITORS — In addition to the class of unsecured creditors specified in ¶ 9, there shall be a separate class of nonpriority unsecured creditors described as follows: debts with codebtors
   a. The debtor estimates that the total claims in this class are $ 5,329 .
   b. The trustee will pay this class $ 5,329 .

9. TIMELY FILED UNSECURED CREDITORS — The trustee will pay holders of nonpriority unsecured claims for which proofs of claim were timely filed the balance of all payments received by the trustee and not paid under ¶ 2, 3, 5, 6, 7, and 8 their pro rata share of approximately $ 29,336 [line 1(d) minus lines 2, 3(e), 5(d), 6(d), 7(d), and 8 (b)].
   a. The debtor estimates that the total unsecured claims held by creditors listed in ¶ 7 are $ 0
   b. The debtor estimates that the debtor's total unsecured claims (excluding those in ¶ 7 and ¶ 8) are $ 29,336 .
   c. Total estimated unsecured claims are $ 29,336 [line 9(a) + line 9(b)].

10. TARDILY FILED UNSECURED CREDITORS — All money paid by the debtor to the trustee under ¶ 1, but not distributed by the trustee under ¶ 2, 3, 5, 6, 7, 8, or 9 shall be paid to holders of nonpriority unsecured claims for which proofs of claim were tardily filed.

11. OTHER PROVISIONS —
   1. We reject our leased timeshare with Summer Vacations Co.
   2. We will file a motion to avoid Ken Williams's judicial lien against our house.
   3. We propose making our regular house and car payments outside the plan.

12. SUMMARY PAYMENTS —

Trustee's Fee [Line 2]	$ 8,940
Priority Claims [Line 3(e)]	$ 33,762
Home Mortgage Defaults [Line 5(d)]	$ 10,800 + 864 (interest)
Long-Term Debt Defaults [Line 6(d)]	$ 372
Other Secured Claims [Line 7(d)]	$ 0
Separate Class [Line 8(b)]	$ 5,329
Unsecured Creditors[Line 9(c)]	$ 29,336
TOTAL [must equal Line 1(d)]	$ 89,403

Signed: *Martin Herchoo*   Signed: *Ellen Herchoo*
DEBTOR   DEBTOR (if joint case)

Filing Your Bankruptcy Papers

Filing your papers with the bankruptcy court clerk should be simple. Most people file all their bankruptcy forms—the court forms and the plan—at the same time, but you don't have to. You can file the official forms in Ch. 6 first, and file your Chapter 13 plan a maximum of 15 days later.

➡️ **Emergency filing.** If you need to stop a foreclosure or have another emergency, you can file the two-page Voluntary Petition, together with a list of the name, address, and zip code of each of your creditors. The automatic stay, which stops all other collection efforts against you—including a foreclosure—will then go into effect. You will have 15 days to file the rest of the forms, including your Chapter 13 plan. (Bankruptcy Rules 1007(c), 3015(b).) See Section C, below.

A. Basic Filing Procedures

You don't have to make a trip to the courthouse to file your bankruptcy papers. Many people prefer to file by mail. You can, however, take your papers to the bankruptcy court clerk. Going to the court will let you correct minor mistakes on the spot.

Filing your bankruptcy papers is an eight-step process.

Step 1: Make sure you have the following information:
- the amount of the filing and administrative fees
- the specific order in which documents should be presented, and
- the number of copies of each document needed.

  If you don't know any of this, check with the bankruptcy court clerk. (See Ch. 6, *Completing the Bankruptcy Forms*, Section B.)

Step 2: Put all your bankruptcy forms in the order required by the bankruptcy court or, if your court doesn't specify the order, in the order they appear in this book. Put each continuation sheet directly after the form to which it applies. Don't staple any forms together.

Bankruptcy Forms Checklist

Unless your court specifies a different order, stack your forms as follows:
- ☐ Form 1—Voluntary Petition
- ☐ Schedule A—Real Property
- ☐ Schedule B—Personal Property
- ☐ Schedule C—Property Claimed as Exempt
- ☐ Schedule D—Creditors Holding Secured Claims
- ☐ Schedule E—Creditors Holding Unsecured Priority Claims
- ☐ Schedule F—Creditors Holding Unsecured Nonpriority Claims
- ☐ Schedule G—Executory Contracts and Unexpired Leases
- ☐ Schedule H—Codebtors
- ☐ Schedule I—Current Income
- ☐ Schedule J—Current Expenditures
- ☐ Summary of Schedules A through J
- ☐ Declaration Concerning Debtor's Schedules
- ☐ Form 7—Statement of Financial Affairs
- ☐ Form 21—Statement of Social Security Number
- ☐ Mailing Matrix (if required)
- ☐ Income Deduction Order (if required)
- ☐ Chapter 13 repayment plan
- ☐ Required local forms

Step 3: Check that you, and your spouse if you're filing a joint petition, have signed and dated each form where required.

Step 4: Make the number of copies required by the court. Usually one copy is required in courts that have electronic filing (for attorneys only) and four in courts that don't. If you are filing by mail, make one additional copy to hold onto in case your papers get lost in the mail. If possible, you're best off filing in person, so that you can correct any minor glitches on the spot rather than having the papers returned to you by the clerk.

Step 5: Unless the court clerk will two-hole punch your papers when you file them, use a standard two-hole punch (copy centers have them) to punch holes in the top of all your bankruptcy papers.

Step 6: If you plan to mail your documents to the court, address a 9" x 12" envelope to yourself. The court clerk will use it to mail back a file-stamped set of your papers. Check whether you need to affix postage.

Step 7: If you can pay the $155 filing fee and $39 administrative fee when you file, clip or staple a $194 money order or cashier's check (courts do not accept personal checks), payable to "U.S. Bankruptcy Court," to the first page of your petition.

If you want to pay the filing fee in installments or through your plan, attach a filled-in Application and Order to Pay Filing Fee in Installments, plus any additional papers required by local court rules, and a money order or cashier's check for the administrative fee ($39). Instructions for paying in installments are in Section B, just below.

Step 8: Take or mail the original and copies of all forms to the correct bankruptcy court.

B. Paying in Installments

You can pay the combined $194 filing fee, however, in up to four installments over 120 days or propose to pay it through your Chapter 13 plan. (Bankruptcy Rule 1006(b)(1).)

You cannot apply for permission to pay in installments if you've paid an attorney or BPP to help you with your bankruptcy.

If you want to pay in installments, you must file a form called an Application to Pay Filing Fee in Installments when you file your petition. A blank copy of this form is in Appendix 2. The Application is easy to fill out. At the top, fill in the name of the court (this is on Form 1—Voluntary Petition), your name (and your spouse's name if you're filing jointly), and "13" in the blank following "Chapter." Leave the Case No. space blank. Then enter:

- the total filing fee you must pay, $194 (item 1)
- the amount you propose to pay when you file the petition, usually 25% of the total fee (item 4, first blank)

- the number of additional installments you need, and
- the amount and date you propose for each installment payment. If you would like to make the payments through your Chapter 13 plan, cross a line through the words "on or before" and type in the blanks that follow "installments to be paid through plan."

You (and your spouse, if you're filing jointly) must sign and date the Application. If you use a BPP (but haven't paid the BBP any money), have that person complete the second section. Leave the bottom section entitled "Order" blank for the judge to fill out. The judge will either approve the application as submitted, or will modify it. You'll be informed of the judge's decision.

Some courts require you to appear before the judge to explain why you need to pay in installments. If that's how your court operates, you may decide that it's easier to just pay up rather than travel to the court and deal with a judge.

C. Emergency Filing

If you want to file for bankruptcy in a hurry to stop your creditors from bugging you, in most places you can accomplish that just by filing Form 1—Voluntary Petition, and a Mailing Matrix—the form on which you list all your creditors. Some courts also require that you file a cover sheet and an Order Dismissing Chapter 13 Case, which will be processed if you don't file the rest of your papers within 15 days. If the bankruptcy court for your district requires either of those forms, you can get it from the court, a local bankruptcy attorney, or bankruptcy petition preparer.

⚠ File the rest of your papers on time. If you don't follow up by filing the additional documents—including your Chapter 13 repayment plan—within 15 days, your bankruptcy case will be dismissed and you may be fined. You can file again, if necessary, but you'll have to pay another filing fee. And if you file and dismiss several times, the court may rule that you are abusing the bankruptcy system and bar you from filing again for months, for years, or, in extreme cases, ever again.

For an emergency filing:

Step 1: Check with your court to find out exactly what forms must be submitted for an emergency filing.

Step 2: Fill in Form 1—Voluntary Petition. (See Ch. 6, *Completing the Bankruptcy Forms*, Section E.)

Step 3: On a mailing matrix (or whatever other form is required by your court), list all your creditors, as well as collection agencies, sheriffs, attorneys, and others who are seeking to collect debts from you. (See Ch. 6, *Completing the Bankruptcy Forms*, Section H.)

Step 4: Fill in any other papers the court requires.

Step 5: File the originals (the copy you signed) and the required number of copies, accompanied by your fee (or an application for payment of fee in installments), and a self-addressed envelope with the bankruptcy court. Keep copies of everything for your records.

Step 6: File all other required forms within 15 days. ■

After You File Your Case

Once you have filed all of your Chapter 13 bankruptcy papers, including your repayment plan, the bankruptcy trustee and the court take over. They will examine your papers and schedule court hearings. Your creditors also get into the act; it's time for them to file their claims, so they can get paid by the trustee once you start making plan payments. They may also object to your plan if they think they are getting shortchanged.

This chapter tells you how to move your bankruptcy case along and deal with any unexpected complications that arise. You will probably have to make two or three brief court appearances and do some negotiating with creditors.

⚠️ **Emergency filing reminder.** If you have not filed all your bankruptcy papers, you must do so within 15 days of when you filed your petition. (Bankruptcy Rules 1007(c), 3015(b).) If you do not, the bankruptcy court will dismiss your case and probably fine you. (See Ch. 6, *Completing the Bankruptcy Forms.*)

A. The Automatic Stay

When you file for bankruptcy, something called the "automatic stay" goes into effect. The automatic stay prohibits virtually all creditors from taking any action directed at collecting the debts you owe them until the court says otherwise. In general, creditors cannot:

- take any collection activities, such as writing letters to you or calling you
- file a lawsuit or proceed with a pending lawsuit against you (with a few exceptions, discussed below)
- terminate utilities or public benefits, such as welfare or food stamps
- withhold money in their possession as a setoff for a debt (they can freeze other accounts in their possession, however)
- record liens against your property, or
- seize your property, such as the money in a bank account.

If a creditor tries to collect a debt in violation of the automatic stay, you can ask the bankruptcy court to

hold the creditor in contempt of court and to fine the creditor. See a lawyer to help you make this request.

There are, however, some notable exceptions to the automatic stay. These proceedings are allowed to continue:

- Criminal proceedings. A criminal proceeding that can be broken down into a criminal component and a debt component will be divided, and only the criminal component will be allowed to continue. For example, if you were convicted of writing a bad check and have been sentenced to community service and ordered to pay a fine, your obligation to do community service will not be stopped by the automatic stay.
- A lawsuit that seeks to establish your paternity of a child or to establish, modify, or collect child support or alimony out of your postfiling assets.
- A tax audit, the issuance of a tax deficiency notice, a demand for a tax return, the issuance of a tax assessment, and the demand for payment of such an assessment by the IRS. The automatic stay, however, does stop the IRS from recording a lien or seizing any of your property.

Creditors won't know to stop their collection efforts until they receive notice of your bankruptcy filing. The notice sent by the court may take several days or weeks to reach your creditors. If you want quicker results, send your own notice to bothersome creditors (and bill collectors, landlords, or sheriffs). A sample letter is shown below. A fill-in-the-blanks copy is in Appendix 2.

How a Typical Chapter 13 Bankruptcy Proceeds	
Step	**When It Happens**
1. You file for Chapter 13 bankruptcy.	
2. The automatic stay takes effect. It bars your creditors, once they learn of your filing, from taking any actions to collect what you owe.	When you file the bankruptcy petition.
3. The court appoints a trustee to oversee your case. You will receive a Notice of Appointment of Trustee from the court.	Within a few days after you file the bankruptcy petition.
4. The trustee sends you a Notice of Commencement of Case, which usually contains: • a summary of your Chapter 13 plan • the date of the meeting of creditors • the date of the confirmation hearing, and • the deadline by which creditors must file their claims.	Within a few days after you file your Chapter 13 plan.
5. You begin making payments under your repayment plan. (If your plan is never approved, the trustee will return your money, less administrative costs.)	Within 30 days after you file the bankruptcy petition.
6. You attend the meeting of the creditors, where the trustee and any creditors who show up can ask you about information in your papers. A creditor may raise objections to your plan with the hope of getting you to modify it before the confirmation hearing.	Within 40 days after you file the bankruptcy petition.
7. You file a modified plan, if you wish.	Anytime before the confirmation hearing. You must send a copy of the modified plan to all creditors. And your creditors are entitled to 20 days' notice before the confirmation hearing. If you send the modified plan with less than 20 days' notice, you will have to schedule a new hearing date.
8. Creditors file written objections to your plan, if they wish. The bankruptcy judge will rule on them at the confirmation hearing.	At least 25 days before the confirmation hearing.
9. You attend the confirmation hearing, where the court addresses any objections raised by creditors or the trustee and approves your repayment plan.	No set time. A few courts hold the hearing after the deadline for creditors to file claims has passed. Most courts hold the hearing right after the meeting of the creditors, which is before the deadline.
10. Creditors file their "proofs of claims," specifying how much they are owed.	Within 90 days after the meeting of the creditors.
11. You or the trustee file written objections to creditors' claims, if you have a reason to object.	As soon as possible after the creditors file their claims. You must notify your creditors at least 30 days in advance of the hearing on your objections.
12. The trustee sends you periodic statements, showing: • who has filed claims and for how much • how much money has been paid to each creditor • the balance due each creditor.	Commonly, twice a year.
13. The court grants your discharge. The court may schedule a brief final court appearance called a "discharge hearing." If there's no discharge hearing, you'll be mailed formal notice of your discharge.	36 to 60 months after you file if you complete your plan payments; sooner if you seek and obtain a hardship discharge.

Notice to Creditor of Filing for Bankruptcy

Lynn Adams
18 Orchard Park Blvd.
East Lansing, MI 48823

June 15, 20xx

Cottons Clothing Store
745 Main Street
Lansing, MI 48915

Dear Cottons Clothing:

On June 14, 20xx, I filed a voluntary petition under Chapter 13 of the U.S. Bankruptcy Code in the Bankruptcy Court for the Eastern District of Michigan. The case number is 123-456-7890. No attorney is representing me. Under 11 U.S.C. § 362(a), you may not:

- take any action against me or my property to collect any debt
- file or pursue any lawsuit against me
- place a lien on my real or personal property
- take any property to satisfy an already recorded lien
- repossess any property in my possession
- discontinue any service or benefit currently being provided to me, or
- take any action to evict me from where I live.

A violation of these prohibitions may be considered contempt of court and punished accordingly.

Very truly yours,

Lynn Adams

Lynn Adams

The court almost always lifts (removes) the stay at the end of the confirmation hearing, because your creditors are now bound by your plan. This means they cannot sue you or take other action to get paid. Their only means of being paid is through the terms of the confirmed plan.

B. Dealing With the Trustee

Within a few days after you file your bankruptcy petition, the bankruptcy court assigns a Chapter 13 trustee to oversee your case. You will receive a Notice of Appointment of Trustee from the court, giving the name, address, and phone number of the trustee. It may also include a list of any financial documents the trustee wants copies of, such as bank statements, canceled checks, and tax returns, and the date by which the trustee wants them.

Within a few days after the trustee is appointed, the trustee will send you a Notice of Commencement of Case. This notice usually contains:

- a summary of your Chapter 13 plan
- an explanation of the automatic stay
- the date, time, and place of the meeting of creditors (see Section E, below)
- the date, time, and place of the confirmation hearing (see Section H, below), and
- the date by which creditors must file their claims (see Section J, below).

⚠ **Some notices are incomplete.** Not all Notices of Commencement of Case include the date, time, and place of the meeting of creditors. If yours does not, call the court clerk to find out.

Along with the notice, the trustee often includes a letter of introduction explaining how this trustee runs a Chapter 13 case. For example, many trustees require you to make your payments by cashier's check or money order, and don't accept personal checks or cash. The letter will probably remind you to make your first payment within 30 days of when you filed your petition.

Many Chapter 13 trustees play a fairly active role in the cases they administer. This is especially true in small suburban or rural judicial districts or districts with a lot of Chapter 13 bankruptcy cases. For example, a trustee may:

- give you financial advice and assistance, such as helping you create a realistic budget (the trustee cannot, however, give you legal advice)
- actively participate in modifying your plan at the meeting of the creditors, and
- participate at any hearing on the value of an item of secured property, possibly even hiring an appraiser.

For more information on the role of the Chapter 13 trustee, see Ch. 2, *An Overview of Chapter 13 Bankruptcy*, Section F.

1. Reporting Expenditures or Acquisitions to the Trustee

Once you file your bankruptcy papers, the property you owned before filing is under the supervision of the bankruptcy court. Don't throw out, give away, sell, or otherwise dispose of any property unless and until the bankruptcy trustee says otherwise.

Despite the trustee's great interest in your finances, your financial relationship with the trustee is not as stifling as it may sound. In general, you still have complete control over money and property you acquire after filing—as long as you make the payments called for under your repayment plan, and you make all regular payments on your secured debts. If you don't make those payments, your creditors may object at the confirmation hearing or even file a motion to dismiss your case.

You can use income you earn after filing that's not going toward your plan payments to make day-to-day purchases such as groceries, personal effects, and clothing. If you have any questions about using your postfiling income, ask the Chapter 13 bankruptcy trustee.

If you receive certain kinds of property (or become entitled to receive it), within 180 days after filing for bankruptcy, you must report it to the bankruptcy trustee. Here's the list:

- property you inherit or become entitled to inherit
- property from a marital settlement agreement or divorce decree, or
- death benefits or life insurance policy proceeds.

If any of this property is nonexempt, you might have to modify your plan to increase the amount your unsecured creditors receive, if they would no longer be receiving at least the value of your nonexempt property.

2. Providing the Trustee With Proof of Insurance

If you are behind on payments on a secured debt, such as a car loan, and you plan to make up the payments and get back on track during your Chapter 13 case, you may have to give the trustee proof that you have adequate insurance on the collateral. This requirement is meant to protect the creditor if the collateral is destroyed or damaged and your plan is not confirmed or you dismiss your case, and you want to give up the property.

C. Make Your First Payment

Within 30 days after you file your petition, you must make the first payment proposed in your Chapter 13 repayment plan. (11 U.S.C. § 1326.) This deadline usually comes up before the meeting of creditors, and always before your confirmation hearing. The reason you must make the payment so early is to establish that you can, in fact, make the payments.

It's crucial that you not miss this first deadline. So that you don't forget, count out 30 days from the date you filed your petition and mark the deadline on a calendar. It might be better, though, to make the payment a little earlier—for example, the day after you get paid, so you'll be sure to have the funds. If your wages are currently subject to a wage attachment, garnishment, or voluntary payroll deduction, call the trustee and ask for help in getting those removed so that you have the money to make your Chapter 13 payments.

If you do not make your first payment on time, the bankruptcy court can convert your case to Chapter 7 bankruptcy, dismiss your case, or deny confirmation of your plan. A few courts consider the failure to make the first payment evidence that the plan was not submitted in good faith and is an abuse of the Chapter 13 bankruptcy system. In that case, the court would lift the automatic stay and allow your creditors to continue their collection efforts. If the court felt you were egregiously abusing the system—for example, this is the fourth Chapter 13 bankruptcy case you've filed without making payments in any of them—the court would likely dismiss your case, and possibly fine you and bar you from ever filing for Chapter 13 bankruptcy again.

D. Keep Your Business Going

If you operate a business, by all means keep running it after you file your Chapter 13 papers. If your business has employees, don't forget to make all required payroll tax and withholding deposits with the IRS and your state taxing authority.

The trustee can require the following from you:

- an inventory of your business property, and
- a report on the recent operation of the business, including a statement of receipts and disbursements, if you didn't include one in your bankruptcy papers (you may have attached one to Schedule I—Current Income of Individual Debtor(s), or Form 7—Statement of Financial Affairs). (11 U.S.C. § 1304; Bankruptcy Rule 2015(c).)

The trustee may also direct you to send notification of your bankruptcy case to all entities who hold money or property that belongs to you. This includes financial institutions where you have accounts, landlords and utility companies who hold security deposits, and insurance companies where you have business insurance with a cash surrender value. If the balance of the money or value of the property is high and your plan provides little or no payment to your unsecured creditors, the trustee might try to take this money or property for them.

E. The Meeting of Creditors

Your first court appearance is a fairly informal one; the bankruptcy judge isn't even present. The purpose of the creditors' meeting is to allow the trustee and your creditors to ask you about the information in your bankruptcy papers, including your repayment plan. The trustee will want to be sure that you can make the payments you've proposed in your plan.

You (and your spouse, if you are filing jointly) must attend. If you don't, you may be fined $100 or so by the judge. Even worse, your case may be dismissed. If you know in advance that you can't attend the creditors' meeting, call the trustee and try to reschedule it.

1. Preparing for the Meeting of the Creditors

Before the meeting, call the trustee. Explain that you're proceeding without a lawyer and ask what records you're required to bring. Some courts require you to bring at least the following documents:

- file-stamped copies of all the papers you've filed with the bankruptcy court

- copies of all documents that describe your debts and property, such as bills, deeds, contracts, and licenses, and
- financial records, such as recent tax returns and checkbooks.

Also be prepared for the trustee to request that you surrender all your major credit cards. (Not all trustees require this.) However, with the advent of the check card, this shouldn't be too traumatic.

If you lack the necessary documents at the creditors meeting, the trustee will postpone the meeting to a later date when you can produce them. Often, if you get the documents to the trustee before the rescheduled meeting, he or she will close the meeting without your having to appear.

You'll have to prove your own identity. To show that you are really who you say you are, you'll need to produce a solid picture ID and official proof of your Social Security number, such as a Social Security card, wage stubs, or a passport. Failure to produce such a document will result in your meeting being reset for a later date. Also, you'll need your picture ID to gain entrance to the federal building where the meeting is being held.

You should also be prepared to bring photo identification (such as a driver's license or passport) and proof of your Social Security number.

If you are feeling anxious about the meeting of creditors, ask the trustee when and where the next scheduled meeting will occur. Then, attend the meeting. That way, you can observe the proceedings and get comfortable with the process before you have to attend your meeting.

The night before the creditors' meeting, thoroughly review the papers you filed with the bankruptcy court. If you discover mistakes, make careful note of them. You'll probably have to correct your papers after the meeting, an easy process. (Instructions are in Section L, below.)

If your papers are internally consistent and there are no problem areas, the trustee is likely to ask you very few questions, perhaps nothing more than whether you have provided complete and accurate information. But sometimes the trustee may delve into a particular subject in more detail. For instance, the trustee may be interested in how you approached the valuation of valuable property such as real estate or a business. Or, if you recently sold some property, the trustee may want to know the details of the transaction and what you did with the proceeds. Or, if one part of your bankruptcy papers shows that you owe a specific debt but that debt hasn't been identified on the appropriate schedule, the trustee will want to know why. And finally, the trustee may want a better understanding of how your plan will pay your creditors.

Clearly there are an infinite number of situations where the trustee may want to go deeper into the facts. So how can you prepare for this? The single best way is to do a complete and accurate job of preparing your bankruptcy papers in the first place. Then, as mentioned, carefully review your papers and make sure you understand all the information they contain and how you arrived at particular estimates and appraisals. Even if you had your papers prepared by someone else, you and you alone are responsible for what goes in them.

2. Getting to the Meeting of the Creditors

Most creditors' meetings take place in a room in or near the bankruptcy courthouse or federal courthouse. The date and time of the meeting are commonly stated on the Notice of Commencement of Case sent to you by the trustee; if they are not call the court clerk to find out. Give yourself at least an extra 30 minutes to find the right place, park, find the right building, go through security, and find the right room.

When you get to the right room, look for the trustee. The trustee will probably be sitting at a table; lawyers may be milling around, waiting to ask questions. Ask the trustee if you have to "check in"—that is, give your name so the trustee knows you are present. Then just sit down and wait your turn.

Tight Court Security

On your way to any court hearing, you will probably spend some time getting through security. Like airports, these days federal courts have metal detectors, but set to an even higher sensitivity. If you set the detector off, you'll have to empty your pockets and take off any offending articles, such as a jacket or belt, and go through again. If you set it off again, the security guard may scan your body with a hand-held metal detector. In addition, items you're carrying—such as a purse, briefcase, or knapsack—must go through an X-ray scanner. The security guard may confiscate objects such as pocket knives; you can reclaim them after your hearing. You should also be prepared to show a picture ID to gain entrance.

---

3. What Happens at the Meeting of the Creditors

Most bankruptcy courts set aside one or two days a month to hold Chapter 13 bankruptcy creditors' meetings. This means that when you show up for your meeting, many other people who have filed for bankruptcy will be there, too. And commonly, everyone was told to come at the same time. That means that 25–30 cases may all be scheduled for 9:00 a.m.

To get a rough idea of when your name will be called, check the schedule that should posted outside the courtroom door. If your name is near the top of the list, you may not have too long to wait. If you're toward the bottom, you may be sitting there for quite some time. This time doesn't have to be wasted. A chance to observe other people at their meetings can be to your advantage; you'll quickly find out what to expect, where to stand, and maybe even what to say. And if you're nervous, watching other cases will probably help you calm down. If you're very nervous, you can visit the bankruptcy court a week or two before your own hearing and watch the proceedings. This should help relax you.

Your creditors' meeting, if it's typical, will last less than 15 minutes. When your name is called, you'll be asked to sit at a table near the front of the courtroom. The court clerk will swear you in and ask your name, address, and other identifying information. The clerk will probably ask to see your photo ID and proof of Social Security number.

The trustee will briefly go over your forms with you, probably asking one or more of the questions mentioned in Section 1 above. Your answers should be both truthful and consistent with your bankruptcy papers. The trustee is likely to be most interested in the fairness of your plan and your ability to make the payments you have proposed.

When the trustee is finished, any creditors who showed up are given a chance to question you. Often, secured creditors come, especially if they have any objections to the plan—for example, that the interest rate you propose is too low, you are taking too long to pay your arrears, or the value you assigned the collateral is wrong. An unsecured creditor who is receiving very little under your plan might show up too, if that creditor thinks you can cut your expenses and increase your disposable income. (See Section G, below, for a discussion on the types of objections creditors raise to repayment plans.)

At the end of the meeting, be ready to negotiate with the creditors. (See Ch. 7, *Writing Your Chapter 13 Bankruptcy Plan*, Section I, for information on negotiating with your creditors.) If you agree to make changes to accommodate their objections, you must submit a modified plan.

F. Modifying Your Plan Before the Confirmation Hearing

You have an absolute right to file modified plans with the bankruptcy court any time before the confirmation hearing, and most Chapter 13 debtors submit at least one. (11 U.S.C. § 1323(a).) You must file the new plan with the bankruptcy court clerk, give a copy to the trustee, and send notice of the new plan to all of your creditors. The new plan replaces the old one.

Here are some common reasons to modify a plan:
- To correct errors—such as to add overlooked creditors or debts.
- To reflect financial changes—such as a new job, raise, inheritance or insurance settlement, reduction in income, or destruction of property secured by a debt.
- To reduce your proposed payments—for example, if you just lost your job or had your income reduced.
- To respond to creditors' objections or include terms you negotiated with a creditor at the end of the meeting of the creditors.
- To add debts you incurred after filing. In general, you should not incur debts after you file, other than day-to-day expenses. You can modify your plan, however, to add any debts that are necessary for you to keep following your plan (such as a medical bill) or unanticipated debts (such as a tax bill). (This is covered in Ch. 10, *After Your Plan is Approved*, Section C.)

Your creditors have a right to be notified about your proposed modifications—and your notice must be fairly specific. At a minimum the notice must:
- identify the debtor (you)
- identify each creditor whose claim is affected by your modification
- describe your proposed modification with particularity (for instance, if you're proposing to reduce your payment to a creditor, your notice has to make that clear), and
- if secured property is involved, state whether you plan to keep making payments or surrender the collateral.

(See *In re Friday*, 304 B.R. 537 (N.D. Ga. 2003).)

G. Creditors' Objections to a Plan

It might seem odd to you that an unsecured creditor would object to your Chapter 13 plan. After all, in Chapter 13 bankruptcy, the creditor may get some money. By contrast, if you ignored the creditor or filed for Chapter 7 bankruptcy, the creditor probably wouldn't get anything.

The creditor isn't trying to derail your bankruptcy, but is trying to get you to modify your plan so that you can really make the payments under your plan. Because so many Chapter 13 debtors eventually dismiss their cases or convert them to Chapter 7 bankruptcy, your creditors have reason to doubt you. A creditor objects to a plan precisely because the creditor wants it to succeed.

A creditor who objects to your plan will probably attend the meeting of the creditors and try to get you to modify your plan before the confirmation hearing. The creditor will probably also file a formal paper, either a motion or an objection, with the bankruptcy court, asking the bankruptcy court to deny confirmation of or modify your plan. That way, in case you and the creditor can't reach an agreement informally, the judge will decide the issue. If the creditor doesn't file a motion or objection, the creditor can't raise the objection at the confirmation hearing. A copy of a Notice of Motion or Objection form is below.

If the Creditor Requests a Deposition

It's rare, but a creditor who thinks you are hiding assets and could pay more into your plan might try to gather evidence about your financial situation through a formal legal process called "discovery." The discovery technique the creditor is most likely to use is a deposition—a proceeding in which you answer questions from the creditor's attorney orally, under oath, before a court reporter. If a creditor sends you a discovery request, the court will postpone the confirmation hearing to give the creditor time to conduct the discovery.

Understanding depositions. For help in preparing for a deposition, see *Nolo's Deposition Handbook,* by Paul Bergman and Albert Moore (Nolo), and *Represent Yourself in Court,* by Paul Bergman and Sara J. Berman-Barrett (Nolo).

This section describes the four most common objections creditors raise to Chapter 13 plans.

1. The Plan Is Not Submitted in Good Faith

Probably the most common objection creditors raise is that a Chapter 13 plan was not proposed in good faith. (11 U.S.C. § 1325(a)(3).) The bankruptcy rules do not define good faith, but bankruptcy courts generally look to see that you have not proposed a plan that obviously will be impossible for you to meet. If you feel confident that you are filing your papers with the honest intention of getting back on your feet and can make the payments under the plan, you probably can overcome a "good faith" objection.

Occasionally, creditors make a good faith objection as a negotiating ploy. They want you to change your plan to satisfy them rather than argue the question of good faith before the bankruptcy court. If you think this is happening, you'll probably need the help of a lawyer to evaluate if any real good faith issues exist concerning your plan.

When creditors pursue good faith objections, most bankruptcy courts look at the following kinds of factors:

- **How often you have filed for bankruptcy.** Filing multiple bankruptcies (file, dismiss, file, dismiss, and file again) in and of itself does not show bad faith. If within one year, however, you've filed and dismissed two or more other bankruptcy cases, the court may find lack of good faith if there are inconsistencies in your papers (except where actual changes occurred) or you cannot show that your circumstances have changed since the previous dismissal. Changed circumstances include:
  - an increase in your income
  - a reduction of your debts
  - a new job that will permit use of an income deduction order
  - your spouse is now filing, too
  - the end of a condition that caused your previous dismissal, such as illness or unemployment.

  Here's another example of lack of good faith. Let's say you received a Chapter 7 bankruptcy discharge, and then file for Chapter 13 less than six years later. In your Chapter 13 plan, you propose paying your unsecured creditors less than 100%. Your plan will not be confirmed because you are using Chapter 13 to circumvent Chapter 7's prohibition on filing a second case within six years of obtaining a discharge in a first case.

- **The accuracy of your bankruptcy papers and oral statements.** The court is likely to find a lack of good faith if you misrepresent your income, debts, expenses, or assets, or you lie at the creditors' meeting or at a deposition. Creditors look for discrepancies by comparing your bankruptcy papers with credit applications and financial data

Form 20A

UNITED STATES BANKRUPTCY COURT

_____ DISTRICT OF _____

In re _____)
      [Set forth here all names including)
      married, maiden, and trade names used)
      by debtor within last 6 years.])
                           Debtor(s)) Case No. _____
Address _____)
)
      _____) Chapter 13
)
Employer's Tax Identification (EIN) No(s). _[if any]_:)
_____)
Last four digits of Social Security No(s): _____)

NOTICE OF [MOTION TO] [OBJECTION TO]

_____ has filed papers with the court to _[relief sought in motion or objection]._

Your rights may be affected. You should read these papers carefully and discuss them with your attorney, if you have one in this bankruptcy case. (If you do not have an attorney, you may wish to consult one.)

If you do not want the court to _[relief sought in motion or objection]_, or if you want the court to consider your views on the _[motion] [objection]_, then on or before _[date]_, you or your attorney must:

    File with the court a written request for a hearing _[or, if the court requires a written response, an answer, explaining your position]_ at:

        [address of the bankruptcy clerk's office]

    If you mail your _[request] [response]_ to the court for filing, you must mail it early enough so the court will receive it on or before the date stated above.

    You must also mail a copy to:

        [movant's attorney's name and address]

        [names and addresses of others to be served]

    _[Attend the hearing scheduled to be held on ___[date]___, [year], at ___ a.m./p.m. in Courtroom _____, United States Bankruptcy Court, [address].]_

    [Other steps required to oppose a motion or objection under local rule or court order.]

If you or your attorney do not take these steps, the court may decide that you do not oppose the relief sought in the motion or objection and may enter an order granting that relief.

Date: _____   Signature: _____

                                       Name: _____

                                       Address: _____

you submitted to them. Even if your mistakes were purely accidental, the appearance of sloppiness (such as failing to mention property, even if it's worthless, failing to mention minor debts, providing the wrong Social Security number, listing insufficient or erroneous information about creditors, or wrongly valuing property) will lead some courts to dismiss your case on the ground that you failed to meet your obligations as a debtor. If you discover any inaccuracy in your papers, be sure to point it out to the trustee at the creditors' meeting and amend your papers. (How to amend your papers is covered in Section L, below.)

- **Your motive for filing for Chapter 13 bankruptcy.** If you want to cure your mortgage default and get back on track with your house payments, pay off a tax debt, or get some breathing room to pay off your creditors, you have nothing to worry about. If the court finds either of the following, however, it might also find bad faith:

  - You filed for bankruptcy for the sole purpose of rejecting a lease or contract, such as a timeshare or car lease.

  - You filed for bankruptcy to handle only one debt (other than mortgage arrears or back taxes). The court might especially find lack of good faith if you file for Chapter 13 only to pay a nondischargeable debt such as a student loan or criminal fine.

- **The length of the plan you've proposed.** If you will pay only a small percentage of your unsecured debts, some courts will find bad faith if your proposed plan is not for five years. An equal number of courts, however, allow small percentage plans that last only three years.

- **Your efforts to repay your debts.** If you will pay your unsecured creditors less than the full amount that you owe, you will have to show the court that you are stretching as much as you can. The court will want to see that you are living frugally and making extraordinary efforts to pay your unsecured creditors. You'll have few problems if you can show that you've eliminated payments on luxury items, depleted your investments, canceled your country club membership, decreased your religious contributions, brought down your living expenses, and increased your hours at work.

- **The cause of your financial trouble.** Bankruptcy courts are reluctant to find bad faith if your financial problems are due to events beyond your control—for example, exceptional medical expenses or an accident, job loss, death or illness in the family.

2. The Plan Is Not Feasible

The second most likely objection is that your plan is not feasible—that is, you won't be able to make the payments or comply with the other terms of the plan. (11 U.S.C. § 1325(a)(6).)

To overcome a feasibility objection, your monthly income must exceed your monthly expenses by at least enough to allow you to make payments. In Ch. 4, *Calculating Your Disposable Income*, you totaled up your income and expenses. If a creditor raises this objection, bring to the confirmation hearing your worksheets and any other documents (such as pay stubs and monthly bills) you have showing your income and expenses.

Your creditors might also question your job stability, the likelihood that you'll incur extraordinary expenses, and whether you have any outside sources of money. The court will likely deny confirmation on the ground that your plan isn't feasible if any of the following is true:

- Your business has been failing, but you've predicted a rebound and intend to use the predicted increase in business income to make your plan payments.

- You propose making plan payments from the proceeds of the sale of certain property, but nothing points to the likelihood of a sale—for example, your house has been on the market for a long time and you've had no offers.

- Your plan includes a balloon payment, but you have not identified a source of money with which to make the payment.

- You owe back alimony or child support and have been held in contempt of court for failing to pay.

- You've been convicted of a crime, and you have not convinced the bankruptcy court that you will stay out of jail.

3. The Plan Fails the Best Interest of the Creditors Test

When you file for Chapter 13 bankruptcy, you must pay your unsecured creditors at least as much as they would have received if you had filed for Chapter 7 bankruptcy. (11 U.S.C. § 1325(a)(4).) (This is explained in Ch. 5, *Calculating the Value of Your Nonexempt Property*.) This is called the "best interest of the creditors" test.

If a creditor raises this objection, bring to the confirmation hearing your worksheets from Ch. 5 and any other documents you have showing the values of your nonexempt items of property, such as a recent appraisal or a publication showing the value of your automobile.

4. The Plan Unfairly Discriminates

In your plan, you must specify which unsecured creditors get paid in full and which, if any, get less. To do that, you can create classes of unsecured creditors, specifying how much (or what percentage) each class will receive, as long as you do not unfairly discriminate against any specific creditor. Ch. 7, *Writing Your Chapter 13 Bankruptcy Plan*, Section J, describes common classes of creditors and creditors' likely objections.

If a creditor objects to classes you've created, you can either fight it out in court at the confirmation hearing (which will require that you research how your bankruptcy court district has ruled in previous cases on the subject) or amend your plan to eliminate the class.

H. The Confirmation Hearing

A judge must approve your Chapter 13 plan for it to be valid. This is done at a confirmation hearing, where the judge addresses any objections raised by creditors or the trustee. You (and your spouse, if you are filing jointly) must attend. In a few courts, the judge schedules a confirmation hearing only if a creditor has filed a formal motion objecting to the plan. If the judge doesn't schedule a hearing, it means your plan is approved as filed.

Often, the court holds the confirmation meeting the same day as the meeting of the creditors, which is before the deadline has passed for creditors to file claims. (As discussed in Section J, below, a creditor must file with the court something called a "proof of claim" in order to get paid through your Chapter 13 plan.) In this situation, the court must approve or deny your plan without knowing exactly which creditors want to be paid through it. If creditors file claims after the court approves your plan, you may need to pay more into the plan than you expected. (See Ch. 10, *After Your Plan Is Approved*, Section A.)

Try Not to Dispute Debts Before Your Confirmation Hearing

If you want to dispute whether you actually owe a particular debt, you'll need to file your objection with the court. The court will issue a ruling on whether you owe the debt. Similarly, you may need to ask the court to rule on whether a nondischargeable debt is dischargeable in your particular circumstances.

Ideally, you want the court to rule on your objection prior to the confirmation of your plan. Otherwise you'll have to modify your plan if the court ultimately agrees with your objection. And until you get the court's ruling, you'll also have to start paying off the debt if these payments come due under your Chapter 13 plan. Unfortunately, many courts hold confirmation hearings early in the case—even as early as the creditors' meeting—so it may be difficult if not impossible to get a ruling prior to confirmation.

---

1. Preparing for the Confirmation Hearing

A few days before the confirmation hearing, review your plan and the objections raised by your creditors or trustee. If you're confident that you can make the payments under your plan and that your plan is fair to your creditors, gather the documents that support your plan—such as pay stubs showing your income. You're ready to go.

If you have lingering feelings that the objections have some merit, you'll probably need to hit the law library. There, you can do a little legal research to see how bankruptcy appeals and federal appeals courts for your district have ruled in similar disputes. Ch. 12, *Help Beyond the Book*, suggests some excellent resources to help you do your bankruptcy research.

If you find cases that support your position, photocopy them and bring them to court. If you find material that supports the objection, be ready to modify your plan.

2. Getting to the Confirmation Hearing

The confirmation hearing is held in a bankruptcy courtroom. The tips in Section E, above, apply here.

3. What Happens at the Confirmation Hearing

Most bankruptcy districts set aside one or two days a month to hold Chapter 13 bankruptcy confirmation hearings—and in many courts, confirmation hearings are scheduled at the same time as other hearings, such as hearings on motions to dismiss, motions to convert to Chapter 7, and motions to establish the value of property. The courtroom will probably be filled with people who have all been told to come at the same time.

Watch the cases before yours so you know where to go when your name is called. If your case is called first, just ask the judge, clerk, or trustee—whoever is calling the cases—where you should stand. The judge or court clerk will ask you to state your name.

Unlike a creditors' meeting, the confirmation hearing is run by the judge. Judges like to get easy cases in and out of their courtrooms as quickly as possible. This means that all uncontested matters will be heard first. Next will be cases where the outcome is fairly obvious—often motions to dismiss in cases where the plans were approved but the debtors have missed several payments. If yours is a case in which the trustee or a creditor has filed an objection, your confirmation hearing will probably be toward the end. Bring a big book with you.

The judge is most interested in your ability to make the payments under your plan, and will question you about that or about plan provisions that are unclear.

After these questions, the judge will ask you whether any objections raised by the trustee or credi-

tors have been resolved. If they haven't been, the judge may ask the trustee or creditors to elaborate on their objections, ask you for any response, and then make a ruling. If the trustee doesn't think your plan is feasible, the trustee will raise that now. If the judge still has a lot of cases to get through, the judge may reschedule the rest of your hearing to a less busy day.

If the judge agrees with an objection, you will probably be allowed to submit a modified plan. (See Section I, below.) But if it's obvious that Chapter 13 bankruptcy just isn't realistic for you—for example, you earn very little money to pay into a plan—the judge will order that your case be dismissed or converted to Chapter 7 bankruptcy.

4. Issuing an Income Deduction Order

If you have a regular job with regular income, the bankruptcy judge may order, at the confirmation hearing, that the monthly payments under your Chapter 13 plan be automatically deducted from your wages and sent to the bankruptcy court. (11 U.S.C. § 1325(c).) This is called an income deduction order. Income deduction orders work if you are regularly paid a salary or wages. They are almost impossible to issue, however, if you are:

- self-employed
- funding your plan with public benefits, such as Social Security—the Social Security Act prohibits the Social Security Administration from complying with an income deduction order, or
- funding your plan with pension benefits—many pension plans prohibit the administrator from paying proceeds to anyone other than the beneficiary (you), which means that the administrator will ignore the income deduction order.

In many districts, the bankruptcy court automatically issues an income deduction order at the confirmation hearing—and possibly even earlier. In some districts, the bankruptcy court leaves it up to the debtor whether or not to issue an order. And in a few districts, the court doesn't issue the order unless you miss a payment in your plan.

You may not like the idea of the order, but the court is likely to deny your plan for lack of feasibility if you refuse to comply with it. And you should realize that the order will probably make it easier for you to complete your plan. The success rate of Chapter 13 cases is higher for debtors with income deduction orders than for debtors who pay the trustee themselves.

One benefit of an income deduction order is that it usually forbids your employer from making other deductions from your paycheck. This means that all wage attachments, garnishments, and voluntary payroll deductions will end (if they haven't already) when the order takes effect.

If the court does issue an income deduction order, you will have to find out from the court clerk or trustee who is responsible for preparing and giving your employer the order—the clerk, the trustee, or you. (If it's you, see Ch. 6, *Completing the Bankruptcy Forms*, Section J.) To avoid having someone from your job accidentally mention your bankruptcy when the income deduction order arrives, you could inform the payroll department that you've filed for Chapter 13 bankruptcy and to expect an income deduction order from the bankruptcy court.

Once the income deduction order takes effect, you will need to tell the trustee if you change jobs. You can just call, or write a letter if you'd prefer.

Your Employer Can't Fire You for Filing for Bankruptcy

Don't be worried that your employer, who learns of your bankruptcy because of an income deduction order, will fire you because you filed for bankruptcy. Employers rarely care. If your employer does punish you for having filed for bankruptcy, let someone in charge know that under the Bankruptcy Act, all private and public employers are prohibited from terminating you or otherwise discriminating against you solely because you filed for bankruptcy. (11 U.S.C. §§ 525(a), 525(b).) (See Ch. 11, *Life After Bankruptcy*, Section C, for more on the laws against this kind of discrimination.)

5. The Judge's Order Confirming Your Plan

A court order granting confirmation of your repayment plan is binding on your creditors; they must accept the payments the trustee will make to them under the terms of your plan. This includes creditors who do not file claims by the deadline and creditors who objected to your plan. (11 U.S.C. § 1327(a).)

In the past, some debtors tried to get student loans discharged by including them in their plan as just another unsecured debt. Because student loans are nondischargeable unless the debtor comes forward to establish hardship, the student loan creditor wouldn't object to the confirmation. The debtor would then argue that the confirmation was final and the debt was discharged as a result. This practice was referred to as "discharge by declaration" and has been rejected by an increasing number of courts. (See *In re Ruehle*, 307 B.R. 28 (6th Cir. B.A.P. Ohio 2004); *In re Banks*, 299 F.3d 296 (4th Cir. 2002).)

When the court approves your plan, you usually must file an Order Confirming Chapter 13 Plan with the bankruptcy court clerk and send notice that your plan was confirmed to all your creditors. If the judge doesn't say anything, ask the judge if you must prepare the order and send notice.

Below are a sample Order and sample Notice form. To complete your own, type up the samples—filling in the information requested in italics. Attach a copy of your confirmed plan to the Order, and then file the Order and Notice with the bankruptcy court clerk. After you've filed the papers, you must send a copy of the Notice to each of your creditors.

I. Modifying Your Plan After the Confirmation Hearing

If your plan isn't confirmed at the hearing, the court will usually give you a certain amount of time in which you can try again. If you don't submit a modified plan by the deadline (or if the court found bad faith or a lack of feasibility), the court will dismiss your case or convert it to a Chapter 7 bankruptcy case. In that situation, the trustee must return your payments to you, less the amount of administrative expenses. (11 U.S.C. § 1326(a)(1).)

If you want to submit a modified plan, call the trustee and ask for an appointment. Then, if you don't already know, find out from the trustee what it will take to get your plan confirmed. If you do know, ask the trustee if the ideas you have to modify your plan are likely to be approved by the judge.

UNITED STATES BANKRUPTCY COURT

_____ DISTRICT OF _____

In re _____   )
        [Set forth here all names including   )
        married, maiden, and trade names used   )
        by debtor within last 6 years.]   )
                        Debtor(s)   )   Case No. *[copy from your Voluntary Petition]*
Address _____   )
)
        _____   )   Chapter _____
)
Employer's Tax Identification (EIN) No(s). *[if any]*:   )
_____   )
Last four digits of Social Security No(s): _____   )

ORDER CONFIRMING CHAPTER 13 PLAN

The Chapter 13 Plan confirmation came on for hearing on _____ *[date and time of hearing]* _____ in the

above-captioned court, the Honorable _____ *[Name of judge]* _____ presiding. _____ *[Your name(s)]* _____ ,

Debtor(s), appeared without counsel. _____ *[Name of trustee]* _____ appeared as the Chapter 13 Trustee.

Upon recommendation of the Trustee, there being no opposition by any creditor, and good cause

appearing therefore,

IT IS HEREBY ORDERED, ADJUDGED, AND DECREED:

Debtor's Chapter 13 Plan, attached as Exhibit A, is confirmed.

Dated: _____   _____
                                        U.S. Bankruptcy Judge

UNITED STATES BANKRUPTCY COURT

_____ DISTRICT OF _____

In re _____   )

         [Set forth here all names including   )
         married, maiden, and trade names used   )
         by debtor within last 6 years.]   )
                        Debtor(s)   )   Case No. _____

Address _____   )

)

_____   )   Chapter _____

)

Employer's Tax Identification (EIN) No(s). *[if any]:*   )

_____   )

Last four digits of Social Security No(s): _____   )

NOTICE OF ENTRY OF ORDER CONFIRMING CHAPTER 13 PLAN

TO ALL INTERESTED PARTIES AND THEIR ATTORNEYS OF RECORD:

NOTICE IS HEREBY GIVEN pursuant to Bankruptcy Rule 3020(c) of the Order Confirming Chapter 13 Plan

entered on ____*[date judge signed order]*____.

Dated: _____   _____
                                           Debtor in Propria Persona

In most cases, you'll need to do one or more of the following to get your modified plan confirmed:

- extend your plan (if it's under five years)
- speed up the time you pay off secured debt arrears
- change an interest rate on secured debt arrears
- increase the secured portion of a debt that is partially secured and partially unsecured
- create or eliminate a class of unsecured creditors, or
- increase the amount a particular class of creditors receives.

After you type up your modified plan, call the court and ask how many copies you need to submit when filing a modified Chapter 13 plan. (You may need to submit more than you did when you filed the original.) Next, call the trustee and ask who sends the modified plan to your creditors—you or the court. (If it's you, ask the trustee the procedure.) As with modifications before confirmation, it's very important that you give your creditors exact notice of your intended modifications. (See *In re Friday*, 304 B.R. 537 (N.D. Ga. 2003).) Otherwise, your modification may not be binding on any creditor who didn't get adequate notice.

After you file the modified plan, the court will schedule a new confirmation hearing. You'll get a notice with the date and time. It will be at least 25 days after you filed the modified plan; your creditors must be given at least 25 days to file any objections.

J. Creditors' Claims

After you file for bankruptcy, the trustee sends a notice of your bankruptcy filing to all the creditors you listed in your papers. In general, creditors who want to be paid must file a claim within 90 days after the meeting of creditors is *scheduled* to be held. If the meeting is rescheduled, the deadline is still 90 days from the originally scheduled date. As explained in Section E, above, the deadline is usually after your confirmation hearing.

Sometimes, a creditor you want to pay through your Chapter 13 plan forgets to file a claim. You then may have to file it for the creditor within 30 days after the deadline the creditor missed. (Bankruptcy Rule 3004.) (Reasons you might want to file a claim for a creditor are explained below.)

1. Filing a Proof of Claim

Most claims are filed on an official court form. Most bankruptcy courts will also accept an informal document or letter, as long as it shows the creditor intends to assert a claim.

A blank proof of claim form is in Appendix 2; a completed sample is shown below. You must attach to the form evidence of your debt, such as your mortgage agreement and any notice of default. Ask the trustee whether you should file it with the court clerk or directly with the trustee.

How the claim procedure works depends on whether the creditor is classified as secured, priority, or unsecured.

Secured creditors. The bankruptcy code does not expressly require secured creditors to file claims to be paid, but few trustees will pay secured creditors unless there's a claim on file. (Even if a secured creditor doesn't file a claim, however, the creditor's lien stays on the property.)

If you want to make up missed payments on a secured debt in your Chapter 13 case and the creditor doesn't file a claim, you will have to file it on the creditor's behalf. For example, if you have missed three house payments, but the lender doesn't file a claim, the trustee won't pay your arrears through your plan. In that event the lender would probably ask the court for permission to proceed with a foreclosure.

Priority creditors. Priority creditors must file a claim to be paid. Most creditors must file the claim within 90 days from the date you filed your case. Government agencies must file a proof of claim within 180 days from the date you filed your case. The government can get an extension if it formally requests one before the 180 days expire. (Bankruptcy Rule 3002(c)(1).) The IRS is notoriously late at filing claims, but it is usually granted extensions.

Many lawyers might advise you to file a claim on behalf of the IRS for a tax debt that would be non-dischargeable if you convert to Chapter 7 bankruptcy. This is an odd strategy, however, because you are assuming that your Chapter 13 case will fail and will convert to a Chapter 7 bankruptcy. Some Chapter 13 cases do succeed, and not all that fail convert to Chapter 7 bankruptcy. If your case succeeds, you will have paid a tax claim that otherwise would have been discharged.

Unsecured creditors. Unsecured creditors must file a claim to be paid. If an unsecured creditor does not, that creditor's debt will be discharged when you complete your plan, unless the debt is nondischargeable.

If you want to pay a nondischargeable unsecured debt through your Chapter 13 plan (to avoid having the debt remain after your case ends) and the creditor doesn't file a claim, you will have to file it on the creditor's behalf.

2. Objecting to a Creditor's Claim

Unless you submit to the court a written objection to a creditor's claim, the trustee will pay the claim. (In bankruptcy legalese, claims the trustee pays are called "allowed" claims.) Your objection can be as informal as a letter. You can file an objection at any time, but the sooner the better. The court will schedule a hearing at which the creditor must prove you owe the claim. This is where you get to contest the validity of a disputed debt, such as a tax debt.

Possible reasons for objecting to a creditor's claim include:

- You owe less than the creditor claims you do.
- A secured creditor has overstated the value of the collateral.
- The creditor has characterized the debt as secured (meaning you'll have to pay it in full), and you think it's unsecured.
- The claim was filed late. Most courts disallow late claims. Some, however, allow late claims if the creditor shows "excusable neglect" or another good reason for the failure to file on time.

Objecting to a Proof of Claim for a Credit Card Debt

The court will presume that a proof of claim submitted on a credit card debt (most likely by your credit card company) is valid if it is accompanied by a summary statement that:

- identifies the debtor's (your) name and account number
- states the amount of the debt before the bankruptcy filing date
- is presented in the form of a business record or other reliable format, and
- breaks down any charges, such as for interest, late fees, and attorney's fees.

If the proof of claim includes this information, then you, the debtor have the burden of refuting the claim as part of your objection. If the proof of claim doesn't include this information, or you refute the claim, the creditor must prove the claim if you object to it. Finally, if the holder of the claim is not the original creditor, the creditor must document the ownership of the claim in addition to providing the other information. (See *In re Armstrong*, 320 B.R. 97 (N.D. Tex. 2005).)

K. Asking the Court to Eliminate Liens

During your Chapter 13 case, you may be able to get the court to reduce or eliminate liens on your property. If you succeed, you'll still owe the debt, but it will be unsecured. You pay the creditor just what you are paying your other unsecured creditors and you keep the property. Even if you're paying your other unsecured creditors 100%, avoiding the lien is still worthwhile, because you get to keep your property with clear title. See *In re Lane*, 280 F.3d 663 (6th Cir. 2002) (wholly unsecured lien on residence).

1. Avoiding a Lien

Lien avoidance is a procedure by which you ask the bankruptcy court to "avoid" (eliminate or reduce) certain liens. If in your Chapter 13 repayment plan

FORM B10 (Official Form 10) (04/04)

UNITED STATES BANKRUPTCY COURT ___XXXX___ DISTRICT OF ___Arizona, Tucson Division___	PROOF OF CLAIM

Name of Debtor	Case Number
Herchoo, Martin & Ellen	C139000417

NOTE: This form should not be used to make a claim for an administrative expense arising after the commencement of the case. A "request" for payment of an administrative expense may be filed pursuant to 11 U.S.C. § 503.

Name of Creditor (The person or other entity to whom the debtor owes money or property):

Big Home Loan Bank

Name and address where notices should be sent:

232 Desert Way

Tucson, AZ 85700

Attn: Ed Mist

Telephone number: (602) 555-1830

☐ Check box if you are aware that anyone else has filed a proof of claim relating to your claim. Attach copy of statement giving particulars.

☐ Check box if you have never received any notices from the bankruptcy court in this case.

☐ Check box if the address differs from the address on the envelope sent to you by the court.

THIS SPACE IS FOR COURT USE ONLY

Account or other number by which creditor identifies debtor:

XX-1149-2081

Check here ☐ replaces
if this claim ☐ amends   a previously filed claim, dated:_____

1. Basis for Claim

- ☒ Goods sold
- ☐ Services performed
- ☐ Money loaned
- ☐ Personal injury/wrongful death
- ☐ Taxes
- ☐ Other _____

- ☐ Retiree benefits as defined in 11 U.S.C. § 1114(a)
- ☐ Wages, salaries, and compensation (fill out below)
  Last four digits of SS #: _____
  Unpaid compensation for services performed
  from _____ to_____
  (date)   (date)

2. Date debt was incurred: 11/27/xx

3. If court judgment, date obtained:

4. Total Amount of Claim at Time Case Filed: $ ___10,800___ | _____ | _____ | _____
(unsecured)   (secured)   (priority)   (Total)

If all or part of your claim is secured or entitled to priority, also complete Item 5 or 7 below.

☐☒ Check this box if claim includes interest or other charges in addition to the principal amount of the claim. Attach itemized statement of all interest or additional charges.

5. Secured Claim.

☒ Check this box if your claim is secured by collateral (including a right of setoff).

Brief Description of Collateral:

☒ Real Estate   ☐ Motor Vehicle
☐ Other_____

Value of Collateral: $ 275,000

Amount of arrearage and other charges at time case filed included in secured claim, if any: $ 10,800

6. Unsecured Nonpriority Claim $_____

☐ Check this box if: a) there is no collateral or lien securing your claim, or b) your claim exceeds the value of the property securing it, or if c) none or only part of your claim is entitled to priority.

7. Unsecured Priority Claim.

☐ Check this box if you have an unsecured priority claim

Amount entitled to priority $_____
Specify the priority of the claim:

- ☐ Wages, salaries, or commissions (up to $4,925),* earned within 90 days before filing of the bankruptcy petition or cessation of the debtor's business, whichever is earlier - 11 U.S.C. § 507(a)(3).
- ☐ Contributions to an employee benefit plan - 11 U.S.C. § 507(a)(4).
- ☐ Up to $2,225* of deposits toward purchase, lease, or rental of property or services for personal, family, or household use - 11 U.S.C. § 507(a)(6).
- ☐ Alimony, maintenance, or support owed to a spouse, former spouse, or child - 11 U.S.C. § 507(a)(7).
- ☐ Taxes or penalties owed to governmental units-11 U.S.C. § 507(a)(8).
- ☐ Other - Specify applicable paragraph of 11 U.S.C. § 507(a)(____).

Amounts are subject to adjustment on 4/1/07 and every 3 years thereafter with respect to cases commenced on or after the date of adjustment.

8. Credits: The amount of all payments on this claim has been credited and deducted for the purpose of making this proof of claim.

9. Supporting Documents: *Attach copies of supporting documents,* such as promissory notes, purchase orders, invoices, itemized statements of running accounts, contracts, court judgments, mortgages, security agreements, and evidence of perfection of lien. DO NOT SEND ORIGINAL DOCUMENTS. If the documents are not available, explain. If the documents are voluminous, attach a summary.

10. Date-Stamped Copy: To receive an acknowledgment of the filing of your claim, enclose a stamped, self-addressed envelope and copy of this proof of claim

THIS SPACE IS FOR COURT USE ONLY

Date	Sign and print the name and title, if any, of the creditor or other person authorized to file this claim (attach copy of power of attorney, if any):
7/8/xx	*Martin Herchoo*

Penalty for presenting fraudulent claim: Fine of up to $500,000 or imprisonment for up to 5 years, or both. 18 U.S.C. §§ 152 and 3571.

you proposed to pay nothing or very little on your unsecured debts, lien avoidance makes a lot of sense. As long as there's a lien, you have to pay it in full to keep your secured property.

Lien avoidance is available only in very limited circumstances. See Ch. 3, *Adding Up Your Secured and Unsecured Debts,* Section A, for a detailed discussion of when lien avoidance is possible.

You request lien avoidance by typing and filing a motion. It is quite simple and can be done without a lawyer. In most courts, you must file your motion with the court within 30 days after you file for bankruptcy. But some courts require it to be filed before the creditors' meeting. Check your local rules.

What goes in your motion papers depends on the kind of lien you're trying to get eliminated. Again, refer to Ch. 3, Section A, to determine whether or not lien avoidance is possible for you and if so, what kind of lien you want the court to avoid.

You will need to fill out one complete set of forms for each affected creditor—generally, each creditor holding a lien on that property. Sample forms are shown below. Some courts have their own forms; if yours does, use them and adapt these instructions to fit.

Most courts consider a motion to avoid a lien as a matter that can be settled by default—in other words, by a ruling based on your motion, in cases where the creditor hasn't bothered to reply. The law is very clear about when a lien can be avoided, and if your papers indicate that you fit within that law, the creditor will most likely see no point in opposing ("contesting") the matter. This means that your first set of papers should notify the creditor that if he or she hasn't filed a response to your motion within a particular period of time—usually 20 days—the court will rule in your favor. Your notice should also explain that if the creditor wants to contest your motion, it's the creditor's job to arrange a hearing on the matter.

Although we provide sample motions to avoid liens below, you'll also need to check the local rules issued by your district's bankruptcy court. Local rules can get into some picayune details, from the exact wording of the notice you must send the creditor to the procedures for setting up a hearing if the creditor contests your motion. In some areas the rules require you to set a hearing, on the assumption that the creditor will want to contest your motion. Local rules also govern such mundane matters as whether numbered papers must be used and how to attach any exhibits that accompany the papers.

If the creditor requests a hearing, the local rules will explain what actions you should take, if any. In addition to procedural actions, such as filing a response to the creditor's request, you'll be required to prove, at a minimum, that the lien would impair your exemption on the property if you were required to pay it.

If the creditor doesn't request a hearing, you'll be required to file a proposed order and a request to enter a default. Your local rules will also govern this procedure.

The sample papers provided below assume that you are in a district where numbered paper is required and where motions to avoid liens may proceed without the creditor's reply ("by default"). The language in the sample notice is based on Local Rule 9014-1 for the Northern District of California bankruptcy court. (See www.canb.uscourts.gov, local rules (on the right), general matters (scroll down).)

In Chapter 13 cases, the most common type of motion to avoid a lien involves a lien that a creditor has placed on a house as a result of a court judgment. This motion is titled Motion to Avoid Judicial Lien on Real Estate, so our samples are based on this scenario. Other types of motions to avoid liens will normally follow the same procedures, although the exact wording of the motions will differ.

Where can you find your local court's rules regarding motions to avoid liens? The rules should be available on your court's website, which you can locate on the Internet at www.bankruptcydata.com (click "Court Links," then choose your closest state court—if you're unsure, call one of the courts). Once you get to your local court's website, it should have a link titled "local rules" or something similar. If you don't find the information you need, call the court clerk for assistance.

Step 1: If your court publishes local rules, refer to them for time limits, format of papers, and other details of a motion proceeding.

Step 2: Type the top half of the pleading form (where you list your name, the court, case number, etc.), following the examples shown below. This part of the form is known as the "caption." It is the same for all pleadings.

Step 3: If you're using a computer to prepare the forms, save the caption portion and reuse it for other pleadings. If you're using a typewriter to prepare the forms, stop when you've typed the caption, and photocopy the page you've made so far, so you can reuse it for other pleadings.

Step 4: Using one of the copies that you just made, start typing again just below the caption and prepare a Notice of Motion and Motion to Avoid Judicial Lien on Real Estate as shown in the sample.

Step 5: Prepare a separate Proof of Service as shown in the example. Note that the proof of service must include the trustee and the U.S. Trustee as well as the creditor. If the creditor is a corporation, the proof of service must identify a specific human being as the object of the service. This involves calling the corporation and asking the name and title of the person who accepts service for it. If the corporation holding the lien is no longer active—for instance it has merged with another corporation—ask the current corporation who should be served for the defunct corporation. You can also often get the name of the person who should be served by contacting the agency responsible for corporate filings in your state (usually the secretary of state). They will usually be able to give you the appropriate person to be served.

Step 6: Make at least three extra copies of all forms.

Step 7: Keep the Proofs of Service. Have your friend mail one copy of the Motion, Notice of Motion, and proposed Order to each affected creditor and the trustee.

How to Serve a Business Creditor

For your service to be effective, you need to serve a live human being who represents the creditor. You can't just send your motion to "Capital One," for example. Here's how to find that warm body:

Call the creditor and ask for the name and address of the person who accepts service of process for the business. If you don't know how to reach the creditor, contact your state's secretary of state and ask for the name and address of the person who is listed as agent for service of process for that company. Some states make this information available online.

Step 8: File (in person or by mail) the original (signed) Notice of Motion, Motion, and Proof of Service with the bankruptcy court. There is no fee.

Step 9: Wait the required period of time for a response from the creditor (usually 20 calendar days). If no response arrives, prepare a Request for Entry of Default, a Proposed Order, and a Proof of Service, as shown in the samples. If you receive a response, the response will, in most districts, provide you with notice of a hearing that has been scheduled by the creditor. Under most local rules, the creditor's response will also contain a Memorandum of Points and Authorities as to why your Motion should be denied. However, your local rules may instead require you to set the hearing and to provide points and authorities as to why your motion should be granted.

Sample Notice of Motion and Motion to Avoid Judicial Lien on Real Estate

```
1   [Debtor's (your) name]
2   [Debtor's address]
    [City, state, and zip code]
    [Phone number]
3   Debtors Representing Themselves
4
            IN THE UNITED STATES BANKRUPTCY COURT
                   [District and Division]
5
6   In the Matter of
7   [Debtor's name]                 ) Case No: [Bankruptcy Case #]
    Debtors                          ) [Special number for Avoidance of
8                                     ) Lien motions, if any]
9                                     ) Chapter 13
10                                    )
11
12          NOTICE OF MOTION AND
        MOTION TO AVOID JUDICIAL LIEN ON REAL ESTATE
13
14      PLEASE TAKE NOTICE that Debtor [debtor's name] is moving the
15  court to avoid a judicial lien held by [name of lien owner] on certain
16  real property owned by the Debtor.
17      This motion is being brought under procedures prescribed by
18  Bankruptcy Local Rule 9414-1 of the United States Bankruptcy Court for
19  the Northern District of California.
20      If you wish to object to the motion, or request a hearing on the
21  motion, your objection and/or request must be filed and served upon
22  Debtor within 20 days of the date this notice was mailed;
23      You must accompany any request you make for a hearing, or any
24  objection to the relief sought by Debtor(s), with any declarations or
25  memoranda of law you wish to present in support of your position.
26      If you do not make a timely objection to the requested relief, or a
27  timely request for hearing, the court may enter an order granting the
28  relief by default and either 1) set a tentative hearing date or 2)
```

Sample Notice of Motion and Motion to Avoid Judicial Lien on Real Estate (cont'd)

```
1   require that Debtors provide you at least 10 days written notice of
2   hearing (in the event an objection or request for hearing is timely made).
3   1.  Debtor [debtor's name] commenced this case on [date of bankruptcy
4   filing] by filing a voluntary petition for relief under Chapter 13 of
5   Title 11 of the United States Bankruptcy Code.
6   2.  This court has jurisdiction over this motion, filed pursuant to 11
7   U.S.C. Sec. 522(f) to avoid and cancel a judicial lien held by [name of
8   lien owner] on real property used as the debtors' residence, under 28
9   U.S.C. Sec. 1334.
10  3.  On [date of lien being recorded], creditors recorded a judicial lien
11  against the debtors' residence at [address]. The said judicial lien is
12  entered of record as follows: [describe how lien appears in public records].
13  4.  The Debtors' interest in the property referred to in the preceding
14  paragraph and encumbered by the lien has been claimed as fully exempt in
15  their bankruptcy case.
16  5.  The existence of [lien owner's name] lien on Debtors' real property
17  impairs exemptions to which the Debtors would be entitled under 11 U.S.C.
18  Sec. 522(b).
19      WHEREFORE, Debtors pray for an order against [lien owner's name]
20  avoiding and canceling the judicial lien in the above-mentioned property,
21  and for such additional or alternative relief as may be just and proper.
22
23  Date:
24  Signed by:
25
26
27
28
```

Sample Request for Entry of Order by Default and Proposed Order

```
1    [Debtor's (your) name]
2    [Debtor's address]
3    [City, state, and zip code]
     [Phone number]
     Debtors Representing Themselves
4
5
6              IN THE UNITED STATES BANKRUPTCY COURT
                      [District and Division]
7
     In the Matter of
8    [Debtor's name]              ) Case No: [Bankruptcy case #]
     Debtors                      )  [Special number for avoidance
9                                 )   of lien motions, if any]
10                                ) Chapter 13
                                  )
11                                )
                                  )
12   REQUEST FOR ENTRY OF ORDER BY DEFAULT AND PROPOSED ORDER
13   Now comes [debtor's name] who declares and says under penalty of
14   perjury this [date of request] that the following statements are true
15   and correct:
16   1. On [date notice and motion served], Debtor [debtor's name] caused a
17      Notice of Motion and Motion to Avoid Judicial Lien on Real Estate to be
18      served on [name of person served on behalf of lien owner].
19   2. A copy of the Notice of Motion and Motion and a proposed order are
20      attached to this request. Also attached is a Proof of Service of this
21      request on [name of lien owner], the Trustee, and the U.S. Trustee.
22   3. The Trustee and the U.S. Trustee were also served with the Notice of
23      Motion and Motion on [date notice and motion served].
24   4. A proof of service duly executed by [name of person who mailed the
25      notice] as to service of the Notice of Motion and Motion is on file
26      with the court.
27
28
```

Sample Request for Entry of Order by Default and Proposed Order (cont'd)

```
1    5. The Notice of Motion and Motion complies in all respects with
2       Bankruptcy Local Rule 9414-1 of the United States Bankruptcy Court
3       for the Northern District of California.
4    6. The Debtor has received no response from any of the served parties
5       as of the date of this request, more than 20 days after the service
6       of the Notice of Motion and Motion.
7    WHEREFORE, Debtor respectfully requests that the court enter by default
8    the attached Order to Avoid Judicial Lien on Real Estate.
9
10   Dated: [date of request]
11   Signed: [debtor's signature] _____
12
13
14
15
16
17
18
19
20
21
22
23
24
25
26
27
28
```

Sample Order to Avoid Judicial Lien on Real Estate

```
1   [Debtor's (your) name]
2   [Debtor's address]
2   [City, state, and zip code]
    [Phone number]
3   Debtors Representing Themselves
4
5                IN THE UNITED STATES BANKRUPTCY COURT
                        [District and Division]
6
7   In the Matter of
    [Debtor's name]
8   Debtors                    ) Case No: [Bankruptcy case #]
                               ) [Special number for avoidance
9                              )  of lien motions, if any]
                               )
10                             )  Chapter 13
                               )
11
12            ORDER TO AVOID JUDICIAL LIEN ON REAL ESTATE
13       Upon request of Debtor for relief by default under Bankruptcy
14   Local Rule 9014(b)(4), and good cause appearing therefore, the motion
15   of the above-named debtor [debtor's name] to avoid the lien of respondent
16   [creditor's name] is sustained.
17       It is hereby ORDED AND DECREED that the judicial lien held by
18   [creditor's name] in and on Debtor's residential real estate at [address
19   of real estate] recorded [date lien recorded and description of lien as
20   it appears in the records] and any other amounts due under the lien be
21   hereby canceled.
22       It is further ORDERED that unless Debtor's bankruptcy case
23   is dismissed, [creditor's name] and its successors shall take all steps
24   necessary and appropriate t release the judicial lien and remove it
25   from the local judgment index.
26
27   Dated: _____
28                                       U.S. Bankruptcy Judge
```

Sample Proof of Service

```
1   [Debtor's (your) name]
    [Debtor's address]
2   [City, state, and zip code]
    [Phone number]
3   Debtors Representing Themselves
4
5                IN THE UNITED STATES BANKRUPTCY COURT
                        [District and Division]
6
7   In the Matter of
    [Debtor's name]
8   Debtors                    ) Case No: [Bankruptcy case #]
                               ) [Special number for avoidance
9                              )  of lien motions, if any]
                               )
10                             )  Chapter 13
                               )
11
12            PROOF OF SERVICE BY MAIL (Bankruptcy Rule 7004)
13       I, [name of server], declare that I am a resident of or employed in the
14   County of [insert county], State of [server's state]. My address is [server's
15   address]. I am over the age of eighteen years of age and am not a party to this
16   case.
17       On [date request served], I served the enclosed Request for Entry of Order
18   by Default on the following parties by placing true and correct copies thereof
19   enclosed in a sealed envelope with postage thereon fully prepaid, in the United
20   States Mail at [city and state], addressed as follows:
21       [name and address of lien owner]
         [name and address of trustee]
22       U.S. Trustee Region [add region #]
23       U.S. Dept. of Justice
24       [address of U.S. Trustee]
25       I declare under penalty of perjury that the foregoing is true and correct,
26   and that this declaration was executed on [date Proof of Service signed].
27
28   _____
         [name of server]
```

Scheduling a Hearing

To schedule a hearing, call the court clerk and give your name and case number. Say that you'd like to file a motion to avoid a lien and need to find out when and where the judge will hear arguments on your motion.

In some districts, the local rules require the clerk to set a hearing date for you; if so, ask for a date at least 31 days in the future, because you'll have to mail notice of your motion to the creditor at least 30 days' in advance of the hearing (unless your local rules state differently). Write down the information the clerk gives you.

If the clerk won't permit you to take care of these matters by phone, go to the court with a copy of your motion filled out. File the form and schedule the hearing. Write down the information about when and where your motion will be heard by the judge.

Step 10: Serve the Request for Entry of Default and Proposed Order on the creditor, trustee, and U.S. Trustee.

Step 11: File the Request for Entry of Default and Proposed Order with the court, including the Proof of Service as shown in the sample.

Step 12: The court should sign your proposed order and mail it back to you.

Step 13: Obtain a certified copy of the order from the court clerk. Ask the clerk what the fees are for this service.

Step 14: Even though the court's order requires the creditor to remove the lien from your records, you should independently record the certified copy of the order with the land records office where your real estate is recorded. This will remove the lien from the official records.

2. Challenging a Tax Lien

If your federal tax debt is secured, you may have a basis for challenging the lien. Quite often, the IRS makes mistakes when it records a notice of federal tax lien.

Help from a lawyer. You will need the help of a tax or bankruptcy attorney—preferably one who has experience in both areas—to challenge a tax lien.

Here are some possible grounds for asking the court to remove the lien:

- The notice of federal tax lien was never recorded, though the IRS claims it was.
- The notice of federal tax lien was recorded after the automatic stay took effect.
- The notice of federal tax lien was recorded in the wrong county—it must be recorded where you own real estate for it to attach to the real estate in that county.
- The notice of federal tax lien was recorded against the wrong assets, such as your child's house, not yours.

Even if the notice of federal tax lien was recorded correctly, you still may have a basis to fight it if:

- the lien expired—liens last only ten years, or
- the lien is based on an invalid tax assessment by the IRS.

L. Amending Your Bankruptcy Forms

You have a right to amend the bankruptcy forms you have filed at any time before your final discharge. (You can also modify your plan after it's confirmed if the judge consents.) This means that if you made a mistake on your schedules, you can correct it easily. Also, you must amend your papers if you receive certain property within 180 days after filing. (These are described in Section B, above.) Some courts have local forms to be used and rules to be followed for this purpose. Otherwise, all you do is file a corrected document, labeling it, for example, "Amended Schedule B."

If the judge says "No." Bankruptcy rules state clearly that you have a right to amend any time before your case is closed. (Bankruptcy Rule 1009.) But judges sometimes balk. For instance, some courts may not let you amend your exemption schedule after if it's too late for creditors to object to the exemptions you claimed. If you run into this problem, consult a bankruptcy attorney.

If your mistake means that notice of your bankruptcy filing must be sent to additional creditors (for instance, if you inadvertently left off a creditor who must be notified), you'll have to pay a fee to file the amendment. If your mistake doesn't require new notice (for example, you just add information about property you owned when you filed), you may not have to pay an additional filing fee. If you amend your schedules to add creditors before the meeting of creditors, you'll usually be required to provide the newly listed creditors with notice of the meeting as well as with notice of your amendment.

If you become aware of debts or property that you should have included in your papers, amending your papers will avoid any suspicion that you're trying to conceal things from the trustee. If you fail to amend your papers in this situation and someone else discovers your error, the judge may dismiss your bankruptcy petition or rule that one or more of your debts is nondischargeable.

1. Common Amendments

Here are some of the more common reasons for amendments and the forms that you may need to amend.

⚠️ **Amend all relevant forms.** Even a simple change in one form may require changes in several other forms. Exactly what forms you'll have to change depends on your court's rules.

a. Add or Delete Exempt Property on Schedule C

If you want to add or delete property from your list of exemptions, you must file an amended Schedule C. You may also need to change:

- Schedule A, if the property is real estate and not listed there
- Schedule B, if the property is personal property and not listed there
- Schedule D, if the property is collateral for a secured debt and isn't already listed
- Form 7—The Statement of Financial Affairs, if any transactions regarding the property weren't described on that form, or

- the Mailing Matrix (if your court requires one), if the exempt item is tied to a particular creditor who isn't listed.

b. Add or Delete Property on Schedules A or B

If you forgot to list some of your property on your schedules or if you receive certain property within six months after filing (see Section B, above), you may need to file amendments to:

- Schedule A, if the property is real estate
- Schedule B, if the property is personal property
- Schedule C, if the property was claimed as exempt or you want to claim it as exempt
- Schedule D, if the property is collateral for a secured debt
- Form 7—The Statement of Financial Affairs, if any transactions regarding the property haven't been described as required by that form, or
- the Mailing Matrix (if your court requires one), if the item is tied to a particular creditor who isn't listed.

c. Correct Your List of Creditors

To correct your list of creditors, you may need to amend:

- Schedule C, if the debt is secured and you plan to claim the collateral as exempt
- Schedule D, if the debt is a secured debt
- Schedule E, if the debt is a priority debt
- Schedule F, if the debt is unsecured
- Form 7—The Statement of Financial Affairs, if any transactions regarding the creditor haven't been described on that form, or
- the Mailing Matrix (if your court uses it), which contains the names and addresses of all your creditors.

2. How to File an Amendment

To make an amendment, take these steps:

Step 1: Fill out the Amendment Cover Sheet in Appendix 2, if no local form is required. Otherwise, use the local form.

Step 2: Make copies of the blank forms you need to amend.

Step 3: Check your local court rules or ask the court clerk whether you must retype the whole form to make the correction, or if you can just type the new information on another blank form. If you can't find the answer, ask a local bankruptcy lawyer or bankruptcy petition preparer. If it's acceptable to just type the new information, precede the information you're typing with "ADD:," "CHANGE:," or "DELETE:" as appropriate. At the bottom of the form, type "AMENDED" in capital letters.

Step 4: Call or visit the court and ask what order it requires the papers in and how many copies it requires for amendments.

Step 5: Make the required number of copies, plus one copy for yourself, one for the trustee, and one for any creditor affected by your amendment.

Step 6: Have a friend or relative mail, first class, a copy of your amended papers to the bankruptcy trustee and to any creditor affected by your amendment.

Step 7: Enter the name and complete address of every new creditor affected by your amendment on the Proof of Service by Mail (a copy is in Appendix 2). Also enter the name and address of the bankruptcy trustee. Then have the person who mailed the Amendments sign and date the Proof of Service.

Step 8: Mail or take the original Amendment and Proof of Service and copies to the bankruptcy court. Enclose or take a money order for the filing fee, if required. If you use the mail, enclose a self-addressed envelope so the clerk can return a file-stamped set of papers to you.

If the meeting of creditors occurred before you file your amendment, the court is likely to schedule another one.

M. Filing a Change of Address

If you move while your bankruptcy case is still open, you must give the court, the trustee, and your creditors your new address. Here's how to do it:

Step 1: Make one or two photocopies of the blank Notice of Change of Address and Proof of Service forms in Appendix 2.

Step 2: Fill in the Change of Address form.

Step 3: Make one photocopy for the trustee, one for your records, and one for each creditor listed in Schedules D, E, and F or the Mailing Matrix.

Step 4: Have a friend or relative mail a copy of the Notice of Change of Address to the trustee and to each creditor.

Step 5: Complete the Proof of Service by Mail form, listing the bankruptcy trustee and the names and addresses of all creditors the Notice was mailed to. Have the person who did the mailing sign it.

Step 6: File the original Notice of Change of Address and original Proof of Service with the bankruptcy court.

N. Dealing With Creditors' Motions

Most Chapter 13 cases progress fairly smoothly, and you'll probably be able to work out minor glitches as they arise. On rare occasions, however, a creditor throws a monkey wrench into the works and files a motion which, if successful, could mean the dismissal of your case.

Take heart in knowing even when a creditor raises these issues, few Chapter 13 trustees want to deal with them. Most Chapter 13 trustees handle thousands of cases a year. They do not want to get involved in drawn-out court battles unless the result is likely to have an impact on many other debtors in your district. So the trustee will encourage you and the creditor to settle the matter without a hearing. Some trustees even discourage creditors from filing a lot of motions (and creditors need to stay on the trustee's good side).

You will have a certain period of time to file a written response. If you don't respond, you will automatically lose the motion. You may need to consult with a bankruptcy lawyer to help you prepare the response.

You should also appear at the hearing. This is your opportunity to explain your position to the judge.

Help from a lawyer. You will need the help of a bankruptcy attorney if you want or need to file a response to a creditor's motion.

1. Objections to Your Eligibility for Chapter 13

A creditor might file a motion claiming that your debts exceed the Chapter 13 bankruptcy limits—$307,675 of unsecured debts and $922,975 of secured debts. (These limits are covered in detail in Ch. 1, *Should You File for Chapter 13 Bankruptcy?*, Section A.) A creditor may raise this kind of objection if your liability for a debt hasn't yet been determined, and the creditor is afraid you'll wipe it out in bankruptcy.

> EXAMPLE: A few years ago, you and a partner started a business. It failed, you both lost a lot of money, and your ex-partner blames you. He has been threatening to sue you for the money he claims you are responsible for him losing. During your business's lean times, you missed several house payments, didn't pay your personal income taxes, and charged up your credit cards. You have filed for Chapter 13 bankruptcy, and your plan proposes to pay only 10% on your unsecured debts. Your ex-partner objects, claiming that you owe him at least $400,000, which exceeds the Chapter 13 limit for unsecured debts.

2. Motion for "Adequate Protection"

Any secured creditor will probably insist that you agree to protect the collateral against loss, damage, or general depreciation. This is called providing "adequate protection." You must do this in case you can't finish your Chapter 13 plan and later want to give the property back to the creditor. The protection you provide could be additional liens or proof of insurance. If you refuse to provide the creditor with sufficient protection, the creditor may file a motion with the court, asking the court to order you to protect the property. So you might as well comply and avoid a court fight that's a clear loser.

3. Motion for Relief From the Automatic Stay

When you file for bankruptcy, the automatic stay prohibits virtually all creditors from taking any action directed toward collecting the debts you owe them until the court says otherwise. (See Section A, above.)

In a Chapter 13 bankruptcy, the automatic stay bars your creditors from going after the property and wages you acquire after you file your petition and before your confirmation hearing. The court almost always lifts (removes) the stay at the end of the confirmation hearing, because your creditors are now bound by your plan. If the confirmation hearing is delayed, your creditors may ask that the stay be lifted early. The court is likely to grant such a motion in any of the following situations:

- You refuse to provide adequate protection to a secured creditor. (See Section 2, above.)
- Your filing is obviously in bad faith or your plan is totally unfeasible. (See Section G, above.)
- You have no equity in an item of secured property, and the creditor (who wants to repossess it) claims you don't need the item to carry out your Chapter 13 plan. You may be able to get around this if:
  - Your plan includes payments on the secured claim.
  - You can show that you do need the property to generate income—for example, if it's a car, you could argue that you need to drive to work, and there is no adequate alternative.
  - The property is your family residence. Many courts rule that the family home is always necessary. Some courts rule otherwise, however, if the creditor shows that comparable housing is available to you for less money. You would need to emphasize to the court your children's ties to their school, your proximity to your job, and the cost of getting new housing and moving. ■

After Your Plan Is Approved

Once the court has approved your repayment plan, you should be in for smooth sailing as long as you make your monthly payments. If an unforeseen problem arises, and you think you're going to have trouble making a payment, notify the trustee as quickly as you can. The trustee wants you to succeed and will help you over the rough spots.

You may be wondering why the trustee cares whether you are successful with your Chapter 13 plan. The answer, of course, is money. Remember, the trustee gets a cut of everything he or she pays to creditors under your plan. If instead of completing your Chapter 13 plan you convert it to Chapter 7 (or dismiss it), the trustee's income from your case will be cut off. Only if you convert to Chapter 7 and have nonexempt assets that the trustee can sell would the trustee continue to make money off your case.

A. Making Plan Payments

By the time your plan is confirmed, you will have made at least one plan payment, and probably more. The hardest part of Chapter 13 bankruptcy is making those payments.

1. Prepare for Postconfirmation Creditor Claims

You probably feel like you are stretching as far as you can to make your plan payments every month and still have enough to take care of your day-to-day needs. But sometimes it's a good idea to reach even a little deeper into your pocket and come up with a few extra dollars to add to each payment. Here's why.

Sometimes creditors file claims with the bankruptcy court after the judge approves your repayment plan at the confirmation hearing. Unless you regularly ask the trustee for a list of claims filed by creditors, you won't know who has filed claims.

Claims filed after your plan is confirmed can cause problems, for a number of reasons:

- If you forgot about a creditor (didn't list the creditor in your papers), but the creditor somehow hears about your bankruptcy and files a claim, the trustee will probably pay that creditor.

- If a creditor files a claim for more than the amount you think you owe, the trustee could end up paying out more than you had anticipated, especially if your plan pays each creditor a percentage of their claim, not a set dollar amount.

- If a creditor files a claim for payment of a secured debt (meaning you'll have to pay it in full) and you mistakenly thought it was unsecured, the trustee will probably pay that creditor more than you planned. This is often the situation with Sears—someone charges items on a Sears card and assumes the debt is unsecured. Sears's paperwork states, however, that Sears takes a security interest in all items paid for using its card, so those debts are secured.

To avoid underpaying your creditors in your Chapter 13 plan, it's a good idea to include an extra few dollars ($5, $10, $25—whatever you can afford) in each payment. Keep this up until the time for making claims has passed. If you're paying the trustee directly, tell the trustee why you're adding a few dollars. If the court has issued an income deduction order, send the trustee a few extra dollars yourself each month.

If no creditor files a claim you hadn't anticipated, you will simply complete your plan early. On the other hand, if you don't add the money and creditors you hadn't thought of do file claims, you will probably still owe some money at the end of your Chapter 13 case. Either you will have to pay a lump sum to make up what you still owe or you will have to ask the court to extend your plan if it was less than five years.

To keep track of the new claims, you can monitor your case file at the bankruptcy court during the 90 days following the meeting of the creditors (the deadline for creditors to file proofs of claims). If you disagree with any of the claims filed, you will have to file a motion objecting to the claim. (See Ch. 9, *After You File Your Case*, Section J, for more information on objecting to a claim.)

2. If Your Income Increases

If the bankruptcy trustee thinks you've had an unanticipated increase in income that could be used to pay your creditors, the trustee might ask you to complete a financial questionnaire or submit copies of your tax return. Some trustees require this of Chapter 13 debtors once a year as a matter of course.

If your financial condition improves to the point that you could afford to pay more to your unsecured creditors (assuming they are not receiving 100% of what you owe), the trustee or an unsecured creditor may file a motion with the bankruptcy court. The motion will request that the court order you to increase each payment, pay a lump sum amount (especially if you've inherited valuable property or won the lottery), or extend your plan. (Section C, below, covers modifications in more detail.) The bankruptcy court will most likely grant the motion.

If You Get a Windfall

If you win the lottery, get a substantial raise, receive an inheritance, or if your house goes way up in value, you may be able to dismiss your case and pay off your debts outside of bankruptcy. But keep in mind that the interest and sometimes the penalties on your debts that stopped accruing while you were in bankruptcy can be added back when you dismiss your case. In addition, before assuming you can use the equity in your home, of course, apply for and obtain the loan. Don't dismiss your case and then apply for the loan. If you are rejected, you'll just have to refile your bankruptcy.

B. Selling Property

Certain property remains under the control of the bankruptcy court even after your plan is approved. (See Ch. 9, *After You File Your Case*, Section B.) If you want to sell any of this property, the court or, in some cases, the trustee will have to approve the sale. And your unsecured creditors might object if after selling the property and paying off the liens, you'd pocket cash rather than use it to pay your unsecured creditors.

C. Modifying Your Plan When Problems Come Up

Chapter 13 bankruptcy isn't easy. You must live under a strict budget for at least three years and possibly as many as five. Problems are bound to arise. Fortunately,

the Chapter 13 bankruptcy system has procedures built into it to handle the disruptions. Any time after your plan is confirmed, you, the trustee, or an unsecured creditor who filed a claim can file a motion with the court, asking permission to modify the plan. (11 U.S.C. § 1329.)

This section discusses four common situations in which you might need to modify your plan. If you think you want to modify your plan, call the trustee and ask for help in filing your motion and scheduling your hearing before the judge. Your creditors will have to be sent notice of your motion at least 20 days before the hearing date. (Bankruptcy Rule 2002(a)(6).) Ask the trustee if you need to send the notice or if the trustee will do it.

The court hearing on modification of the plan is just like the original confirmation hearing. The rules and procedures are discussed in Ch. 9, *After You File Your Case*, Section H.

Your modified plan cannot last more than five years from the date your plan originally began.

1. You Miss a Payment

If the trustee doesn't receive a plan payment, expect a phone call. Sometimes, the problem will be easy to solve—the payment got lost in the mail, your employer forgot to send it (if there is an income deduction order), or you changed jobs and forgot to change the income deduction order.

If you missed the payment because you are struggling to make ends meet, resolving the problem may be more complicated. But don't lose heart. If the problem looks temporary, and you are several months or years into your plan, the trustee may suggest that you modify your plan to do any of the following:

- skip a few payments altogether, meaning your unsecured creditors would receive less than you originally proposed
- skip a few payments now and extend your plan to make them up, assuming your plan is for less than five years
- make a lump sum payment to make up the payments you've missed, or
- increase several payments to cover the payments you missed.

If the problem looks likely to continue, or it happens very early in your Chapter 13 case, the trustee is less likely to support a modification of your plan. Instead, the trustee (or a creditor) is likely to file a motion to have your case dismissed or require you to convert to a Chapter 7 case as an alternative. (See Section E, below.)

If you file a motion to modify your plan because you've missed some payments, a creditor may ask that the modified plan contain what is called a "drop dead" clause. Such a clause provides that if you miss another payment, your case will automatically convert to Chapter 7 bankruptcy or be dismissed by the court. Many courts include drop dead clauses in modified plans.

Your plan payment isn't the only payment you might miss. If the court approved your request to make direct payments to certain creditors (such as a mortgage lender) and you miss a payment, the creditor will run to the court. Most likely, the creditor will file a motion to have the automatic stay lifted, which would let the creditor go after any property you've acquired since filing for bankruptcy. Alternatively, the creditor may ask the court to dismiss your case or, as an alternative, convert it to a Chapter 7 case. If it's early in your plan and you haven't missed any other payments, ask the court for permission to modify your plan to pay the new arrears immediately.

2. Your Disposable Income Goes Down

You wouldn't have filed for Chapter 13 bankruptcy if you hadn't had debt problems in your past—perhaps because of job losses or reduced work hours. Filing for bankruptcy doesn't make those kind of problems go away.

If your income goes down, you or your spouse suffer a serious illness, go on maternity leave, or incur an extraordinary expense, call the trustee. The trustee is likely to suggest that you suspend payments for a month or two. You can make up the difference by modifying your plan to:

- make a lump sum payment when your income goes back up
- extend your plan, if it is for less than five years, or
- decrease the amount or percentage that a certain class of creditor receives—for example, you might have originally proposed to pay your

general unsecured creditors 75% of what you owe but will now file a modified plan that calls for them to get only 45%.

Creditors rarely object to a short suspension in payments, and bankruptcy courts routinely grant those modifications. If you propose a longer-term suspension, however, your secured creditors may object, especially if the collateral is decreasing in value. You may have to continue your payments on secured debts and suspend only the unsecured portion for a while.

3. You Need to Replace Your Car

A lot can go wrong with a car during the three to five years you're paying into your Chapter 13 plan—especially if you bought a used car before you filed to minimize your expenses. Chapter 13 trustees often hear from debtors whose cars have died or are on their last legs. This situation raises several issues in a Chapter 13 bankruptcy case.

Taking out a new loan. Let's say your car dies, you need another one, and you want to take out a loan to pay for it. You file a motion to modify your plan to include payments for the new loan. Will the court confirm the new plan? The court is likely to say "yes" if you *must* have the car to complete your plan—for example, you're a salesperson. If, however, the car is just a convenience, the payments will significantly increase your monthly expenses, and you've had trouble making your plan payments, the court will probably say "no."

For most people, the need for a car isn't all or nothing. In that case, the court will probably allow you to take out the loan if the effect is to lower your bills (for example, you were still making payments on your previous car and the loan will reduce your payments) or to increase your income (for instance, it would take two hours each way to get to work by public transit and only 35 minutes by car, so with a car you can get paid for three more hours' work a day).

Giving back a wrecked car. Now let's assume that after your plan is confirmed, your car is wrecked or won't run. You want to give the car back to the lender and modify your plan to treat the balance due (called a deficiency) as an unsecured claim. Several courts have allowed this. (*In re Hernandez*, 282 B.R. 200

(Bankr. S.D. Tex. 2002; *In re Knappen*, 281 B.R. 714 (Bankr. D. N.M. 2002); *In re Townley*, 256 B.R. 697 (Bankr. D. N.J. 2000); *In re Rincon*, 133 B.R. 594 (N.D. Tex. 1991).)

Several other courts and the Sixth Circuit Court of Appeals have ruled that a secured creditor cannot be reclassified into an unsecured creditor after a plan has been confirmed, and that the debtor still must pay the full balance owed the lender. (*In re Nolan*, 232 F.3d 528 (6th Cir. 2000); *In re Wilcox*, 295 B.R. 155 (Bankr. W.D. Okla. 2003); *In re Meeks*, 237 B.R. 856 (Bankr. M.D. Fla. 1999); *In re Coleman*, 231 B.R. 397 (Bankr. S.D. Ga. 1999); *In re Dunlap*, 215 B.R. 867 (Bankr. E.D. Ark. 1997); *In re Holt*, 136 B.R. 260 (Bankr. D. Idaho 1992); and *In re Abercrombie*, 39 B.R. 178 (N.D. Ga. 1984).

A court might look at how you got into the situation. If your negligence or recklessness caused the problem, the court may be more inclined to deny modification of your plan.

What happens to insurance proceeds. If your car was all paid off and is damaged in an accident, you get any insurance money. The court will probably want you to use that money to get the new car you need. If your car wasn't paid off, the insurance money will go to pay off your lender. If the insurance proceeds exceed what you owe the lender under your plan, you get the difference. Remember, once the court determines the amount a secured creditor is entitled to get under the plan, that's all the creditor gets.

4. You Incur New Debt

If you fail to pay debts you incur after your plan is confirmed, you can amend your plan so these creditors are paid through your plan. You may have anticipated this by creating a class of postpetition creditors in your plan. If so, your plan should specify that these creditors receive 100% of what they are owed, plus interest. If you didn't create such a class, you'll have to handle postpetition debts as they arise.

No matter what your plan provides, your postpetition creditors will need to file a claim with the trustee in order to get paid through your plan.

a. Your Plan Includes a Class of Postpetition Creditors

If your plan includes 100% payment of your postpetition debts, your postpetition creditors are unlikely to object to being paid through the trustee.

If, however, the creditor disagrees with the terms of your plan or you miss a plan payment, the creditor might object. If this happens, you will have to modify your plan to handle the creditor's objection. If the creditor is still not satisfied, the creditor might file a motion with the bankruptcy court asking the court to lift the automatic stay. If the court grants the motion, the creditor would be allowed to go after your postpetition property and income for payment.

EXAMPLE: For the first year and one-half of your plan, you will be paying your priority tax debt and your mortgage arrears. Not until month 19 will the trustee pay your unsecured creditors, including a class of postpetition creditors. Three months into your plan, the court lets you incur a medical debt. The doctor objects to being paid through the plan because the first payment won't come for at least 16 months. You will probably have to amend your plan to pay your tax debt, mortgage arrears, and the medical debt during the first several months of your plan.

b. Your Plan Does Not Include a Class of Postpetition Creditors

If your plan does not include a class of postpetition creditors, and you want to pay a new creditor through your plan, you will have to modify your plan. Sometimes, postpetition creditors themselves file a motion to be included in a modified Chapter 13 plan. The motion is likely to be granted.

If you don't modify your plan to include postpetition creditors to whom you default, the creditor may be able to take collection efforts against property you acquired after filing for bankruptcy.

D. Attempts to Revoke Your Confirmation

If a creditor or the trustee thinks you obtained your confirmation fraudulently—for example, because you used a false name, address, or Social Security number—one of them may file something called an "adversary proceeding" asking the court to revoke your confirmation. (11 U.S.C. § 1330.) This is extremely rare. An adversary proceeding to revoke a confirmation must be filed within 180 days of the confirmation.

An adversary proceeding is much more formal than a motion. It creates an entirely new lawsuit, separate from your bankruptcy case, and proceeds like any other lawsuit. You will need a lawyer to help you.

The bankruptcy court won't revoke your confirmation because of fraud unless it finds that:

- you made a material (significant) false statement in your papers, in a deposition, or in court
- you either knew the statement was false or made the statement with reckless disregard to its truth
- you intended to induce the court into relying on the statement, and
- the court did rely on the statement.

E. If You Cannot Complete Your Plan

Despite your best efforts to keep a handle on your finances and make your regular plan payments, you may come to a point where you realize that it's impossible for you to complete your plan. You won't be alone—a significant percentage of Chapter 13 debtors eventually find themselves in this position. If it happens to you, you have three options: dismiss your case, convert it to a Chapter 7 bankruptcy, or ask the court to grant you a hardship discharge.

1. Dismiss Your Case

Except if the bankruptcy court believes that you filed for bankruptcy in bad faith (see Ch. 9, Section G1), you have the absolute right to dismiss your Chapter 13 bankruptcy case at any time, as long as it did not start out as a different type of case which you converted to Chapter 13 bankruptcy. You dismiss your case by filing a simple motion with the court. (The court may have a preprinted dismissal form you can use; if it does not,

ask the trustee for help.) There won't be any court hearing, and your motion will automatically be granted. A creditor or the trustee can also file a motion to have your case dismissed. Approximately 50% of all Chapter 13 bankruptcy cases filed are eventually dismissed.

If your case started as a different kind of bankruptcy and you converted to Chapter 13 bankruptcy, you have to ask the court for permission to dismiss it. The court may deny your request—and order you to convert to Chapter 7 bankruptcy—if it feels that you are abusing the bankruptcy system. Or, it may grant your request, but sanction (fine) you or issue an order barring you from filing for bankruptcy again for a certain period of time.

If your case is dismissed, there are several important consequences:

- You cannot refile for bankruptcy—Chapter 13, Chapter 7, or any other kind—within 180 days if you dismissed your bankruptcy case because a creditor filed a motion with the bankruptcy court asking for relief from the automatic stay.
- All liens on your property are reinstated.
- All money you have paid the trustee that has not yet been disbursed to your creditors will be returned to you, less the trustee's expenses.
- The automatic stay ends, meaning your creditors are free to go after you and your assets for payment.
- Interest (and in some cases penalties) that stopped accruing during your bankruptcy will be added on to your debts.

If you change your mind and decide you want your case to proceed, you can file a motion with the bankruptcy court within ten days of the dismissal asking that your case be reinstated. Unless you have a history of filing and dismissing, or you've had serious problems making the payments under this plan, the court will probably grant your motion.

2. Convert Your Case to Chapter 7 Bankruptcy

You have the absolute right to convert your Chapter 13 bankruptcy case to a Chapter 7 bankruptcy case at any time, as long as you haven't received a Chapter 7 discharge within the previous six years. (Chapter 7 bankruptcy is discussed in Ch. 1, *Should You File for Chapter 13 Bankruptcy?*, Section B.)

You convert your case by filing a simple motion with the court. (The court may have a preprinted form you can use; if it does not, ask the trustee for help.) There won't be a court hearing, and your motion will automatically be granted. A creditor or the trustee can also file a motion to have your case converted. (11 U.S.C. § 1307.) Approximately 15% of all Chapter 13 bankruptcy cases convert to Chapter 7 bankruptcy.

If you want to convert your case, ask the trustee whether or not you must notify your creditors. When you convert your case, all money you have paid the trustee which has not yet been disbursed to your creditors will be returned to you, less the trustee's expenses.

In addition, the bankruptcy forms you filed for your Chapter 13 case will usually become a part of your new case. (These are the forms in Ch. 6 of this book.) A few bankruptcy courts, however, require that you file an entire new set of schedules, even if nothing has changed. Within 30 days after you convert, you must file one additional bankruptcy form called the Statement of Intention. It tells the court what you plan to do with your secured debts. You will also have to attend a new meeting of creditors.

Because all debts you incurred after filing your Chapter 13 case can be discharged in your Chapter 7 case (if they are otherwise dischargeable), you must amend the appropriate forms:

- Schedule D (if you've incurred new secured debts)
- Schedule E (if you've incurred new unsecured priority debts)
- Schedule F (if you've incurred new unsecured nonpriority debts)
- Schedule G (if you entered into any new contracts or leases), and
- Schedule H (if you have new codebtors).
(11 U.S.C. § 348(d).)

If, in your Chapter 13 case, the court established a value for certain items of property or determined the amount of a secured claim, those values and amounts will apply in the converted case. (11 U.S.C. § 348(f)(1)(B).)

Some courts determine your exemptions based on the date you filed your Chapter 13 bankruptcy, while other courts determine them as of the date of conversion. In the latter situation, if you've acquired nonexempt property after filing your Chapter 13 case, you will be

at risk of losing it in your Chapter 7 case. In addition, if the court determines that your conversion to Chapter 7 bankruptcy is in bad faith, the court can order that the new property be included in your Chapter 7 bankruptcy estate. (11 U.S.C. § 348(f)(2).)

If your creditors have filed proofs of claim, those claims carry over to your Chapter 7 case. If you dismiss your Chapter 13 case and refile a Chapter 7 case, your creditors will have to file new claims, assuming you have assets to be distributed. Some people use this strategy (dismissing one case and refiling a second one) with the hope that creditors won't file new claims and therefore won't be paid in the Chapter 7 case.

Resource for Chapter 7 bankruptcy. *How to File for Chapter 7 Bankruptcy*, by Stephen Elias, Albin Renauer, and Robin Leonard (Nolo), contains detailed information on Chapter 7 bankruptcy. It includes the forms and instructions you will need to file the additional form (the "Statement of Intention") and to amend the forms you've already filed.

3. Seek a Hardship Discharge

If you cannot complete your Chapter 13 repayment plan, you can file a motion with the bankruptcy court asking for a hardship discharge. (11 U.S.C. § 1328(b).) The court will grant your request only if three conditions are met:

1. Your failure to complete the payments under your plan is due to circumstances "for which you should not justly be held accountable." Your burden is to show the maximum possible misery and the worst of awfuls—that is, more than just a temporary job loss or temporary physical disability. Permanence of the condition is usually key; you may need to bring medical evidence to court.

2. Based on what you have already paid into the plan, your unsecured creditors have received at least the amount they would have received if you had filed for Chapter 7—that is, the value of your nonexempt property. (This is a hard condition to meet unless you have little or no nonexempt property.)

3. Modification of your plan is not practical. To meet this requirement, you do not have to file a motion for modification and lose it; you just have

to show the bankruptcy court that you wouldn't be able to make payments under a modified plan.

If the court grants your motion for a hardship discharge, only your unsecured nonpriority dischargeable debts are discharged. You won't be eliminating arrears on your secured debts or any of the other debts listed below. (11 U.S.C. §§ 1322(b)(5), 523(a).)

Nondischargeable debts. Extensive information on the nondischargeable debts listed above is contained in *How to File for Chapter 7 Bankruptcy*, by Stephen Elias, Albin Renauer, and Robin Leonard (Nolo).

F. When You Complete Your Plan

It's quite an accomplishment and something to be proud of—to stick with a Chapter 13 plan to the end. After you have made all of your payments under your plan, the court grants a "full payment" discharge. (11 U.S.C. § 1328(a).) In most courts, the trustee simply files the discharge order on behalf of the court after determining that all payments have been made. In other courts, you must ask the trustee (by phone is fine) to file the discharge order.

1. Debts Covered by the Discharge

Your Chapter 13 discharge wipes out the balance owed on all of your debts, as long as your plan contains some provision describing the debt and the debt does not fall into one of these categories:

- Long-term obligations for which the last payment is still due—that is, it will be paid after you've made the final payment on your plan.
- Nondischargeable debts, described in Ch. 2, *An Overview of Chapter 13 Bankruptcy*, Section D.
- Debts you incurred after filing your Chapter 13 case, if the creditor was not paid or was only partially paid through the plan.

2. The Discharge Hearing

After struggling for years to repay your debts, the long-awaited end of your bankruptcy case may be a little anticlimactic. The court may hold a brief hearing,

---

Debts Not Included in a Hardship Discharge

Debts Generally Not Included in the Hardship Discharge:

- priority debts
- secured debts
- debts you didn't list in your bankruptcy papers
- student loans
- most federal, state, and local taxes and any money borrowed or charged on a credit card to pay those taxes
- child support, alimony, and debts in the nature of support
- fines imposed in a criminal-type proceeding
- debts resulting from intoxicated driving
- debts for dues or special assessments owed to a condominium or cooperative association
- debts you couldn't discharge in a previous bankruptcy that was dismissed due to fraud or misfeasance.

Debts Not Included If the Creditor Successfully Objects in Court:

- debts incurred on the basis of fraudulent acts, including using a credit card when payment is impossible
- debts from willful or malicious injury to a person or property
- debts from embezzlement, larceny, or breach of trust (fiduciary duty)
- debts (other than support) arising from a marital settlement agreement or divorce decree.

If you have a debt that falls into the second category, your best approach is to do nothing and hope the creditor does the same. If the creditor does object, the court will examine the circumstances under which you incurred the debt to determine whether or not it can be legally eliminated. You should respond if you want the debt to be included in your hardship discharge. If the debt is large enough to justify the fees you'll have to pay, hire a bankruptcy attorney to handle it, or do some legal research yourself. See Ch. 12, *Help Beyond the Book.*

called a discharge hearing, and require you to attend. At the hearing, the judge explains the effects of discharging your debts in bankruptcy and may lecture you about staying clear of debt.

Few courts, however, schedule a discharge hearing in Chapter 13 cases. Whether or not you must attend a discharge hearing, you'll receive a copy of your discharge order from the court within about four weeks after you complete your payments. If you don't, call the trustee. Make several photocopies of the order and keep them in a safe place. If it's necessary, send copies to creditors who attempt to collect their debt after your case is over or to credit bureaus that still list you as owing a discharged debt.

3. Ending the Income Deduction Order

The trustee will probably remember to stop your income deduction order after you've made your last payment. If, however, the trustee forgets, you may need to call and remind him.

4. Debtor Rehabilitation Program

A few Chapter 13 bankruptcy courts have created Debtor Rehabilitation/Credit Re-establishment programs. The purpose is to reward people who choose Chapter 13 bankruptcy instead of Chapter 7 bankruptcy and who succeed in completing their Chapter 13 cases.

If you have paid off a high percentage of your unsecured debts (often 75% or more), you may attend money management seminars and apply for credit from certain creditors.

In the typical program, the court staff includes a person called a "credit liaison." This person will help you:

- acquire, review, and correct your credit file—in particular, to get your credit file to show that you completed a Chapter 13 bankruptcy in which you paid back a high percentage of your debts
- set up a budget
- analyze your ability to repay new debts
- understand the different types of credit
- identify possible sources of credit and credit limits
- fill out credit applications
- obtain information to support your application, such as your Chapter 13 payment history and completed plan
- prepare for any in-person interview with a creditor (for a car loan, for example), and
- understand how creditors make their decisions about extending credit.

Ask the trustee whether your court has a rehabilitation program. If it doesn't, find out from the trustee if a nearby bankruptcy court does in which you might participate. If there's nothing nearby, you'll have to take your own steps to rebuild your credit. (See Ch. 11, *Life After Bankruptcy*, Section A.) ■

11

Life After Bankruptcy

Congratulations! After you receive your final discharge and your case is closed, you can get on with your life and enjoy the fresh start that bankruptcy offers. This chapter explains how you can start to rebuild your credit, and how to deal with any problems that come up.

A. Rebuilding Your Credit

A bankruptcy filing can legally remain on your credit record for ten years from the date you filed your papers, although most credit bureaus remove a Chapter 13 bankruptcy filing after seven years. (Major creditors, such as banks and department stores, have pressured bureaus to remove the notations after seven years as an incentive to debtors to choose Chapter 13 bankruptcy over Chapter 7 bankruptcy.) Many creditors disregard Chapter 13 bankruptcy after about five years.

In about two years, you can probably rebuild your credit to the point that you won't be turned down for a major credit card or loan. Most creditors look for steady employment and a history, since bankruptcy, of making and paying for purchases on credit.

Resource for rebuilding credit. For more information on rebuilding your credit—including obtaining a copy of your credit file, requesting that the credit bureau correct mistakes, contacting creditors directly for help in cleaning up your credit, and getting positive information into your credit file—see *Credit Repair*, by Robin Leonard (Nolo).

Using a check card instead of a credit card. Many people mistakenly believe that they have to have a regular credit card to do simple things like charge a meal in a restaurant, get gas at the pump, or buy a book on the Internet. In fact, simply by maintaining a checking account with your bank, you will usually be issued a "check card" that doubles as a Visa or MasterCard—except that your ability to charge things on the card is limited by how much you have in your bank account when the card is used. Alas, the check card doesn't work for everything. Car rental companies usually require a major credit card and won't accept your check card unless you post a sizable deposit. Also, check cards make it easier to overdraw your account, often resulting in steep penalties.

Don't Take on Too Much Debt Too Soon

Habitual overspending can be just as hard to overcome as excessive gambling or drinking. If you think you may be a compulsive spender, one of the worst things you might do is rebuild your credit. Instead, you need to get a handle on your spending habits.

Debtors Anonymous, a 12-step support program similar to Alcoholics Anonymous, has programs nationwide. If a Debtors Anonymous group or a therapist recommends that you stay out of the credit system for a while, follow that advice. Even if you don't feel you're a compulsive spender, paying as you spend may still be the way to go.

To find a Debtors Anonymous meeting close by, go to www.debtorsanonymous.org or call 781-453-2743.

1. Create a Budget

The first step in rebuilding your credit is to create a budget. Making a budget will help you control impulses to overspend and help you start saving money—an essential part of rebuilding your credit.

Before you try to limit how much you spend, take some time to find out exactly how much money you spend now, using a Daily Expenses form like the one shown below. Make copies of the form, which is in Appendix 2, and fill one out for 30 days. Write down every cent you spend—50¢ for the paper, $2 for your morning coffee and muffin, $5 for lunch, $3 for the bridge or tunnel toll, and so on. If you omit any money spent, your picture of how much you spend, and your budget, will be inaccurate. If you're married or combine your finances with someone, make sure each person fills out the Daily Expense forms.

At the end of the 30 days, review your sheets. Are you surprised? Are you impulsively buying things, or do you tend to buy the same types of things consistently? If the latter, you'll have an easier time planning a budget than if your spending varies tremendously from day to day.

Think about the changes you need to make to put away a few dollars at the end of every week. Even if you think there's nothing to spare, try to set a small goal—even $5 a week. It will help. If you spend $2

Daily Expenses

Date: 8/1

Item	Cost
coffee	1.20
paper	.35
lunch	6.16
toll	3.00
rent	650.00
Daily total	844.89

Date: 8/2

Item	Cost
coffee	2.75
paper	.35
toll	3.00
CD	17.58
Daily total	23.68

Date: 8/3

Item	Cost
coffee	1.20
paper	.35
lunch	3.00
toll	3.00
hardware store—light switches	17.11
fabric store—sewing gadgets	19.06
Daily total	43.72

Date: 8/4

Item	Cost
brunch	11.50
haircut	25.00
movie rental	2.99
Daily total	39.49

each day on coffee and a muffin, that adds up to $10 per week and at least $40 per month. Eating breakfast at home might save you most of that amount. If you buy the newspaper at the corner store every day, consider subscribing. A subscription doesn't involve extending credit; if you don't pay, they simply stop delivering.

Once you understand your spending habits and identify what changes you need to make, you're ready to make a budget. At the top of a sheet of paper, write down your monthly net income—that is, the amount you bring home after taxes and other mandatory deductions. At the left, list everything you spend money on in a month, any investments you plan to make (including into a savings or money market account), and any nondischargeable or other debts you make payments on. To the right of each item, write down the amount of money you spend, deposit, or pay each month. Finally, total up the amount. If it exceeds your monthly income, make some changes—eliminate or reduce expenditures for nonnecessities—and start over. Once your budget is final, stick to it.

2. Keep Your Credit File Accurate

When you apply for credit, the creditor will contact a credit reporting agency (also called credit bureau) and request a copy of your credit file. The information in the file—and the numerical score the agency will compute from that information—is primarily what a creditor uses to decide whether to grant or deny your credit request. In addition, some insurance companies, landlords, and employers obtain credit reports when evaluating the potential insurance policyholder, tenant, or employee.

So that creditors and other users of credit files see you in the best light, you want to keep incorrect and outdated information out of your credit file, and get current positive information into your file.

Start by obtaining a copy of your file from one of the "big three" credit reporting agencies or, if available in your state, the centralized resource for reports from any of the three (see "Centralized Credit Reporting System in the Works," below):

- Equifax, 800-685-1111; www.equifax.com
- Experian, 888-EXPERIAN; www.experian.com
- TransUnion, 800-888-4213, www.transunion.com.

Avoiding Financial Problems

These nine rules, suggested by people who have been through bankruptcy, will help you stay out of financial hot water.

1. Create a realistic budget and stick to it.
2. Don't impulse buy. When you see something you hadn't planned to purchase, go home and think it over. It's unlikely you'll return to the store and buy it.
3. Avoid sales unless you are looking for something you absolutely need. Buying a $500 item on sale for $400 isn't a $100 savings if you didn't need the item in the first place—it's spending $400 unnecessarily.
4. Get medical insurance. You can't avoid medical emergencies, but living without medical insurance is an invitation to financial ruin.
5. Charge items only if you could pay for them now. Don't charge based on future income—sometimes that income doesn't materialize.
6. Avoid large house payments. Obligate yourself only for what you can now afford and increase your mortgage payments only as your income increases. Again, don't obligate yourself based on future income that you might not have.
7. Think long and hard before agreeing to cosign or guarantee a loan for someone. Your signature obligates you as if you were the primary borrower. You can't be sure that the other person will pay.
8. If possible, avoid joint obligations with people who have questionable spending habits. If you incur a joint debt, you're probably liable for it all if the other person defaults.
9. Avoid high-risk investments, such as speculative real estate, penny stocks, and junk bonds. Invest conservatively in things such as certificates of deposit, money market funds, and government bonds. And never invest more than you can afford to lose.

Centralized Credit Reporting Service in the Works

Obtaining a copy of your credit report is about to get much easier and cheaper. In 2004, the Federal Trade Commission (FTC) approved a rule allowing consumers to receive a free copy of their credit report from each of the major credit reporting agencies every 12 months. (While some states already mandate that credit reports be provided free of charge, consumers in most states have, up to now, had to pay a nominal fee, usually $8–$9, for the report.) If you stagger your requests to the different agencies, you can actually get three credit reports over the course of a year.

The FTC's ruling forced the three major credit bureaus, Experian, TransUnion, and Equifax, to create a "centralized source" for accepting credit report requests. The service will be accessible via a toll-free number (877-322-8228), a dedicated website (www.annualcreditreport.com), and a postal address (Credit Report Service, P.O. Box 105281, Atlanta, GA 30348-5281).

The centralized source is already available to consumers in some states. It is being rolled out from west to east over a period of nine months, as follows:

December 1, 2004: Alaska, Arizona, California, Colorado, Hawaii, Idaho, Montana, Nevada, New Mexico, Oregon, Utah, Washington, and Wyoming.

March 1, 2005: Illinois, Indiana, Iowa, Kansas, Michigan, Minnesota, Missouri, Nebraska, North Dakota, Ohio, South Dakota, and Wisconsin.

June 1, 2005: Alabama, Arkansas, Florida, Georgia, Kentucky, Louisiana, Mississippi, Oklahoma, South Carolina, Tennessee, and Texas.

September 1, 2005: Connecticut, Delaware, District of Columbia, Maine, Maryland, Massachusetts, New Hampshire, New Jersey, New York, North Carolina, Pennsylvania, Rhode Island, Vermont, Virginia, West Virginia, Puerto Rico, and all U.S. territories.

You will need to send the agency your name and any previous names, addresses for the last two years, telephone number, year or date of birth, employer, and Social Security number. If you're married, enclose the same information for your spouse.

In addition to your credit history, your credit report will contain the sources of the information and the names of people who have received your file within the last year, or within the last two years if those people sought your file for employment reasons. (15 U.S.C. §§ 1681g(a)(3)(A), 1681g(a)(3)(B).)

Credit files can contain negative information for up to seven years, except for bankruptcy filings, which can stay for ten. As mentioned earlier, most credit bureaus report Chapter 13 bankruptcies for only seven years. You will want to challenge outdated, as well as incorrect or incomplete, information. The bureau must investigate the accuracy of anything you challenge within 30 days. Then the bureau must either correct it, or if it can't verify the item, remove it.

If, after the investigation, the bureau keeps information in your file you still believe is wrong, you are entitled to write a brief statement giving your version, to be included in your file. Be sure the statement is tied to a particular item in your file. When the item eventually is removed from your file or corrected, the statement will be taken out. If you write a general "my life was a mess and I got into debt" statement, however, it will stay for a full seven years from the date you place it, even if the negative items come out sooner. An example of a statement is shown below.

Sample Statement to Credit Bureau

September 12, 20xx

Your records show that I am unemployed. That's incorrect. I am a self-employed cabinetmaker and carpenter. I work out of my home and take orders from people who are referred to me through various sources. My work is known in the community and that's how I earn my living.

Denny Porter
Denny Porter

The agency must give the statement, or a summary of it, to anyone who's given your credit file. In addition, if you request it, the agency must pass on a copy or summary of your statement to any person who received your report within the past year, or two years if it involved employment.

You also want to keep new negative information out of your file. To do this, remain current on your bills. What you owe, as well as how long it takes you to pay, are in that file.

In addition to information about credit accounts, credit reports also contain information from public records, including criminal records. After receiving your bankruptcy discharge, be sure to modify public records to reflect what occurred in the bankruptcy, so wrong information won't appear in your credit file. For example, if a court case was pending against you at the time you filed for bankruptcy, and, as part of the bankruptcy, the potential judgment against you was discharged, be sure the court case is formally dismissed. You may need the help of an attorney. (See Ch. 12, *Help Beyond the Book*.)

Avoid Credit Repair Agencies

You've probably seen ads for companies that claim they can fix your credit, qualify you for a loan, and get you a credit card. Stay clear of these companies. Their practices are almost always deceptive and sometimes illegal. Some steal the credit files or Social Security numbers of people who have died or live in places like Guam or the U.S. Virgin Islands and replace your file with these other files. Others create new identities for debtors by applying to the IRS for a taxpayer I.D. number and telling debtors to use it in place of their Social Security number.

Even the legitimate companies can't do anything for you that you can't do yourself. If items in your credit file are correct, these companies cannot get them removed. About the only difference between using a legitimate credit repair agency and doing it yourself is the money you save by doing it yourself.

3. Negotiate With Current Creditors

If you owe any debts that show up as past due on your credit file (perhaps the debt wasn't discharged in bankruptcy or was incurred after you filed), you can take steps to make them current. Contact the creditor and ask that the item be removed in exchange for full or partial payment. On a revolving account (such as a department store), ask the creditor to "re-age" the account so that is shown as current. For help in negotiating with your creditors, consider contacting a local Consumer Credit Counseling Service office. (See Ch. 1, *Should You File for Chapter 13 Bankruptcy?*, Section C.)

4. Stabilize Your Income and Employment

Your credit history and score are not the only thing lenders will consider in deciding whether to give you credit. They also look carefully at the stability of your income and employment. Plus, if you start getting new credit before you're back on your feet financially, you'll end up in the same mess that led you to file for bankruptcy in the first place.

5. Get a Credit Card

Once you have your budget and some money saved, you can begin to get some positive information in your credit file. One way is to get a secured credit card. In a few years, banks and other large creditors will be more apt to grant you credit if, since your bankruptcy, you've made and paid for purchases on credit.

Some banks will give you a credit card and a line of credit if you deposit money into a savings account. In exchange, you cannot remove the money from your account. If you don't pay your bill, the bank uses the money in your account to cover what you owe. Get such a card if you truly believe you'll control any impulses to overuse it.

A major drawback with these cards is that the interest rate often nears 25%–30%. So use the card only to cash checks, buy inexpensive items you can pay for when the bill arrives, or guarantee a hotel reservation or car rental. Otherwise, you're going to pay a bundle in interest and may end up in financial trouble again.

Be sure to shop around before signing up for a secured credit card. Even though you just filed for bankruptcy, you'll probably still get lots of offers for unsecured cards in the mail. Often, these cards have better terms than do secured cards. If you do choose a secured credit card, be sure it isn't secured by your home.

⚠️ **Avoid look-alike credit cards.** Some lesser-known mail-order companies issue cards that look like credit cards, but allow you to make purchases only from their own catalogues. The items in the catalogue tend to be overpriced and of mediocre (if not poor) quality. And your use of the card isn't reported to credit bureaus, so you won't be rebuilding your credit.

6. Borrow From a Bank

Bank loans provide an excellent way to rebuild credit. A few banks offer something called a passbook savings loan, which is a lot like a secured credit card. You deposit a sum of money into a savings account, and in exchange the bank makes you a loan. You have no access to your savings account while your loan is outstanding. If you don't repay it, the bank will use the money in your savings account. The amount you can borrow depends on how much the bank requires you to deposit.

In most cases, though, you'll have to apply for a standard bank loan. You probably won't qualify unless you bring in a cosigner, offer some property as collateral, or agree to a very high rate of interest.

Banks that offer passbook loans typically give you one to three years to repay the loan. But don't pay the loan back too soon—give it about six to nine months to appear on your credit file. Standard bank loans are paid back on a monthly schedule, usually for a year or two.

Before you take out any loan, be sure you understand the terms:

- **Interest rate.** The interest rate on the loan is usually between two and six percentage points over what the bank charges its customers with the best credit.
- **Prepayment penalties.** Usually, you can pay the loan back as soon as you want without incurring

any prepayment penalties. Prepayment penalties are fees banks sometimes charge if you pay back a loan early and the bank doesn't collect as much interest from you as it had expected. The penalty is usually a small percentage of the loan amount.

- **Whether the bank reports the loan to a credit bureau.** This is key; the whole reason you take out the loan is to rebuild your credit. You may have to make several calls to find a bank that reports the loan.

7. Work With a Local Merchant

Another step to consider in rebuilding your credit is to approach a local merchant, such as a jewelry or furniture store, about purchasing an item on credit. Many local stores will work with you in setting up a payment schedule, but be prepared to put down a deposit of up to 30%, to pay a high rate of interest, or to find someone to cosign the loan. This isn't an ideal way to rebuild your credit, but if all other lenders turn you down, it may be your only option.

B. Attempts to Collect Clearly Discharged Debts

If a debt was discharged in bankruptcy, the law prohibits creditors from filing a lawsuit, sending you collection letters, calling you, withholding credit, or threatening to file or actually filing a criminal complaint against you. (11 U.S.C. § 524.) If a creditor tries to collect a debt that clearly was discharged in your bankruptcy, you should respond at once with a letter like the one shown below.

Letter to Creditor

1905 Fifth Road
N. Miami Beach, FL 35466

March 18, 20xx

Bank of Miami
2700 Finances Highway
Miami, FL 36678

To Whom It May Concern:

I've been contacted once by letter and once by phone by Rodney Moore of your bank. Mr. Moore claims that I owe $4,812 on Visa account number 1234 567 890 123.

As you're well aware, this debt was discharged in bankruptcy (case number 111-999 in the Western District of Tennessee) on February 1, 20xx. Thus, your collection efforts violate federal law, 11 U.S.C. § 524. If they continue, I won't hesitate to pursue my legal rights, including bringing a lawsuit against you for harassment.

Sincerely,

Dawn Schaffer
Dawn Schaffer

The court doesn't give you a list of debts that were discharged. But you can assume a debt was discharged if you listed it in your bankruptcy papers, the creditor didn't successfully object to its discharge, and it isn't in one of the nondischargeable categories listed in Ch. 2, *An Overview of Chapter 13 Bankruptcy*, Section D. Also, if you live in a community property state and your spouse filed alone, your share of the community debts was discharged.

If the collection efforts don't immediately stop, you may want to hire a lawyer to write the creditor again—sometimes, a lawyer's letterhead gets results. If that doesn't work, you can sue the creditor for harassment. You can bring a lawsuit in state court or in the bankruptcy court. The bankruptcy court should be more familiar with the prohibitions against collection and more sympathetic to you.

If the creditor sues you over the debt, you'll want to raise the discharge as a defense and sue the creditor yourself to stop the illegal collection efforts. The court has the power to hold the creditor in contempt of court. The court may also fine the creditor for the humiliation, inconvenience, and anguish caused you and order the creditor to pay your attorney's fees. For example, a bankruptcy court in North Carolina fined a creditor $900 for attempting to collect a discharged debt. (*In re Barbour*, 77 B.R. 530 (E.D. N.C. 1987).)

If the creditor sues you (almost certainly in state court), you or your attorney can file papers requesting that the case be transferred ("removed") to the bankruptcy court.

Anticipating Postbankruptcy Debt Collections

Sometimes you can anticipate when a particular creditor will consider a debt to be nondischargeable and go after you for it after your bankruptcy case is closed. In that event, you can file an action in the bankruptcy court while your case is still open to obtain a determination of whether the debt is dischargeable. If the court rules in your favor, the creditor will be prevented from pursuing the debt in state court. Telling you how to do this is beyond the scope of this book. However, *Represent Yourself in Court*, by Bergman and Barrett (Nolo), has a chapter on the subject, and instructions are also available in *Getting Paid: How to Collect From Bankrupt Debtors*, by Stephen R. Elias (Nolo).

C. Postbankruptcy Discrimination

Although filing bankruptcy has serious consequences, it might not be as bad as you think. There are laws that will protect you from most types of postbankruptcy discrimination by the government and by private employers.

1. Government Discrimination

All federal, state, and local governmental units are prohibited from discriminating against you solely because you filed for bankruptcy. (11 U.S.C. § 525(a).) This includes denying, revoking, suspending, or refusing to renew a license, permit, charter, franchise, or other similar grant. This part of the Bankruptcy Code provides important protections, but it does not insulate debtors from all adverse consequences of filing for bankruptcy. Lenders, for example, can consider a debtor's bankruptcy filing when reviewing an application for a government loan or extension of credit. (See, for example, *Watts v. Pennsylvania Housing Finance Co.*, 876 F.2d 1090 (3rd Cir. 1989) and *Toth v. Michigan State Housing Development Authority,* 136 F.3d 477 (6th Cir. 1998).) Still, under this provision of the Bankruptcy Code, the government cannot:

- deny you a job or fire you
- deny you or terminate your public benefits
- evict you from public housing (although if you have a Section 8 voucher, you may not be protected)
- deny you or refuse to renew your state liquor license
- withhold your college transcript
- deny you a driver's license, or
- deny you a contract, such as a contract for a construction project.

In addition, the Bankruptcy Code bars a lender from excluding you from participating in a government-guaranteed student loan program. (11 U.S.C. § 525 (c).)

In general, once any government-related debt has been discharged, all acts against you that arise out of that debt also must end. If, for example, you lost your driver's license because you didn't pay a court judgment that resulted from a car accident, once the debt is discharged, you must be granted a license. If your license was also suspended because you didn't have state-required insurance, you may not get your license back until you meet the requirements set forth in your state's law. If, however, the judgment wasn't discharged, you can still be denied your license until you pay up.

Keep in mind that only denials based solely on your bankruptcy are prohibited. You may be denied a loan, job, or apartment for reasons unrelated to the bankruptcy or for reasons related to your future credit-worthiness—for example, because the government concludes you won't be able to repay a Small Business Administration loan.

2. Nongovernment Discrimination

Private employers may not fire you or otherwise discriminate against you solely because you filed for bankruptcy. (11 U.S.C. § 525(b).) While the Bankruptcy Code expressly prohibits employers from firing you, it is unclear whether or not the act prohibits employers from not hiring you because you went through bankruptcy.

Other forms of discrimination in the private sector aren't illegal. If you seek to rent an apartment and the landlord does a credit check, sees your bankruptcy, and refuses to rent to you, there's not much you can do other than try to show that you'll pay your rent and be a responsible tenant. Paying several months rent in advance can work wonders in these situations.

If you suffer illegal discrimination because of your bankruptcy, you can sue in state court or in the bankruptcy court. You'll probably need the assistance of an attorney.

D. Attempts to Revoke Your Discharge

In extremely rare instances, the trustee or a creditor can ask the bankruptcy court to revoke your discharge. The trustee or creditor must file a complaint within one year of your discharge.

Your discharge can be revoked only if the creditor or trustee proves that you obtained the discharge through fraud, which was discovered after your discharge. If your discharge is revoked, you'll owe your creditors as if you had not filed for bankruptcy. Any payment your creditors received from the trustee, however, will be credited against what you owe.

 Help from a lawyer. If someone asks the bankruptcy court to revoke your discharge, consult a bankruptcy attorney right away. ∎

Help Beyond the Book

Although this book covers routine Chapter 13 bankruptcy procedures in some detail, it doesn't come close to covering everything. That would require a 1,000-page treatise, most of which would be irrelevant for nearly all readers. That said, here are some suggestions if you need more information or advice than this book provides.

The major places to go for follow-up are:

- **Lawyers.** When you want information, advice, or legal representation.
- **Bankruptcy Petition Preparers.** When you're ready to file for bankruptcy, but want help typing the forms.
- **The law library.** When you want more information on an issue raised in the course of your bankruptcy.

A. Bankruptcy Lawyers

Even if you want, for personal or financial reasons, to handle your Chapter 13 bankruptcy yourself, you may want at least limited help from a bankruptcy lawyer. Here are some of the things a bankruptcy lawyer can do for you:

- negotiate with your creditors
- speak for you in court
- coach you on how to prepare your papers
- coach you on appearing in court
- review your bankruptcy papers after you prepare them
- prepare your bankruptcy plan for you, or
- answer your legal questions as they arise.

1. How to Find a Bankruptcy Lawyer

Where there's a bankruptcy court, there are bankruptcy lawyers. They're listed in the Yellow Pages under attorneys and often advertise in newspapers. You should use an experienced bankruptcy lawyer, not a general practitioner.

There are several ways to find a bankruptcy lawyer suited to your job:

- **Personal referrals.** This is your best approach. If you know someone who was pleased with the services of a lawyer, call that lawyer first. If that

lawyer doesn't handle bankruptcies or can't take on your case, she may recommend someone else who's experienced, competent, and available.

- **Bankruptcy Petition Preparers.** Reputable bankruptcy petition preparers commonly work closely with bankruptcy attorneys who are both competent and sympathetic to self-helpers. If there's a bankruptcy petition preparer in your area, ask for a recommendation.
- **Legal Aid.** Legal Aid offices are partially funded by the federal Legal Services Corporation and offer legal assistance in many areas; many offices do bankruptcies. To qualify for Legal Aid, you must be low income. To find a Legal Aid office, look in your local phone book.
- **Legal clinic.** Many law schools sponsor legal clinics and provide free legal advice to consumers. Some legal clinics have the same income requirements as Legal Aid; others offer free services to low- to moderate-income people.
- **Group legal plans.** Some unions, employers, and consumer action organizations offer group plans to their members or employees, who can obtain comprehensive legal assistance free or for low rates. If you're a member of such a plan, and the plan covers bankruptcies, check with it first for a lawyer.
- **Prepaid legal insurance.** Prepaid "legal insurance" plans offer some services for a low monthly fee and charge more for additional or different work. That means that participating lawyers may use the plan as a way to get clients, who are attracted by the low-cost basic services, and then sell them more expensive services.

  If a plan offers extensive free advice, your initial membership fee may be worth the consultation you receive, even if you use it only once. You can always join a plan for a specific service and then not renew. For bankruptcy purposes, however, a plan won't be much help unless it offers the services of bankruptcy attorneys.

  There's no guarantee that the lawyers available through these plans are of the best caliber; sometimes they aren't. As with any consumer transaction, check out the plan carefully before signing up. Ask about the plan's complaint system, whether you get to choose your lawyer, and whether or not the lawyer will represent you in court.

- **Lawyer referral panels.** Most county bar associations will give you the names of some bankruptcy attorneys who practice in your area. But bar associations usually provide only minimal screening for the attorneys listed, which means those who participate may not be the most experienced or competent. You may find a skilled attorney willing to work for a reasonable fee this way, but take the time to check out the credentials and experience of the person to whom you're referred.

2. What to Look for in a Lawyer

Once you have the names of a few bankruptcy lawyers, do a little screening before you commit yourself to hiring someone.

It's important that you be as comfortable as possible with any lawyer you hire. When making an appointment, ask to talk directly to the lawyer. If you can't, this may give you a hint as to how accessible he or she is. Of course, if you're told that a paralegal will be handling the routine aspects of your case under the supervision of a lawyer, you may be satisfied with that arrangement.

If you do talk directly to the lawyer, ask some specific questions. Do you get clear, concise answers? If not, try someone else.

Finally, once you find a lawyer you like, make an hour-long appointment to discuss your situation fully. Your goal at the initial conference is to find out what the lawyer recommends and how much it will cost. Go home and think about the lawyer's suggestions. If they don't make complete sense or you have other reservations, call someone else.

Don't let the lawyer take over. Fight any urge you may have to surrender your will and be intimidated by a lawyer. You should be the one who decides what you feel comfortable doing about your legal and financial affairs. Don't hire a lawyer who wants you to be a passive client. Also, pay attention to how the lawyer responds to your considerable knowledge. By getting this book and learning about Chapter 13 bankruptcy, you're already better informed about the law than most clients (and some lawyers). Many lawyers are threatened when the client knows too much, or in some cases, anything.

3. What Bankruptcy Attorneys Charge

Bankruptcy attorneys generally charge about $1,000 to $2,000 (plus the $194 filing and administrative fee) to handle an entire Chapter 13 bankruptcy case. The lawyer's fee is usually paid through the Chapter 13 plan. This means you do not have to come up with all the money up front in order to have a lawyer file a Chapter 13 bankruptcy for you. But you will probably have to come up with a major portion of it. This is because you might convert from Chapter 13 to Chapter 7 after a month or two, in which case the lawyer's fee would be discharged. So, expect to pay up front the amount you would pay to have a Chapter 7 case filed (roughly $600 to $1,000).

If you hire an attorney to perform a limited task, such as to represent you at court hearings, or to coach you on certain aspects of your case, expect to be charged somewhere between $150 and $250 an hour.

Fortunately, there are some limitations on what a bankruptcy attorney can charge. Because every penny you pay a bankruptcy lawyer is a penny not available to your creditors, the attorney must obtain approval of the fee from the bankruptcy court. The court has the legal authority to call the attorney in to justify the fee. This rarely happens, because attorneys know what local bankruptcy judges will allow and set their fees accordingly.

Commonly, bankruptcy attorneys charge a basic fee for a routine case and then add set amounts for necessary additional procedures. For instance, the basic fee may be $1,000, but it will cost you $150 more to respond to a motion brought by a creditor and $250 more to file a motion to establish the fair market value of secured property.

B. Bankruptcy Petition Preparers

Even though you should be able to handle routine bankruptcy procedures yourself, you may want help with form preparation. In that case, you don't have to hire a lawyer. For this level of assistance, a bankruptcy petition preparer (BPP) can help you. BPPs are not lawyers, but they are familiar with the bankruptcy courts in your area. They can:

* prepare your forms
* provide some basic information about local procedures and requirements, and
* help you prepare for negotiations with your creditors.

BPPs will use a computer program (there are many on the market) to create a clean set of your bankruptcy papers. BBPs charge about $75 to $150 for this service. Many BPPs won't file the papers for you, though, because the Bankruptcy Code prohibits them from taking the filing fee from you. (11 U.S.C. § 110(g)(1).) In this situation, you'll have to take the forms to the court for filing. Some BPPs will let you give them a cashier's check, made out to the court, to cover the filing fee. In this case, the BPP will also file your papers for you.

BPPs are very different from lawyers. They can't give legal advice or represent you in court—only lawyers are allowed to do those things. That means they cannot advise you to file or not file for bankruptcy, tell you what to include or not include on your forms, tell you which exemption schedule to use, or recommend a particular course of action regarding a debt or piece of property. If you need help doing any of these things, you should see an attorney.

BPPs are springing up all over the country to help people who don't want or can't afford to hire a lawyer, but you're still more likely to find a BPP if you live on the West Coast. A recommendation from someone who has used a particular BPP is the best way to find a reputable one in your area.

BPPs often advertise in classified sections of local newspapers and in the Yellow Pages. You may have to look hard to find BPPs, however, because the Bankruptcy Code bars them from using the term "legal" or any similar term in their advertisements or from advertising under any category that contains the word "legal" or a similar term. And many BPPs have display ads in local throwaway papers like the *Classified Flea Market* or *Giant Nickel*.

Know what you're getting. A small percentage of BPPs can only be described as rip-off artists. They promise to prepare and file your bankruptcy case for you—but, in fact, complete and file only the bankruptcy petition. Filing this two-page document will get your case started, but you must file the remaining 12 forms and your repayment plan within 15 days or your case will be dismissed. These BPPs don't tell you that you must complete and file the other papers.

C. The Law Library

Often, you can handle a problem yourself if you're willing to do some research in a law library. The trick is in knowing what types of information you can find there. Sometimes, what you need to know isn't written down. For instance, if you want to know whether the local bankruptcy judge is strict or generous when you put together your monthly budget, you can't find out by going to the law library. You'll probably have to talk to a bankruptcy lawyer, a petition preparer, or the trustee.

Bankruptcy Code Sections (Title 11 of the United States Code)

§ 109 Who may file for which type of bankruptcy

§ 110 Nonattorney bankruptcy petition preparers

§ 302 Who qualifies for filing joint cases

§ 341 Meeting of the creditors

§ 342 Giving notice of the meeting of the creditors

§ 343 Examination of the debtor at the meeting of the creditors

§ 348 Converting from one type of bankruptcy to another

§ 349 Dismissing a case

§ 350 Closing and reopening a case

§ 361 Providing adequate protection to a secured creditor

§ 362 The automatic stay

§ 365 Executory contracts and unexpired leases

§ 366 Continuing or reconnecting utility service

§ 501 Filing of proofs of claims

§ 502 Establishing the amount of a creditor's claim

§ 506 Determining secured claims and avoiding liens

§ 507 Claims having priority

§ 522 Exemptions

§ 523 Nondischargeable debts

§ 524 Reaffirmation of debts

§ 525 Prohibited postbankruptcy discrimination

§ 541 Property of the estate (general)

§ 547 Preferences

§ 548 Fraudulent transfers

§ 553 Setoffs

§ 1301 Codebtor stay

§ 1304 Debtor engaged in business

§ 1305 Postpetition claims

§ 1306 Property of the estate (unique to Chapter 13)

§ 1307 Converting or dismissing a Chapter 13 case

§ 1322 Contents of the Chapter 13 plan

§ 1323 Modifying the plan before confirmation

§ 1325 Confirmation hearing

§ 1326 Making plan payments

§ 1327 Rights and obligations after confirmation

§ 1328 Discharge

§ 1329 Modifying the plan after confirmation

The library can help you, however, if your question involves a legal interpretation, such as how the judge is likely to rule if a creditor objects to your plan for a particular reason. You can find out how similar questions have been decided by bankruptcy courts and courts of appeal.

Here's what you can find in the average law library:

- books and articles by bankruptcy experts on almost every aspect of bankruptcy law and practice, including many of the local procedures peculiar to each court
- federal bankruptcy statutes (the Bankruptcy Code)
- federal bankruptcy rules, which govern bankruptcy court procedure
- published decisions of bankruptcy court judges and appellate courts that interpret the bankruptcy statutes and rules
- specific instructions for handling routine and nonroutine bankruptcy procedures, and
- cross-reference tools to help you get from one statute, rule, or case to another and to help you make sure the material you find is up to date.

Here, briefly, are the basic steps of researching bankruptcy questions.

1. Find a Law Library

To do legal research, you need to find a law library that's open to the public. Public law libraries are often found in county courthouses, public law schools, and state capitals. If you can't find one, ask a public library reference librarian, court clerk, or lawyer.

2. Use a Good Legal Research Resource

To find the answer to a legal question, or look up a statute or case, you need some guidance in basic legal research techniques. Any of the following resources that may be available in your law library will tell you how to do legal research:

- *Legal Research: How to Find & Understand the Law*, by Steve Elias and Susan Levinkind (Nolo)
- *How to Find the Law*, by Morris Cohen, Robert Berring, and Kent Olson (West Publishing Co.)
- *The Legal Research Manual: A Game Plan for Legal Research and Analysis*, by Christopher and Jill Wren.

3. Use *Collier on Bankruptcy*

It's a good idea to get an overview of your subject before trying to find a precise answer to a precise question. The best way to do this is to find a general commentary on your subject by a bankruptcy expert. For example, if you want to find out whether a particular debt is nondischargeable, you should start by reading a general discussion about the type of debt you're dealing with.

The most complete source of this type of background information is a multivolume treatise known as *Collier on Bankruptcy,* by Lawrence P. King, et al. (Matthew Bender). It's available in virtually all law libraries. *Collier* is both incredibly thorough and meticulously up-to-date; semiannual supplements, with all the latest developments, are located at the front of each volume. In addition to comments on every aspect of bankruptcy law, *Collier* contains the bankruptcy statutes, rules, and exemption lists for every state.

Collier is organized according to the bankruptcy statutes. This means that the quickest way to find information in it is to know which section of the Bankruptcy Code relates to your question. If you don't know, start with the *Collier* subject-matter index. Be warned, however, that the index can be difficult to use; it contains a lot of bankruptcy jargon you may be unfamiliar with.

4. Use Other Background Resources

For general discussions of bankruptcy issues, there are several other good places to start.

- *Consumer Bankruptcy Law and Practice.* This excellent all-around resource, published by the National Consumer Law Center, is updated every year. It contains a complete discussion of Chapter 13 bankruptcy procedures, the official bankruptcy forms, and a marvelous bibliography.
- *Chapter 13 Bankruptcy*, by Keith M. Lundin (Wiley Law). Judge Lundin is one of the nation's most respected Chapter 13 bankruptcy judges. (He sits in Nashville, Tennessee, and was a Chapter 13 bankruptcy trustee before being appointed judge.) His three-volume treatise contains thorough information on every aspect of Chapter 13 bankruptcy. Although it is written

for lawyers, laypeople will find it is easy to understand.

- *Chapter 13 Practice Guide*, by Keith M. Lundin (Wiley Law). Judge Lundin's second book contains the required, preferred, or a sample Chapter 13 repayment plan for every bankruptcy court in the nation. It also contains information on bankruptcy court procedures.
- Commerce Clearing House (CCH) *Bankruptcy Law Reporter* (BLR). In this loose-leaf publication, you can find all three primary source materials relating to bankruptcy: statutes, rules, and cases. BLR is multivolume and looks scary to use. Don't be intimidated. Clear and complete instructions on using this extremely helpful resource are at the beginning of BLR Volume 1.
- If you are looking for information on adversary proceedings (such as how to defend against a creditor's challenge to the dischargeability of a debt), turn to *Represent Yourself in Court,* by Paul Bergman and Sara J. Berman-Barrett (Nolo). It has an entire chapter on representing yourself in adversary proceedings in bankruptcy court.

5. Find and Read Relevant Statutes

After consulting *Collier* or one of the other background resources, you may need to read a statute for yourself.

Statutes passed by Congress apply to the bankruptcy courts, and your first step should be to figure out which statute governs the issue you're interested in. Sometimes you'll know this from the references (citations) in this book. For instance, the discussion of income deduction orders (Ch. 9, *After You File Your Case*) refers to 11 U.S.C. § 1325(c). The citation means Title 11 of the United States Code, Section 1325(c).

Federal statutes are collected in a multivolume set of books known as the United States Code (U.S.C.) and divided into 50 numbered titles. Title 11 contains the bankruptcy statutes.

If you need to research a question and don't know what statute to start with, there are two ways to find out. First, use the list above, which tells you what's covered by most of the bankruptcy statutes that might affect your case.

If the list doesn't help, two different publications of the United States Code contain not only the statutes, but also various types of clarifying information.

- *United States Code Annotated* (U.S.C.A., published by West Publishing Co.), and
- *United States Code Service* (U.S.C.S., published by Bancroft-Whitney/Lawyer's Cooperative).

The statutes are the same in both publications—for instance, you can find Section 506 in Title 11 of either the U.S.C.A. or the U.S.C.S. The accompanying material, however, varies. Some libraries carry only one of these publications; larger libraries carry both.

To read a bankruptcy statute, find the U.S.C.A. or U.S.C.S. in your law library. Find Title 11, turn to the section number, and begin reading. After you read the statute in the hardcover portion of the book, turn to the very back of the book. There should be an insert pamphlet (called a pocket part) for the current year. Look to see if the statute is in the pocket part as well, to see whether it has been amended since the hardcover volume was published.

When you first read a bankruptcy statute you'll probably be totally confused, if not in tears. Relax. No one understands these statutes as they're written. You can go either to *Collier on Bankruptcy* and read its interpretation (remember, it's organized according to the bankruptcy statutes), or directly to court opinions that have interpreted the statute. You can locate these opinions in the case summaries that directly follow the statute in the U.S.C.A. or U.S.C.S. (See Section 7, below.)

6. Read Procedural Rules

If you have a question about court procedures—for example, the time in which a creditor may withdraw a claim—then you'll need to look at the federal bankruptcy rules. They govern the procedural aspects of bankruptcy cases, such as time limits and the process of filing your papers. The rules cover other issues, too, which may seem like questions of substance, not procedure, such as paying the fee in installments. If you can't find your answer in the Bankruptcy Code, it may be in the rules.

You can find the bankruptcy rules in *Collier, Consumer Bankruptcy Law and Practice*, and *Chapter 13 Practice Guide*.

7. Find and Read Relevant Cases

To understand bankruptcy statutes and rules, it's usually necessary to read a case (court decision) or two that has dealt with how the particular statute applies to situations like yours. Published court decisions are of two types: those decided by a single bankruptcy judge and those decided by a court of appeal.

A bankruptcy judge who resolves a particular issue in a case may write a statement explaining the decision. If this statement, usually called a "memorandum opinion" or "findings of fact and conclusions of law," appears to be of interest to those who practice bankruptcy law, it will be published. If you want to persuade your bankruptcy judge of a particular point, it's to your advantage to find a supportive case which has been decided by another bankruptcy judge considering similar facts.

Several publications include bankruptcy cases; the one most commonly found in law libraries is the *Bankruptcy Reports* (West Publishing Co.), abbreviated as B.R. You can find summaries of cases published in the *Bankruptcy Reports* directly following each bankruptcy statute.

If one of the parties to a bankruptcy dispute appeals the bankruptcy judge's ruling, the appeal is decided by a federal district court or a bankruptcy appellate panel. These decisions are published in the *Bankruptcy Reports* or the *Federal Reporter*, 2nd and 3rd Series (West Publishing Co.), abbreviated as F.2d and F.3d.

Once you find a relevant case or two, you can find similar cases by using cross-reference tools known as digests and *Shepards*. These are explained in *Legal Research: How to Find & Understand the Law*, by Steve Elias and Susan Levinkind (Nolo Press), and other legal research texts.

D. Resources on the Internet

You can accomplish a good deal of legal and practical research through the Internet. But you can't do it all—not every court decision or state statute is available online. Furthermore, unless you know what you are looking for—the case name and citation or the code section—you may have difficulty finding it.

Still, there are a number of useful sites:

- **www.nolo.com**

  The "Help With Legal Research" section of Nolo's website provides links to state cases, as well as statutes, United States Supreme Court cases, and the federal code (the bankruptcy laws are in Title 11 of the code). Go to www.nolo.com/statute/index.cfm. Nolo's website also contains free articles about bankruptcy. Finally, check Nolo's Legal Updates for recent changes in bankruptcy laws (such as filing fee changes). On the home page, click "View All Products," scroll down and click on this book's title, look under "Product Details," then click "Updates."

- **www.uscourts.gov/bkforms/index.html**

  You can download all bankruptcy forms from this site.

- **http://bankruptcymedia.com/bkfinder/bankruptcyreformnews.html**

  This site includes daily news updates, information, and commentary on bankruptcy legislation.

- **www.bernsteinlaw.com/publications/index_pubs.html**

  The law firm of Bernstein and Bernstein provides an online version of their handy book, *A Dictionary of Bankruptcy Terminology*.

- **www.lawtrove.com/bankruptcy**

  This site provides an extensive list of online bankruptcy-related materials, such as frequently asked questions (FAQs), important bankruptcy cases, United States Bankruptcy Code, federal bankruptcy rules, background on bankruptcy lawyers, and links to other online bankruptcy sites.

- **http://nacba.com**

  This is the site for the National Association of Consumer Bankruptcy Attorneys. In addition to information about the organization and its activities, you can find the text of recent articles, cases, and legislative developments.

- **www.findlaw.com**

  FindLaw links to each state's online legal information, such as statutes and cases, as well as to federal statutes and cases. It also links to many online bankruptcy resources, including government documents, journals, and newsletters.

- **www.13network.com**

  Get a peek at how trustees do their work. This site, sponsored by a bank, has wide participation among Chapter 13 trustees. ■

State and Federal Exemption Tables

Using the Exemption Tables

Every state lets people who file for bankruptcy keep certain property, called exemptions. Ch. 5, *Calculating the Value of Your Nonexempt Property*, discusses exemptions in detail.

1. What This Appendix Contains

- lists of each state's exemptions
- list of the federal bankruptcy exemptions (available as a choice in a handful of states and the District of Columbia)
- list of the federal nonbankruptcy exemptions (available as additional exemptions when the state exemptions are chosen).

Each list is divided into three columns. Column 1 lists the major exemption categories: homestead, insurance, miscellaneous, pensions, personal property, public benefits, tools of the trade, wages, and wildcard. (These categories differ on the federal nonbankruptcy exemptions chart.)

Column 2 gives the specific property that falls into each large category, with noted limitations.

For example, the federal bankruptcy exemptions allow married couples filing jointly to each claim a full set of exemptions. This is called "doubling." Many state exemption systems do not allow doubling or do not allow doubling for certain types of property, such as the homestead exemption (which exempts equity in your residence). In some states, the legislature has expressly allowed or prohibited doubling. In others, the courts have allowed or prohibited doubling. In still others, neither the courts nor the legislature has addressed the issue. If that is the case, doubling is probably allowed. In Column 2, we've noted whether a court or state legislature has expressly allowed or prohibited doubling. If the chart doesn't say, it is probably safe to double. However, keep in mind that this area of the law changes rapidly—legislation or court decisions regarding doubling issued after the publication date of this book will not be reflected in the chart.

Column 3 lists the applicable law, which must be included on Schedule C.

These charts can't reflect every exception to the exemption laws. The information in the following tables is general in nature. Additional limitations or exceptions exist—unfortunately, we can't list them all here. For example, the exemptions noted in the charts may not shield you against claims for child support or tax debts, or they may have been altered by related state statutes or court decisions. Consider doing further legal research or consulting a local attorney about your own exemptions, particularly if someone challenges the amounts you claim. And if a large amount of property is at stake, you may wish to consult a lawyer or accountant experienced in asset protection strategies in your state.

2. Choosing Between State and Federal Exemptions

Each state chart indicates whether the federal exemptions are available for that state. The list of federal exemptions follows Wyoming.

3. Houses and Pensions

If you own a house, you should also read Ch. 6, *Completing the Bankruptcy Forms.*

With pensions, some states exempt only the money building up in the pension fund, and a few exempt only payments actually being received. Most exempt both. If the pension listing doesn't indicate otherwise, it means the state exempts both.

4. Wages, Benefits, and Other Payments

Many states exempt insurance proceeds, pension payments, alimony and child support payments, public benefits, or wages. This means that payments you received before filing are exempt if you haven't mixed them with other money or, if you have mixed them, if you can trace the exempt portion back to its source.

If, when you file for bankruptcy, you're entitled to receive an exempt payment but haven't yet received it, you can exempt the payment when it comes in by amending Schedules B (personal property you own or possess) and C (property you claim as exempt).

Alabama

Federal Bankruptcy Exemptions not available. All law references are to Alabama Code.

ASSET	EXEMPTION	LAW
homestead	Real property or mobile home to $5,000; property cannot exceed 160 acres	6-10-2
	Must record homestead declaration before attempted sale of home	6-10-20
insurance	Annuity proceeds or avails to $250 per month	27-14-32
	Disability proceeds or avails to an average of $250 per month	27-14-31
	Fraternal benefit society benefits	27-34-27
	Life insurance proceeds or avails	6-10-8; 27-14-29
	Life insurance proceeds or avails if clause prohibits proceeds from being used to pay beneficiary's creditors	27-15-26
	Mutual aid association benefits	27-30-25
pensions	IRAs & other retirement accounts	19-3-1
	Judges (only payments being received)	12-18-10(a),(b)
	Law enforcement officers	36-21-77
	State employees	36-27-28
	Teachers	16-25-23
personal property	Books of debtor & family	6-10-6
	Burial place for self & family	6-10-5
	Church pew for self & family	6-10-5
	Clothing of debtor & family	6-10-6
	Family portraits or pictures	6-10-6
public benefits	Aid to blind, aged, disabled; & other public assistance	38-4-8
	Crime victims' compensation	15-23-15(e)
	Southeast Asian War POWs' benefits	31-7-2
	Unemployment compensation	25-4-140
	Workers' compensation	25-5-86(b)
tools of trade	Arms, uniforms, equipment that state military personnel are required to keep	31-2-78
wages	With respect to consumer loans, consumer credit sales, & consumer leases, 75% of weekly net earnings or 30 times the federal minimum hourly wage; all other cases, 75% of earned but unpaid wages; bankruptcy judge may authorize more for low-income debtors	5-19-15; 6-10-7
wildcard	$3,000 of any personal property, except wages	6-10-6

Alaska

Alaska law states that only the items found in Alaska Statutes §§ 9.38.010, 9.38.015(a), 9.38.017, 9.38.020, 9.38.025, and 9.38.030 may be exempted in bankruptcy. In *In re McNutt*, 87 B.R. 84 (9th Cir. 1988), however, an Alaskan debtor used the federal bankruptcy exemptions. All law references are to Alaska Statutes.

Alaska exemption amounts are adjusted regularly by administrative order. Current amounts are found at 8 Alaska Admin. Code tit. 8, § 95.030.

ASSET	EXEMPTION	LAW
homestead	$67,500 (joint owners may each claim a portion, but total can't exceed $67,500)	09.38.010(a)
insurance	Disability benefits	09.38.015(b); 09.38.030(e)(1),(5)
	Fraternal benefit society benefits	21.84.240
	Life insurance or annuity contracts, total aggregate cash surrender value to $12,500	09.38.025
	Medical, surgical, or hospital benefits	09.38.015(a)(3)
miscellaneous	Alimony, to extent wages exempt	09.38.030(e)(2)
	Child support payments made by collection agency	09.38.015(b)
	Liquor licenses	09.38.015(a)(7)
	Property of business partnership	09.38.100(b)
pensions	Elected public officers (only benefits building up)	09.38.015(b)
	ERISA-qualified benefits deposited more than 120 days before filing bankruptcy	09.38.017
	Judicial employees (only benefits building up)	09.38.015(b)
	Public employees (only benefits building up)	09.38.015(b); 39.35.505
	Roth & traditional IRAs, medical savings accounts	09.38.017(e)(3)
	Teachers (only benefits building up)	09.38.015(b)
	Other pensions, to extent wages exempt (only payments being received)	09.38.030(e)(5)
personal property	Books, musical instruments, clothing, family portraits, household goods, & heirlooms to $3,750 total	09.38.020(a)
	Building materials	34.35.105
	Burial plot	09.38.015(a)(1)
	Cash or other liquid assets to $1,750; for sole wage earner in household, $2,750 (restrictions apply—see *wages*)	09.38.030(b)
	Deposit in apartment or condo owners' association	09.38.010(e)
	Health aids needed	09.38.015(a)(2)
	Jewelry to $1,250	09.38.020(b)
	Motor vehicle to $3,750; vehicle's market value can't exceed $25,000	09.38.020(e)
	Personal injury recoveries, to extent wages exempt	09.38.030(e)(3)
	Pets to $1,250	09.38.020(d)
	Proceeds for lost, damaged, or destroyed exempt property	09.38.060
	Tuition credits under an advance college tuition payment contract	09.38.015(a)(8)
	Wrongful death recoveries, to extent wages exempt	09.38.030(e)(3)
public benefits	Adult assistance to elderly, blind, disabled	47.25.550
	Alaska longevity bonus	09.38.015(a)(5)
	Crime victims' compensation	09.38.015(a)(4)
	Federally exempt public benefits paid or due	09.38.015(a)(6)
	General relief assistance	47.25.210
	20% of permanent fund dividends	43.23.065
	Unemployment compensation	09.38.015(b); 23.20.405
	Workers' compensation	23.30.160
tools of trade	Implements, books, & tools of trade to $3,500	09.38.020(c)
wages	Weekly net earnings to $438; for sole wage earner in a household, $688; if you don't receive weekly or semimonthly pay, can claim $1,750 in cash or liquid assets paid any month; for sole wage earner in household, $2,750	9.38.030(a),(b); 9.38.050(b)
wildcard	None	

Be sure to read the caution about exceptions to exemptions in the introduction to this appendix.

Arizona

Federal Bankruptcy Exemptions not available. All law references are to Arizona Revised Statutes unless otherwise noted.

ASSET	EXEMPTION	LAW
homestead	Real property, an apartment, or mobile home you occupy to $150,000; sale proceeds exempt 18 months after sale or until new home purchased, whichever occurs first (husband & wife may not double)	33-1101(A)
	May record homestead declaration to clarify which one of multiple eligible parcels is being claimed as homestead	33-1102
insurance	Fraternal benefit society benefits	20-877
	Group life insurance policy or proceeds	20-1132
	Health, accident, or disability benefits	33-1126(A)(4)
	Life insurance cash value or proceeds to $25,000 total if beneficiary is spouse or child & owned at least two years	33-1126(A)(6); 20-1131(D)
	Life insurance proceeds to $20,000 if beneficiary is spouse or child	33-1126(A)(1)
miscellaneous	Alimony, child support needed for support	33-1126(A)(3)
	Minor child's earnings, unless debt is for child	33-1126(A)(2)
pensions *see also wages*	Board of regents members, faculty & administrative officers under board's jurisdiction	15-1628(I)
	District employees	48-227
	ERISA-qualified benefits deposited over 120 days before filing	33-1126(C)
	IRAs & Roth IRAs	33-1126(c) *In re Herrscher,* 121 B.R. 29 (D. Ariz. 1989)
	Firefighters	9-968
	Police officers	9-931
	Rangers	41-955
	State employees retirement & disability	38-792; 38-797.11
personal property *husband & wife may double all personal property*	2 beds & bedding; 1 living room chair per person; 1 dresser, table, lamp; kitchen table; dining room table & 4 chairs (1 more per person); living room carpet or rug; couch; 3 lamps; 3 coffee or end tables; pictures, paintings, personal drawings, family portraits; refrigerator, stove, washer, dryer, vacuum cleaner; TV, radio, stereo, alarm clock to $4,000 total	33-1123
	Bank deposit to $150 in one account	33-1126(A)(8)
	Bible; bicycle; sewing machine; typewriter; burial plot; rifle, pistol, or shotgun to $500 total	33-1125
	Books to $250; clothing to $500; wedding & engagement rings to $1,000; watch to $100; pets, horses, milk cows, & poultry to $500; musical instruments to $250	33-1125
	Food & fuel to last 6 months	33-1124
	Funeral deposits to $5,000	32-1391.05(4)
	Health aids	33-1125(9)
	Motor vehicle to $5,000 ($10,000, if disabled)	33-1125(8)
	Prepaid rent or security deposit to $1,000 or 1-1/2 times your rent, whichever is less, in lieu of homestead	33-1126(D)
	Proceeds for sold or damaged exempt property	33-1126(A)(5),(7)
	Wrongful death awards	12-592
public benefits	Unemployment compensation	23-783(A)
	Welfare benefits	46-208
	Workers' compensation	23-1068(B)
tools of trade *husband & wife may double*	Arms, uniforms, & accoutrements of profession or office required by law	33-1130(3)
	Farm machinery, utensils, seed, instruments of husbandry, feed, grain, & animals to $2,500 total	33-1130(2)
	Library & teaching aids of teacher	33-1127
	Tools, equipment, instruments, & books to $2,500	33-1130(1)
wages	75% of earned but unpaid weekly net earnings or 30 times the federal minimum hourly wage; 50% of wages for support orders; bankruptcy judge may authorize more for low-income debtors	33-1131
wildcard	None	

Arkansas

Federal Bankruptcy Exemptions available. All law references are to Arkansas Code Annotated unless otherwise noted.

Note: *In re Holt,* 894 F.2d 1005 (8th Cir. 1990) held that Arkansas residents are limited to exemptions in the Arkansas Constitution. Statutory exemptions can still be used within Arkansas for nonbankruptcy purposes, but they cannot be claimed in bankruptcy

ASSET	EXEMPTION	LAW
homestead *choose option 1 or 2*	1. For married person or head of family: unlimited exemption on real or personal property used as residence to 1/4 acre in city, town, or village, or 80 acres elsewhere; if property is between 1/4–1 acre in city, town, or village, or 80-160 acres elsewhere, additional limit is $2,500; homestead may not exceed 1 acre in city, town, or village, or 160 acres elsewhere (husband & wife may not double)	Constitution 9-3; 9-4, 9-5; 16-66-210; 16-66-218(b)(3), (4) *In re Stevens,* 829 F.2d 693 (8th Cir. 1987)
	2. Real or personal property used as residence to $800 if single; $1,250 if married	16-66-218(a)(1)
insurance	Annuity contract	23-79-134
	Disability benefits	23-79-133
	Fraternal benefit society benefits	23-74-403
	Group life insurance	23-79-132
	Life, health, accident, or disability cash value or proceeds paid or due to $500	16-66-209; Constitution 9-1, 9-2; *In re Holt,* 894 F. 2d 1005 (7th Cir. 1990)
	Life insurance proceeds if clause prohibits proceeds from being used to pay beneficiary's creditors	23-79-131
	Life insurance proceeds or avails if beneficiary isn't the insured	23-79-131
	Mutual assessment life or disability benefits to $1,000	23-72-114
	Stipulated insurance premiums	23-71-112
miscellaneous	Property of business partnership (will be repealed in 2005)	4-42-502
pensions	Disabled firefighters	24-11-814
	Disabled police officers	24-11-417
	Firefighters	24-10-616
	IRA deposits to $20,000 if deposited over 1 year before filing for bankruptcy	16-66-218(b)(16)
	Police officers	24-10-616
	School employees	24-7-715
	State police officers	24-6-205; 24-6-223
personal property	Burial plot to 5 acres, if choosing federal homestead exemption (option 2)	16-66-207; 16-66-218(a)(1)
	Clothing	Constitution 9-1, 9-2
	Motor vehicle to $1,200	16-66-218(a)(2)
	Prepaid funeral trusts	23-40-117
	Wedding rings	16-66-219
public benefits	Crime victims' compensation	16-90-716(e)
	Unemployment compensation	11-10-109
	Workers' compensation	11-9-110
tools of trade	Implements, books, & tools of trade to $750	16-66-218(a)(4)
wages	Earned but unpaid wages due for 60 days; in no event less than $25 per week	16-66-208; 16-66-218(b)(6)
wildcard	$500 of any personal property if married or head of family; $200 if not married	Constitution 9-1, 9-2; 16-66-218(b)(1),(2)

Be sure to read the caution about exceptions to exemptions in the introduction to this appendix.

California—System 1

Federal Bankruptcy Exemptions not available. California has two systems; you must select one or the other. All law references are to California Code of Civil Procedure unless otherwise noted. Many exemptions do not apply to claims for child support.

Note: California's exemption amounts are no longer updated in the statutes themselves. California Code of Civil Procedure Section 740.150 deputized the California Judicial Council to update the exemption amounts every three years. (The next revision will be in 2007.) As a result, the amounts listed in this chart will not match the amounts that appear in the cited statutes. The current exemption amounts can be found on the California Judicial Council website, www.courtinfo.ca.gov/forms/documents/exemptions.pdf.

ASSET	EXEMPTION	LAW
homestead	Real or personal property you occupy including mobile home, boat, stock cooperative, community apartment, planned development, or condo to $50,000 if single & not disabled; $75,000 for families if no other member has a homestead (if only one spouse files, may exempt one-half of amount if home held as community property & all of amount if home held as tenants in common); $150,000 if 65 or older, or physically or mentally disabled; $150,000 if 55 or older, single, & earn under $15,000 or married & earn under $20,000 & creditors seek to force the sale of your home; forced sale proceeds received exempt for 6 months after. (Husband & wife may not double.)	704.710; 704.720; 704.730 *In re McFall,* 112 B.R. 336 (9th Cir. B.A.P. 1990)
	May file homestead declaration to protect exemption amount from attachment of judicial liens and to protect proceeds of voluntary sale for 6 months	704.920
insurance	Disability or health benefits	704.130
	Fidelity bonds	Labor 404
	Fraternal benefit society benefits	704.170
	Fraternal unemployment benefits	704.120
	Homeowners' insurance proceeds for 6 months after received, to homestead exemption amount	704.720(b)
	Life insurance proceeds if clause prohibits proceeds from being used to pay beneficiary's creditors	Ins. 10132; Ins. 10170; Ins. 10171
	Matured life insurance benefits needed for support	704.100(c)
	Unmatured life insurance policy cash surrender value completely exempt. Loan value exempt to $9,700	704.100(b)
miscellaneous	Business or professional licenses	695.060
	Inmates' trust funds to $1,225 (husband & wife may not double)	704.090
	Property of business partnership	Corp. 16501-04
pensions	County employees	Gov't 31452
	County firefighters	Gov't 32210
	County peace officers	Gov't 31913
	Private retirement benefits, including IRAs & Keoghs	704.115
	Public employees	Gov't 21255
	Public retirement benefits	704.110
personal property	Appliances, furnishings, clothing, & food	704.020
	Bank deposits from Social Security Administration to $2,425 ($3,650 for husband & wife); unlimited if SS funds are not commingled with other funds Bank deposits of other public benefits to $1,225 ($1,825 for husband & wife)	704.080
	Building materials to repair or improve home to $2,425 (husband & wife may not double)	704.030
	Burial plot	704.200
	Funds held in escrow	Fin. 17410
	Health aids	704.050
	Jewelry, heirlooms, & art to $6,075 total (husband & wife may not double)	704.040
	Motor vehicles to $2,300, or $2,300 in auto insurance for loss or damages (husband & wife may not double)	704.010
	Personal injury & wrongful death causes of action	704.140(a); 704.150(a)
	Personal injury & wrongful death recoveries needed for support; if receiving installments, at least 75%	704.140(b),(c),(d); 704.150(b),(c)
public benefits	Aid to blind, aged, disabled; public assistance	704.170
	Financial aid to students	704.190
	Relocation benefits	704.180
	Unemployment benefits	704.120
	Union benefits due to labor dispute	704.120(b)(5)
	Workers' compensation	704.160
tools of trade	Tools, implements, materials, instruments, uniforms, books, furnishings, & equipment to $6,075 total ($12,150 total if used by both spouses in same occupation)	704.060
	Commercial vehicle (Vehicle Code § 260) to $4,850 ($9,700 total if used by both spouses in same occupation)	704.060
wages	Minimum 75% of wages paid within 30 days prior to filing	704.070
	Public employees' vacation credits; if receiving installments, at least 75%	704.113
wildcard	None	

California—System 2

Refer to the notes for California—System 1, above.

Note: Married couples may not double any exemptions. (*In re Talmadge,* 832 F.2d 1120 (9th Cir. 1987); *In re Baldwin,* 70 B.R. 612 (9th Cir. B.A.P. 1987).)

ASSET	EXEMPTION	LAW
homestead	Real or personal property, including co-op, used as residence to $18,675; unused portion of homestead may be applied to any property	703.140(b)(1)
insurance	Disability benefits	703.140(b)(10)(C)
	Life insurance proceeds needed for support of family	703.140(b)(11)(C)
	Unmatured life insurance contract accrued avails to $9,975	703.140(b)(8)
	Unmatured life insurance policy other than credit	703.140(b)(7)
miscellaneous	Alimony, child support needed for support	703.140(b)(10)(D)
pensions	ERISA-qualified benefits needed for support	703.140(b)(10)(E)
personal property	Animals, crops, appliances, furnishings, household goods, books, musical instruments, & clothing to $475 per item	703.140(b)(3)
	Burial plot to $18,675, in lieu of homestead	703.140(b)(1)
	Health aids	703.140(b)(9)
	Jewelry to $1,225	703.140(b)(4)
	Motor vehicle to $2,975	703.140(b)(2)
	Personal injury recoveries to $18,675 (not to include pain & suffering; pecuniary loss)	703.140(b)(11)(D),(E)
	Wrongful death recoveries needed for support	703.140(b)(11)(B)
public benefits	Crime victims' compensation	703.140(b)(11)(A)
	Public assistance	703.140(b)(10)(A)
	Social Security	703.140(b)(10)(A)
	Unemployment compensation	703.140(b)(10)(A)
	Veterans' benefits	703.140(b)(10)(B)
tools of trade	Implements, books, & tools of trade to $1,875	703.140(b)(6)
wages	None (use federal nonbankruptcy wage exemption)	
wildcard	$1,000 of any property	703.140(b)(5)
	Unused portion of homestead or burial exemption of any property	703.140(b)(5)

Be sure to read the caution about exceptions to exemptions in the introduction to this appendix.

Colorado

Federal Bankruptcy Exemptions not available. All law references are to Colorado Revised Statutes.

ASSET	EXEMPTION	LAW
homestead	Real property, mobile home, manufactured home, or house trailer you occupy to $45,000; sale proceeds exempt 1 year after received	38-41-201; 38-41-201.6; 38-41-203; 38-41-207; In re Pastrana, 216 B.R. 948 (Colo., 1998)
	Spouse or child of deceased owner may claim homestead exemption	38-41-204
insurance	Disability benefits to $200 per month; if receive lump sum, entire amount exempt	10-16-212
	Fraternal benefit society benefits	10-14-403
	Group life insurance policy or proceeds	10-7-205
	Homeowners' insurance proceeds for 1 year after received, to homestead exemption amount	38-41-209
	Life insurance cash surrender value to $50,000, except contributions to policy within past 48 months	13-54-102(1)(l)
	Life insurance proceeds if clause prohibits proceeds from being used to pay beneficiary's creditors	10-7-106
miscellaneous	Child support	13-54-102.5
	Property of business partnership	7-60-125
pensions see also wages	ERISA-qualified benefits, including IRAs & Roth IRAs	13-54-102(1)(s)
	Firefighters & police officers	31-30.5-208; 31-31-203
	Public employees' pensions & defined contribution plans as of 2006	24-51-212
	Public employees' deferred compensation	24-52-105
	Teachers	22-64-120
	Veteran's pension for veteran, spouse, or dependents if veteran served in war or armed conflict	13-54-102(1)(h); 13-54-104
personal property	1 burial plot per family member	13-54-102(1)(d)
	Clothing to $1,500	13-54-102(1)(a)
	Food & fuel to $600	13-54-102(1)(f)
	Health aids	13-54-102(1)(p)
	Household goods to $3,000	13-54-102(1)(e)
	Jewelry & articles of adornment to $1,000	13-54-102(1)(b)
	Motor vehicles or bicycles used for work to $3,000; to $6,000 if used by a debtor or by a dependent who is disabled or 65 or over	13-54-102(j)(I), (II)
	Personal injury recoveries	13-54-102(1)(n)
	Family pictures & books to $1,500	13-54-102(1)(c)
	Proceeds for damaged exempt property	13-54-102(1)(m)
	Security deposits	13-54-102(1)(r)
public benefits	Aid to blind, aged, disabled; public assistance	26-2-131
	Crime victims' compensation	13-54-102(1)(q); 24-4.1-114
	Earned income tax credit	13-54-102(1)(o)
	Unemployment compensation	8-80-103
	Veteran's benefits for veteran, spouse, or child if veteran served in war or armed conflict	13-54-102(1)(h)
	Workers' compensation	8-42-124
tools of trade	Livestock or other animals, machinery, tools, equipment, & seed of person engaged in agriculture, to $25,000 total	13-54-102(1)(g)
	Professional's library to $3,000 (if not claimed under other tools of trade exemption)	13-54-102(1)(k)
	Stock in trade, supplies, fixtures, tools, machines, electronics, equipment, books, & other business materials, to $10,000 total	13-54-102(1)(i)
	Military equipment personally owned by members of the National Guard	13-54-102(1)(h.5)
wages	Minimum 75% of weekly net earnings or 30 times the federal minimum wage, whichever is greater, including pension & insurance payments	13-54-104
wildcard	None	

Connecticut

Federal Bankruptcy Exemptions available. All law references are to Connecticut General Statutes Annotated.

ASSET	EXEMPTION	LAW
homestead	Real property, including mobile or manufactured home, to $75,000; applies only to claims arising after 1993, but to $125,000 in the case of a money judgment arising out of services provided at a hospital	52-352a(e); 52-352b(t)
insurance	Disability benefits paid by association for its members	52-352b(p)
	Fraternal benefit society benefits	38a-637
	Health or disability benefits	52-352b(e)
	Life insurance proceeds if clause prohibits proceeds from being used to pay beneficiary's creditors	38a-454
	Life insurance proceeds or avails	38a-453
	Unmatured life insurance policy loan value to $4,000	52-352b(s)
miscellaneous	Alimony, to extent wages exempt	52-352b(n)
	Child support	52-352b(h)
	Farm partnership animals & livestock feed reasonably required to run farm where at least 50% of partners are members of same family	52-352d
pensions	ERISA-qualified benefits, including IRAs, Roth IRAs, & Keoghs, to extent wages exempt	52-321a; 52-352b(m)
	Medical savings account	52-321a
	Municipal employees	7-446
	State employees	5-171; 5-192w
	Teachers	10-183q
personal property	Appliances, food, clothing, furniture, bedding	52-352b(a)
	Burial plot	52-352b(c)
	Health aids needed	52-352b(f)
	Motor vehicle to $1,500	52-352b(j)
	Proceeds for damaged exempt property	52-352b(q)
	Residential utility & security deposits for 1 residence	52-3252b(l)
	Spendthrift trust funds required for support of debtor & family	52-321(d)
	Transfers to a nonprofit debt adjuster	52-352b(u)
	Wedding & engagement rings	52-352b(k)
public benefits	Crime victims' compensation	52-352b(o); 54-213
	Public assistance	52-352b(d)
	Social Security	52-352b(g)
	Unemployment compensation	31-272(c); 52-352b(g)
	Veterans' benefits	52-352b(g)
	Workers' compensation	52-352b(g)
tools of trade	Arms, military equipment, uniforms, musical instruments of military personnel	52-352b(i)
	Tools, books, instruments, & farm animals needed	52-352b(b)
wages	Minimum 75% of earned but unpaid weekly disposable earnings, or 40 times the state or federal hourly minimum wage, whichever is greater	52-361a(f)
wildcard	$1,000 of any property	52-352b(r)

Be sure to read the caution about exceptions to exemptions in the introduction to this appendix.

Delaware

Federal Bankruptcy Exemptions not available. All law references are to Delaware Code Annotated (in the form title number-section number) unless otherwise noted.

Note: A single person may exempt no more than $5,000 total in all exemptions (not including retirement plans); a husband & wife may exempt no more than $10,000 total (10-4914).

ASSET	EXEMPTION	LAW
homestead	None; however, property held as tenancy by the entirety may be exempt against debts owed by only one spouse	*In re Kelley*, 289 B.R. 38 (Bankr. D. Del. 2003)
insurance	Annuity contract proceeds to $350 per month	18-2728
	Fraternal benefit society benefits	18-6218
	Group life insurance policy or proceeds	18-2727
	Health or disability benefits	18-2726
	Life insurance proceeds if clause prohibits proceeds from being used to pay beneficiary's creditors	18-2729
	Life insurance proceeds or avails	18-2725
pensions	IRAs, Roth IRAs, & any other retirement plans	*In re Yuhas*, 104 F.3d 612 (3rd Cir. 1997)
	Kent County employees	9-4316
	Police officers	11-8803
	State employees	29-5503
	Volunteer firefighters	16-6653
personal property	Bible, books, & family pictures	10-4902(a)
	Burial plot	10-4902(a)
	Church pew or any seat in public place of worship	10-4902(a)
	Clothing, includes jewelry	10-4902(a)
	College investment plan account (limit for year before filing is $5,000 or average of past two years' contribution, whichever is more)	10-4916
	Income from spendthrift trusts	12-3536
	Pianos & leased organs	10-4902(d)
	Sewing machines	10-4902(c)
public benefits	Aid to blind	31-2309
	Aid to aged, disabled, general assistance	31-513
	Crime victims' compensation	11-9011
	Unemployment compensation	19-3374
	Workers' compensation	19-2355
tools of trade	Tools, implements, & fixtures to $75 in New Castle & Sussex Counties; to $50 in Kent County	10-4902(b)
wages	85% of earned but unpaid wages	10-4913
wildcard	$500 of any personal property, except tools of trade, if head of family	10-4903

District of Columbia

Federal Bankruptcy Exemptions available. All law references are to District of Columbia Code unless otherwise noted.

ASSET	EXEMPTION	LAW
homestead	Any property used as a residence or co-op that debtor or debtor's dependent uses as a residence	15-501(a)(14)
	Property held as tenancy by the entirety may be exempt against debts owed by only one spouse	*Estate of Wall*, 440 F.2d 215 (D.C. Cir. 1971)
insurance	Disability benefits	15-501(a)(7)
	Fraternal benefit society benefits	31-5315
	Group life insurance policy or proceeds	31-4717
	Life insurance payments	15-501(a)(11)
	Life insurance proceeds if clause prohibits proceeds from being used to pay beneficiary's creditors	31-4719
	Life insurance proceeds or avails	31-4716
	Other insurance proceeds to $200 per month, maximum 2 months, for head of family; else $60 per month	15-503
	Unmatured life insurance contract other than credit life insurance	15-501(a)(5)
miscellaneous	Alimony or child support	15-501(a)(7)
pensions *see also wages*	ERISA-qualified benefits, IRAs, Keoghs, etc. to maximum deductible contribution	15-501(b)(9)
	Any stock bonus, annuity, pension, or profit-sharing plan	15-501(a)(7)
	Judges	11-1570(d)
	Public school teachers	38-2001.17; 38-2021.17
personal property	Appliances, books, clothing, household furnishings, goods, musical instruments, pets to $425 per item or $8,625 total	15-501(a)(2)
	Cemetery & burial funds	27-111
	Cooperative association holdings to $50	29-928
	Food for 3 months	15-501(a)(12)
	Health aids	15-501(a)(6)
	Higher education tuition savings account	47-4510
	Residential condominium deposit	42-1904.09
	All family pictures; & all the family library, to $400	15-501(a)(8)
	Motor vehicle to $2,575	15-501(a)(1)
	Payment including pain & suffering for loss of debtor or person depended on	15-501(a)(11)
	Uninsured motorist benefits	31-2408.01(h)
	Wrongful death damages	15-501(a)(11)
public benefits	Aid to blind, aged, disabled; general assistance	4-215.01
	Crime victims' compensation	15-501(a)(11)
	Social Security	15-501(a)(7)
	Unemployment compensation	51-118
	Veterans' benefits	15-501(a)(7)
	Workers' compensation	32-1517
tools of trade	Library, furniture, tools of professional, or artist to $300	15-501(a)(13)
	Tools of trade or business to $1,625	15-501(a)(5)
	Mechanic's tools to $200	15-503(b)
	Seal & documents of notary public	1-1206
wages	Minimum 75% of earned but unpaid wages, pension payments; bankruptcy judge may authorize more for low-income debtors	16-572
	Nonwage (including pension & retirement) earnings to $200/mo for head of family; else $60/mo for a maximum of two months	15-503
	Payment for loss of future earnings	15-501(e)(11)
wildcard	Up to $850 in any property, plus up to $8,075 of unused homestead exemption	15-501(a)(3)

Be sure to read the caution about exceptions to exemptions in the introduction to this appendix.

Florida

Federal Bankruptcy Exemptions not available. All law references are to Florida Statutes Annotated unless otherwise noted.

ASSET	EXEMPTION	LAW
homestead	Real or personal property including mobile or modular home to unlimited value; cannot exceed half acre in municipality or 160 acres elsewhere; spouse or child of deceased owner may claim homestead exemption	222.01; 222.02; 222.03; 222.05; Constitution 10-4 *In re Colwell,* 196 F.3d 1225 (11th Cir. 1999)
	May file homestead declaration	222.01
	Property held as tenancy by the entirety may be exempt against debts owed by only one spouse	*Havoco of America, Ltd. v. Hill,* 197 F.3d 1135 (11th Cir Fla.,1999)
insurance	Annuity contract proceeds; does not include lottery winnings	222.14; *In re Pizzi,* 153 B.R. 357 (S.D. Fla. 1993)
	Death benefits payable to a specific beneficiary, not the deceased's estate	222.13
	Disability or illness benefits	222.18
	Fraternal benefit society benefits	632.619
	Life insurance cash surrender value	222.14
miscellaneous	Alimony, child support needed for support	222.201
	Damages to employees for injuries in hazardous occupations	769.05
pensions *see also wages*	County officers, employees	122.15
	ERISA-qualified benefits, including IRAs & Roth IRAs	222.21(2)
	Firefighters	175.241
	Police officers	185.25
	State officers, employees	121.131
	Teachers	238.15
personal property	Any personal property to $1,000 (husband & wife may double)	Constitution 10-4 *In re Hawkins,* 51 B.R. 348 (S.D. Fla. 1985)
	Federal income tax refund or credit	222.25
	Health aids	222.25
	Motor vehicle to $1,000	222.25
	Pre-need funeral contract deposits	497.413(8)
	Prepaid college education trust deposits	222.22(1)
	Prepaid medical savings account deposits	222.22(2)
public benefits	Crime victims' compensation, unless seeking to discharge debt for treatment of injury incurred during the crime	960.14
	Public assistance	222.201
	Social Security	222.201
	Unemployment compensation	222.201; 443.051(2),(3)
	Veterans' benefits	222.201; 744.626
	Workers' compensation	440.22
tools of trade	None	
wages	100% of wages for heads of family up to $500 per week either unpaid or paid & deposited into bank account for up to 6 months	222.11
	Federal government employees' pension payments needed for support & received 3 months prior	222.21
wildcard	See personal property	

Georgia

Federal Bankruptcy Exemptions not available. All law references are to the Official Code of Georgia Annotated, not to the Georgia Code Annotated.

ASSET	EXEMPTION	LAW
homestead	Real or personal property, including co-op, used as residence to $10,000; up to $5,000 of unused portion of homestead may be applied to any property	44-13-100(a)(1); 44-13-100(a)(6)
insurance	Annuity & endowment contract benefits	33-28-7
	Disability or health benefits to $250 per month	33-29-15
	Fraternal benefit society benefits	33-15-62
	Group insurance	33-30-10
	Proceeds & avails of life insurance	33-26-5; 33-25-11
	Life insurance proceeds if policy owned by someone you depended on, needed for support	44-13-100(a)(11)(C)
	Unmatured life insurance contract	44-13-100(a)(8)
	Unmatured life insurance dividends, interest, loan value, or cash value to $2,000 if beneficiary is you or someone you depend on	44-13-100(a)(9)
miscellaneous	Alimony, child support needed for support	44-13-100(a)(2)(D)
pensions	Employees of nonprofit corporations	44-13-100(a)(2.1)(B)
	ERISA-qualified benefits & IRAs	18-4-22
	Public employees	44-13-100(a)(2.1)(A); 47-2-332
	Payments from IRA necessary for support	44-13-100(a)(2)(F)
	Other pensions needed for support	18-4-22; 44-13-100(a)(2)(E); 44-13-100(a)(2.1)(C)
personal property	Animals, crops, clothing, appliances, books, furnishings, household goods, musical instruments to $300 per item, $5,000 total	44-13-100(a)(4)
	Burial plot, in lieu of homestead	44-13-100(a)(1)
	Compensation for lost future earnings needed for support to $7,500	44-13-100(a)(11)(E)
	Health aids	44-13-100(a)(10)
	Jewelry to $500	44-13-100(a)(5)
	Motor vehicles to $3,500	44-13-100(a)(3)
	Personal injury recoveries to $10,000	44-13-100(a)(11)(D)
	Wrongful death recoveries needed for support	44-13-100(a)(11)(B)
public benefits	Aid to blind	49-4-58
	Aid to disabled	49-4-84
	Crime victims' compensation	44-13-100(a)(11)(A)
	Local public assistance	44-13-100(a)(2)(A)
	Old age assistance	49-4-35
	Social Security	44-13-100(a)(2)(A)
	Unemployment compensation	44-13-100(a)(2)(A)
	Veterans' benefits	44-13-100(a)(2)(B)
	Workers' compensation	34-9-84
tools of trade	Implements, books, & tools of trade to $1,500	44-13-100(a)(7)
wages	Minimum 75% of earned but unpaid weekly disposable earnings, or 40 times the state or federal hourly minimum wage, whichever is greater, for private & federal workers; bankruptcy judge may authorize more for low-income debtors	18-4-20; 18-4-21
wildcard	$600 of any property	44-13-100(a)(6)
	Unused portion of homestead exemption to $5,000	44-13-100(a)(6)

Be sure to read the caution about exceptions to exemptions in the introduction to this appendix.

Hawaii

Federal Bankruptcy Exemptions available. All law references are to Hawaii Revised Statutes unless otherwise noted.

ASSET	EXEMPTION	LAW
homestead	Head of family or over 65 to $30,000; all others to $20,000; property cannot exceed 1 acre; sale proceeds exempt for 6 months after sale (husband & wife may not double)	651-91; 651-92; 651-96
	Property held as tenancy by the entirety may be exempt against debts owed by only one spouse	*Security Pacific Bank v. Chang*, 818 F.Supp. 1343 (D. Haw. 1993)
insurance	Annuity contract or endowment policy proceeds if beneficiary is insured's spouse, child, or parent	431:10-232(b)
	Accident, health, or sickness benefits	431:10-231
	Fraternal benefit society benefits	432:2-403
	Group life insurance policy or proceeds	431:10-233
	Life insurance proceeds if clause prohibits proceeds from being used to pay beneficiary's creditors	431:10D-112
	Life or health insurance policy for spouse or child	431:10-234
miscellaneous	Property of business partnership	425-125
pensions	ERISA-qualified benefits deposited over 3 years before filing bankruptcy	651-124
	Firefighters	88-169
	Police officers	88-169
	Public officers & employees	88-91; 653-3
personal property	Appliances & furnishings	651-121(1)
	Books	651-121(1)
	Burial plot to 250 sq. ft. plus tombstones, monuments, & fencing	651-121(4)
	Clothing	651-121(1)
	Jewelry, watches, & articles of adornment to $1,000	651-121(1)
	Motor vehicle to wholesale value of $2,575	651-121(2)
	Proceeds for sold or damaged exempt property; sale proceeds exempt for 6 months after sale	651-121(5)
public benefits	Crime victims' compensation & special accounts created to limit commercial exploitation of crimes	351-66; 351-86
	Public assistance paid by Dept. of Health Services for work done in home or workshop	346-33
	Temporary disability benefits	392-29
	Unemployment compensation	383-163
	Unemployment work relief funds to $60 per month	653-4
	Workers' compensation	386-57
tools of trade	Tools, implements, books, instruments, uniforms, furnishings, fishing boat, nets, motor vehicle, & other property needed for livelihood	651-121(3)
wages	Prisoner's wages held by Dept. of Public Safety (except for restitution, child support, & other claims)	353-22.5
	Unpaid wages due for services of past 31 days	651-121(6)
wildcard	None	

Idaho

Federal Bankruptcy Exemptions not available. All law references are to Idaho Code.

ASSET	EXEMPTION	LAW
homestead	Real property or mobile home to $50,000; sale proceeds exempt for 6 months (husband & wife may not double)	55-1003; 55-1113
	Must record homestead exemption for property that is not yet occupied	55-1004
insurance	Annuity contract proceeds to $1,250 per month	41-1836
	Death or disability benefits	11-604(1)(a); 41-1834
	Fraternal benefit society benefits	41-3218
	Group life insurance benefits	41-1835
	Homeowners' insurance proceeds to amount of homestead exemption	55-1008
	Life insurance proceeds if clause prohibits proceeds from being used to pay beneficiary's creditors	41-1930
	Life insurance proceeds or avails for beneficiary other than the insured	11-604(d); 41-1833
	Medical, surgical, or hospital care benefits	11-603(5)
	Unmatured life insurance contract, other than credit life insurance, owned by debtor	11-605(8)
	Unmatured life insurance contract interest or dividends to $5,000 owned by debtor or person debtor depends on	11-605(9)
miscellaneous	Alimony, child support	11-604(1)(b)
	Liquor licenses	23-514
pension *see also wages*	ERISA-qualified benefits	55-1011
	Firefighters	72-1422
	Government & private pensions, retirement plans, IRAs, Roth IRAs, Keoghs, etc.	11-604A
	Police officers	50-1517
	Public employees	59-1317
personal property	Appliances, furnishings, books, clothing, pets, musical instruments, 1 firearm, family portraits, & sentimental heirlooms to $500 per item, $5,000 total	11-605(1)
	Building materials	45-514
	Burial plot	11-603(1)
	College savings program account	11-604A(4)(b)
	Crops cultivated on maximum of 50 acres, to $1,000; water rights to 160 inches	11-605(6)
	Health aids	11-603(2)
	Jewelry to $1,000	11-605(2)
	Motor vehicle to $3,000	11-605(3)
	Personal injury recoveries	11-604(1)(c)
	Proceeds for damaged exempt property for 3 months after proceeds received	11-606
	Wrongful death recoveries	11-604(1)(c)
public benefits	Aid to blind, aged, disabled	56-223
	Federal, state, & local public assistance	11-603(4)
	General assistance	56-223
	Social Security	11-603(3)
	Unemployment compensation	11-603(6)
	Veterans' benefits	11-603(3)
	Workers' compensation	72-802
tools of trade	Arms, uniforms, & accoutrements that peace officer, National Guard, or military personnel is required to keep	11-605(5)
	Implements, books, & tools of trade to $1,500	11-605(3)
wages	Minimum 75% of earned but unpaid weekly disposable earnings, or 30 times the federal hourly minimum wage, whichever is greater; pension payments; bankruptcy judge may authorize more for low-income debtors	11-207
wildcard	$800 in any tangible personal property	11-605(10)

Be sure to read the caution about exceptions to exemptions in the introduction to this appendix.

Illinois

Federal Bankruptcy Exemptions not available. All law references are to Illinois Annotated Statutes.

ASSET	EXEMPTION	LAW
homestead	Real or personal property including a farm, lot, & buildings, condo, co-op, or mobile home to $7,500; sale proceeds exempt for 1 year	735-5/12-901; 735-5/12-906
	Spouse or child of deceased owner may claim homestead exemption	735-5/12-902
	Illinois recognizes tenancy by the entirety, with limitations	750-65/22; 765-1005/1c; *In re Gillissie*, 215 B.R. 370 (Bankr. N.D. Ill. 1998); *Great Southern Co. v. Allard*, 202 B.R. 938 (N.D. Ill. 1996)
insurance	Fraternal benefit society benefits	215-5/299.1a
	Health or disability benefits	735-5/12-1001(g)(3)
	Homeowners' proceeds if home destroyed, to $7,500	735-5/12-907
	Life insurance, annuity proceeds, or cash value if beneficiary is insured's child, parent, spouse, or other dependent	215-5/238; 735-5/12-1001(f)
	Life insurance proceeds to a spouse or dependent of debtor to extent needed for support	735-5/12-1001(f),(g)(3)
miscellaneous	Alimony, child support	735-5/12-1001(g)(4)
	Property of business partnership	805-205/25
pensions	Civil service employees	40-5/11-223
	County employees	40-5/9-228
	Disabled firefighters; widows & children of firefighters	40-5/22-230
	ERISA-qualified benefits	735-5/12-1006
	Firefighters	40-5/4-135; 40-5/6-213
	General assembly members	40-5/2-154
	House of correction employees	40-5/19-117
	Judges	40-5/18-161
	Municipal employees	40-5/7-217(a); 40-5/8-244
	Park employees	40-5/12-190
	Police officers	40-5/3-144.1; 40-5/5-218
	Public employees	735-5/12-1006
	Public library employees	40-5/19-218
	Sanitation district employees	40-5/13-805
	State employees	40-5/14-147
	State university employees	40-5/15-185
	Teachers	40-5/16-190; 40-5/17-151
personal property	Bible, family pictures, schoolbooks, & clothing	735-5/12-1001(a)
	Health aids	735-5/12-1001(e)
	Motor vehicle to $1,200	735-5/12-1001(c)
	Personal injury recoveries to $7,500	735-5/12-1001(h)(4)
	Pre-need cemetery sales funds, care funds, & trust funds	235-5/6-1; 760-100/4; 815-390/16
	Prepaid tuition trust fund	110-979/45(g)
	Proceeds of sold exempt property	735-5/12-1001
	Wrongful death recoveries	735-5/12-1001(h)(2)
public benefits	Aid to aged, blind, disabled; public assistance	305-5/11-3
	Crime victims' compensation	735-5/12-1001(h)(1)
	Restitution payments on account of WWII relocation of Aleuts & Japanese-Americans	735-5/12-1001(12)(h)(5)
	Social Security	735-5/12-1001(g)(1)
	Unemployment compensation	735-5/12-1001(g)(1),(3)
	Veterans' benefits	735-5/12-1001(g)(2)
	Workers' compensation	820-305/21
	Workers' occupational disease compensation	820-310/21
tools of trade	Implements, books, & tools of trade to $750	735-5/12-1001(d)
wages	Minimum 85% of earned but unpaid weekly wages or 45 times the federal minimum hourly wage; bankruptcy judge may authorize more for low-income debtors	740-170/4
wildcard	$2,000 of any personal property (does not include wages)	735-5/12-1001(b)

Be sure to read the caution about exceptions to exemptions in the introduction to this appendix.

Indiana

Federal Bankruptcy Exemptions not available. All law references are to Indiana Statutes Annotated.

ASSET	EXEMPTION	LAW
homestead *see also wildcard*	Real or personal property used as residence to $7,500; homestead plus personal property—except health aids—can't exceed $10,000	34-55-10-2(b)(1); 34-55-10-2(c)
	Property held as tenancy by the entirety may be exempt against debts incurred by only one spouse	34-55-10-2(b)(5)
insurance	Employer's life insurance policy on employee	27-1-12-17.1
	Fraternal benefit society benefits	27-11-6-3
	Group life insurance policy	27-1-12-29
	Life insurance policy, proceeds, cash value, or avails if beneficiary is insured's spouse or dependent	27-1-12-14
	Life insurance proceeds if clause prohibits proceeds to be used to pay beneficiary's creditors	27-2-5-1
	Mutual life or accident proceeds	27-8-3-23
miscellaneous	Property of business partnership	23-4-1-25
pensions	Firefighters	36-8-7-22 36-8-8-17
	Police officers	36-8-8-17; 10-12-2-10
	Public employees	5-10.3-8-9
	Public or private retirement benefits & contributions	34-55-10-2(b)(6)
	Sheriffs	36-8-10-19
	State teachers	21-6.1-5-17
personal property *see also wildcard*	Health aids	34-55-10-2(b)(4)
	Money in medical care savings account	34-55-10-2(b)(7)
	Spendthrift trusts	30-4-3-2
	$100 of any intangible personal property, except money owed to you	34-55-10-2(b)(3)
public benefits	Crime victims' compensation, unless seeking to discharge the debts for which the victim was compensated	5-2-6.1-38
	Unemployment compensation	22-4-33-3
	Workers' compensation	22-3-2-17
tools of trade	National Guard uniforms, arms, & equipment	10-16-10-3
wages	Minimum 75% of earned but unpaid weekly disposable earnings, or 30 times the federal hourly minimum wage; bankruptcy judge may authorize more for low-income debtors	24-4.5-5-105
wildcard	$4,000 of any real estate or tangible personal property, but wildcard plus homestead cannot exceed $10,000	34-55-10-2(b)(2)

Iowa

Federal Bankruptcy Exemptions not available. All law references are to Iowa Code Annotated.

ASSET	EXEMPTION	LAW
homestead	May record homestead declaration	561.4
	Real property or an apartment to an unlimited value; property cannot exceed 1/2 acre in town or city, 40 acres elsewhere (husband & wife may not double)	499A.18; 561.2; 561.16
insurance	Accident, disability, health, illness, or life proceeds or avails	627.6(6)
	Disability or illness benefit	627.6(8)(c)
	Employee group insurance policy or proceeds	509.12
	Fraternal benefit society benefits	512B.18
	Life insurance proceeds if clause prohibits proceeds from being used to pay beneficiary's creditors	508.32
	Life insurance proceeds paid to spouse, child, or other dependent (limited to $10,000 if acquired within 2 years of filing for bankruptcy)	627.6(6)
	Upon death of insured, up to $15,000 total proceeds from all matured life, accident, health, or disability policies exempt from beneficiary's debts contracted before insured's death	627.6(6)
miscellaneous	Alimony, child support needed for support	627.6(8)(d)
	Liquor licenses	123.38
pensions *see also wages*	Disabled firefighters, police officers (only payments being received)	410.11
	Federal government pension	627.8
	Firefighters	411.13
	Other pensions, annuities, & contracts fully exempt; however, contributions made within 1 year prior to filing for bankruptcy not exempt to the extent they exceed normal & customary amounts	627.6(8)(e)
	Peace officers	97A.12
	Police officers	411.13
	Public employees	97B.39
	Retirement plans, Keoghs, IRAs, Roth IRAs, ERISA-qualified benefits	627.6(8)(f)
personal property	Appliances, furnishings, & household goods to $2,000 total	627.6(5)
	Bibles, books, portraits, pictures, & paintings to $1,000 total	627.6(3)
	Burial plot to 1 acre	627.6(4)
	Clothing & its storage containers to $1,000	627.6(1)
	Health aids	627.6(7)
	Motor vehicle, musical instruments, tax refund, & accrued wages to $5,000 total; no more than $1,000 from tax refunds & accrued wages	627.6(9)
	Residential security or utility deposit, or advance rent, to $500	627.6(14)
	Rifle or musket; shotgun	627.6(2)
	Wedding or engagement rings	627.6(1)
public benefits	Adopted child assistance	627.19
	Aid to dependent children	239B.6
	Any public assistance benefit	627.6(8)(a)
	Social Security	627.6(8)(a)
	Unemployment compensation	627.6(8)(a)
	Veterans' benefits	627.6(8)(b)
	Workers' compensation	627.13
tools of trade	Farming equipment; includes livestock, feed to $10,000	627.6(11)
	Nonfarming equipment to $10,000	627.6(10)
wages	Expected annual earnings / Amount NOT exempt per year: $0 to $12,000 → $250; $12,000 to $16,000 → $400; $16,000 to $24,000 → $800; $24,000 to $35,000 → $1,000; $35,000 to $50,000 → $2,000; More than $50,000 → 10%. Not exempt from spousal or child support	642.21
	Wages or salary of a prisoner	356.29
wildcard	$100 of any personal property, including cash	627.6(13)

Be sure to read the caution about exceptions to exemptions in the introduction to this appendix.

Kansas

Federal Bankruptcy Exemptions not available. All law references are to Kansas Statutes Annotated unless otherwise noted.

ASSET	EXEMPTION	LAW
homestead	Real property or mobile home you occupy or intend to occupy to unlimited value; property cannot exceed 1 acre in town or city, 160 acres on farm	60-2301; Constitution 15-9
insurance	Cash value of life insurance; not exempt if obtained within 1 year prior to bankruptcy with fraudulent intent.	60-2313(a)(7); 40-414(b)
	Disability & illness benefits	60-2313(a)(1)
	Fraternal life insurance benefits	60-2313(a)(8)
	Life insurance proceeds	40-414(a)
miscellaneous	Alimony, maintenance, & support	60-2312(b)
	Liquor licenses	60-2313(a)(6); 41-326
pensions	Elected & appointed officials in cities with populations between 120,000 & 200,000	13-14a10
	ERISA-qualified benefits	60-2308(b)
	Federal government pension needed for support & paid within 3 months of filing for bankruptcy (only payments being received)	60-2308(a)
	Firefighters	12-5005(e); 14-10a10
	Judges	20-2618
	Police officers	12-5005(e); 13-14a10
	Public employees	74-4923; 74-49,105
	State highway patrol officers	74-4978g
	State school employees	72-5526
	Payment under a stock bonus, pension, profit-sharing, annuity, or similar plan or contract on account of illness, disability, death, age, or length of service, to the extent reasonably necessary for support	60-2312(b)
personal property	Burial plot or crypt	60-2304(d)
	Clothing to last 1 year	60-2304(a)
	Food & fuel to last 1 year	60-2304(a)
	Funeral plan prepayments	60-2313(a)(10); 16-310(d)
	Furnishings & household equipment	60-2304(a)
	Jewelry & articles of adornment to $1,000	60-2304(b)
	Motor vehicle to $20,000; if designed or equipped for disabled person, no limit	60-2304(c)
public benefits	Crime victims' compensation	60-2313(a)(7); 74-7313(d)
	General assistance	39-717(c)
	Social Security	60-2312(b)
	Unemployment compensation	60-2313(a)(4); 44-718(c)
	Veterans' benefits	60-2312(b)
	Workers' compensation	60-2313(a)(3); 44-514
tools of trade	Books, documents, furniture, instruments, equipment, breeding stock, seed, grain, & stock to $7,500 total	60-2304(e)
	National Guard uniforms, arms, & equipment	48-245
wages	Minimum 75% of disposable weekly wages or 30 times the federal minimum hourly wage per week, whichever is greater; bankruptcy judge may authorize more for low-income debtors	60-2310
wildcard	None	

Kentucky

Federal Bankruptcy Exemptions not available. All law references are to Kentucky Revised Statutes.

ASSET	EXEMPTION	LAW
homestead	Real or personal property used as residence to $5,000; sale proceeds exempt	427.060; 427.090
insurance	Annuity contract proceeds to $350 per month	304.14-330
	Cooperative life or casualty insurance benefits	427.110(1)
	Fraternal benefit society benefits	427.110(2)
	Group life insurance proceeds	304.14-320
	Health or disability benefits	304.14-310
	Life insurance policy if beneficiary is a married woman	304.14-340
	Life insurance proceeds if clause prohibits proceeds from being used to pay beneficiary's creditors	304.14-350
	Life insurance proceeds or cash value if beneficiary is someone other than insured	304.14-300
miscellaneous	Alimony, child support needed for support	427.150(1)
	Property of business partnership	362.270
pensions	ERISA-qualified benefits, including IRAs, SEPs, & Keoghs deposited more than 120 days before filing	427.150
	Firefighters	67A.620; 95.878
	Police officers	427.120; 427.125
	State employees	61.690
	Teachers	161.700
	Urban county government employees	67A.350
personal property	Burial plot to $5,000, in lieu of homestead	427.060
	Clothing, jewelry, articles of adornment, & furnishings to $3,000 total	427.010(1)
	Health aids	427.010(1)
	Lost earnings payments needed for support	427.150(2)(d)
	Medical expenses paid & reparation benefits received under motor vehicle reparation law	304.39-260
	Motor vehicle to $2,500	427.010(1)
	Personal injury recoveries to $7,500 (not to include pain & suffering or pecuniary loss)	427.150(2)(c)
	Prepaid tuition payment fund account	164A.707(3)
	Wrongful death recoveries for person you depended on, needed for support	427.150(2)(b)
public benefits	Aid to blind, aged, disabled; public assistance	205.220(c)
	Crime victims' compensation	427.150(2)(a)
	Unemployment compensation	341.470(4)
	Workers' compensation	342.180
tools of trade	Library, office equipment, instruments, & furnishings of minister, attorney, physician, surgeon, chiropractor, veterinarian, or dentist to $1,000	427.040
	Motor vehicle of auto mechanic, mechanical, or electrical equipment servicer, minister, attorney, physician, surgeon, chiropractor, veterinarian, or dentist to $2,500	427.030
	Tools, equipment, livestock, & poultry of farmer to $3,000	427.010(1)
	Tools of nonfarmer to $300	427.030
wages	Minimum 75% of disposable weekly earnings or 30 times the federal minimum hourly wage per week, whichever is greater; bankruptcy judge may authorize more for low-income debtors	427.010(2),(3)
wildcard	$1,000 of any property	427.160

Be sure to read the caution about exceptions to exemptions in the introduction to this appendix.

Louisiana

Federal Bankruptcy Exemptions not available. All law references are to Louisiana Revised Statutes Annotated unless otherwise noted.

ASSET	EXEMPTION	LAW
homestead	Property you occupy to $25,000 (if debt is result of catastrophic or terminal illness or injury, limit is full value of property as of 1 year before filing); cannot exceed 5 acres in city or town, 200 acres elsewhere (husband & wife may not double)	20:1(A)(1),(2),(3)
	Spouse or child of deceased owner may claim homestead exemption; spouse given home in divorce gets homestead	20:1(B)
insurance	Annuity contract proceeds & avails	22:647
	Fraternal benefit society benefits	22:558
	Group insurance policies or proceeds	22:649
	Health, accident, or disability proceeds or avails	22:646
	Life insurance proceeds or avails; if policy issued within 9 months of filing, exempt only to $35,000	22:647
miscellaneous	Property of minor child	13:3881(A)(3); Civil Code Art. 223
pensions	Assessors	11:1403
	Court clerks	11:1526
	District attorneys	11:1583
	ERISA-qualified benefits, including IRAs, Roth IRAs, & Keoghs, if contributions made over 1 year before filing for bankruptcy	13:3881(D)(1); 20:33(1)
	Firefighters	11:2263
	Gift or bonus payments from employer to employee or heirs whenever paid	20:33(2)
	Judges	11:1378
	Louisiana University employees	11:952.3
	Municipal employees	11:1735
	Parochial employees	11:1905
	Police officers	11:3513
	School employees	11:1003
	Sheriffs	11:2182
	State employees	11:405
	Teachers	11:704
	Voting registrars	11:2033
personal property	Arms, military accoutrements; bedding; dishes, glassware, utensils, silverware (nonsterling); clothing, family portraits, musical instruments; bedroom, living room, & dining room furniture; poultry, 1 cow, household pets; heating & cooling equipment, refrigerator, freezer, stove, washer & dryer, iron, sewing machine	13:3881(A)(4)
	Cemetery plot, monuments	8:313
	Engagement & wedding rings to $5,000	13:3881(A)(5)
	Spendthrift trusts	9:2004
public benefits	Aid to blind, aged, disabled; public assistance	46:111
	Crime victims' compensation	46:1811
	Earned Income tax credit	13:3881 (A)(6)
	Unemployment compensation	23:1693
	Workers' compensation	23:1205
tools of trade	Tools, instruments, books, $7,500 of equity in a motor vehicle, one firearm to $500, needed to work	13:3881(A)(2)
wages	Minimum 75% of disposable weekly earnings or 30 times the federal minimum hourly wage per week, whichever is greater; bankruptcy judge may authorize more for low-income debtors	13:3881(A)(1)
wildcard	None	

Maine

Federal Bankruptcy Exemptions not available. All law references are to Maine Revised Statutes Annotated, in the form title number-section number.

ASSET	EXEMPTION	LAW
homestead	Real or personal property (including cooperative) used as residence to $35,000; if debtor has minor dependents in residence, to $70,000; if debtor over age 60 or physically or mentally disabled, $70,000; proceeds of sale exempt for six months	14-4422(1)
insurance	Annuity proceeds to $450 per month	24-A-2431
	Death benefit for police, fire, or emergency medical personnel who die in the line of duty	25-1612
	Disability or health proceeds, benefits, or avails	14-4422(13)(A),(C); 24-A-2429
	Fraternal benefit society benefits	24-A-4118
	Group health or life policy or proceeds	24-A-2430
	Life, endowment, annuity, or accident policy, proceeds or avails	14-4422(14)(C); 24-A-2428
	Life insurance policy, interest, loan value, or accrued dividends for policy from person you depended on, to $4,000	14-4422(11)
	Unmatured life insurance policy, except credit insurance policy	14-4422(10)
miscellaneous	Alimony & child support needed for support	14-4422(13)(D)
	Property of business partnership	31-305
pensions	ERISA-qualified benefits	14-4422(13)(E)
	Judges	4-1203
	Legislators	3-703
	State employees	5-17054
personal property	Animals, crops, musical instruments, books, clothing, furnishings, household goods, appliances to $200 per item	14-4422(3)
	Balance due on repossessed goods; total amount financed can't exceed $2,000	9-A-5-103
	Burial plot in lieu of homestead exemption	14-4422(1)
	Cooking stove; furnaces & stoves for heat	14-4422(6)(A),(B)
	Food to last 6 months	14-4422(7)(A)
	Fuel not to exceed 10 cords of wood, 5 tons of coal, or 1,000 gal. of heating oil	14-4422(6)(C)
	Health aids	14-4422(12)
	Jewelry to $750; no limit for one wedding & one engagement ring	14-4422(4)
	Lost earnings payments needed for support	14-4422(14)(E)
	Military clothes, arms, & equipment	37-B-262
	Motor vehicle to $5,000	14-4422(2)
	Personal injury recoveries to $12,500	14-4422(14)(D)
	Seeds, fertilizers, & feed to raise & harvest food for 1 season	14-4422(7)(B)
	Tools & equipment to raise & harvest food	14-4422(7)(C)
	Wrongful death recoveries needed for support	14-4422(14)(B)
public benefits	Maintenance under the Rehabilitation Act	26-1411-H
	Crime victims' compensation	14-4422(14)(A)
	Public assistance	22-3180, 22-3766
	Social Security	14-4422(13)(A)
	Unemployment compensation	14-4422(13)(A),(C)
	Veterans' benefits	14-4422(13)(B)
	Workers' compensation	39-A-106
tools of trade	Books, materials, & stock to $5,000	14-4422(5)
	Commercial fishing boat, 5-ton limit	14-4422(9)
	One of each farm implement (& its maintenance equipment needed to harvest & raise crops	14-4422(8)
wages	None (use federal nonbankruptcy wage exemption)	
wildcard	Unused portion of exemption in homestead to $6,000; or unused exemption in animals, crops, musical instruments, books, clothing, furnishings, household goods, appliances, tools of the trade, & personal injury recoveries	14-4422(15)
	$400 of any property	14-4422(15)

Be sure to read the caution about exceptions to exemptions in the introduction to this appendix.

Maryland

Federal Bankruptcy Exemptions not available. All law references are to Maryland Code of Courts & Judicial Proceedings unless otherwise noted.

ASSET	EXEMPTION	LAW
homestead	None; however, property held as tenancy by the entirety is exempt against debts owed by only one spouse	In re Birney, 200 F.3d 225 (4th Cir. 1999)
insurance	Disability or health benefits, including court awards, arbitrations, & settlements	11-504(b)(2)
	Fraternal benefit society benefits	Ins. 8-431; Estates & Trusts 8-115
	Life insurance or annuity contract proceeds or avails if beneficiary is insured's dependent, child, or spouse	Ins. 16-111(a); Estates & Trusts 8-115
	Medical insurance benefits deducted from wages plus medical insurance payments to $145 per week or 75% of disposable wages	Commercial Law 15-601.1(3)
pensions	ERISA-qualified benefits, including IRAs, Roth IRAs, & Keoghs	11-504(h)(1), (4)
	State employees	State Pers. & Pen. 21-502
personal property	Appliances, furnishings, household goods, books, pets, & clothing to $1,000 total	11-504(b)(4)
	Burial plot	Bus. Reg. 5-503
	Health aids	11-504(b)(3)
	Perpetual care trust funds	Bus. Reg. 5-602
	Prepaid college trust funds	Educ. 18-1913
	Lost future earnings recoveries	11-504(b)(2)
public benefits	Baltimore Police death benefits	Code of 1957 art. 24, 16-103
	Crime victims' compensation	Crim. Proc. 11-816(b)
	General assistance	Code of 1957 88A-73
	Unemployment compensation	Labor & Employment 8-106
	Workers' compensation	Labor & Employment 9-732
tools of trade	Clothing, books, tools, instruments, & appliances to $5,000	11-504(b)(1)
wages	Earned but unpaid wages, the greater of 75% or $145 per week; in Kent, Caroline, & Queen Anne's of Worcester Counties, the greater of 75% or 30 times federal minimum hourly wage	Commercial Law 15-601.1
wildcard	$6,000 in cash or any property, if claimed within 30 days of attachment or levy	11-504(b)(5)
	An additional $5,000 in real or personal property	11-504(f)

Massachusetts

Federal Bankruptcy Exemptions available. All law references are to Massachusetts General Laws Annotated, in the form title number-section number.

ASSET	EXEMPTION	LAW
homestead	If statement of homestead is not in title to property, must record homestead declaration before filing bankruptcy	188-2
	Property held as tenancy by the entirety may be exempt against debt for nonnecessity owed by only one spouse.	209-1
	Property you occupy or intend to occupy (including mobile home) to $500,000; if over 65 or disabled, $300,000	188-1; 188-1A
	Spouse or children of deceased owner may claim homestead exemption	188-4
insurance	Disability benefits to $400 per week	175-110A
	Fraternal benefit society benefits	176-22
	Group annuity policy or proceeds	175-132C
	Group life insurance policy	175-135
	Life insurance or annuity contract proceeds if clause prohibits proceeds from being used to pay beneficiary's creditors	175-119A
	Life insurance policy if beneficiary is married woman	175-126
	Life or endowment policy, proceeds, or cash value	175-125
	Medical malpractice self-insurance	175F-15
miscellaneous	Property of business partnership	108A-25
pensions *see also wages*	Credit union employees	171-84
	ERISA-qualified benefits, including IRAs & Keoghs to specified limits	235-34A; 246-28
	Private retirement benefits	32-41
	Public employees	32-19
	Savings bank employees	168-41; 168-44
personal property	Bank deposits to $125	235-34
	Beds & bedding; heating unit; clothing	235-34
	Bibles & books to $200 total; sewing machine to $200	235-34
	Burial plots, tombs, & church pew	235-34
	Cash for fuel, heat, water, or light to $75 per month	235-34
	Cash to $200/month for rent, in lieu of homestead	235-34
	Cooperative association shares to $100	235-34
	Food or cash for food to $300	235-34
	Furniture to $3,000; motor vehicle to $700	235-34
	Moving expenses for eminent domain	79-6A
	Trust company, bank, or credit union deposits to $500	246-28A
	2 cows, 12 sheep, 2 swine, 4 tons of hay	235-34
public benefits	Aid to families with dependent children	118-10
	Public assistance	235-34
	Unemployment compensation	151A-36
	Veterans' benefits	115-5
	Workers' compensation	152-47
tools of trade	Arms, accoutrements, & uniforms required	235-34
	Fishing boats, tackle, & nets to $500	235-34
	Materials you designed & procured to $500	235-34
	Tools, implements, & fixtures to $500 total	235-34
wages	Earned but unpaid wages to $125 per week	246-28
wildcard	None	

Be sure to read the caution about exceptions to exemptions in the introduction to this appendix.

Michigan

Federal Bankruptcy Exemptions available. All law references are to Michigan Compiled Laws Annotated unless otherwise noted.

ASSET	EXEMPTION	LAW
homestead	Property held as tenancy by the entirety may be exempt against debts owed by only one spouse	In re Smith, 246 B.R. 540 (E.D. Mich., 2000); In re Spears, 313 B.R. 212 (W.D. Mich. 2004)
	Real property including condo to $3,500; property cannot exceed 1 lot in town, village, city, or 40 acres elsewhere; spouse or children of deceased owner may claim homestead exemption	559.214; 600.6023(1)(h),(i); 600.6023(3)
insurance	Disability, mutual life, or health benefits	600.6023(1)(f)
	Employer-sponsored life insurance policy or trust fund	500.2210
	Fraternal benefit society benefits	500.8181
	Life, endowment, or annuity proceeds if clause prohibits proceeds from being used to pay beneficiary's creditors	500.4054
	Life insurance	500.2207
miscellaneous	Property of business partnership	449.25
pensions	ERISA-qualified benefits, except contributions within last 120 days	600.6023(1)(l)
	Firefighters, police officers	38.559(6); 38.1683
	IRAs & Roth IRAs, except contributions within last 120 days	600.6023(1)(k)
	Judges	38.2308; 38.1683
	Legislators	38.1057; 38.1683
	Probate judges	38.2308; 38.1683
	Public school employees	38.1346; 38.1683
	State employees	38.40; 38.1683
personal property	Appliances, utensils, books, furniture, & household goods to $1,000 total	600.6023(1)(b)
	Building & loan association shares to $1,000 par value, in lieu of homestead	600.6023(1)(g)
	Burial plots, cemeteries; church pew, slip, seat for entire family	600.6023(1)(c)
	Clothing; family pictures	600.6023(1)(a)
	Food & fuel to last family for 6 months	600.6023(1)(a)
	2 cows, 100 hens, 5 roosters, 10 sheep, 5 swine, & feed to last 6 months	600.6023(1)(d)
public benefits	Crime victims' compensation	18.362
	Social welfare benefits	400.63
	Unemployment compensation	421.30
	Veterans' benefits for Korean War veterans	35.977
	Veterans' benefits for Vietnam veterans	35.1027
	Veterans' benefits for WWII veterans	35.926
	Workers' compensation	418.821
tools of trade	Arms & accoutrements required	600.6023(1)(a)
	Tools, implements, materials, stock, apparatus, team, motor vehicle, horse, & harness to $1,000 total	600.6023(1)(e)
wages	Head of household may keep 60% of earned but unpaid wages (no less than $15/week), plus $2/week per nonspouse dependent; if not head of household may keep 40% (no less than $10/week)	600.5311
wildcard	None	

Minnesota

Federal Bankruptcy Exemptions available. All law references are to Minnesota Statutes Annotated.

NOTE: Section 550.37(4)(a) requires certain exemptions to be adjusted for inflation on July 1 of even-numbered years; this table includes all changes made through July 1, 2004. Exemptions are published in the May 1 issue of the *Minnesota State Register*, www.comm.media.state.mn.us/bookstore/stateregister.asp, or call the Minnesota Dept. of Commerce at 651-296-7977.

ASSET	EXEMPTION	LAW
homestead	Home & land on which it is situated to $200,000; if homestead is used for agricultural purposes, $500,000; cannot exceed 1/2 acre in city, 160 acres elsewhere (husband & wife may not double);	510.01; 510.02
	Manufactured home to an unlimited value	550.37 subd. 12
insurance	Accident or disability proceeds	550.39
	Fraternal benefit society benefits	64B.18
	Life insurance proceeds to $38,000, if beneficiary is spouse or child of insured, plus $9,500 per dependent	550.37 subd. 10
	Police, fire, or beneficiary association benefits	550.37 subd. 11
	Unmatured life insurance contract dividends, interest, or loan value to $7,600 if insured is debtor or person debtor depends on	550.37 subd. 23
miscellaneous	Earnings of minor child	550.37 subd. 15
pensions	ERISA-qualified benefits or needed for support, up to $57,000 in present value	550.37 subd. 24
	IRAs or Roth IRAs needed for support, up to $57,000 in present value	550.37 subd. 24
	Public employees	353.15
	State employees	352.96 subd. 6
	State troopers	352B.071
personal property	Appliances, furniture, jewelry, radio, phonographs, & TV to $8,550 total	550.37 subd. 4(b)
	Bible & books	550.37 subd. 2
	Burial plot; church pew or seat	550.37 subd. 3
	Clothing, one watch, food, & utensils for family	550.37 subd. 4(a)
	Motor vehicle to $3,800 (up to $38,000 if vehicle has been modified for disability)	550.37 subd. 12(a)
	Personal injury recoveries	550.37 subd. 22
	Proceeds for damaged exempt property	550.37 subds. 9, 16
	Wrongful death recoveries	550.37 subd. 22
public benefits	Crime victims' compensation	611A.60
	Public benefits	550.37 subd. 14
	Unemployment compensation	268.192 subd. 2
	Veterans' benefits	550.38
	Workers' compensation	176.175
tools of trade total (except teaching materials) can't exceed $13,000	Farm machines, implements, livestock, produce, & crops	550.37 subd. 5
	Teaching materials of college, university, public school, or public institution teacher	550.37 subd. 8
	Tools, machines, instruments, stock in trade, furniture, & library to $9,500 total	550.37 subd. 6
wages	Minimum 75% of weekly disposable earnings or 40 times federal minimum hourly wage, whichever is greater	571.922
	Wages deposited into bank accounts for 20 days after depositing	550.37 subd. 13
	Wages, paid within 6 mos. of returning to work, after receiving welfare or after incarceration; includes earnings deposited in a financial institution in the last 60 days	550.37 subd. 14
wildcard	None	

NOTE: In cases of suspected fraud, the Minnesota constitution permits courts to cap exemptions that would otherwise be unlimited. *In re Tveten*, 402 N.W.2d 551 (Minn. 1987); *In re Medill*, 119 B.R. 685 (Bankr. D. Minn. 1990); *In re Sholdan*, 217 F.3d 1006 (8th Cir. 2000).

Be sure to read the caution about exceptions to exemptions in the introduction to this appendix.

Mississippi

Federal Bankruptcy Exemptions not available. All law references are to Mississippi Code.

ASSET	EXEMPTION	LAW
homestead	May file homestead declaration	85-3-27; 85-3-31
	Mobile home does not qualify as homestead unless you own land on which it is located (see personal property)	In re Cobbins, 234 B.R. 882 (S.D. Miss. 1999)
	Property you own & occupy to $75,000; if over 60 & married or widowed may claim a former residence; property cannot exceed 160 acres; sale proceeds exempt	85-3-1(b)(i); 85-3-21; 85-3-23
insurance	Disability benefits	85-3-1(b)(ii)
	Fraternal benefit society benefits	83-29-39
	Homeowners' insurance proceeds to $75,000	85-3-23
	Life insurance proceeds if clause prohibits proceeds from being used to pay beneficiary's creditors	83-7-5
miscellaneous	Property of business partnership	79-12-49
pensions	ERISA-qualified benefits, IRAs, Keoghs deposited over 1 yr. before filing bankruptcy	85-3-1(f)
	Firefighters (includes death benefits)	21-29-257; 45-2-1
	Highway patrol officers	25-13-31
	Law enforcement officers' death benefits	45-2-1
	Police officers (includes death benefits)	21-29-257; 45-2-1
	Private retirement benefits to extent tax-deferred	71-1-43
	Public employees retirement & disability benefits	25-11-129
	State employees	25-14-5
	Teachers	25-11-201(1)(d)
	Volunteer firefighters' death benefits	45-2-1
personal property	Mobile home to $20,000	85-3-1(e)
	Personal injury judgments to $10,000	85-3-17
	Sale or insurance proceeds for exempt property	85-3-1(b)(i)
	Tangible personal property to $10,000: any item worth less than $200; furniture, dishes, kitchenware, household goods, appliances, 1 radio & 1 TV, 1 firearm, 1 lawnmower, clothing, wedding rings, motor vehicles, tools of the trade, books, crops, health aids, domestic animals (does not include works of art, antiques, jewelry, or electronic entertainment equipment)	85-3-1(a)
public benefits	Assistance to aged	43-9-19
	Assistance to blind	43-3-71
	Assistance to disabled	43-29-15
	Crime victims' compensation	99-41-23(7)
	Social Security	25-11-129
	Unemployment compensation	71-5-539
	Workers' compensation	71-3-43
tools of trade	See personal property	
wages	Earned but unpaid wages owed for 30 days; after 30 days, minimum 75% of earned but unpaid weekly disposable earnings, or 30 times the federal hourly minimum wage, whichever is greater (bankruptcy judge may authorize more for low-income debtors)	85-3-4
wildcard	See personal property	

Missouri

Federal Bankruptcy Exemptions not available. All law references are to Annotated Missouri Statutes unless otherwise noted.

ASSET	EXEMPTION	LAW
homestead	Property held as tenancy by the entirety may be exempt against debts owed by only one spouse	In re Eads, 271 B.R. 371 (Bankr. W.D. Mo. 2002).
	Real property to $15,000 or mobile home to $5,000 (joint owners may not double)	513.430(6); 513.475 In re Smith, 254 B.R. 751 (Bank. W.D. Mo. 2000)
insurance	Assessment plan or life insurance proceeds	377.090
	Disability or illness benefits	513.430(10)(c)
	Fraternal benefit society benefits to $5,000, bought over 6 months before filing	513.430(8)
	Life insurance dividends, loan value, or interest to $150,000, bought over 6 months before filing	513.430(8)
	Life insurance proceeds if policy owned by a woman & insures her husband	376.530
	Life insurance proceeds if policy owned by unmarried woman & insures her father or brother	376.550
	Stipulated insurance premiums	377.330
	Unmatured life insurance policy	513.430(7)
miscellaneous	Alimony, child support to $750 per month	513.430(10)(d)
	Property of business partnership	358.250
pensions	Employee benefit spendthrift trust	456.072
	Employees of cities with 100,000 or more people	71.207
	ERISA-qualified benefits, IRAs, Roth IRAs, & other retirement accounts needed for support	513.430(10)(e), (f)
	Firefighters	87.090; 87.365; 87.485
	Highway & transportation employees	104.250
	Police department employees	86.190; 86.353; 86.493; 86.780
	Public officers & employees	70.695; 70.755
	State employees	104.540
	Teachers	169.090
personal property	Appliances, household goods, furnishings, clothing, books, crops, animals, & musical instruments to $3,000 total	513.430(1)
	Burial grounds to 1 acre or $100	214.190
	Health aids	513.430(9)
	Motor vehicle to $3,000	513.430(5)
	Personal injury causes of action	In re Mitchell, 73 B.R. 93 (Bankr. E.D. Mo. 1987)
	Wedding ring to $1,500, & other jewelry to $500	513.430(2)
	Wrongful death recoveries for person you depended on	513.430(11)
public benefits	Crime victim's compensation	595.025
	Public assistance	513.430(10)(a)
	Social Security	513.430(10)(a)
	Unemployment compensation	288.380(10)(l); 513.430(10)(c)
	Veterans' benefits	513.430(10)b)
	Workers' compensation	287.260
tools of trade	Implements, books, & tools of trade to $3,000	513.430(4)
wages	Minimum 75% of weekly earnings (90% of weekly earnings for head of family), or 30 times the federal minimum hourly wage, whichever is more; bankruptcy judge may authorize more for low-income debtors	525.030
	Wages of servant or common laborer to $90	513.470
wildcard	$1,250 of any property if head of family, else $600; head of family may claim additional $350 per child	513.430(3); 513.440

Be sure to read the caution about exceptions to exemptions in the introduction to this appendix.

Montana

Federal Bankruptcy Exemptions not available. All law references are to Montana Code Annotated.

ASSET	EXEMPTION	LAW
homestead	Must record homestead declaration before filing for bankruptcy	70-32-105
	Real property or mobile home you occupy to $100,000; sale, condemnation, or insurance proceeds exempt for 18 months	70-32-104; 70-32-201; 70-32-213
insurance	Annuity contract proceeds to $350 per month	33-15-514
	Disability or illness proceeds, avails, or benefits	25-13-608(1)(d); 33-15-513
	Fraternal benefit society benefits	33-7-522
	Group life insurance policy or proceeds	33-15-512
	Hail insurance benefits	80-2-245
	Life insurance proceeds if clause prohibits proceeds from being used to pay beneficiary's creditors	33-20-120
	Medical, surgical, or hospital care benefits	25-13-608(1)(f)
	Unmatured life insurance contracts to $4,000	25-13-609(4)
miscellaneous	Alimony, child support	25-13-608(1)(g)
pensions	ERISA-qualified benefits deposited over 1 year before filing bankruptcy or up to 15% of debtor's gross annual income	31-2-106
	Firefighters	19-18-612(1)
	IRA & Roth IRA contributions & earnings made before judgment filed	25-13-608(1)(e)
	Police officers	19-19-504(1)
	Public employees	19-2-1004; 25-13-608(i)
	Teachers	19-20-706(2); 25-13-608(j)
	University system employees	19-21-212
personal property	Appliances, household furnishings, goods, animals with feed, crops, musical instruments, books, firearms, sporting goods, clothing, & jewelry to $600 per item, $4,500 total	25-13-609(1)
	Burial plot	25-13-608(1)(h)
	Cooperative association shares to $500 value	35-15-404
	Health aids	25-13-608(1)(a)
	Motor vehicle to $2,500	25-13-609(2)
	Proceeds from sale or for damage or loss of exempt property for 6 mos. after received	25-13-610
public benefits	Aid to aged, disabled needy persons	53-2-607
	Crime victims' compensation	53-9-129
	Local public assistance	25-13-608(1)(b)
	Silicosis benefits	39-73-110
	Social Security	25-13-608(1)(b)
	Subsidized adoption payments to needy persons	53-2-607
	Unemployment compensation	31-2-106(2); 39-51-3105
	Veterans' benefits	25-13-608(1)(c)
	Vocational rehabilitation to blind needy persons	53-2-607
	Workers' compensation	39-71-743
tools of trade	Implements, books, & tools of trade to $3,000	25-13-609(3)
	Uniforms, arms, accoutrements needed to carry out government functions	25-13-613(b)
wages	Minimum 75% of earned but unpaid weekly disposable earnings, or 30 times the federal hourly minimum wage, whichever is greater; bankruptcy judge may authorize more for low-income debtors	25-13-614
wildcard	None	

Nebraska

Federal Bankruptcy Exemptions not available. All law references are to Revised Statutes of Nebraska.

ASSET	EXEMPTION	LAW
homestead	$12,500 for married debtor or head of household; cannot exceed 2 lots in city or village, 160 acres elsewhere; sale proceeds exempt 6 months after sale (husband & wife may not double)	40-101; 40-111; 40-113
	May record homestead declaration	40-105
insurance	Fraternal benefit society benefits to $10,000 loan value unless beneficiary convicted of a crime related to benefits	44-1089
	Life insurance or annuity contract proceeds to $10,000 loan value	44-371
pensions *see also wages*	County employees	23-2322
	Deferred compensation of public employees	48-1401
	ERISA-qualified benefits including IRAs & Roth IRAs needed for support	25-1563.01
	Military disability benefits	25-1559
	School employees	79-948
	State employees	84-1324
personal property	Burial plot	12-517
	Clothing	25-1556(2)
	Crypts, lots, tombs, niches, vaults	12-605
	Furniture, household goods & appliances, household electronics, personal computers, books, & musical instruments to $1,500	25-1556(3)
	Health aids	25-1556(5)
	Perpetual care funds	12-511
	Personal injury recoveries	25-1563.02
	Personal possessions	25-1556
public benefits	Aid to disabled, blind, aged; public assistance	68-1013
	General assistance to poor persons	68-148
	Unemployment compensation	48-647
	Workers' compensation	48-149
tools of trade	Equipment or tools including a vehicle used in/or for commuting to principal place of business to $2,400 (husband & wife may double)	25-1556(4); *In re Keller*, 50 B.R. 23 (D. Neb. 1985)
wages	Minimum 85% of earned but unpaid weekly disposable earnings or pension payments for head of family; minimum 75% of earned but unpaid weekly disposable earnings, or 30 times the federal hourly minimum wage, whichever is greater, for all others; bankruptcy judge may authorize more for low-income debtors	25-1558
wildcard	$2,500 of any personal property, except wages, in lieu of homestead	25-1552

Be sure to read the caution about exceptions to exemptions in the introduction to this appendix.

Nevada

Federal Bankruptcy Exemptions not available. All law references are to Nevada Revised Statutes Annotated.

ASSET	EXEMPTION	LAW
homestead	Must record homestead declaration before filing for bankruptcy	115.020
	Real property or mobile home to $200,000	115.010; 21.090(1)(m)
insurance	Annuity contract proceeds to $350 per month	687B.290
	Fraternal benefit society benefits	695A.220
	Group life or health policy or proceeds	687B.280
	Health proceeds or avails	687B.270
	Life insurance policy or proceeds if annual premiums not over $1,000	21.090(1)(k); In re Bower, 234 B.R. 109 (Nev. 1999)
	Life insurance proceeds if you're not the insured	687B.260
miscellaneous	Alimony & child support	21.090(1)(r)
	Property of business partnership	87.250
pensions	ERISA-qualified benefits, deferred compensation, SEP IRA, or IRAs to $500,000	21.090(1)(q)
	Public employees	286.670
personal property	Appliances, household goods, furniture, home & yard equipment to $10,000 total	21.090(1)(b)
	Books to $1,500	21.090(1)(a)
	Burial plot purchase money held in trust	689.700
	Funeral service contract money held in trust	689.700
	Health aids	21.090(1)(p)
	Keepsakes & pictures	21.090(1)(a)
	Metal-bearing ores, geological specimens, art curiosities, or paleontological remains; must be arranged, classified, catalogued, & numbered in reference books	21.100
	Mortgage impound accounts	645B.180
	Motor vehicle to $15,000; no limit on vehicle equipped for disabled person	21.090(1)(f),(o)
	One gun	21.090(1)(i)
	Personal injury compensation to $16,500	21.090(t)
	Restitution received for criminal act	21.090(w)
	Wrongful death awards to survivors	21.090(u)
public benefits	Aid to blind, aged, disabled; public assistance	422.291
	Crime victim's compensation	21.090
	Industrial insurance (workers' compensation)	616C.205
	Public assistance for children	432.036
	Unemployment compensation	612.710
	Vocational rehabilitation benefits	615.270
tools of trade	Arms, uniforms, & accoutrements you're required to keep	21.090(1)(j)
	Cabin or dwelling of miner or prospector; mining claim, cars, implements, & appliances to $4,500 total (for working claim only)	21.090(1)(e)
	Farm trucks, stock, tools, equipment, & seed to $4,500	21.090(1)(c)
	Library, equipment, supplies, tools, & materials to $4,500	21.090(1)(d)
wages	Minimum 75% of disposable weekly earnings or 30 times the federal minimum hourly wage per week, whichever is more; bankruptcy judge may authorize more for low-income debtors	21.090(1)(g)
wildcard	None	

New Hampshire

Federal Bankruptcy Exemptions available. All law references are to New Hampshire Revised Statutes Annotated.

ASSET	EXEMPTION	LAW
homestead	Real property or manufactured housing (& the land it's on if you own it) to $100,000	480:1
insurance	Firefighters' aid insurance	402:69
	Fraternal benefit society benefits	418:17
	Homeowners' insurance proceeds to $5,000	512:21(VIII)
miscellaneous	Jury, witness fees	512:21(VI)
	Property of business partnership	304-A:25
	Wages of minor child	512:21(III)
pensions	ERISA-qualified retirement accounts including IRAs & Roth IRAs	512:2 (XIX)
	Federally created pension (only benefits building up)	512:21(IV)
	Firefighters	102:23
	Police officers	103:18
	Public employees	100-A:26
personal property	Beds, bedding, & cooking utensils	511:2(II)
	Bibles & books to $800	511:2(VIII)
	Burial plot, lot	511:2(XIV)
	Church pew	511:2(XV)
	Clothing	511:2(I)
	Cooking & heating stoves, refrigerator	511:2(IV)
	Domestic fowl to $300	511:2(XIII)
	Food & fuel to $400	511:2(VI)
	Furniture to $3,500	511:2(III)
	Jewelry to $500	511:2(XVII)
	Motor vehicle to $4,000	511:2(XVI)
	Proceeds for lost or destroyed exempt property	512:21(VIII)
	Sewing machine	511:2(V)
	1 cow, 6 sheep & their fleece, 4 tons of hay	511:2(XI); (XII)
	1 hog or pig or its meat (if slaughtered)	511:2(X)
public benefits	Aid to blind, aged, disabled; public assistance	167:25
	Unemployment compensation	282-A:159
	Workers' compensation	281-A:52
tools of trade	Tools of your occupation to $5,000	511:2(IX)
	Uniforms, arms, & equipment of military member	511:2(VII)
	Yoke of oxen or horse needed for farming or teaming	511:2(XII)
wages	50 times the federal minimum hourly wage per week	512:21(II)
	Deposits in any account designated a payroll account	512:21(XI)
	Earned but unpaid wages of spouse	512:21(III)
wildcard	$1,000 of any property	511:2(XVIII)
	Unused portion of bibles & books, food & fuel, furniture, jewelry, motor vehicle, & tools of trade exemptions to $7,000	511:2(XVIII)

Be sure to read the caution about exceptions to exemptions in the introduction to this appendix.

New Jersey

Federal Bankruptcy Exemptions available. All law references are to New Jersey Statutes Annotated.

ASSET	EXEMPTION	LAW
homestead	None, but survivorship interest of a spouse in property held as tenancy by the entirety is exempt from creditors of a single spouse	*Freda v. Commercial Trust Co. of New Jersey,* 570 A.2d 409 (N.J.,1990)
insurance	Annuity contract proceeds to $500 per month	17B:24-7
	Disability benefits	17:18-12
	Disability, death, medical, or hospital benefits for civil defense workers	App. A:9-57.6
	Disability or death benefits for military member	38A:4-8
	Group life or health policy or proceeds	17B:24-9
	Health or disability benefits	17:18-12; 17B:24-8
	Life insurance proceeds if clause prohibits proceeds from being used to pay beneficiary's creditors	17B:24-10
	Life insurance proceeds or avails if you're not the insured	17B:24-6b
pensions	Alcohol beverage control officers	43:8A-20
	City boards of health employees	43:18-12
	Civil defense workers	App. A:9-57.6
	County employees	43:10-57; 43:10-105
	ERISA-qualified benefits for city employees	43:13-9
	Firefighters, police officers, traffic officers	43:16-7; 43:16A-17
	IRAs	*In re Yuhas,* 104 F.3d 612 (3rd Cir. 1997)
	Judges	43:6A-41
	Municipal employees	43:13-44
	Prison employees	43:7-13
	Public employees	43:15A-53
	School district employees	18A:66-116
	State police	53:5A-45
	Street & water department employees	43:19-17
	Teachers	18A:66-51
	Trust containing personal property created pursuant to federal tax law, including 401(k) plans, IRAs, Roth IRAs, & higher education (529) savings plans	25:2-1; *In re Yuhas,* 104 F.3d 612 (3d Cir. 1997)
personal property	Burial plots	45:27-21
	Clothing	2A:17-19
	Furniture & household goods to $1,000	2A:26-4
	Personal property & possessions of any kind, stock or interest in corporations to $1,000 total	2A:17-19
public benefits	Old age, permanent disability assistance	44:7-35
	Unemployment compensation	43:21-53
	Workers' compensation	34:15-29
tools of trade	None	
wages	90% of earned but unpaid wages if annual income under $7,500; if annual income over $7,500, judge decides amount that is exempt	2A:17-56
	Wages or allowances received by military personnel	38A:4-8
wildcard	None	

New Mexico

Federal Bankruptcy Exemptions available. All law references are to New Mexico Statutes Annotated.

ASSET	EXEMPTION	LAW
homestead	$30,000	42-10-9
insurance	Benevolent association benefits to $5,000	42-10-4
	Fraternal benefit society benefits	59A-44-18
	Life, accident, health, or annuity benefits, withdrawal or cash value, if beneficiary is a New Mexico resident	42-10-3
	Life insurance proceeds	42-10-5
miscellaneous	Ownership interest in unincorporated association	53-10-2
	Property of business partnership	54-1A-501
pensions	Pension or retirement benefits	42-10-1; 42-10-2
	Public school employees	22-11-42A
personal property	Books & furniture	42-10-1; 42-10-2
	Building materials	48-2-15
	Clothing	42-10-1; 42-10-2
	Cooperative association shares, minimum amount needed to be member	53-4-28
	Health aids	42-10-1; 42-10-2
	Jewelry to $2,500	42-10-1; 42-10-2
	Materials, tools, & machinery to dig, drill, complete, operate, or repair oil line, gas well, or pipeline	70-4-12
	Motor vehicle to $4,000	42-10-1; 42-10-2
public benefits	Crime victims' compensation (will be repealed in 2006)	31-22-15
	General assistance	27-2-21
	Occupational disease disablement benefits	52-3-37
	Unemployment compensation	51-1-37
	Workers' compensation	52-1-52
tools of trade	$1,500	42-10-1; 42-10-2
wages	Minimum 75% of disposable earnings or 40 times the federal hourly minimum wage, whichever is more; bankruptcy judge may authorize more for low-income debtors	35-12-7
wildcard	$500 of any personal property	42-10-1
	$2,000 of any real or personal property, in lieu of homestead	42-10-10

New York

Federal Bankruptcy Exemptions not available. Law references to Consolidated Laws of New York; Civil Practice Law & Rules are abbreviated C.P.L.R.

ASSET	EXEMPTION	LAW
homestead	Real property including co-op, condo, or mobile home, to $10,000	C.P.L.R. 5206(a); *In re Pearl*, 723 F.2d 193 (2nd Cir. 1983)
insurance	Annuity contract benefits due the debtor, if debtor paid for the contract; $5,000 limit if purchased within 6 mos. prior to filing & not tax-deferred	Ins. 3212(d); Debt. & Cred. 283(1)
	Disability or illness benefits to $400/month	Ins. 3212(c)
	Life insurance proceeds & avails if the beneficiary is not the debtor, or if debtor's spouse has taken out policy	Ins. 3212(b)
	Life insurance proceeds left at death with the insurance company, if clause prohibits proceeds from being used to pay beneficiary's creditors	Est. Powers & Trusts 7-1.5(a)(2)
miscellaneous	Alimony, child support	C.P.L.R. 5205 (d)(3); Debt. & Cred. 282(2)(d)
	Property of business partnership	Partnership 51
pensions	ERISA-qualified benefits, IRAs, Roth IRAs, & Keoghs & income needed for support	C.P.L.R. 5205(c); Debt. & Cred. 282(2)(e)
	Public retirement benefits	Ins. 4607
	State employees	Ret. & Soc. Sec. 10
	Teachers	Educ. 524
	Village police officers	Unconsolidated 5711-o
	Volunteer ambulance workers' benefits	Vol. Amb. Wkr. Ben. 23
	Volunteer firefighters' benefits	Vol. Firefighter Ben. 23
personal property	Bible, schoolbooks, other books to $50; pictures; clothing; church pew or seat; sewing machine, refrigerator, TV, radio; furniture, cooking utensils & tableware, dishes; food to last 60 days; stoves with fuel to last 60 days; domestic animal with food to last 60 days, to $450; wedding ring; watch to $35; exemptions may not exceed $5,000 total (including tools of trade & limited annuity)	C.P.L.R. 5205(a)(1)-(6); Debt. & Cred. 283(1)
	Burial plot without structure to 1/4 acre	C.P.L.R. 5206(f)
	Cash (including savings bonds, tax refunds, bank & credit union deposits) to $2,500, or to $5,000 after exemptions for personal property taken, whichever amount is less (for debtors who do not claim homestead)	Debt. & Cred. 283(2)
	College tuition savings program trust fund	C.P.L.R. 5205(j)
	Health aids, including service animals with food	C.P.L.R. 5205(h)
	Lost future earnings recoveries needed for support	Debt. & Cred. 282(3)(iv)
	Motor vehicle to $2,400	Debt. & Cred. 282(1); *In re Miller*, 167 B.R. 782 (S.D. N.Y. 1994)
	Personal injury recoveries up to 1 year after receiving	Debt. & Cred. 282(3)(iii)
	Recovery for injury to exempt property up to 1 year after receiving	C.P.L.R. 5205(b)
	Savings & loan savings to $600	Banking 407
	Security deposit to landlord, utility company	C.P.L.R. 5205(g)
	Spendthrift trust fund principal, 90% of income if not created by debtor	C.P.L.R. 5205(c),(d)
	Wrongful death recoveries for person you depended on	Debt. & Cred. 282(3)(ii)
public benefits	Aid to blind, aged, disabled	Debt. & Cred. 282(2)(c)
	Crime victims' compensation	Debt. & Cred. 282(3)(i)
	Home relief, local public assistance	Debt. & Cred. 282(2)(a)
	Public assistance	Soc. Serv. 137
	Social Security	Debt. & Cred. 282(2)(a)
	Unemployment compensation	Debt. & Cred. 282(2)(a)
	Veterans' benefits	Debt. & Cred. 282(2)(b)
	Workers' compensation	Debt. & Cred. 282(2)(c); Work. Comp. 33, 218
tools of trade	Farm machinery, team, & food for 60 days; professional furniture, books, & instruments to $600 total	C.P.L.R. 5205(a),(b)
	Uniforms, medal, emblem, equipment, horse, arms, & sword of member of military	C.P.L.R. 5205(e)
wages	90% of earned but unpaid wages received within 60 days before & anytime after filing	C.P.L.R. 5205(d)
	90% of earnings from dairy farmer's sales to milk dealers	C.P.L.R. 5205(f)
	100% of pay of noncommissioned officer, private, or musician in U.S. or N.Y. state armed forces	C.P.L.R. 5205(e)
wildcard	None	

North Carolina

Federal Bankruptcy Exemptions not available. All law references are to General Statutes of North Carolina unless otherwise noted.

ASSET	EXEMPTION	LAW
homestead	Property held as tenancy by the entirety may be exempt against debts owed by only one spouse	*In re Chandler*, 148 B.R. 13 (E.D. N.C., 1992)
	Real or personal property, including co-op, used as residence to $10,000; up to $3,500 of unused portion of homestead may be applied to any property	1C-1601(a)(1),(2)
insurance	Employee group life policy or proceeds	58-58-165
	Fraternal benefit society benefits	58-24-85
	Life insurance on spouse or children	1C-1601(a)(6); Const. Art. X § 5
miscellaneous	Property of business partnership	59-55
	Support received by a surviving spouse for 1 year, up to $10,000	30-15
pensions	Firefighters & rescue squad workers	58-86-90
	IRAs	1C-1601(a)(9)
	Law enforcement officers	143-166.30(g)
	Legislators	120-4.29
	Municipal, city, & county employees	128-31
	Teachers & state employees	135-9; 135-95
personal property	Animals, crops, musical instruments, books, clothing, appliances, household goods & furnishings to $3,500 total; may add $750 per dependent, up to $3,000 total additional (all property must have been purchased at least 90 days before filing)	1C-1601(a)(4),(d)
	Burial plot to $10,000, in lieu of homestead	1C-1601(a)(1)
	Health aids	1C-1601(a)(7)
	Motor vehicle to $1,500	1C-1601(a)(3)
	Personal injury & wrongful death recoveries for person you depended on	1C-1601(a)(8)
public benefits	Aid to blind	111-18
	Crime victims' compensation	15B-17
	Public adult assistance under work first program	108A-36
	Unemployment compensation	96-17
	Workers' compensation	97-21
tools of trade	Implements, books, & tools of trade to $750	1C-1601(a)(5)
wages	Earned but unpaid wages received 60 days before filing for bankruptcy, needed for support	1-362
wildcard	$3,500 less any amount claimed for homestead or burial exemption, of any property	1C-1601(a)(2)
	$500 of any personal property	Constitution Art. X § 1

Be sure to read the caution about exceptions to exemptions in the introduction to this appendix.

North Dakota

Federal Bankruptcy Exemptions not available. All law references are to North Dakota Century Code.

ASSET	EXEMPTION	LAW
homestead	Real property, house trailer, or mobile home to $80,000 (husband & wife may not double)	28-22-02(10); 47-18-01
insurance	Fraternal benefit society benefits	26.1-15.1-18; 26.1-33-40
	Life insurance proceeds payable to deceased's estate, not to a specific beneficiary	26.1-33-40
	Life insurance surrender value to $100,000 per policy, if beneficiary is insured's dependent & policy was owned over 1 year before filing for bankruptcy; limit does not apply if more needed for support	28-22-03.1(3)
miscellaneous	Child support payments	14-09-09.31
pensions	Disabled veterans' benefits, except military retirement pay	28-22-03.1(4)(d)
	ERISA-qualified benefits, IRAs, Roth IRAs, & Keoghs to $100,000 per plan; no limit if more needed for support; total exemption (with life insurance surrender value) cannot exceed $200,000	28-22-03.1(3)
	Public employees deferred compensation	54-52.2-06
	Public employees pensions	28-22-19(1)
personal property	1. All debtors may exempt:	
	Bible, schoolbooks; other books to $100	28-22-02(4)
	Burial plots, church pew	28-22-02(2),(3)
	Clothing & family pictures	28-22-02(1),(5)
	Crops or grain raised by debtor on 160 acres where debtor resides	28-22-02(8)
	Food & fuel to last 1 year	28-22-02(6)
	Insurance proceeds for exempt property	28-22-02(9)
	Motor vehicle to $1,200 (or $32,000 for vehicle that has been modified to accommodate owner's disability)	28-22-03.1(2)
	Personal injury recoveries to $7,500	28-22-03.1(4)(b)
	Wrongful death recoveries to $7,500	28-22-03.1(4)(a)
	2. Head of household not claiming crops or grain may claim $5,000 of any personal property or:	28-22-03
	Books & musical instruments to $1,500	28-22-04(1)
	Household & kitchen furniture, beds & bedding, to $1,000	28-22-04(2)
	Library & tools of professional, tools of mechanic, & stock in trade, to $1,000	28-22-04(4)
	Livestock & farm implements to $4,500	28-22-04(3)
	3. Non-head of household not claiming crops or grain may claim $2,500 of any personal property	28-22-05
public benefits	Crime victims' compensation	28-22-19(2)
	Old age & survivor insurance program benefits	52-09-22
	Public assistance	28-22-19(3)
	Social Security	28-22-03.1(4)(c)
	Unemployment compensation	52-06-30
	Workers' compensation	65-05-29
tools of trade	See personal property, option 2	
wages	Minimum 75% of disposable weekly earnings or 40 times the federal minimum wage, whichever is more; bankruptcy judge may authorize more for low-income debtors	32-09.1-03
wildcard	$7,500 of any property in lieu of homestead	28-22-03.1(1)

Ohio

Federal Bankruptcy Exemptions not available. All law references are to Ohio Revised Code unless otherwise noted.

ASSET	EXEMPTION	LAW
homestead	Property held as tenancy by the entirety may be exempt against debts owed by only one spouse	In re Pernus, 143 B.R. 856 (N.D. Ohio, 1992)
	Real or personal property used as residence to $5,000	2329.66(A)(1)(b)
insurance	Benevolent society benefits to $5,000	2329.63; 2329.66(A)(6)(a)
	Disability benefits to $600 per month	2329.66(A)(6)(e); 3923.19
	Fraternal benefit society benefits	2329.66(A)(6)(d); 3921.18
	Group life insurance policy or proceeds	2329.66(A)(6)(c); 3917.05
	Life, endowment, or annuity contract avails for your spouse, child, or dependent	2329.66(A)(6)(b); 3911.10
	Life insurance proceeds for a spouse	3911.12
	Life insurance proceeds if clause prohibits proceeds from being used to pay beneficiary's creditors	3911.14
miscellaneous	Alimony, child support needed for support	2329.66(A)(11)
	Property of business partnership	1775.24; 2329.66(A)(14)
pensions	ERISA-qualified benefits needed for support	2329.66(A)(10)(b)
	Firefighters, police officers	742.47
	IRAs, Roth IRAs, & Keoghs needed for support	2329.66(A)(10)(c), (a)
	Public employees	145.56
	Public safety officers' death benefit	2329.66(A)(10)(a)
	Public school employees	3309.66
	State highway patrol employees	5505.22
	Volunteer firefighters' dependents	146.13
personal property	Animals, crops, books, musical instruments, appliances, household goods, furnishings, firearms, hunting & fishing equipment to $200 per item; jewelry to $400 for 1 item, $200 for all others; $1,500 total ($2,000 if no homestead exemption claimed)	2329.66(A)(4)(b),(c),(d); In re Szydlowski, 186 B.R. 907 (N.D. Ohio 1995)
	Beds, bedding, clothing to $200 per item	2329.66(A)(3)
	Burial plot	517.09; 2329.66(A)(8)
	Cash, money due within 90 days, tax refund, bank, security, & utility deposits to $400 total	2329.66(A)(4)(a); In re Szydlowski, 186 B.R. 907 (N.D. Ohio 1995)
	Compensation for lost future earnings needed for support, received during 12 months before filing	2329.66(A)(12)(d)
	Cooking unit & refrigerator to $300 each	2329.66(A)(3)
	Health aids (professionally prescribed)	2329.66(A)(7)
	Motor vehicle to $1,000	2329.66(A)(2)(b)
	Personal injury recoveries to $5,000, received during 12 months before filing	2329.66(A)(12)(c)
	Tuition credit or payment	2329.66(A)(16)
	Wrongful death recoveries for person debtor depended on, needed for support, received during 12 months before filing	2329.66(A)(12)(b)
public benefits	Crime victim's compensation, received during 12 months before filing	2329.66(A)(12)(a); 2743.66(D)
	Disability assistance payments	2329.66(A)(9)(f); 5115.07
	Public assistance	2329.66(A)(9)(d); 5107.12, 5108.08
	Unemployment compensation	2329.66(A)(9)(c); 4141.32
	Vocational rehabilitation benefits	2329.66(A)(9)(a); 3304.19
	Workers' compensation	2329.66(A)(9)(b); 4123.67
tools of trade	Implements, books, & tools of trade to $750	2329.66(A)(5)
wages	Minimum 75% of disposable weekly earnings or 30 times the federal hourly minimum wage, whichever is higher; bankruptcy judge may authorize more for low-income debtors	2329.66(A)(13)
wildcard	$400 of any property	2329.66(A)(18)

Be sure to read the caution about exceptions to exemptions in the introduction to this appendix.

Oklahoma

Federal Bankruptcy Exemptions not available. All law references are to Oklahoma Statutes Annotated, in the form title number-section number.

ASSET	EXEMPTION	LAW
homestead	Real property or manufactured home to unlimited value; property cannot exceed 1 acre in city, town, or village, or 160 acres elsewhere; $5,000 limit if more than 25% of total sq. ft. area used for business purposes; okay to rent homestead as long as no other residence is acquired	31-1(A)(1); 31-1(A)(2); 31-2
insurance	Annuity benefits & cash value	36-3631.1
	Assessment or mutual benefits	36-2410
	Fraternal benefit society benefits	36-2718.1
	Funeral benefits prepaid & placed in trust	36-6125
	Group life policy or proceeds	36-3632
	Life, health, accident, & mutual benefit insurance proceeds & cash value, if clause prohibits proceeds from being used to pay beneficiary's creditors	36-3631.1
	Limited stock insurance benefits	36-2510
miscellaneous	Alimony, child support	31-1(A)(19)
	Beneficiary's interest in a statutory support trust	6-3010
	Liquor license	37-532
	Property of business partnership	54-1-504
pensions	County employees	19-959
	Disabled veterans	31-7
	ERISA-qualified benefits, IRAs, Roth IRAs, Education IRAs, & Keoghs	31-1(A)(20),(23),(24)
	Firefighters	11-49-126
	Judges	20-1111
	Law enforcement employees	47-2-303.3
	Police officers	11-50-124
	Public employees	74-923
	Tax-exempt benefits	60-328
	Teachers	70-17-109
personal property	Books, portraits, & pictures	31-1(A)-7
	Burial plots	31-1(A)(4); 8-7
	Clothing to $4,000	31-1(A)(8)
	College savings plan interest	31-1(24)
	Deposits in an IDA (Individual Development Account)	31-1(22)
	Federal earned income tax credit	31-1(A)(25)
	Food & seed for growing to last 1 year	31-1(A)(17)
	Health aids (professionally prescribed)	31-1(A)(9)
	Household & kitchen furniture	31-1(A)(3)
	Livestock for personal or family use: 5 dairy cows & calves under 6 months; 100 chickens; 20 sheep; 10 hogs; 2 horses, bridles, & saddles; forage & feed to last 1 year	31-1(A)(10),(11),(12), (15),(16),(17)
	Motor vehicle to $3,000	31-1(A)(13)
	Personal injury & wrongful death recoveries to $50,000	31-1(A)(21)
	Prepaid funeral benefits	36-6125(H)
	War bond payroll savings account	51-42
	1 gun	31-1(A)(14)
public benefits	Crime victims' compensation	21-142.13
	Public assistance	56-173
	Social Security	56-173
	Unemployment compensation	40-2-303
	Workers' compensation	85-48
tools of trade	Implements needed to farm homestead, tools, books, & apparatus to $5,000 total	31-1(A)(5),(6); 31-1(C)
wages	75% of wages earned in 90 days before filing bankruptcy; bankruptcy judge may allow more if you show hardship	12-1171.1; 31-1(A)(18); 31-1.1
wildcard	None	

Oregon

Federal Bankruptcy Exemptions not available. All law references are to Oregon Revised Statutes.

ASSET	EXEMPTION	LAW
homestead	Prepaid rent & security deposit for renter's dwelling	In re Casserino, 379 F.3d 1069 (9th Cir. 2004)
	Real property of a soldier or sailor during time of war	408.440
	Real property you occupy or intend to occupy to $25,000 ($33,000 for joint owners); mobile home on property you own or houseboat to $23,000 ($30,000 for joint owners); mobile home not on your land to $20,000 ($27,000 for joint owners); property cannot exceed 1 block in town or city or 160 acres elsewhere; sale proceeds exempt 1 year from sale, if you intend to purchase another home	18.428; 18.395; 18.402
	Tenancy by entirety not exempt, but subject to survivorship rights of nondebtor spouse	In re Pletz, 225 B.R. 206 (D. Ore., 1997)
insurance	Annuity contract benefits to $500 per month	743.049
	Fraternal benefit society benefits to $7,500	748.207; 18.348
	Group life policy or proceeds not payable to insured	743.047
	Health or disability proceeds or avails	743.050
	Life insurance proceeds or cash value if you are not the insured	743.046, 743.047
miscellaneous	Alimony, child support needed for support	18.345(1)(i)
	Liquor licenses	471.292 (1)
pensions	ERISA-qualified benefits, including IRAs & SEPs; & payments to $7,500	18.358; 18.348
	Public officers, employees pension payments to $7,500	237.980; 238.445; 18.348 (2)
personal property	Bank deposits to $7,500; cash for sold exempt property	18.348; 18.345(2)
	Books, pictures, & musical instruments to $600 total	18.345(1)(a)
	Building materials for construction of an improvement	87.075
	Burial plot	65.870
	Clothing, jewelry, & other personal items to $1,800 total	18.345(1)(b)
	Compensation for lost earnings payments for debtor or someone debtor depended on, to extent needed	18.345(1)(L),(3)
	Domestic animals, poultry, & pets to $1,000 plus food to last 60 days	18.345(1)(e)
	Federal earned income tax credit	18.345(1)(n)
	Food & fuel to last 60 days if debtor is householder	18.345(1)(f)
	Furniture, household items, utensils, radios, & TVs to $3,000 total	18.345(1)(f)
	Health aids	18.345(1)(h)
	Higher education savings account to $7,500	348.863; 18.348(1)
	Motor vehicle to $1,700	18.345(1)(d),(3)
	Personal injury recoveries to $10,000	18.345(1)(k),(3)
	Pistol; rifle or shotgun (owned by person over 16) to $1,000	18.362
public benefits	Aid to blind to $7,500	412.115; 18.348
	Aid to disabled to $7,500	412.610; 18.348
	Civil defense & disaster relief to $7,500	401.405; 18.348
	Crime victims' compensation	18.345(1)(j)(A),(3); 147.325
	General assistance to $7,500	411.760; 18.348
	Injured inmates' benefits to $7,500	655.530; 18.348
	Medical assistance to $7,500	414.095; 18.348
	Old-age assistance to $7,500	413.130; 18.348
	Unemployment compensation to $7,500	657.855; 18.348
	Veterans' benefits & proceeds of Veterans loans	407.125; 407.595; 18.348(m)
	Vocational rehabilitation to $7,500	344.580; 18.348
	Workers' compensation to $7,500	656.234; 18.348
tools of trade	Tools, library, team with food to last 60 days, to $3,000	18.345(1)(c),(3)
wages	75% of disposable wages or $170 per week, whichever is greater; bankruptcy judge may authorize more for low-income debtors	18.385
	Wages withheld in state employee's bond savings accounts	292.070
wildcard	$400 of any personal property not already covered by existing exemption	18.348(1)(o)

Be sure to read the caution about exceptions to exemptions in the introduction to this appendix.

Pennsylvania

Federal Bankruptcy Exemptions available. All law references are to Pennsylvania Consolidated Statutes Annotated.

ASSET	EXEMPTION	LAW
homestead	None; however, property held as tenancy by the entirety may be exempt against debts owed by only one spouse	*In re Martin*, 259 B.R. 119 (M.D. Pa. 2001)
insurance	Accident or disability benefits	42-8124(c)(7)
	Fraternal benefit society benefits	42-8124(c)(1),(8)
	Group life policy or proceeds	42-8124(c)(5)
	Insurance policy or annuity contract payments, where insured is the beneficiary, cash value or proceeds to $100 per month	42-8124(c)(3)
	Life insurance & annuity proceeds if clause prohibits proceeds from being used to pay beneficiary's creditors	42-8214(c)(4)
	Life insurance annuity policy cash value or proceeds if beneficiary is insured's dependent, child, or spouse	42-8124(c)(6)
	No-fault automobile insurance proceeds	42-8124(c)(9)
miscellaneous	Property of business partnership	15-8342
pensions	City employees	53-13445; 53-23572; 53-39383; 42-8124(b)(1)(iv)
	County employees	16-4716
	Municipal employees	53-881.115; 42-8124(b)(1)(vi)
	Police officers	53-764; 53-776; 53-23666; 42-8124(b)(1)(iii)
	Private retirement benefits to extent tax-deferred, if clause prohibits proceeds from being used to pay beneficiary's creditors; exemption limited to deposits of $15,000 per year made at least 1 year before filing (limit does not apply to rollovers from other exempt funds or accounts)	42-8124(b)(1)(vii), (viii),(ix)
	Public school employees	24-8533; 42-8124(b)(1)(i)
	State employees	71-5953; 42-8124(b)(1)(ii)
personal property	Bibles & schoolbooks	42-8124(a)(2)
	Clothing	42-8124(a)(1)
	Military uniforms & accoutrements	42-8124(a)(4); 51-4103
	Sewing machines	42-8124(a)(3)
public benefits	Crime victims' compensation	18-11.708
	Korean conflict veterans' benefits	51-20098
	Unemployment compensation	42-8124(a)(10); 43-863
	Veterans' benefits	51-20012; 20048; 20098; 20127
	Workers' compensation	42-8124(c)(2)
tools of trade	Seamstress's sewing machine	42-8124(a)(3)
wages	Earned but unpaid wages	42-8127
	Prison inmates wages	61-1054
	Wages of victims of abuse	42-8127(f)
wildcard	$300 of any property, including cash, real property, securities, or proceeds from sale of exempt property	42-8123

Rhode Island

Federal Bankruptcy Exemptions available. All law references are to General Laws of Rhode Island.

ASSET	EXEMPTION	LAW
homestead	$200,000 in land & buildings you occupy or intend to occupy as a principal residence (husband & wife may not double)	9-26-4.1
insurance	Accident or sickness proceeds, avails, or benefits	27-18-24
	Fraternal benefit society benefits	27-25-18
	Life insurance proceeds if clause prohibits proceeds from being used to pay beneficiary's creditors	27-4-12
	Temporary disability insurance	28-41-32
miscellaneous	Earnings of a minor child	9-26-4(9)
	Property of business partnership	7-12-36
pensions	ERISA-qualified benefits	9-26-4(12)
	Firefighters	9-26-5
	IRAs & Roth IRAs	9-26-4(11)
	Police officers	9-26-5
	Private employees	28-17-4
	State & municipal employees	36-10-34
personal property	Beds, bedding, furniture, household goods, & supplies, to $8,600 total (husband & wife may not double)	9-26-4(3); *In re Petrozella*, 247 B.R. 591 (R.I. 2000)
	Bibles & books to $300	9-26-4(4)
	Burial plot	9-26-4(5)
	Clothing	9-26-4(1)
	Consumer cooperative association holdings to $50	7-8-25
	Debt secured by promissory note or bill of exchange	9-26-4(7)
	Jewelry to $1,000	9-26-4 (14)
	Motor vehicles to $10,000	9-26-4 (13)
	Prepaid tuition program or tuition savings account	9-26-4 (15)
public benefits	Aid to blind, aged, disabled; general assistance	40-6-14
	Crime victims' compensation	12-25.1-3(b)(2)
	Family assistance benefits	40-5.1-15
	State disability benefits	28-41-32
	Unemployment compensation	28-44-58
	Veterans' disability or survivors' death benefits	30-7-9
	Workers' compensation	28-33-27
tools of trade	Library of practicing professional	9-26-4(2)
	Working tools to $1,200	9-26-4(2)
wages	Earned but unpaid wages due military member on active duty	30-7-9
	Earned but unpaid wages due seaman	9-26-4(6)
	Earned but unpaid wages to $50	9-26-4(8)(iii)
	Wages of any person who had been receiving public assistance are exempt for 1 year after going off of relief	9-26-4(8)(ii)
	Wages of spouse & minor children	9-26-4(9)
	Wages paid by charitable organization or fund providing relief to the poor	9-26-4(8)(i)
wildcard	None	

Be sure to read the caution about exceptions to exemptions in the introduction to this appendix.

South Carolina

Federal Bankruptcy Exemptions not available. All law references are to Code of Laws of South Carolina.

ASSET	EXEMPTION	LAW
homestead	Real property, including co-op, to $5,000	15-41-30(1)
insurance	Accident & disability benefits	38-63-40(D)
	Benefits accruing under life insurance policy after death of insured, where proceeds left with insurance company pursuant to agreement; benefits not exempt from action to recover necessaries if parties agree	38-63-50
	Disability or illness benefits	15-41-30(10)(C)
	Fraternal benefit society benefits	38-38-330
	Group life insurance proceeds; cash value to $50,000	38-63-40(C); 38-65-90
	Life insurance avails from policy for person you depended on to $4,000	15-41-30(8)
	Life insurance proceeds from policy for person you depended on, needed for support	15-41-30(11)(C)
	Proceeds & cash surrender value of life insurance payable to beneficiary other than insured's estate & for the express benefit of insured's spouse, children, or dependents (must be purchased 2 years before filing)	38-63-40(A)
	Proceeds of life insurance or annuity contract	38-63-40(B)
	Unmatured life insurance contract, except credit insurance policy	15-41-30(7)
miscellaneous	Alimony, child support	15-41-30(10)(D)
	Property of business partnership	33-41-720
pensions	ERISA-qualified benefits; your share of the pension plan fund	15-41-30(10)(E),(13)
	Firefighters	9-13-230
	General assembly members	9-9-180
	IRAs & Roth IRAs needed for support	15-41-30(12)
	Judges, solicitors	9-8-190
	Police officers	9-11-270
	Public employees	9-1-1680
personal property	Animals, crops, appliances, books, clothing, household goods, furnishings, musical instruments to $2,500 total	15-41-30(3)
	Burial plot to $5,000, in lieu of homestead	15-41-30(1)
	Cash & other liquid assets to $1,000, in lieu of burial or homestead exemption	15-41-30(5)
	College investment program trust fund	59-2-140
	Health aids	15-41-30(9)
	Jewelry to $500	15-41-30(4)
	Motor vehicle to $1,200	15-41-30(2)
	Personal injury & wrongful death recoveries for person you depended on for support	15-41-30(11)(B)
public benefits	Crime victims' compensation	15-41-30(11)(A); 16-3-1300
	General relief; aid to aged, blind, disabled	43-5-190
	Local public assistance	15-41-30(10)(A)
	Social Security	15-41-30(10)(A)
	Unemployment compensation	15-41-30(10)(A)
	Veterans' benefits	15-41-30(10)(B)
	Workers' compensation	42-9-360
tools of trade	Implements, books, & tools of trade to $750	15-41-30(6)
wages	None (use federal nonbankruptcy wage exemption)	
wildcard	None	

South Dakota

Federal Bankruptcy Exemptions not available. All law references are to South Dakota Codified Laws.

ASSET	EXEMPTION	LAW
homestead	Gold or silver mine, mill, or smelter not exempt	43-31-5
	May file homestead declaration	43-31-6
	Real property to unlimited value or mobile home (larger than 240 sq. ft. at its base & registered in state at least 6 months before filing) to unlimited value; property cannot exceed 1 acre in town or 160 acres elsewhere; sale proceeds to $30,000 ($170,000 if over age 70 or widow or widower who hasn't remarried) exempt for 1 year after sale (husband & wife may not double)	43-31-1; 43-31-2; 43-31-3; 43-31-4 43-45-3
	Spouse or child of deceased owner may claim homestead exemption	43-31-13
insurance	Annuity contract proceeds to $250 per month	58-12-6; 58-12-8
	Endowment, life insurance, policy proceeds to $20,000; if policy issued by mutual aid or benevolent society, cash value to $20,000	58-12-4
	Fraternal benefit society benefits	58-37A-18
	Health benefits to $20,000	58-12-4
	Life insurance proceeds, if clause prohibits proceeds from being used to pay beneficiary's creditors	58-15-70
	Life insurance proceeds to $10,000, if beneficiary is surviving spouse or child	43-45-6
pensions	City employees	9-16-47
	ERISA-qualified benefits, limited to income & distribution on $250,000	43-45-16
	Public employees	3-12-115
personal property	Bible, schoolbooks; other books to $200	43-45-2(4)
	Burial plots, church pew	43-45-2(2),(3)
	Cemetery association property	47-29-25
	Clothing	43-45-2(5)
	Family pictures	43-45-2(1)
	Food & fuel to last 1 year	43-45-2(6)
public benefits	Crime victim's compensation	23A-28B-24
	Public assistance	28-7A-18
	Unemployment compensation	61-6-28
	Workers' compensation	62-4-42
tools of trade	None	
wages	Earned wages owed 60 days before filing bankruptcy, needed for support of family	15-20-12
	Wages of prisoners in work programs	24-8-10
wildcard	Head of family may claim $6,000, or non-head of family may claim $4,000 of any personal property	43-45-4

Tennessee

Federal Bankruptcy Exemptions not available. All law references are to Tennessee Code Annotated unless otherwise noted.

ASSET	EXEMPTION	LAW
homestead	$5,000; $7,500 for joint owners (if 62 or older, $12,500 if single; $20,000 if married; $25,000 if spouse is also 62 or older)	26-2-301
	2–15 year lease	26-2-303
	Life estate	26-2-302
	Property held as tenancy by the entirety may be exempt against debts owed by only one spouse, but survivorship right is not exempt	In re Arango, 136 B.R. 740 aff'd, 992 F.2d 611 (6th Cir. 1993); In re Arwood, 289 B.R. 889 (Bankr. E.D. Tenn. 2003)
	Spouse or child of deceased owner may claim homestead exemption	26-2-301
insurance	Accident, health, or disability benefits for resident & citizen of Tennessee	26-2-110
	Disability or illness benefits	26-2-111(1)(C)
	Fraternal benefit society benefits	56-25-1403
	Life insurance or annuity	56-7-203
miscellaneous	Alimony, child support owed for 30 days before filing for bankruptcy	26-2-111(1)(E)
	Educational scholarship trust funds & pre-payment plans	49-4-108; 49-7-822
pensions	ERISA-qualified benefits, IRAs, & Roth IRAs	26-2-111(1)(D)
	Public employees	8-36-111
	State & local government employees	26-2-105
	Teachers	49-5-909
personal property	Bible, schoolbooks, family pictures, & portraits	26-2-104
	Burial plot to 1 acre	26-2-305; 46-2-102
	Clothing & storage containers	26-2-104
	Health aids	26-2-111(5)
	Lost future earnings payments for you or person you depended on	26-2-111(3)
	Personal injury recoveries to $7,500; wrongful death recoveries to $10,000 ($15,000 total for personal injury, wrongful death, & crime victims' compensation)	26-2-111(2)(B),(C)
	Wages of debtor deserting family, in hands of family	26-2-109
public benefits	Aid to blind	71-4-117
	Aid to disabled	71-4-1112
	Crime victims' compensation to $5,000 (see personal property)	26-2-111(2)(A); 29-13-111
	Local public assistance	26-2-111(1)(A)
	Old-age assistance	71-2-216
	Relocation assistance payments	13-11-115
	Social Security	26-2-111(1)(A)
	Unemployment compensation	26-2-111(1)(A)
	Veterans' benefits	26-2-111(1)(B)
	Workers' compensation	50-6-223
tools of trade	Implements, books, & tools of trade to $1,900	26-2-111(4)
wages	Minimum 75% of disposable weekly earnings or 30 times the federal minimum hourly wage, whichever is more, plus $2.50 per week per child; bankruptcy judge may authorize more for low-income debtors	26-2-106,107
wildcard	$4,000 of any personal property including deposits on account with any bank or financial institution	26-2-103

Texas

Federal Bankruptcy Exemptions available. All law references are to Texas Revised Civil Statutes Annotated unless otherwise noted.

ASSET	EXEMPTION	LAW
homestead	Unlimited; property cannot exceed 10 acres in town, village, city or 100 acres (200 for families) elsewhere; sale proceeds exempt for 6 months after sale (renting okay if another home not acquired, Prop. 41.003)	Prop. 41.001; 41.002; Const. Art. 16 §§ 50, 51
	Must file homestead declaration, or court will file it for you & charge you for doing so	Prop. 41.005(f); 41.021 to 41.023
insurance	Church benefit plan benefits	1407a (6)
	Fraternal benefit society benefits	Ins. 885.316
	Life, health, accident, or annuity benefits, monies, policy proceeds, & cash values due or paid to beneficiary or insured	Ins. 1108.051
	Texas employee uniform group insurance	Ins. 1551.011
	Texas public school employees group insurance	Ins. 1575.006
	Texas state college or university employee benefits	Ins. 1601.008
miscellaneous	Alimony & child support	Prop. 42.001(b)(3)
	Higher education savings plan trust account	Educ. 54.709(e)
	Liquor licenses & permits	Alco.Bev.Code 11.03
	Prepaid tuition plans	Educ. 54.639
	Property of business partnership	6132b-5.01
pensions	County & district employees	Gov't. 811.006
	ERISA-qualified government or church benefits, including Keoghs & IRAs	Prop. 42.0021
	Firefighters	6243e(5); 6243a-1(8.03); 6243b(15); 6243e(5); 6243e.1(1.04)
	Judges	Gov't. 831.004
	Law enforcement officers, firefighters, emergency medical personnel survivors	Gov't. 615.005
	Municipal employees & elected officials, state employees	6243h(22); Gov't. 811.005
	Police officers	6243d-1(17); 6243j(20); 6243a-1(8.03); 6243b(15); 6243d-1(17)
	Retirement benefits to extent tax-deferred	Prop. 42.0021
	Teachers	Gov't. 821.005
personal property to $60,000 total for family, $30,000 for single adult (see also tools of trade)	Athletic & sporting equipment, including bicycles	Prop. 42.002(a)(8)
	Burial plots (exempt from total)	Prop. 41.001
	Clothing & food	Prop. 42.002(a)(2),(5)
	Health aids (exempt from total)	Prop. 42.001(b)(2)
	Home furnishings including family heirlooms	Prop. 42.002(a)(1)
	Jewelry (limited to 25% of total exemption)	Prop. 42.002(a)(6)
	Pets & domestic animals plus their food: 2 horses, mules, or donkeys & tack; 12 head of cattle; 60 head of other livestock; 120 fowl	Prop. 42.002(a)(10),(11)
	1 two-, three- or four-wheeled motor vehicle per family member or per single adult who holds a driver's license; or, if not licensed, who relies on someone else to operate vehicle	Prop. 42.002(a)(9)
	2 firearms	Prop. 42.002(a)(7)
public benefits	Crime victims' compensation	Crim. Proc. 56.49
	Medical assistance	Hum. Res. 32.036
	Public assistance	Hum. Res. 31.040
	Unemployment compensation	Labor 207.075
	Workers' compensation	Labor 408.201
tools of trade included in aggregate dollar limits for personal property	Farming or ranching vehicles & implements	Prop. 42.002(a)(3)
	Tools, equipment (includes boat & motor vehicles used in trade), & books	Prop. 42.002(a)(4)
wages	Earned but unpaid wages	Prop. 42.001(b)(1)
	Unpaid commissions not to exceed 25% of total personal property exemptions	Prop. 42.001(d)
wildcard	None	

Be sure to read the caution about exceptions to exemptions in the introduction to this appendix.

Utah

Federal Bankruptcy Exemptions not available. All law references are to Utah Code.

ASSET	EXEMPTION	LAW
homestead	Must file homestead declaration before attempted sale of home	78-23-4
	Real property, mobile home, or water rights to $20,000 if primary residence; $5,000 if not primary residence	78-23-3(1),(2),(4)
	Sale proceeds exempt for 1 year	78-23-3(5)(b)
insurance	Disability, illness, medical, or hospital benefits	78-23-5(1)(a)(iii)
	Fraternal benefit society benefits	31A-9-603
	Life insurance policy cash surrender value to $5,000	78-23-7
	Life insurance proceeds if beneficiary is insured's spouse or dependent, as needed for support	78-23-6(2)
	Medical, surgical, & hospital benefits	78-23-5(1)(a)(iv)
miscellaneous	Alimony needed for support	78-23-5(1)(a)(vi); 78-23-6(1)
	Child support	78-23-5(1)(f),(k)
	Property of business partnership	48-1-22
pensions	ERISA-qualified benefits, IRAs, Roth IRAs, & Keoghs (benefits that have accrued & contributions that have been made at least 1 year prior to filing)	78-23-5(1)(a)(x)
	Other pensions & annuities needed for support	78-23-6(3)
	Public employees	49-11-612
personal property	Animals, books, & musical instruments to $500	78-23-8(1)(c)
	Artwork depicting, or done by, a family member	78-23-5(1)(a)(viii)
	Bed, bedding, carpets	78-23-5(1)(a)(vii)
	Burial plot	78-23-5(1)(a)(i)
	Clothing (cannot claim furs or jewelry)	78-23-5(1)(a)(vii)
	Dining & kitchen tables & chairs to $500	78-23-8(1)(b)
	Food to last 12 months	78-23-5(1)(a)(vii)
	Health aids	78-23-5(1)(a)(ii)
	Heirlooms to $500	78-23-8(1)(d)
	Motor vehicle to $2,500	78-23-8(3)
	Personal injury, wrongful death recoveries for you or person you depended on	78-23-5(1)(a)(ix)
	Proceeds for sold, lost, or damaged exempt property	78-23-9
	Refrigerator, freezer, microwave, stove, sewing machine, washer & dryer	78-23-5(1)(a)(vii)
	Sofas, chairs, & related furnishings to $500	78-23-8(1)(a)
public benefits	Crime victims' compensation	63-25a-421(4)
	General assistance	35A-3-112
	Occupational disease disability benefits	34A-3-107
	Unemployment compensation	35A-4-103(4)(b)
	Veterans' benefits	78-23-5(1)(a)(v)
	Workers' compensation	34A-2-422
tools of trade	Implements, books, & tools of trade to $3,500	78-23-8(2)
	Military property of National Guard member	39-1-47
wages	Minimum 75% of disposable weekly earnings or 30 times the federal hourly minimum wage, whichever is more; bankruptcy judge may authorize more for low-income debtors	70C-7-103
wildcard	None	

Vermont

Federal Bankruptcy Exemptions available. All law references are to Vermont Statutes Annotated unless otherwise noted.

ASSET	EXEMPTION	LAW
homestead	Property held as tenancy by the entirety may be exempt against debts owed by only one spouse	In re McQueen, 21 B.R. 736 (D. Ver. 1982)
	Real property or mobile home to $75,000; may also claim rents, issues, profits, & outbuildings	27-101
	Spouse of deceased owner may claim homestead exemption	27-105
insurance	Annuity contract benefits to $350 per month	8-3709
	Disability benefits that supplement life insurance or annuity contract	8-3707
	Disability or illness benefits needed for support	12-2740(19)(C)
	Fraternal benefit society benefits	8-4478
	Group life or health benefits	8-3708
	Health benefits to $200 per month	8-4086
	Life insurance proceeds for person you depended on	12-2740(19)(H)
	Life insurance proceeds if clause prohibits proceeds from being used to pay beneficiary's creditors	8-3705
	Life insurance proceeds if beneficiary is not the insured	8-3706
	Unmatured life insurance contract other than credit	12-2740(18)
miscellaneous	Alimony, child support	12-2740(19)(D)
pensions	Municipal employees	24-5066
	Other pensions	12-2740(19)(J)
	Self-directed accounts (IRAs, Roth IRAs, Keoghs); contributions must be made 1 year before filing	12-2740(16)
	State employees	3-476
	Teachers	16-1946
personal property	Appliances, furnishings, goods, clothing, books, crops, animals, musical instruments to $2,500 total	12-2740(5)
	Bank deposits to $700	12-2740(15)
	Cow, 2 goats, 10 sheep, 10 chickens, & feed to last 1 winter; 3 swarms of bees plus honey; 5 tons coal or 500 gal. heating oil, 10 cords of firewood; 500 gal. bottled gas; growing crops to $5,000; yoke of oxen or steers, plow & ox yoke; 2 horses with harnesses, halters, & chains	12-2740(6),(9)-(14)
	Health aids	12-2740(17)
	Jewelry to $500; wedding ring unlimited	12-2740(3),(4)
	Motor vehicles to $2,500	12-2740(1)
	Personal injury, lost future earnings, wrongful death recoveries for you or person you depended on	12-2740(19)(F), (G),(I)
	Stove, heating unit, refrigerator, freezer, water heater, & sewing machines	12-2740(8)
public benefits	Aid to blind, aged, disabled; general assistance	33-124
	Crime victims' compensation needed for support	12-2740(19)(E)
	Social Security needed for support	12-2740(19)(A)
	Unemployment compensation	21-1367
	Veterans' benefits needed for support	12-2740(19)(B)
	Workers' compensation	21-681
tools of trade	Books & tools of trade to $5,000	12-2740(2)
wages	Entire wages, if you received welfare during 2 months before filing	12-3170
	Minimum 75% of weekly disposable earnings or 30 times the federal minimum hourly wage, whichever is greater; bankruptcy judge may authorize more for low-income debtors	12-3170
wildcard	Unused exemptions for motor vehicle, tools of trade, jewelry, household furniture, appliances, clothing, & crops to $7,000	12-2740(7)
	$400 of any property	12-2740(7)

Be sure to read the caution about exceptions to exemptions in the introduction to this appendix.

Virginia

Federal Bankruptcy Exemptions not available. All law references are to Code of Virginia unless otherwise noted.

ASSET	EXEMPTION	LAW
homestead	$5,000 plus $500 per dependent; rents & profits; sale proceeds exempt to $5,000 (unused portion of homestead may be applied to any personal property)	*Cheeseman v. Nachman,* 656 F.2d 60 (4th Cir. 1981); 34-4; 34-18; 34-20
	May include mobile home	*In re Goad,* 161 B.R. 161 (W.D. Va. 1993)
	Must file homestead declaration before filing for bankruptcy	34-6
	Property held as tenancy by the entirety may be exempt against debts owed by only one spouse	*In re Bunker,* 312 F.3d 145 (4th Cir., 2002)
	Surviving spouse may claim $15,000; if no surviving spouse, minor children may claim exemption	64.1-151.3
insurance	Accident or sickness benefits	38.2-3406
	Burial society benefits	38.2-4021
	Cooperative life insurance benefits	38.2-3811
	Fraternal benefit society benefits	38.2-4118
	Group life or accident insurance for government officials	51.1-510
	Group life insurance policy or proceeds	38.2-3339
	Industrial sick benefits	38.2-3549
	Life insurance proceeds	38.2-3122
miscellaneous	Property of business partnership	50-73.108
pensions *see also wages*	City, town, & county employees	51.1-802
	ERISA-qualified benefits to $17,500	34-34
	Judges	51.1-300
	State employees	51.1-124.4(A)
	State police officers	51.1-200
personal property	Bible	34-26(1)
	Burial plot	34-26(3)
	Clothing to $1,000	34-26(4)
	Family portraits & heirlooms to $5,000 total	34-26(2)
	Health aids	34-26(6)
	Household furnishings to $5,000	34-26(4a)
	Motor vehicle to $2,000	34-26(8)
	Personal injury causes of action & recoveries	34-28.1
	Pets	34-26(5)
	Prepaid tuition contracts	23-38.81(E)
	Spendthrift trusts not created by debtor	55-19
	Wedding & engagement rings	34-26(1a)
public benefits	Aid to blind, aged, disabled; general relief	63.2-506
	Crime victims' compensation unless seeking to discharge debt for treatment of injury incurred during crime	19.2-368.12
	Payments to tobacco farmers	3.1-1111.1
	Unemployment compensation	60.2-600
	Workers' compensation	65.2-531
tools of trade	For farmer, pair of horses, or mules with gear; one wagon or cart, one tractor to $3,000; 2 plows & wedges, one drag, harvest cradle, pitchfork, rake; fertilizer to $1,000	34-27
	Tools, books, & instruments of trade, including motor vehicles, to $10,000, needed in your occupation or education	34-26(7)
	Uniforms, arms, equipment of military member	44-96
wages	Minimum 75% of weekly disposable earnings or 30 times the federal minimum hourly wage, whichever is greater; bankruptcy judge may authorize more for low-income debtors	34-29
wildcard	Unused portion of homestead or personal property exemption	34-13
	$2,000 of any property for disabled veterans	34-4.1

Washington

Federal Bankruptcy Exemptions available. All law references are to Revised Code of Washington Annotated.

ASSET	EXEMPTION	LAW
homestead	Must record homestead declaration before sale of home if property unimproved or home unoccupied	6.15.040
	Real property or mobile home to $40,000; unimproved property intended for residence to $15,000 (husband & wife may not double)	6.13.010; 6.13.030
insurance	Annuity contract proceeds to $250 per month	48.18.430
	Disability proceeds, avails, or benefits	48.36A.180
	Fraternal benefit society benefits	48.18.400
	Group life insurance policy or proceeds	48.18.420
	Life insurance proceeds or avails if beneficiary is not the insured	48.18.410
miscellaneous	Child support payments	6.15.010(3)(d)
pensions	City employees	41.28.200; 41.44.240
	ERISA-qualified benefits, IRAs, Roth IRAs, & Keoghs	6.15.020
	Judges	2.10.180; 2.12.090
	Law enforcement officials & firefighters	41.26.053
	Police officers	41.20.180
	Public & state employees	41.40.052
	State patrol officers	43.43.310
	Teachers	41.32.052
	Volunteer firefighters	41.24.240
personal property	Appliances, furniture, household goods, home & yard equipment to $2,700 total for individual ($5,400 for community)	6.15.010(3)(a)
	Books to $1,500	6.15.010(2)
	Burial ground	68.24.220
	Burial plots sold by nonprofit cemetery association	68.20.120
	Clothing, no more than $1,000 in furs, jewelry, ornaments	6.15.010(1)
	Fire insurance proceeds for lost, stolen, or destroyed exempt property	6.15.030
	Food & fuel for comfortable maintenance	6.15.010(3)(a)
	Health aids prescribed	6.15.010(3)(e)
	Keepsakes & family pictures	6.15.010(2)
	Motor vehicle to $2,500 total for individual (two vehicles to $5,000 for community)	6.15.010(3)(c)
	Personal injury recoveries to $16,150	6.15.010(3)(f)
public benefits	Child welfare	74.13.070
	Crime victims' compensation	7.68.070(10)
	General assistance	74.04.280
	Industrial insurance (workers' compensation)	51.32.040
	Old-age assistance	74.08.210
	Unemployment compensation	50.40.020
tools of trade	Farmer's trucks, stock, tools, seed, equipment, & supplies to $5,000 total	6.15.010(4)(a)
	Library, office furniture, office equipment, & supplies of physician, surgeon, attorney, clergy, or other professional to $5,000 total	6.15.010(4)(b)
	Tools & materials used in any other trade to $5,000	6.15.010(4)(c)
wages	Minimum 75% of weekly disposable earnings or 30 times the federal minimum hourly wage, whichever is greater; bankruptcy judge may authorize more for low-income debtors	6.27.150
wildcard	$2,000 of any personal property (no more than $200 in cash, bank deposits, bonds, stocks, & securities)	6.15.010(3)(b)

Be sure to read the caution about exceptions to exemptions in the introduction to this appendix.

West Virginia

Federal Bankruptcy Exemptions not available. All law references are to West Virginia Code.

ASSET	EXEMPTION	LAW
homestead	Real or personal property used as residence to $25,000; unused portion of homestead may be applied to any property	38-10-4(a)
insurance	Fraternal benefit society benefits	33-23-21
	Group life insurance policy or proceeds	33-6-28
	Health or disability benefits	38-10-4(j)(3)
	Life insurance payments from policy for person you depended on, needed for support	38-10-4(k)(3)
	Unmatured life insurance contract, except credit insurance policy	38-10-4(g)
	Unmatured life insurance contract's accrued dividend, interest, or loan value to $8,000, if debtor owns contract & insured is either debtor or a person on whom debtor is dependent	38-10-4(h)
miscellaneous	Alimony, child support needed for support	38-10-4(j)(4)
pensions	ERISA-qualified benefits, IRAs needed for support	38-10-4(j)(5)
	Public employees	5-10-46
	Teachers	18-7A-30
personal property	Animals, crops, clothing, appliances, books, household goods, furnishings, musical instruments to $400 per item, $8,000 total	38-10-4(c)
	Burial plot to $25,000, in lieu of homestead	38-10-4(a)
	Health aids	38-10-4(i)
	Jewelry to $1,000	38-10-4(d)
	Lost earnings payments needed for support	38-10-4(k)(5)
	Motor vehicle to $2,400	38-10-4(b)
	Personal injury recoveries to $15,000	38-10-4(k)(4)
	Prepaid higher education tuition trust fund & savings plan payments	38-10-4(k)(6)
	Wrongful death recoveries for person you depended on, needed for support	38-10-4(k)(2)
public benefits	Aid to blind, aged, disabled; general assistance	9-5-1
	Crime victims' compensation	38-10-4(k)(1)
	Social Security	38-10-4(j)(1)
	Unemployment compensation	38-10-4(j)(1)
	Veterans' benefits	38-10-4(j)(2)
	Workers' compensation	23-4-18
tools of trade	Implements, books, & tools of trade to $1,500	38-10-4(f)
wages	Minimum 30 times the federal minimum hourly wage per week; bankruptcy judge may authorize more for low-income debtors	38-5A-3
wildcard	$800 plus unused portion of homestead or burial exemption, of any property	38-10-4(e)

Wisconsin

Federal Bankruptcy Exemptions available. All law references are to Wisconsin Statutes Annotated.

ASSET	EXEMPTION	LAW
homestead	Property you occupy or intend to occupy to $40,000; sale proceeds exempt for 2 years if you intend to purchase another home (husband & wife may not double)	815.20
insurance	Federal disability insurance benefits	815.18(3)(ds)
	Fraternal benefit society benefits	614.96
	Life insurance proceeds for someone debtor depended on, needed for support	815.18(3)(i)(a)
	Life insurance proceeds held in trust by insurer, if clause prohibits proceeds from being used to pay beneficiary's creditors	632.42
	Unmatured life insurance contract (except credit insurance contract) if debtor owns contract & insured is debtor or dependents, or someone debtor is dependent on	815.18(3)(f)
	Unmatured life insurance contract's accrued dividends, interest, or loan value to $4,000 total, if debtor owns contract & insured is debtor or dependents, or someone debtor is dependent on	815.18(3)(f)
miscellaneous	Alimony, child support needed for support	815.18(3)(c)
	Property of business partnership	178.21(3)(c)
pensions	Certain municipal employees	62.63(4)
	Firefighters, police officers who worked in city with population over 100,000	815.18(3)(ef)
	Military pensions	815.18(3)(n)
	Private or public retirement benefits	815.18(3)(j)
	Public employees	40.08(1)
personal property	Burial plot, tombstone, coffin	815.18(3)(a)
	College savings account or tuition trust fund	14.64(7); 14.63(8)
	Deposit accounts to $1,000	815.18(3)(k)
	Fire & casualty proceeds for destroyed exempt property for 2 years from receiving	815.18(3)(e)
	Household goods & furnishings, clothing, keepsakes, jewelry, appliances, books, musical instruments, firearms, sporting goods, animals, & other tangible personal property to $5,000 total	815.18(3)(d)
	Lost future earnings recoveries, needed for support	815.18(3)(i)(d)
	Motor vehicles to $1,200; unused portion of $5,000 personal property exemption may be added	815.18(3)(g)
	Personal injury recoveries to $25,000	815.18(3)(i)(c)
	Tenant's lease or stock interest in housing co-op, to homestead amount	182.004(6)
	Wages used to purchase savings bonds	20.921(1)(e)
	Wrongful death recoveries, needed for support	815.18(3)(i)(b)
public benefits	Crime victims' compensation	949.07
	Social services payments	49.96
	Unemployment compensation	108.13
	Veterans' benefits	45.35(8)(b)
	Workers' compensation	102.27
tools of trade	Equipment, inventory, farm products, books, & tools of trade to $7,500 total	815.18(3)(b)
wages	75% of weekly net income or 30 times the greater of the federal or state minimum hourly wage; bankruptcy judge may authorize more for low-income debtors	815.18(3)(h)
	Wages of county jail prisoners	303.08(3)
	Wages of county work camp prisoners	303.10(7)
	Wages of inmates under work-release plan	303.065(4)(b)
wildcard	None	

Be sure to read the caution about exceptions to exemptions in the introduction to this appendix.

Wyoming

Federal Bankruptcy Exemptions not available. All law references are to Wyoming Statutes Annotated unless otherwise noted.

ASSET	EXEMPTION	LAW
homestead	Property held as tenancy by the entirety may be exempt against debts owed by only one spouse	*In re Anselmi,* 52 B.R. 479 (D. Wyo. 1985)
	Real property you occupy to $10,000 or house trailer you occupy to $6,000	1-20-101; 102; 104
	Spouse or child of deceased owner may claim homestead exemption	1-20-103
insurance	Annuity contract proceeds to $350 per month	26-15-132
	Disability benefits if clause prohibits proceeds from being used to pay beneficiary's creditors	26-15-130
	Fraternal benefit society benefits	26-29-218
	Group life or disability policy or proceeds, cash surrender & loan values, premiums waived, & dividends	26-15-131
	Individual life insurance policy proceeds, cash surrender & loan values, premiums waived, & dividends	26-15-129
	Life insurance proceeds held by insurer, if clause prohibits proceeds from being used to pay beneficiary's creditors	26-15-133
miscellaneous	Liquor licenses & malt beverage permits	12-4-604
pensions	Criminal investigators, highway officers	9-3-620
	Firefighters' death benefits	15-5-209
	Game & fish wardens	9-3-620
	Police officers	15-5-313(c)
	Private or public retirement funds & accounts	1-20-110
	Public employees	9-3-426
personal property	Bedding, furniture, household articles, & food to $2,000 per person in the home	1-20-106(a)(iii)
	Bible, schoolbooks, & pictures	1-20-106(a)(i)
	Burial plot	1-20-106(a)(ii)
	Clothing & wedding rings to $1,000	1-20-105
	Medical savings account contributions	1-20-111
	Motor vehicle to $2,400	1-20-106(a)(iv)
	Prepaid funeral contracts	26-32-102
public benefits	Crime victims' compensation	1-40-113
	General assistance	42-2-113(b)
	Unemployment compensation	27-3-319
	Workers' compensation	27-14-702
tools of trade	Library & implements of profession to $2,000 or tools, motor vehicle, implements, team & stock in trade to $2,000	1-20-106(b)
wages	Earnings of National Guard members	19-9-401
	Minimum 75% of disposable weekly earnings or 30 times the federal hourly minimum wage, whichever is more	1-15-511
	Wages of inmates in adult community corrections program	7-18-114
	Wages of inmates in correctional industries program	25-13-107
	Wages of inmates on work release	7-16-308
wildcard	None	

Federal Bankruptcy Exemptions

Married couples filing jointly may double all exemptions. All references are to 11 U.S.C. § 522. These exemptions were last adjusted in 2004. Every three years ending on April 1, these amounts will be adjusted to reflect changes in the Consumer Price Index. Debtors in the following states may select the Federal Bankruptcy Exemptions:

Arkansas	Massachusetts	New Jersey	Texas
Connecticut	Michigan	New Mexico	Vermont
District of Columbia	Minnesota	Pennsylvania	Washington
Hawaii	New Hampshire	Rhode Island	Wisconsin

ASSET	EXEMPTION	SUBSECTION
homestead	Real property, including co-op or mobile home, or burial plot to $18,450; unused portion of homestead to $9,250 may be applied to any property	(d)(1)
insurance	Disability, illness, or unemployment benefits	(d)(10)(C)
	Life insurance payments for person you depended on, needed for support	(d)(11)(C)
	Life insurance policy with loan value, in accrued dividends or interest, to $9,850	(d)(8)
	Unmatured life insurance contract, except credit insurance policy	(d)(7)
miscellaneous	Alimony, child support needed for support	(d)(10)(D)
pensions	ERISA-qualified benefits needed for support; may include IRAs	Awaiting decision in *Rousey v. Jacoway,* 347 F.3d 689 (8th Cir. 2003), *cert. granted,* 73 U.S.L.W. 3204 (U.S. Sept. 28, 2004) (No. 03-1407)
personal property	Animals, crops, clothing, appliances, books, furnishings, household goods, musical instruments to $475 per item, $9,850 total	(d)(3)
	Health aids	(d)(9)
	Jewelry to $1,225	(d)(4)
	Lost earnings payments	(d)(11)(E)
	Motor vehicle to $2,950	(d)(2)
	Personal injury recoveries to $17,425 (not to include pain & suffering or pecuniary loss)	(d)(11)(D)
	Wrongful death recoveries for person you depended on	(d)(11)(B)
public benefits	Crime victims' compensation	(d)(11)(A)
	Public assistance	(d)(10)(A)
	Social Security	(d)(10)(A)
	Unemployment compensation	(d)(10)(A)
	Veterans' benefits	(d)(10)(A)
tools of trade	Implements, books, & tools of trade to $1,850	(d)(6)
wages	None	
wildcard	$975 of any property	(d)(5)
	Up to $9,250 of unused homestead exemption amount, for any property	(d)(5)

Be sure to read the caution about exceptions to exemptions in the introduction to this appendix.

Federal Nonbankruptcy Exemptions

These exemptions are available only if you select your state exemptions. You may use them for any exemptions in addition to those allowed by your state, but they cannot be claimed if you file using federal bankruptcy exemptions. All law references are to the United States Code.

ASSET	EXEMPTION	LAW
death & disability benefits	Government employees	5 § 8130
	Longshoremen & harbor workers	33 § 916
	War risk, hazard, death, or injury compensation	42 § 1717
retirement	Civil service employees	5 § 8346
	Foreign Service employees	22 § 4060
	Military Medal of Honor roll pensions	38 § 1562(c)
	Military service employees	10 § 1440
	Railroad workers	45 § 231m
	Social Security	42 § 407
	Veterans' benefits	38 § 5301
survivor's benefits	Judges, U.S. court & judicial center directors, administrative assistants to U.S. Supreme Court Chief Justice	28 § 376
	Lighthouse workers	33 § 775
	Military service	10 § 1450
miscellaneous	Indian lands or homestead sales or lease proceeds	25 § 410
	Klamath Indians tribe benefits for Indians residing in Oregon	25 §§ 543; 545
	Military deposits in savings accounts while on permanent duty outside U.S.	10 §§ 1035
	Military group life insurance	38 § 1970(g)
	Railroad workers' unemployment insurance	45 § 352(e)
	Seamen's clothing	46 § 11110
	Seamen's wages (while on a voyage) pursuant to a written contract	46 § 11109
	Minimum 75% of disposable weekly earnings or 30 times the federal minimum hourly wage, whichever is more; bankruptcy judge may authorize more for low-income debtors	15 § 1673

Be sure to read the caution about exceptions to exemptions in the introduction to this appendix.

APPENDIX

2

Tear-Out Forms

Form	Chapter

Worksheet 1: How Much Will You Have to Repay?

1. Total value of your nonexempt property (Worksheet 8), plus any
    increase for priority debts or to pay back a higher percentage $ _____

2. Amount overdue to mortgage lender (Worksheet 2); add interest if loan
    was obtained before October 20, 1994 $ _____

3. Amount overdue to other secured creditors (Worksheets 2 and 3), or
    the value of the collateral, plus interest $ _____

4. Compensation for lost interest on payments on unsecured debts $ _____

5. **Subtotal of lines 1 through 4** $ _____

6. Trustee's fee (3% to 10% of line 5) $ _____

7. **Minimum Amount You Will Pay Into Your Plan** $ _____

Worksheet 2: Secured Debts With Voluntary Security Interests

1 Description of debt/ name of creditor	2 Total outstanding balance	3 Regular monthly payment	4 Total amount of arrears	5 Present value of collateral
Mortgages and home equity loans				
Motor vehicle loans				
Personal loans				
Department store charges with security agreements				
Other				

Total $ _____

Worksheet 3: Secured Debts Created Without Your Consent

1 Description of debt/ name of creditor	2 Amount of debt	3 Property affected by lien	4 Present value of property
Judicial liens			
Statutory liens			
Tax liens			

Total $ _____

Worksheet 4: Unsecured Debts

1 Description of debt/ name of creditor	2 Total outstanding balance	3 Regular monthly payment	4 Total amount of arrears
Student loans			
Unsecured consolidation loans			
Unsecured personal loans			
Medical (doctors', dentists', and hospital) bills			
Lawyers' and accountants' bills			
Credit and charge cards			
Department store and gasoline credit cards			

Worksheet 4: Unsecured Debts (continued)

1 Description of debt/ name of creditor	2 Total outstanding balance	3 Regular monthly payment	4 Total amount of arrears
Alimony or child support arrears			
Back rent			
Unpaid utility bills (gas, electric, water, phone, cable, garbage)			
Tax debts (no lien recorded on undersecured portion)			
Other			

Total $ _____

If your unsecured debts add up to more than $307,675 you cannot file for Chapter 13 bankruptcy.

Worksheet 5: Your Total Monthly Income

1 Source of Income	2 Amount of each payment	3 Period covered by each payment	4 Amount per month

A. Wages or Salary

Job 1: _____

Gross pay, including overtime $ _____ _____

Subtract:

    Federal taxes _____

    State taxes _____

    Social Security (FICA) _____

    Union dues _____

    Insurance payments _____

    Child support wage withholding _____

    Other mandatory deductions (specify):

    _____ _____

              Subtotal $ _____ _____

Job 2: _____

Gross pay, including overtime $ _____ _____

Subtract:

    Federal taxes _____

    State taxes _____

    Social Security (FICA) _____

    Union dues _____

    Insurance payments _____

    Child support wage withholding _____

    Other mandatory deductions (specify):

    _____ _____

              Subtotal $ _____ _____

Job 3: _____

Gross pay, including overtime $ _____ _____

Subtract:

    Federal taxes _____

    State taxes _____

    Social Security (FICA) _____

    Union dues _____

    Insurance payments _____

    Child support wage withholding _____

    Other mandatory deductions (specify):

    _____ _____

              Subtotal $ _____ _____

Worksheet 5: Your Total Monthly Income (continued)

1 Source of Income	2 Amount of each payment	3 Period covered by each payment	4 Amount per month

B. Self-Employment Income

Job 1: _____

Pay $ _____ _____

   Subtract:

   Federal taxes   _____

   State taxes   _____

   Self-employment taxes   _____

   Other mandatory deductions (specify):

_____ _____

Subtotal $ _____   _____

Job 2: _____

Pay $ _____ _____

Subtract:

   Federal taxes   _____

   State taxes   _____

   Self-employment taxes   _____

   Other mandatory deductions (specify):

_____ _____

Subtotal $ _____   _____

C. Other Sources

Bonuses _____ _____ _____ _____

Dividends and interest _____ _____ _____ _____

Rent, lease, or license income _____ _____ _____ _____

Royalties _____ _____ _____ _____

Note or trust income _____ _____ _____ _____

Alimony or child support you receive ____ _____ _____ _____

Pension or retirement income _____ _____ _____ _____

Social Security _____ _____ _____ _____

Other public assistance _____ _____ _____ _____

Other (specify): _____ _____ _____ _____

Other (specify): _____ _____ _____ _____

Other (specify): _____ _____ _____ _____

Total monthly income $ _____

Worksheet 6: Your Total Monthly Expenses

1 Expenses	2 Amount per month
A. Your residence	
Rent or mortgage	_____
Second mortgage or home equity loan	_____
Homeowners' association fee	_____
Property taxes	_____
Homeowners' or renters' insurance	_____
Maintenance and upkeep	_____
B. Utilities	
Telephone	_____
Gas, heating fuel, electricity	_____
Water and sewer	_____
Garbage	_____
Cable	_____
C. Food	
At home	_____
Restaurants	_____
D. Personal effects	
Toiletries	_____
Drugstore items	_____
Personal grooming (haircuts)	_____
Other	_____
E. Clothing	
Purchases	_____
Laundry/dry cleaning	_____
F. Medical	
Medical or health insurance	_____
Dental insurance	_____
Deductibles and copayments	_____
Doctor	_____
Dentist	_____
Eye doctor	_____
Medicines/prescriptions	_____
Hospital	_____
Therapist	_____
G. Transportation	
Car payment	_____
Gasoline	_____
Tolls and parking	_____
Auto insurance	_____

1 Expenses	2 Amount per month
Maintenance	_____
Registration	_____
H. Dependents	
Child care	_____
Allowances	_____
Clothes	_____
Tuition	_____
School books	_____
I. Your or your spouse's education	
(Do not include student loan payment)	
Tuition	_____
Books and fees	_____
J. Miscellaneous personal expenses	
Entertainment	_____
Recreation/hobbies	_____
Newspapers and magazines	_____
Books	_____
Gifts	_____
Memberships	_____
Pet supplies/veterinarian	_____
K. Charitable contributions	_____
L. Insurance	
(Do not include health, home, or motor vehicle insurance)	
Disability	_____
Life	_____
Other	_____
M. Support payments	
Alimony, maintenance, or spousal support	_____
Child support	_____
Support of other dependents not living at home	_____
N. Regular business expenses	_____
O. Other	
(Do not include back income taxes or	_____
unsecured installment debts, such as	_____
student loan, personal loan, or credit	_____
card accounts. These debts will be	
paid through your plan.)	_____
Total monthly expenses	$ _____

Worksheet 7: Your Disposable Income

1. **Total Monthly Income** (from Worksheet 5) $ _____

2. Subtract Total Monthly Expenses (from Worksheet 6)   – _____

3. **Total Monthly Disposable Income** $ _____

Total Amount Proposed to Pay Unsecured Creditors

Typical Chapter 13 repayment plan: _____   x   36 months   = $ _____
                                          Line 3

Extended Chapter 13 repayment plan: _____   x   60 months   = $ _____
                                          Line 3

Worksheet 8: Your Exempt and Nonexempt Property

1 Your property	2 Value of property (actual dollar or garage sale value)	3 Your ownership share (%, $)	4 Amount of liens	5 Amount of your equity	6 Exempt? If not, enter nonexempt amount
1. Real estate					
2. Cash on hand (state source, such as wages, public benefits, etc.)					
3. Deposits of money (state source, such as wages, public benefits, etc.)					
4. Security deposits					
5. Household goods, supplies, and furnishings					
6. Books, pictures, art objects; stamp, coin, and other collections					

Worksheet 8: Your Exempt and Nonexempt Property (continued)

1 Your property	2 Value of property (actual dollar or garage sale value)	3 Your ownership share (%, $)	4 Amount of liens	5 Amount of your equity	6 Exempt? If not, enter nonexempt amount
7. Apparel					
8. Jewelry					
9. Firearms, sports equipment, and other hobby equipment					
10. Interests in insurance policies					
11. Annuities					
12. Pension or profit-sharing plans (do not include ERISA-qualified pensions; see Chapter 5, Section A3)					
13. Stocks and interests in incorporated and unincorporated companies					

Worksheet 8: Your Exempt and Nonexempt Property (continued)

1 Your property	2 Value of property (actual dollar or garage sale value)	3 Your ownership share (%, $)	4 Amount of liens	5 Amount of your equity	6 Exempt? If not, enter nonexempt amount

14. Interests in partnerships

15. Government and corporate bonds and other investment instruments

16. Accounts receivable

17. Family support

18. Other debts owed you where the amount owed is known and definite

19. Powers exercisable for your benefit other than those listed under real estate

20. Interests due to another person's death

Worksheet 8: Your Exempt and Nonexempt Property (continued)

1 Your property	2 Value of property (actual dollar or garage sale value)	3 Your ownership share (%, $)	4 Amount of liens	5 Amount of your equity	6 Exempt? If not, enter nonexempt amount

21. All other contingent claims and claims where the amount owed you is not known

22. Patents, copyrights, and other intellectual property

23. Licenses, franchises, and other general intangibles

24. Automobiles and other vehicles

25. Boats, motors, and accessories

26. Aircraft and accessories

27. Office equipment, furnishings, and supplies

28. Machinery, fixtures, equipment, and supplies used in business

1 Your property	2 Value of property (actual dollar or garage sale value)	3 Your ownership share (%, $)	4 Amount of liens	5 Amount of your equity	6 Exempt? If not, enter nonexempt amount
29. Business inventory					
30. Livestock, poultry, and other animals					
31. Crops					
32. Farming equipment and implements					
33. Farm supplies, chemicals, and feed					
34. Other personal property					

Subtotal	_____
Wildcard Exemption	− _____
Total Value of Nonexempt Property	_____
This is the minimum amount you will have to pay your unsecured creditors through your Chapter 13 plan.	_____

United States Bankruptcy Court

TO THE COURT CLERK:

Please send me the following materials or information:

- A copy of all local forms published by this court for filing a Chapter 13 bankruptcy, such as:
  - ☐ Chapter 13 bankruptcy cover sheet
  - ☐ Chapter 13 plan
  - ☐ worksheet showing the Chapter 13 plan calculation
  - ☐ summary of the Chapter 13 plan
  - ☐ separate creditor mailing list (matrix)
  - ☐ income deduction order and information on when to submit it
  - ☐ business report for debtor engaged in business
  - ☐ proof of claim (in case I must file claim on behalf of a creditor).
- Copies of all local rules applicable in a Chapter 13 case—rules for the judicial district, this bankruptcy court, and any applicable division.
- A copy of the court's calendar.
- The number of copies or sets of all forms I must file.
- The order in which forms should be submitted.

I have additional questions:

1. Is the filing fee still $155? Is the administrative fee still $39?
2. Can I make my plan payments with a personal check? If not, can I use cash or am I limited to cashier's checks and money orders?
3. Is there more than one division for this bankruptcy court? If so, in which division should I file?
4. Must I submit a mailing matrix?
5. Must I submit an income deduction order?
6. Should I two-hole punch my papers or is that done by the court?

I've enclosed a self-addressed envelope for your reply. Thank you.

Sincerely,

FORM B1	United States Bankruptcy Court _____District of_____	Voluntary Petition

Name of Debtor (if individual, enter Last, First, Middle):	Name of Joint Debtor (Spouse) (Last, First, Middle):
All Other Names used by the Debtor in the last 6 years (include married, maiden, and trade names):	All Other Names used by the Joint Debtor in the last 6 years (include married, maiden, and trade names):
Last four digits of Soc. Sec. No./Complete EIN or other Tax I.D. No. (if more than one, state all):	Last four digits of Soc. Sec.No./Complete EIN or other Tax I.D. No. (if more than one, state all):
Street Address of Debtor (No. & Street, City, State & Zip Code):	Street Address of Joint Debtor (No. & Street, City, State & Zip Code):
County of Residence or of the Principal Place of Business:	County of Residence or of the Principal Place of Business:
Mailing Address of Debtor (if different from street address):	Mailing Address of Joint Debtor (if different from street address):

Location of Principal Assets of Business Debtor
(if different from street address above):

Information Regarding the Debtor (Check the Applicable Boxes)

Venue (Check any applicable box)

☐ Debtor has been domiciled or has had a residence, principal place of business, or principal assets in this District for 180 days immediately preceding the date of this petition or for a longer part of such 180 days than in any other District.

☐ There is a bankruptcy case concerning debtor's affiliate, general partner, or partnership pending in this District.

Type of Debtor (Check all boxes that apply)	**Chapter or Section of Bankruptcy Code Under Which the Petition is Filed** (Check one box)
☐ Individual(s) ☐ Railroad ☐ Corporation ☐ Stockbroker ☐ Partnership ☐ Commodity Broker ☐ Other_____ ☐ Clearing Bank	☐ Chapter 7 ☐ Chapter 11 ☐ Chapter 13 ☐ Chapter 9 ☐ Chapter 12 ☐ Sec. 304 - Case ancillary to foreign proceeding
Nature of Debts (Check one box) ☐ Consumer/Non-Business ☐ Business	**Filing Fee** (Check one box) ☐ Full Filing Fee attached ☐ Filing Fee to be paid in installments (Applicable to individuals only) Must attach signed application for the court's consideration certifying that the debtor is unable to pay fee except in installments. Rule 1006(b). See Official Form No. 3.
Chapter 11 Small Business (Check all boxes that apply) ☐ Debtor is a small business as defined in 11 U.S.C. § 101 ☐ Debtor is and elects to be considered a small business under 11 U.S.C. § 1121(e) (Optional)	

Statistical/Administrative Information (Estimates only)

☐ Debtor estimates that funds will be available for distribution to unsecured creditors.

☐ Debtor estimates that, after any exempt property is excluded and administrative expenses paid, there will be no funds available for distribution to unsecured creditors.

THIS SPACE IS FOR COURT USE ONLY

Estimated Number of Creditors	1-15	16-49	50-99	100-199	200-999	1000-over
	☐	☐	☐	☐	☐	☐

Estimated Assets							
$0 to $50,000	$50,001 to $100,000	$100,001 to $500,000	$500,001 to $1 million	$1,000,001 to $10 million	$10,000,001 to $50 million	$50,000,001 to $100 million	More than $100 million
☐	☐	☐	☐	☐	☐	☐	☐

Estimated Debts							
$0 to $50,000	$50,001 to $100,000	$100,001 to $500,000	$500,001 to $1 million	$1,000,001 to $10 million	$10,000,001 to $50 million	$50,000,001 to $100 million	More than $100 million
☐	☐	☐	☐	☐	☐	☐	☐

Voluntary Petition
(This page must be completed and filed in every case)

Name of Debtor(s):

Prior Bankruptcy Case Filed Within Last 6 Years (If more than one, attach additional sheet)

Location Where Filed:	Case Number:	Date Filed:

Pending Bankruptcy Case Filed by any Spouse, Partner or Affiliate of this Debtor (If more than one, attach additional sheet)

Name of Debtor:	Case Number:	Date Filed:
District:	Relationship:	Judge:

Signatures

Signature(s) of Debtor(s) (Individual/Joint)

I declare under penalty of perjury that the information provided in this petition is true and correct.
[If petitioner is an individual whose debts are primarily consumer debts and has chosen to file under chapter 7] I am aware that I may proceed under chapter 7, 11, 12 or 13 of title 11, United States Code, understand the relief available under each such chapter, and choose to proceed under chapter 7.
I request relief in accordance with the chapter of title 11, United States Code, specified in this petition.

X _____
Signature of Debtor

X _____
Signature of Joint Debtor

_____
Telephone Number (If not represented by attorney)

_____
Date

Signature of Attorney

X _____
Signature of Attorney for Debtor(s)

_____
Printed Name of Attorney for Debtor(s)

_____
Firm Name

_____
Address

_____
Telephone Number

_____
Date

Signature of Debtor (Corporation/Partnership)

I declare under penalty of perjury that the information provided in this petition is true and correct, and that I have been authorized to file this petition on behalf of the debtor.

The debtor requests relief in accordance with the chapter of title 11, United States Code, specified in this petition.

X _____
Signature of Authorized Individual

_____
Printed Name of Authorized Individual

_____
Title of Authorized Individual

_____
Date

Exhibit A

(To be completed if debtor is required to file periodic reports (e.g., forms 10K and 10Q) with the Securities and Exchange Commission pursuant to Section 13 or 15(d) of the Securities Exchange Act of 1934 and is requesting relief under chapter 11)

☐ Exhibit A is attached and made a part of this petition.

Exhibit B

(To be completed if debtor is an individual whose debts are primarily consumer debts)

I, the attorney for the petitioner named in the foregoing petition, declare that I have informed the petitioner that [he or she] may proceed under chapter 7, 11, 12, or 13 of title 11, United States Code, and have explained the relief available under each such chapter.

X _____
Signature of Attorney for Debtor(s)   Date

Exhibit C

Does the debtor own or have possession of any property that poses or is alleged to pose a threat of imminent and identifiable harm to public health or safety?

☐ Yes, and Exhibit C is attached and made a part of this petition.
☐ No

Signature of Non-Attorney Petition Preparer

I certify that I am a bankruptcy petition preparer as defined in 11 U.S.C. § 110, that I prepared this document for compensation, and that I have provided the debtor with a copy of this document.

_____
Printed Name of Bankruptcy Petition Preparer

_____
Social Security Number (Required by 11 U.S.C.§ 110)

_____
Address

Names and Social Security numbers of all other individuals who prepared or assisted in preparing this document:

If more than one person prepared this document, attach additional sheets conforming to the appropriate official form for each person.

X _____
Signature of Bankruptcy Petition Preparer

_____
Date

A bankruptcy petition preparer's failure to comply with the provisions of title 11 and the Federal Rules of Bankruptcy Procedure may result in fines or imprisonment or both 11 U.S.C. §110; 18 U.S.C. §156.

Exhibit "C"

[If, to the best of the debtor's knowledge, the debtor owns or has possession of property that poses or is alleged to pose a threat of imminent and identifiable harm to the public health or safety, attach this Exhibit "C" to the petition.]

[Caption as in Form 16B]

Exhibit "C" to Voluntary Petition

1. Identify and briefly describe all real or personal property owned by or in possession of the debtor that, to the best of the debtor's knowledge, poses or is alleged to pose a threat of imminent and identifiable harm to the public health or safety (attach additional sheets if necessary):

....
....
....
....

2. With respect to each parcel of real property or item of personal property identified in question 1, describe the nature and location of the dangerous condition, whether environmental or otherwise, that poses or is alleged to pose a threat of imminent and identifiable harm to the public health or safety (attach additional sheets if necessary):

....
....
....
....

In re _____ ,   Case No._____
                    Debtor   (If known)

SCHEDULE A—REAL PROPERTY

Except as directed below, list all real property in which the debtor has any legal, equitable, or future interest, including all property owned as a co-tenant, community property, or in which the debtor has a life estate. Include any property in which the debtor holds rights and powers exercisable for the debtor's own benefit. If the debtor is married, state whether husband, wife, or both own the property by placing an "H," "W," "J," or "C" in the column labeled "Husband, Wife, Joint, or Community." If the debtor holds no interest in real property, write "None" under "Description and Location of Property."

Do not include interests in executory contracts and unexpired leases on this schedule. List them in Schedule G—Executory Contracts and Unexpired Leases.

If an entity claims to have a lien or hold a secured interest in any property, state the amount of the secured claim. See Schedule D. If no entity claims to hold a secured interest in the property, write "None" in the column labeled "Amount of Secured Claim."

If the debtor is an individual or if a joint petition is filed, state the amount of any exception claimed in the property only in Schedule C—Property Claimed as Exempt.

DESCRIPTION AND LOCATION OF PROPERTY	NATURE OF DEBTOR'S INTEREST IN PROPERTY	HUSBAND, WIFE, JOINT, OR COMMUNITY	CURRENT MARKET VALUE OF DEBTOR'S INTEREST IN PROPERTY WITHOUT DEDUCTING ANY SECURED CLAIM OR EXEMPTION	AMOUNT OF SECURED CLAIM

Total ➡ $

(Report also on Summary of Schedules.)

FORM B6B
(10/89)

In re _____,
　　　　　　　Debtor

Case No._____
　　　　　　　(If known)

SCHEDULE B—PERSONAL PROPERTY

Except as directed below, list all personal property of the debtor of whatever kind. If the debtor has no property in one or more of the categories, place an "X" in the appropriate position in the column labeled "None." If additional space is needed in any category, attach a separate sheet properly identified with the case name, case number, and the number of the category. If the debtor is married, state whether husband, wife, or both own the property by placing an "H," "W," "J," or "C" in the column labeled "Husband, Wife, Joint, or Community." If the debtor is an individual or a joint petition is filed, state the amount of any exemptions claimed only in Schedule C—Property Claimed as Exempt.

Do not include interests in executory contracts and unexpired leases on this schedule. List them in Schedule G—Executory Contracts and Unexpired Leases.

If the property is being held for the debtor by someone else, state that person's name and address under "Description and Location of Property."

TYPE OF PROPERTY	NONE	DESCRIPTION AND LOCATION OF PROPERTY	HUSBAND, WIFE, JOINT, OR COMMUNITY	CURRENT MARKET VALUE OF DEBTOR'S INTEREST IN PROPERTY, WITHOUT DEDUCTING ANY SECURED CLAIM OR EXEMPTION
1. Cash on hand.				
2. Checking, savings or other financial accounts, certificates of deposit, or shares in banks, savings and loan, thrift, building and loan, and homestead associations, or credit unions, brokerage houses, or cooperatives.				
3. Security deposits with public utilities, telephone companies, landlords, and others.				
4. Household goods and furnishings, including audio, video, and computer equipment.				

In re _____,   Case No._____
                          Debtor   (If known)

SCHEDULE B—PERSONAL PROPERTY
(Continuation Sheet)

TYPE OF PROPERTY	NONE	DESCRIPTION AND LOCATION OF PROPERTY	HUSBAND, WIFE, JOINT, OR COMMUNITY	CURRENT MARKET VALUE OF DEBTOR'S INTEREST IN PROPERTY, WITHOUT DEDUCTING ANY SECURED CLAIM OR EXEMPTION
5. Books, pictures and other art objects, antiques, stamp, coin, record, tape, compact disc, and other collections or collectibles.				
6. Wearing apparel.				
7. Furs and jewelry.				
8. Firearms and sports, photo-graphic, and other hobby equipment.				
9. Interests in insurance policies. Name insurance company of each policy and itemize surrender or refund value of each.				
10. Annuities. Itemize and name each issuer.				
11. Interests in IRA, ERISA, Keogh, or other pension or profit sharing plans. Itemize.				
12. Stock and interests in incor-porated and unincorporated businesses. Itemize.				
13. Interests in partnerships or joint ventures. Itemize.				

In re _____, Case No._____
　　　　　　Debtor   (If known)

SCHEDULE B—PERSONAL PROPERTY
(Continuation Sheet)

TYPE OF PROPERTY	NONE	DESCRIPTION AND LOCATION OF PROPERTY	HUSBAND, WIFE, JOINT, OR COMMUNITY	CURRENT MARKET VALUE OF DEBTOR'S INTEREST IN PROPERTY, WITHOUT DEDUCTING ANY SECURED CLAIM OR EXEMPTION
14. Government and corporate bonds and other negotiable and non-negotiable instruments.				
15. Accounts receivable.				
16. Alimony, maintenance, sup-port, and property settlements to which the debtor is or may be entitled. Give particulars.				
17. Other liquidated debts owing debtor including tax refunds. Give particulars.				
18. Equitable or future interest, life estates, and rights or powers exercisable for the benefit of the debtor other than those listed in Schedule of Real Property.				
19. Contingent and noncontin-gent interests in estate of a decedent, death benefit plan, life insurance policy, or trust.				
20. Other contingent and unliqui-dated claims of every nature, including tax refunds, counter claims of the debtor, and rights to setoff claims. Give estimated value of each.				
21. Patents, copyrights, and other intellectual property. Give particulars.				
22. Licenses, franchises, and other general intangibles. Give particulars.				

FORM B6B-cont.
(10/89)

In re _____,   Case No._____
                           Debtor   (If known)

SCHEDULE B—PERSONAL PROPERTY
(Continuation Sheet)

TYPE OF PROPERTY	NONE	DESCRIPTION AND LOCATION OF PROPERTY	HUSBAND, WIFE, JOINT, OR COMMUNITY	CURRENT MARKET VALUE OF DEBTOR'S INTEREST IN PROPERTY, WITHOUT DEDUCTING ANY SECURED CLAIM OR EXEMPTION
23. Automobiles, trucks, trailers, and other vehicles and accessories.				
24. Boats, motors, and accessories.				
25. Aircraft and accessories.				
26. Office equipment, furnishings, and supplies.				
27. Machinery, fixtures, equipment, and supplies used in business.				
28. Inventory.				
29. Animals.				
30. Crops—growing or harvested. Give particulars.				
31. Farming equipment and implements.				
32. Farm supplies, chemicals, and feed.				
33. Other personal property of any kind not already listed, such as season tickets. Itemize.				
			Total ➡	$

_____ continuation sheets attached

(Include amounts from any continuation sheets attached. Report total also on Summary of Schedules.)

In re _____ ,   Case No. _____
                        Debtor   (If known)

SCHEDULE C—PROPERTY CLAIMED AS EXEMPT

Debtor elects the exemptions to which debtor is entitled under:

(Check one box)

☐ 11 U.S.C. § 522(b)(1):   Exemptions provided in 11 U.S.C. § 522(d). **Note: These exemptions are available only in certain states.**

☐ 11 U.S.C. § 522(b)(2):   Exemptions available under applicable nonbankruptcy federal laws, state or local law where the debtor's domicile has been located for the 180 days immediately preceding the filing of the petition, or for a longer portion of the 180-day period than in any other place, and the debtor's interest as a tenant by the entirety or joint tenant to the extent the interest is exempt from process under applicable nonbankruptcy law.

DESCRIPTION OF PROPERTY	SPECIFY LAW PROVIDING EACH EXEMPTION	VALUE OF CLAIMED EXEMPTION	CURRENT MARKET VALUE OF PROPERTY WITHOUT DEDUCTING EXEMPTIONS

Form B6D
(12/03)

In re _____ ,   Case No. _____
                    Debtor   **(If known)**

SCHEDULE D - CREDITORS HOLDING SECURED CLAIMS

State the name, mailing address, including zip code and last four digits of any account number of all entities holding claims secured by property of the debtor as of the date of filing of the petition. The complete account number of any account the debtor has with the creditor is useful to the trustee and the creditor and may be provided if the debtor chooses to do so. List creditors holding all types of secured interests such as judgment liens, garnishments, statutory liens, mortgages, deeds of trust, and other security interests. List creditors in alphabetical order to the extent practicable. If all secured creditors will not fit on this page, use the continuation sheet provided.

If any entity other than a spouse in a joint case may be jointly liable on a claim, place an "X" in the column labeled "Codebtor," include the entity on the appropriate schedule of creditors, and complete Schedule H - Codebtors. If a joint petition is filed, state whether husband, wife, both of them, or the marital community may be liable on each claim by placing an "H," "W," "J," or "C" in the column labeled "Husband, Wife, Joint, or Community."

If the claim is contingent, place an "X" in the column labeled "Contingent." If the claim is unliquidated, place an "X" in the column labeled "Unliquidated." If the claim is disputed, place an "X" in the column labeled "Disputed." (You may need to place an "X" in more than one of these three columns.)

Report the total of all claims listed on this schedule in the box labeled "Total" on the last sheet of the completed schedule. Report this total also on the Summary of Schedules.

☐   Check this box if debtor has no creditors holding secured claims to report on this Schedule D.

CREDITOR'S NAME, MAILING ADDRESS INCLUDING ZIP CODE, AND ACCOUNT NUMBER (See instructions above.)	CODEBTOR	HUSBAND, WIFE, JOINT, OR COMMUNITY	DATE CLAIM WAS INCURRED, NATURE OF LIEN, AND DESCRIPTION AND MARKET VALUE OF PROPERTY SUBJECT TO LIEN	CONTINGENT	UNLIQUIDATED	DISPUTED	AMOUNT OF CLAIM WITHOUT DEDUCTING VALUE OF COLLATERAL	UNSECURED PORTION, IF ANY
ACCOUNT NO.								
			VALUE $					
ACCOUNT NO.								
			VALUE $					
ACCOUNT NO.								
			VALUE $					
ACCOUNT NO.								
			VALUE $					

_____ continuation sheets attached

Subtotal• • $ _____
(Total of this page)

Total• • $ _____
(Use only on last page)

(Report total also on Summary of Schedules)

In re _____,   Case No. _____

          Debtor   (If known)

SCHEDULE D - CREDITORS HOLDING SECURED CLAIMS
(Continuation Sheet)

CREDITOR'S NAME, MAILING ADDRESS INCLUDING ZIP CODE AND ACCOUNT NUMBER (See instructions.)	CODEBTOR	HUSBAND, WIFE, JOINT, OR COMMUNITY	DATE CLAIM WAS INCURRED, NATURE OF LIEN, AND DESCRIPTION AND MARKET VALUE OF PROPERTY SUBJECT TO LIEN	CONTINGENT	UNLIQUIDATED	DISPUTED	AMOUNT OF CLAIM WITHOUT DEDUCTING VALUE OF COLLATERAL	UNSECURED PORTION, IF ANY
ACCOUNT NO.								
			VALUE $					
ACCOUNT NO.								
			VALUE $					
ACCOUNT NO.								
			VALUE $					
ACCOUNT NO.								
			VALUE $					
ACCOUNT NO.								
			VALUE $					

Sheet no. ___ of ___ continuation sheets attached to Schedule of Creditors Holding Secured Claims   Subtotal• •
(Total of this page) $

Total• $
(Use only on last page)

(Report total also on Summary of Schedules)

In re _____ 　　　　Case No._____
　　　　　　　　　Debtor 　　　　　　　　　　　　　　　　　　　　(if known)

SCHEDULE E - CREDITORS HOLDING UNSECURED PRIORITY CLAIMS

A complete list of claims entitled to priority, listed separately by type of priority, is to be set forth on the sheets provided. Only holders of unsecured claims entitled to priority should be listed in this schedule. In the boxes provided on the attached sheets, state the name, mailing address, including zip code, and last four digits of the account number, if any, of all entities holding priority claims against the debtor or the property of the debtor, as of the date of the filing of the petition. The complete account number of any account the debtor has with the creditor is useful to the trustee and the creditor and may be provided if the debtor chooses to do so.

If any entity other than a spouse in a joint case may be jointly liable on a claim, place an "X" in the column labeled "Codebtor," include the entity on the appropriate schedule of creditors, and complete Schedule H-Codebtors. If a joint petition is filed, state whether husband, wife, both of them or the marital community may be liable on each claim by placing an "H,""W,""J," or "C" in the column labeled "Husband, Wife, Joint, or Community."

If the claim is contingent, place an "X" in the column labeled "Contingent." If the claim is unliquidated, place an "X" in the column labeled "Unliquidated." If the claim is disputed, place an "X" in the column labeled "Disputed." (You may need to place an "X" in more than one of these three columns.)

Report the total of claims listed on each sheet in the box labeled "Subtotal" on each sheet. Report the total of all claims listed on this Schedule E in the box labeled "Total" on the last sheet of the completed schedule. Repeat this total also on the Summary of Schedules.

☐ Check this box if debtor has no creditors holding unsecured priority claims to report on this Schedule E.

TYPES OF PRIORITY CLAIMS (Check the appropriate box(es) below if claims in that category are listed on the attached sheets)

☐ **Extensions of credit in an involuntary case**

Claims arising in the ordinary course of the debtor's business or financial affairs after the commencement of the case but before the earlier of the appointment of a trustee or the order for relief. 11 U.S.C. § 507(a)(2).

☐ **Wages, salaries, and commissions**

Wages, salaries, and commissions, including vacation, severance, and sick leave pay owing to employees and commissions owing to qualifying independent sales representatives up to $4,925* per person earned within 90 days immediately preceding the filing of the original petition, or the cessation of business, whichever occurred first, to the extent provided in 11 U.S.C. § 507(a)(3).

☐ **Contributions to employee benefit plans**

Money owed to employee benefit plans for services rendered within 180 days immediately preceding the filing of the original petition, or the cessation of business, whichever occurred first, to the extent provided in 11 U.S.C. § 507(a)(4).

☐ **Certain farmers and fishermen**

Claims of certain farmers and fishermen, up to $4,925* per farmer or fisherman, against the debtor, as provided in 11 U.S.C. § 507(a)(5).

☐ **Deposits by individuals**

Claims of individuals up to $2,225* for deposits for the purchase, lease, or rental of property or services for personal, family, or household use, that were not delivered or provided. 11 U.S.C. § 507(a)(6).

Form B6E
(04/04)

In re _____ ,   Case No._____
        Debtor   (if known)

☐ **Alimony, Maintenance, or Support**

Claims of a spouse, former spouse, or child of the debtor for alimony, maintenance, or support, to the extent provided in 11 U.S.C. § 507(a)(7).

☐ **Taxes and Certain Other Debts Owed to Governmental Units**

Taxes, customs duties, and penalties owing to federal, state, and local governmental units as set forth in 11 U.S.C. § 507(a)(8).

☐ **Commitments to Maintain the Capital of an Insured Depository Institution**

Claims based on commitments to the FDIC, RTC, Director of the Office of Thrift Supervision, Comptroller of the Currency, or Board of Governors of the Federal Reserve System, or their predecessors or successors, to maintain the capital of an insured depository institution. 11 U.S.C. § 507 (a)(9).

* Amounts are subject to adjustment on April 1, 2007, and every three years thereafter with respect to cases commenced on or after the date of adjustment.

_____ continuation sheets attached

Form B6E - Cont.
(04/04)

In re _____,   Case No. _____
                        Debtor   (If known)

SCHEDULE E - CREDITORS HOLDING UNSECURED PRIORITY CLAIMS
(Continuation Sheet)

_____
TYPE OF PRIORITY

CREDITOR'S NAME, MAILING ADDRESS INCLUDING ZIP CODE, AND ACCOUNT NUMBER (See instructions.)	CODEBTOR	HUSBAND, WIFE, JOINT, OR COMMUNITY	DATE CLAIM WAS INCURRED AND CONSIDERATION FOR CLAIM	CONTINGENT	UNLIQUIDATED	DISPUTED	AMOUNT OF CLAIM	AMOUNT ENTITLED TO PRIORITY
ACCOUNT NO.								
ACCOUNT NO.								
ACCOUNT NO.								
ACCOUNT NO.								
ACCOUNT NO.								

Sheet no. ____ of ____ sheets attached to Schedule of Creditors Holding Priority Claims

Subtotal ➤ $ _____
(Total of this page)
Total ➤ $ _____
(Use only on last page of the completed Schedule E.)
(Report total also on Summary of Schedules)

Form B6F (12/03)

In re _____,   Case No. _____
                      Debtor   (If known)

SCHEDULE F- CREDITORS HOLDING UNSECURED NONPRIORITY CLAIMS

State the name, mailing address, including zip code, and last four digits of any account number, of all entities holding unsecured claims without priority against the debtor or the property of the debtor, as of the date of filing of the petition. The complete account number of any account the debtor has with the creditor is useful to the trustee and the creditor and may be provided if the debtor chooses to do so. Do not include claims listed in Schedules D and E. If all creditors will not fit on this page, use the continuation sheet provided.

If any entity other than a spouse in a joint case may be jointly liable on a claim, place an "X" in the column labeled "Codebtor," include the entity on the appropriate schedule of creditors, and complete Schedule H - Codebtors. If a joint petition is filed, state whether husband, wife, both of them, or the marital community maybe liable on each claim by placing an "H," "W," "J," or "C" in the column labeled "Husband, Wife, Joint, or Community."

If the claim is contingent, place an "X" in the column labeled "Contingent." If the claim is unliquidated, place an "X" in the column labeled "Unliquidated." If the claim is disputed, place an "X" in the column labeled "Disputed." (You may need to place an "X" in more than one of these three columns.)

Report total of all claims listed on this schedule in the box labeled "Total" on the last sheet of the completed schedule. Report this total also on the Summary of Schedules.

☐ Check this box if debtor has no creditors holding unsecured claims to report on this Schedule F.

CREDITOR'S NAME, MAILING ADDRESS INCLUDING ZIP CODE, AND ACCOUNT NUMBER (See instructions, above.)	CODEBTOR	HUSBAND, WIFE, JOINT, OR COMMUNITY	DATE CLAIM WAS INCURRED AND CONSIDERATION FOR CLAIM. IF CLAIM IS SUBJECT TO SETOFF, SO STATE.	CONTINGENT	UNLIQUIDATED	DISPUTED	AMOUNT OF CLAIM WITHOUT DEDUCTING VALUE OF COLLATERAL
ACCOUNT NO.							
ACCOUNT NO.							
ACCOUNT NO.							
ACCOUNT NO.							

_____ continuation sheets attached   Subtotal • • $ _____
                         Total • • $ _____
(Report also on Summary of Schedules)

Form B6F - Cont.
(12/03)

In re _____,　　　　Case No. _____
　　　　　　　Debtor　　　　　　　　　　　　　　　　　　　　　　　　　(If known)

SCHEDULE F - CREDITORS HOLDING UNSECURED NONPRIORITY CLAIMS
(Continuation Sheet)

CREDITOR'S NAME, MAILING ADDRESS INCLUDING ZIP CODE, AND ACCOUNT NUMBER	CODEBTOR	HUSBAND, WIFE, JOINT, OR COMMUNITY	DATE CLAIM WAS INCURRED AND CONSIDERATION FOR CLAIM. IF CLAIM IS SUBJECT TO SETOFF, SO STATE.	CONTINGENT	UNLIQUIDATED	DISPUTED	AMOUNT OF CLAIM WITHOUT DEDUCTING VALUE OF COLLATERAL
ACCOUNT NO.							
ACCOUNT NO.							
ACCOUNT NO.							
ACCOUNT NO.							
ACCOUNT NO.							

Sheet no. ____ of ____ sheets attached to Schedule of
Creditors Holding Unsecured Nonpriority Claims

Subtotal ▸ ▸　　　$
(Total of this page)
Total　　▸ ▸　　$
(Use only on last page of the completed Schedule E.)
(Report total also on Summary of Schedules)

In re _____ ,   Case No._____
                          Debtor   **(if known)**

SCHEDULE G - EXECUTORY CONTRACTS AND UNEXPIRED LEASES

   Describe all executory contracts of any nature and all unexpired leases of real or personal property. Include any timeshare interests.
   State nature of debtor's interest in contract, i.e., "Purchaser," "Agent," etc. State whether debtor is the lessor or lessee of a lease.
   Provide the names and complete mailing addresses of all other parties to each lease or contract described.

   NOTE: A party listed on this schedule will not receive notice of the filing of this case unless the party is also scheduled in the appropriate schedule of creditors.

☐   Check this box if debtor has no executory contracts or unexpired leases.

NAME AND MAILING ADDRESS, INCLUDING ZIP CODE, OF OTHER PARTIES TO LEASE OR CONTRACT.	DESCRIPTION OF CONTRACT OR LEASE AND NATURE OF DEBTOR'S INTEREST. STATE WHETHER LEASE IS FOR NONRESIDENTIAL REAL PROPERTY. STATE CONTRACT NUMBER OF ANY GOVERNMENT CONTRACT.

B6H
(6/90)

In re _____ ,   Case No. _____
            Debtor   **(if known)**

SCHEDULE H - CODEBTORS

Provide the information requested concerning any person or entity, other than a spouse in a joint case, that is also liable on any debts listed by debtor in the schedules of creditors. Include all guarantors and co-signers. In community property states, a married debtor not filing a joint case should report the name and address of the nondebtor spouse on this schedule. Include all names used by the nondebtor spouse during the six years immediately preceding the commencement of this case.

☐ Check this box if debtor has no codebtors.

NAME AND ADDRESS OF CODEBTOR	NAME AND ADDRESS OF CREDITOR

In re _____ ,   Case No._____
           Debtor   **(if known)**

SCHEDULE I - CURRENT INCOME OF INDIVIDUAL DEBTOR(S)

The column labeled "Spouse" must be completed in all cases filed by joint debtors and by a married debtor in a chapter 12 or 13 case whether or not a joint petition is filed, unless the spouses are separated and a joint petition is not filed.

Debtor's Marital Status:	DEPENDENTS OF DEBTOR AND SPOUSE	
	RELATIONSHIP	AGE

Employment:	DEBTOR	SPOUSE
Occupation		
Name of Employer		
How long employed		
Address of Employer		

Income: (Estimate of average monthly income)	DEBTOR	SPOUSE
Current monthly gross wages, salary, and commissions (pro rate if not paid monthly.)	$ _____	$ _____
Estimated monthly overtime	$ _____	$ _____
SUBTOTAL	$_____	$ _____
LESS PAYROLL DEDUCTIONS		
a. Payroll taxes and social security	$ _____	$ _____
b. Insurance	$ _____	$ _____
c. Union dues	$ _____	$ _____
d. Other (Specify: _____)	$ _____	$ _____
SUBTOTAL OF PAYROLL DEDUCTIONS	$_____	$ _____
TOTAL NET MONTHLY TAKE HOME PAY	$_____	$ _____
Regular income from operation of business or profession or farm (attach detailed statement)	$ _____	$ _____
Income from real property	$ _____	$ _____
Interest and dividends	$ _____	$ _____
Alimony, maintenance or support payments payable to the debtor for the debtor's use or that of dependents listed above.	$ _____	$ _____
Social security or other government assistance (Specify) _____	$ _____	$ _____
Pension or retirement income	$ _____	$ _____
Other monthly income	$ _____	$ _____
(Specify) _____	$ _____	$ _____
_____	$ _____	$ _____
TOTAL MONTHLY INCOME	$_____	$ _____

TOTAL COMBINED MONTHLY INCOME $_____   (Report also on Summary of Schedules)

Describe any increase or decrease of more than 10% in any of the above categories anticipated to occur within the year following the filing of this document:

FORM B6J
(6/90)

In re _____,   Case No._____
                          Debtor   (If known)

SCHEDULE J—CURRENT EXPENDITURES OF INDIVIDUAL DEBTOR(S)

Complete this schedule by estimating the average monthly expenses of the debtor and the debtor's family. Pro rate any payments made bi-weekly, quarterly, semi-annually, or annually to show monthly rate.

☐ Check this box if a joint petition is filed and debtor's spouse maintains a separate household. Complete a separate schedule of expenditures labeled "Spouse."

Rent or home mortgage payment (include lot rented for mobile home) $ _____

Are real estate taxes included?   Yes _____   No _____

Is property insurance included?   Yes _____   No _____

Utilities: Electricity and heating fuel $ _____

            Water and sewer $ _____

            Telephone $ _____

            Other _____ $ _____

Home maintenance (repairs and upkeep) $ _____

Food $ _____

Clothing $ _____

Laundry and dry cleaning $ _____

Medical and dental expenses $ _____

Transportation (not including car payments) $ _____

Recreation, clubs and entertainment, newspapers, magazines, etc. $ _____

Charitable contributions $ _____

Insurance (not deducted from wages or included in home mortgage payments)

            Homeowner's or renter's $ _____

            Life $ _____

            Health $ _____

            Auto $ _____

            Other _____ $ _____

Taxes (not deducted from wages or included in home mortgage payments)

(Specify: _____) $ _____

Installment payments: (In Chapter 12 and 13 cases, do not list payments to be included in the plan)

            Auto $ _____

            Other _____ $ _____

            Other _____ $ _____

Alimony, maintenance, and support paid to others $ _____

Payments for support of additional dependents not living at your home $ _____

Regular expenses from operation of business, profession, or farm (attach detailed statement) $ _____

Other _____ $ _____

TOTAL MONTHLY EXPENSES (Report also on Summary of Schedules) $ _____

[FOR CHAPTER 12 AND CHAPTER 13 DEBTORS ONLY]
Provide the information requested below, including whether plan payments are to be made bi-weekly, monthly, annually, or at some other regular interval.

A. Total projected monthly income $ _____

B. Total projected monthly expenses $ _____

C. Excess income (A minus B) $ _____

D. Total amount to be paid into plan each _____ $ _____
                          (interval)

United States Bankruptcy Court

_____ District of _____

In re _____,   Case No._____
        Debtor   (If known)

SUMMARY OF SCHEDULES

Indicate as to each schedule whether that schedule is attached and state the number of pages in each. Report the totals from Schedules A, B, D, E, F, I and J in the boxes provided. Add the amounts from Schedules A and B to determine the total amount of the debtor's assets. Add the amounts from Schedules D, E and F to determine the total amount of the debtor's liabilities.

NAME OF SCHEDULE	ATTACHED (YES/NO)	NUMBER OF SHEETS	AMOUNTS SCHEDULED		
			ASSETS	LIABILITIES	OTHER
A Real Property			$		
B Personal Property			$		
C Property Claimed as Exempt					
D Creditors Holding Secured Claims				$	
E Creditors Holding Unsecured Priority Claims				$	
F Creditors Holding Unsecured Nonpriority Claims				$	
G Executory Contracts and Unexpired Leases					
H Codebtors					
I Current Income of Individual Debtor(s)					$
J Current Expenditures of Individual Debtor(s)					$

Total Number of Sheets of All Schedules ➡ _____

Total Assets ➡ $_____

Total Liabilities ➡ $_____

In re _____ ,   Case No. _____
                Debtor   (If known)

DECLARATION CONCERNING DEBTOR'S SCHEDULES

DECLARATION UNDER PENALTY OF PERJURY BY INDIVIDUAL DEBTOR

I declare under penalty of perjury that I have read the foregoing summary and schedules, consisting of _____
                                                                                                    (Total shown on summary page plus 1.)

sheets, and that they are true and correct to the best of my knowledge, information, and belief.

Date _____   Signature: _____
                                                                        Debtor

Date _____   Signature:_____
                                                                  (Joint Debtor, if any)

                                                        [If joint case, both spouses must sign.]

- -

CERTIFICATION AND SIGNATURE OF NON-ATTORNEY BANKRUPTCY PETITION PREPARER (See 11 U.S.C. § 110)

I certify that I am a bankruptcy petition preparer as defined in 11 U.S.C. § 110, that I prepared this document for compensation, and that I have provided the debtor with a copy of this document.

_____   _____
Printed or Typed Name of Bankruptcy Petition Preparer   Social Security No.
                                                             (Required by 11 U.S.C. § 110(c).)

_____

_____
Address

Names and Social Security numbers of all other individuals who prepared or assisted in preparing this document:

If more than one person prepared this document, attach additional signed sheets conforming to the appropriate Official Form for each person.

X _____   _____
Signature of Bankruptcy Petition Preparer   Date

*A bankruptcy petition preparer's failure to comply with the provisions of title 11 and the Federal Rules of Bankruptcy Procedure may result in fines or imprisonment or both. 11 U.S.C. §
110; 18 U.S.C. § 156.*
- -

DECLARATION UNDER PENALTY OF PERJURY ON BEHALF OF A CORPORATION OR PARTNERSHIP

I, the _____ [the president or other officer or an authorized agent of the corporation or a member or an authorized agent of the
partnership] of the _____ [corporation or partnership] named as debtor in this case, declare under penalty of perjury that I have
read the foregoing summary and schedules, consisting of _____ sheets, and that they are true and correct to the
best of my knowledge, information, and belief.   *(Total shown on summary page plus 1.)*

Date _____   Signature:_____

                                                        _____
                                                        [Print or type name of individual signing on behalf of debtor.]

[An individual signing on behalf of a partnership or corporation must indicate position or relationship to debtor.]

_____

Penalty for making a false statement or concealing property: Fine of up to $500,000 or imprisonment for up to 5 years or both. 18 U.S.C. §§ 152 and 3571.

FORM 7. STATEMENT OF FINANCIAL AFFAIRS

UNITED STATES BANKRUPTCY COURT

_____ **DISTRICT OF** _____

In re: _____ ,   Case No. _____
          (Name)   (if known)
                    Debtor

STATEMENT OF FINANCIAL AFFAIRS

This statement is to be completed by every debtor. Spouses filing a joint petition may file a single statement on which the information for both spouses is combined. If the case is filed under chapter 12 or chapter 13, a married debtor must furnish information for both spouses whether or not a joint petition is filed, unless the spouses are separated and a joint petition is not filed. An individual debtor engaged in business as a sole proprietor, partner, family farmer, or self-employed professional, should provide the information requested on this statement concerning all such activities as well as the individual's personal affairs.

Questions 1 - 18 are to be completed by all debtors. Debtors that are or have been in business, as defined below, also must complete Questions 19 - 25. **If the answer to an applicable question is "None," mark the box labeled "None."** If additional space is needed for the answer to any question, use and attach a separate sheet properly identified with the case name, case number (if known), and the number of the question.

DEFINITIONS

"In business." A debtor is "in business" for the purpose of this form if the debtor is a corporation or partnership. An individual debtor is "in business" for the purpose of this form if the debtor is or has been, within the six years immediately preceding the filing of this bankruptcy case, any of the following: an officer, director, managing executive, or owner of 5 percent or more of the voting or equity securities of a corporation; a partner, other than a limited partner, of a partnership; a sole proprietor or self-employed.

"Insider." The term "insider" includes but is not limited to: relatives of the debtor; general partners of the debtor and their relatives; corporations of which the debtor is an officer, director, or person in control; officers, directors, and any owner of 5 percent or more of the voting or equity securities of a corporate debtor and their relatives; affiliates of the debtor and insiders of such affiliates; any managing agent of the debtor. 11 U.S.C. § 101.

_____

1. **Income from employment or operation of business**

None
☐

State the gross amount of income the debtor has received from employment, trade, or profession, or from operation of the debtor's business from the beginning of this calendar year to the date this case was commenced. State also the gross amounts received during the **two years** immediately preceding this calendar year. (A debtor that maintains, or has maintained, financial records on the basis of a fiscal rather than a calendar year may report fiscal year income. Identify the beginning and ending dates of the debtor's fiscal year.) If a joint petition is filed, state income for each spouse separately. (Married debtors filing under chapter 12 or chapter 13 must state income of both spouses whether or not a joint petition is filed, unless the spouses are separated and a joint petition is not filed.)

AMOUNT   SOURCE (if more than one)

2. Income other than from employment or operation of business

None ☐

State the amount of income received by the debtor other than from employment, trade, profession, or operation of the debtor's business during the **two years** immediately preceding the commencement of this case. Give particulars. If a joint petition is filed, state income for each spouse separately. (Married debtors filing under chapter 12 or chapter 13 must state income for each spouse whether or not a joint petition is filed, unless the spouses are separated and a joint petition is not filed.)

AMOUNT   SOURCE

---

3. Payments to creditors

None ☐

a. List all payments on loans, installment purchases of goods or services, and other debts, aggregating more than $600 to any creditor, made within **90 days** immediately preceding the commencement of this case. (Married debtors filing under chapter 12 or chapter 13 must include payments by either or both spouses whether or not a joint petition is filed, unless the spouses are separated and a joint petition is not filed.)

NAME AND ADDRESS OF CREDITOR	DATES OF PAYMENTS	AMOUNT PAID	AMOUNT STILL OWING

None ☐

b. List all payments made within **one year** immediately preceding the commencement of this case to or for the benefit of creditors who are or were insiders. (Married debtors filing under chapter 12 or chapter 13 must include payments by either or both spouses whether or not a joint petition is filed, unless the spouses are separated and a joint petition is not filed.)

NAME AND ADDRESS OF CREDITOR AND RELATIONSHIP TO DEBTOR	DATE OF PAYMENT	AMOUNT PAID	AMOUNT STILL OWING

---

4. Suits and administrative proceedings, executions, garnishments and attachments

None ☐

a. List all suits and administrative proceedings to which the debtor is or was a party within **one year** immediately preceding the filing of this bankruptcy case. (Married debtors filing under chapter 12 or chapter 13 must include information concerning either or both spouses whether or not a joint petition is filed, unless the spouses are separated and a joint petition is not filed.)

CAPTION OF SUIT AND CASE NUMBER	NATURE OF PROCEEDING	COURT OR AGENCY AND LOCATION	STATUS OR DISPOSITION

None ☐ b. Describe all property that has been attached, garnished or seized under any legal or equitable process within **one year** immediately preceding the commencement of this case. (Married debtors filing under chapter 12 or chapter 13 must include information concerning property of either or both spouses whether or not a joint petition is filed, unless the spouses are separated and a joint petition is not filed.)

NAME AND ADDRESS OF PERSON FOR WHOSE BENEFIT PROPERTY WAS SEIZED	DATE OF SEIZURE	DESCRIPTION AND VALUE OF PROPERTY

5. Repossessions, foreclosures and returns

None ☐ List all property that has been repossessed by a creditor, sold at a foreclosure sale, transferred through a deed in lieu of foreclosure or returned to the seller, within **one year** immediately preceding the commencement of this case. (Married debtors filing under chapter 12 or chapter 13 must include information concerning property of either or both spouses whether or not a joint petition is filed, unless the spouses are separated and a joint petition is not filed.)

NAME AND ADDRESS OF CREDITOR OR SELLER	DATE OF REPOSSESSION, FORECLOSURE SALE, TRANSFER OR RETURN	DESCRIPTION AND VALUE OF PROPERTY

6. Assignments and receiverships

None ☐ a. Describe any assignment of property for the benefit of creditors made within **120 days** immediately preceding the commencement of this case. (Married debtors filing under chapter 12 or chapter 13 must include any assignment by either or both spouses whether or not a joint petition is filed, unless the spouses are separated and a joint petition is not filed.)

NAME AND ADDRESS OF ASSIGNEE	DATE OF ASSIGNMENT	TERMS OF ASSIGNMENT OR SETTLEMENT

None ☐ b. List all property which has been in the hands of a custodian, receiver, or court-appointed official within **one year** immediately preceding the commencement of this case. (Married debtors filing under chapter 12 or chapter 13 must include information concerning property of either or both spouses whether or not a joint petition is filed, unless the spouses are separated and a joint petition is not filed.)

NAME AND ADDRESS OF CUSTODIAN	NAME AND LOCATION OF COURT CASE TITLE & NUMBER	DATE OF ORDER	DESCRIPTION AND VALUE OF PROPERTY

7. Gifts

List all gifts or charitable contributions made within **one year** immediately preceding the commencement of this case except ordinary and usual gifts to family members aggregating less than $200 in value per individual family member and charitable contributions aggregating less than $100 per recipient. (Married debtors filing under chapter 12 or chapter 13 must include gifts or contributions by either or both spouses whether or not a joint petition is filed, unless the spouses are separated and a joint petition is not filed.)

NAME AND ADDRESS OF PERSON OR ORGANIZATION	RELATIONSHIP TO DEBTOR, IF ANY	DATE OF GIFT	DESCRIPTION AND VALUE OF GIFT

8. Losses

List all losses from fire, theft, other casualty or gambling within **one year** immediately preceding the commencement of this case **or since the commencement of this case**. (Married debtors filing under chapter 12 or chapter 13 must include losses by either or both spouses whether or not a joint petition is filed, unless the spouses are separated and a joint petition is not filed.)

DESCRIPTION AND VALUE OF PROPERTY	DESCRIPTION OF CIRCUMSTANCES AND, IF LOSS WAS COVERED IN WHOLE OR IN PART BY INSURANCE, GIVE PARTICULARS	DATE OF LOSS

9. Payments related to debt counseling or bankruptcy

List all payments made or property transferred by or on behalf of the debtor to any persons, including attorneys, for consultation concerning debt consolidation, relief under the bankruptcy law or preparation of a petition in bankruptcy within **one year** immediately preceding the commencement of this case.

NAME AND ADDRESS OF PAYEE	DATE OF PAYMENT, NAME OF PAYOR IF OTHER THAN DEBTOR	AMOUNT OF MONEY OR DESCRIPTION AND VALUE OF PROPERTY

10. Other transfers

List all other property, other than property transferred in the ordinary course of the business or financial affairs of the debtor, transferred either absolutely or as security within **one year** immediately preceding the commencement of this case. (Married debtors filing under chapter 12 or chapter 13 must include transfers by either or both spouses whether or not a joint petition is filed, unless the spouses are separated and a joint petition is not filed.)

NAME AND ADDRESS OF TRANSFEREE, RELATIONSHIP TO DEBTOR	DATE	DESCRIBE PROPERTY TRANSFERRED AND VALUE RECEIVED

11. Closed financial accounts

None
☐

List all financial accounts and instruments held in the name of the debtor or for the benefit of the debtor which were closed, sold, or otherwise transferred within **one year** immediately preceding the commencement of this case. Include checking, savings, or other financial accounts, certificates of deposit, or other instruments; shares and share accounts held in banks, credit unions, pension funds, cooperatives, associations, brokerage houses and other financial institutions. (Married debtors filing under chapter 12 or chapter 13 must include information concerning accounts or instruments held by or for either or both spouses whether or not a joint petition is filed, unless the spouses are separated and a joint petition is not filed.)

NAME AND ADDRESS OF INSTITUTION	TYPE OF ACCOUNT, LAST FOUR DIGITS OF ACCOUNT NUMBER, AND AMOUNT OF FINAL BALANCE	AMOUNT AND DATE OF SALE OR CLOSING

12. Safe deposit boxes

None
☐

List each safe deposit or other box or depository in which the debtor has or had securities, cash, or other valuables within **one year** immediately preceding the commencement of this case. (Married debtors filing under chapter 12 or chapter 13 must include boxes or depositories of either or both spouses whether or not a joint petition is filed, unless the spouses are separated and a joint petition is not filed.)

NAME AND ADDRESS OF BANK OR OTHER DEPOSITORY	NAMES AND ADDRESSES OF THOSE WITH ACCESS TO BOX OR DEPOSITORY	DESCRIPTION OF CONTENTS	DATE OF TRANSFER OR SURRENDER, IF ANY

13. Setoffs

None
☐

List all setoffs made by any creditor, including a bank, against a debt or deposit of the debtor within **90 days** preceding the commencement of this case. (Married debtors filing under chapter 12 or chapter 13 must include information concerning either or both spouses whether or not a joint petition is filed, unless the spouses are separated and a joint petition is not filed.)

NAME AND ADDRESS OF CREDITOR	DATE OF SETOFF	AMOUNT OF SETOFF

14. Property held for another person

None
☐

List all property owned by another person that the debtor holds or controls.

NAME AND ADDRESS OF OWNER	DESCRIPTION AND VALUE OF PROPERTY	LOCATION OF PROPERTY

15. Prior address of debtor

None ☐ If the debtor has moved within the **two years** immediately preceding the commencement of this case, list all premises which the debtor occupied during that period and vacated prior to the commencement of this case. If a joint petition is filed, report also any separate address of either spouse.

ADDRESS   NAME USED   DATES OF OCCUPANCY

16. Spouses and Former Spouses

None ☐ If the debtor resides or resided in a community property state, commonwealth, or territory (including Alaska, Arizona, California, Idaho, Louisiana, Nevada, New Mexico, Puerto Rico, Texas, Washington, or Wisconsin) within the **six-year period** immediately preceding the commencement of the case, identify the name of the debtor's spouse and of any former spouse who resides or resided with the debtor in the community property state.

NAME

17. Environmental Information.

For the purpose of this question, the following definitions apply:

"Environmental Law" means any federal, state, or local statute or regulation regulating pollution, contamination, releases of hazardous or toxic substances, wastes or material into the air, land, soil, surface water, groundwater, or other medium, including, but not limited to, statutes or regulations regulating the cleanup of these substances, wastes, or material.

"Site" means any location, facility, or property as defined under any Environmental Law, whether or not presently or formerly owned or operated by the debtor, including, but not limited to, disposal sites.

"Hazardous Material" means anything defined as a hazardous waste, hazardous substance, toxic substance, hazardous material, pollutant, or contaminant or similar term under an Environmental Law

None ☐ a. List the name and address of every site for which the debtor has received notice in writing by a governmental unit that it may be liable or potentially liable under or in violation of an Environmental Law. Indicate the governmental unit, the date of the notice, and, if known, the Environmental Law:

SITE NAME   NAME AND ADDRESS   DATE OF   ENVIRONMENTAL
AND ADDRESS   OF GOVERNMENTAL UNIT   NOTICE   LAW

None ☐ b. List the name and address of every site for which the debtor provided notice to a governmental unit of a release of Hazardous Material. Indicate the governmental unit to which the notice was sent and the date of the notice.

SITE NAME   NAME AND ADDRESS   DATE OF   ENVIRONMENTAL
AND ADDRESS   OF GOVERNMENTAL UNIT   NOTICE   LAW

None ☐ c. List all judicial or administrative proceedings, including settlements or orders, under any Environmental Law with respect to which the debtor is or was a party. Indicate the name and address of the governmental unit that is or was a party to the proceeding, and the docket number.

NAME AND ADDRESS OF GOVERNMENTAL UNIT	DOCKET NUMBER	STATUS OR DISPOSITION

---

18 . Nature, location and name of business

None ☐ a. If the debtor is an individual, list the names, addresses, taxpayer identification numbers, nature of the businesses, and beginning and ending dates of all businesses in which the debtor was an officer, director, partner, or managing executive of a corporation, partnership, sole proprietorship, or was a self-employed professional within the **six years** immediately preceding the commencement of this case, or in which the debtor owned 5 percent or more of the voting or equity securities within the **six years** immediately preceding the commencement of this case.

If the debtor is a partnership, list the names, addresses, taxpayer identification numbers, nature of the businesses, and beginning and ending dates of all businesses in which the debtor was a partner or owned 5 percent or more of the voting or equity securities, within the **six years** immediately preceding the commencement of this case.

If the debtor is a corporation, list the names, addresses, taxpayer identification numbers, nature of the businesses, and beginning and ending dates of all businesses in which the debtor was a partner or owned 5 percent or more of the voting or equity securities within the **six years** immediately preceding the commencement of this case.

NAME	TAXPAYER I.D. NO. (EIN)	ADDRESS	NATURE OF BUSINESS	BEGINNING AND ENDING DATES

None ☐ b. Identify any business listed in response to subdivision a., above, that is "single asset real estate" as defined in 11 U.S.C. § 101.

NAME	ADDRESS

The following questions are to be completed by every debtor that is a corporation or partnership and by any individual debtor who is or has been, within the **six years** immediately preceding the commencement of this case, any of the following: an officer, director, managing executive, or owner of more than 5 percent of the voting or equity securities of a corporation; a partner, other than a limited partner, of a partnership; a sole proprietor or otherwise self-employed.

*(An individual or joint debtor should complete this portion of the statement **only** if the debtor is or has been in business, as defined above, within the six years immediately preceding the commencement of this case. A debtor who has not been in business within those six years should go directly to the signature page.)*

19. Books, records and financial statements

None ☐   a.   List all bookkeepers and accountants who within the **two years** immediately preceding the filing of this bankruptcy case kept or supervised the keeping of books of account and records of the debtor.

NAME AND ADDRESS   DATES SERVICES RENDERED

None ☐   b.   List all firms or individuals who within the **two years** immediately preceding the filing of this bankruptcy case have audited the books of account and records, or prepared a financial statement of the debtor.

NAME   ADDRESS   DATES SERVICES RENDERED

None ☐   c.   List all firms or individuals who at the time of the commencement of this case were in possession of the books of account and records of the debtor. If any of the books of account and records are not available, explain.

NAME   ADDRESS

None ☐   d.   List all financial institutions, creditors and other parties, including mercantile and trade agencies, to whom a financial statement was issued within the **two years** immediately preceding the commencement of this case by the debtor.

NAME AND ADDRESS   DATE ISSUED

20. Inventories

None ☐   a.   List the dates of the last two inventories taken of your property, the name of the person who supervised the taking of each inventory, and the dollar amount and basis of each inventory.

                                            DOLLAR AMOUNT OF INVENTORY
DATE OF INVENTORY   INVENTORY SUPERVISOR   (Specify cost, market or other basis)

None ☐   b.   List the name and address of the person having possession of the records of each of the two inventories reported in a., above.

                                     NAME AND ADDRESSES OF CUSTODIAN
DATE OF INVENTORY   OF INVENTORY RECORDS

21 . Current Partners, Officers, Directors and Shareholders

None ☐   a.   If the debtor is a partnership, list the nature and percentage of partnership interest of each member of the partnership.

NAME AND ADDRESS	NATURE OF INTEREST	PERCENTAGE OF INTEREST

None ☐   b.   If the debtor is a corporation, list all officers and directors of the corporation, and each stockholder who directly or indirectly owns, controls, or holds 5 percent or more of the voting or equity securities of the corporation.

NAME AND ADDRESS	TITLE	NATURE AND PERCENTAGE OF STOCK OWNERSHIP

22 . Former partners, officers, directors and shareholders

None ☐   a.   If the debtor is a partnership, list each member who withdrew from the partnership within **one year** immediately preceding the commencement of this case.

NAME	ADDRESS	DATE OF WITHDRAWAL

None ☐   b.   If the debtor is a corporation, list all officers, or directors whose relationship with the corporation terminated within **one year** immediately preceding the commencement of this case.

NAME AND ADDRESS	TITLE	DATE OF TERMINATION

23 . Withdrawals from a partnership or distributions by a corporation

None ☐   If the debtor is a partnership or corporation, list all withdrawals or distributions credited or given to an insider, including compensation in any form, bonuses, loans, stock redemptions, options exercised and any other perquisite during **one year** immediately preceding the commencement of this case.

NAME & ADDRESS OF RECIPIENT, RELATIONSHIP TO DEBTOR	DATE AND PURPOSE OF WITHDRAWAL	AMOUNT OF MONEY OR DESCRIPTION AND VALUE OF PROPERTY

24. Tax Consolidation Group.

None ☐ If the debtor is a corporation, list the name and federal taxpayer identification number of the parent corporation of any consolidated group for tax purposes of which the debtor has been a member at any time within the **six-year period** immediately preceding the commencement of the case.

NAME OF PARENT CORPORATION   TAXPAYER IDENTIFICATION NUMBER (EIN)

---

25. Pension Funds.

None ☐ If the debtor is not an individual, list the name and federal taxpayer identification number of any pension fund to which the debtor, as an employer, has been responsible for contributing at any time within the **six-year period** immediately preceding the commencement of the case.

NAME OF PENSION FUND   TAXPAYER IDENTIFICATION NUMBER (EIN)

---

* * * * * *

[If completed by an individual or individual and spouse]

I declare under penalty of perjury that I have read the answers contained in the foregoing statement of financial affairs and any attachments thereto and that they are true and correct.

Date _____   Signature _____
                                           of Debtor

Date _____   Signature_____
                                           of Joint Debtor
                                           (if any)

_____

[If completed on behalf of a partnership or corporation]

I, declare under penalty of perjury that I have read the answers contained in the foregoing statement of financial affairs and any attachments thereto and that they are true and correct to the best of my knowledge, information and belief.

Date _____   Signature _____

                                   _____
                                   Print Name and Title

[An individual signing on behalf of a partnership or corporation must indicate position or relationship to debtor.]

_____ continuation sheets attached

Penalty for making a false statement: Fine of up to $500,000 or imprisonment for up to 5 years, or both. 18 U.S.C. § 152 and 3571

CERTIFICATION AND SIGNATURE OF NON-ATTORNEY BANKRUPTCY PETITION PREPARER (See 11 U.S.C. § 110)

I certify that I am a bankruptcy petition preparer as defined in 11 U.S.C. § 110, that I prepared this document for compensation, and that I have provided the debtor with a copy of this document.

_____   _____
Printed or Typed Name of Bankruptcy Petition Preparer   Social Security No.
                                                          (Required by 11 U.S.C. § 110(c).)

_____

_____
Address

Names and Social Security numbers of all other individuals who prepared or assisted in preparing this document:

If more than one person prepared this document, attach additional signed sheets conforming to the appropriate Official Form for each person.

X _____   _____
Signature of Bankruptcy Petition Preparer   Date

A bankruptcy petition preparer's failure to comply with the provisions of title 11 and the Federal Rules of Bankruptcy Procedure may result in fines or imprisonment or both. 18 U.S.C. § 156.

In Re:

Debtor
In a joint case,
debtor means debtors in this plan.

1. PAYMENTS BY DEBTOR —

   a. As of this date of this plan, the debtor has paid the trustee $ _____ .

   b. After the date of this plan, the debtor will pay the trustee $ _____ per _____ for _____ months, beginning within 30 days after the filing of this plan for a total of $ _____ .

   c. The debtor will also pay the trustee _____ _____

   d. The debtor will pay the trustee a total of $ _____ [line 1(a) + line 1(b) + line 1(c)].

2. PAYMENTS BY TRUSTEE — The trustee will make payments only to creditors for which proofs of claim have been filed, make payments monthly as available, and collect the trustee's percentage fee of 10% for a total of $_____ [line 1 (d) x .10] or such lesser percentage as may be fixed by the Attorney General. For purposes of this plan, month one (1) is the month following the month in which the debtor makes the debtor's first payment. Unless ordered otherwise, the trustee will not make any payments until the plan is confirmed. Payments will accumulate and be paid following confirmation.

3. PRIORITY CLAIMS — The trustee shall pay in full all claims entitled to priority under § 507, including the following. The amounts listed are estimates only. The trustee will pay the amounts actually allowed.

Creditor	Estimated Claim	Monthly Payment	Beginning in Month #	Number of Payments	TOTAL PAYMENTS
a. Attorney Fees	$ _____	$ _____	_____	_____	$ _____
b. Internal Revenue Service	$ _____	$ _____	_____	_____	$ _____
c. State Dept. of Revenue	$ _____	$ _____	_____	_____	$ _____
d. _____	$ _____	$ _____	_____	_____	$ _____
e. TOTAL					$ _____

4. LONG-TERM SECURED CLAIMS NOT IN DEFAULT — The following creditors have secured claims. Payments are current and the debtor will continue to make all payments which come due after the date the petition was filed directly to the creditors. The creditors will retain their liens.

   a. _____

   b. _____

5. HOME MORTGAGES IN DEFAULT [§ 1322 (b)(5)] — The trustee will cure defaults (plus interest at the rate of 8 per cent per annum) on claims secured only by a security interest in real property that is the debtor's principal residence as follows. The debtor will maintain the regular payments which come due after the date the petition was filed. The creditors will retain their liens. The amounts of default are estimates only. The trustee will pay the actual amounts of default.

Creditor	Amount of Default	Monthly Payment	Beginning in Month #	Number of Payments	TOTAL PAYMENTS
a. _____	$ _____	$ _____	$ _____	$ _____	$ _____
b. _____	$ _____	$ _____	$ _____	$ _____	$ _____
c. _____	$ _____	$ _____	$ _____	$ _____	$ _____
d. TOTAL					$ _____

6. OTHER LONG-TERM SECURED CLAIMS IN DEFAULT [§ 1322 (b)(5)] — The trustee will cure defaults (plus interest at the rate of 8 per cent per annum) on other claims as follows and the debtor will maintain the regular payments which come due after the date the petition was filed. The creditors will retain their liens. The amounts of default are estimates only. The trustee will pay the actual amounts of default.

Creditor	Amount of Default	Monthly Payment	Beginning in Month #	Number of Payments	TOTAL PAYMENTS
a. _____	$ _____	$ _____	_____	_____	$ _____
b. _____	$ _____	$ _____	_____	_____	$ _____
c. _____	$ _____	$ _____	_____	_____	$ _____
d. TOTAL					$ _____

7. OTHER SECURED CLAIMS [§ 1325 (a)(5)] — The trustee will make payments to the following secured creditors having a value as of confirmation equal to the allowed amount of the creditor's secured claim using a discount rate of 8 percent. The creditor's allowed secured claim shall be the creditor's allowed claim or the value of the creditor's interest in the debtor's property, whichever is less. The creditors shall retain their liens. NOTE: NOTWITHSTANDING A CREDITOR'S PROOF OF CLAIM FILED BEFORE OR AFTER CONFIRMATION, THE AMOUNT LISTED IN THIS PARAGRAPH AS A CREDITOR'S SECURED CLAIM BINDS THE CREDITOR PURSUANT TO 11 U.S.C. § 1327 AND CONFIRMATION OF THE PLAN WILL BE CONSIDERED A DETERMINATION OF THE CREDITOR'S ALLOWED SECURED CLAIM UNDER 11 U.S.C. § 506 (a).

Creditor	Claim Amount	Secured Claim	Monthly Payment	Beginning in Month #	Number of Payments	TOTAL PAYMENTS
a. _____	$ _____	$ _____	$ _____	_____	_____	$ _____
b. _____	$ _____	$ _____	$ _____	_____	_____	$ _____
c. _____	$ _____	$ _____	$ _____	_____	_____	$ _____
d. TOTAL						$ _____

8. SEPARATE CLASS OF UNSECURED CREDITORS — In addition to the class of unsecured creditors specified in ¶ 9, there shall be a separate class of nonpriority unsecured creditors described as follows: _____
   a. The debtor estimates that the total claims in this class are $ _____ .
   b. The trustee will pay this class $ _____ .

9. TIMELY FILED UNSECURED CREDITORS — The trustee will pay holders of nonpriority unsecured claims for which proofs of claim were timely filed the balance of all payments received by the trustee and not paid under ¶ 2, 3, 5, 6, 7, and 8 their pro rata share of approximately $ _____ [line 1(d) minus lines 2, 3(e), 5(d), 6(d), 7(d), and 8 (b)].
   a. The debtor estimates that the total unsecured claims held by creditors listed in ¶ 7 are $ _____
   b. The debtor estimates that the debtor's total unsecured claims (excluding those in ¶ 7 and ¶ 8) are $ _____ .
   c. Total estimated unsecured claims are $ _____ [line 9(a) + line 9(b)].

10. TARDILY FILED UNSECURED CREDITORS — All money paid by the debtor to the trustee under ¶ 1, but not distributed by the trustee under ¶ 2, 3, 5, 6, 7, 8, or 9 shall be paid to holders of nonpriority unsecured claims for which proofs of claim were tardily filed.

11. OTHER PROVISIONS —

12. SUMMARY PAYMENTS —
   Trustee's Fee [Line 2] .... $ _____
   Priority Claims [Line 3(e)] .... $ _____
   Home Mortgage Defaults [Line 5(d)] .... $ _____
   Long-Term Debt Defaults [Line 6(d)] .... $ _____
   Other Secured Claims [Line 7(d)] .... $ _____
   Separate Class [Line 8(b)] .... $ _____
   Unsecured Creditors[Line 9(c)] .... $ _____
   TOTAL [must equal Line 1(d)] .... $ _____

Signed: _____ Signed: _____
   DEBTOR   DEBTOR (if joint case)

(ATTORNEY NAME:) _____

(ADDRESS:) _____

(CITY:) _____ (STATE:) _____

(ZIP:) _____

(PHONE NUMBER:) (____) _____

(BAR NUMBER:) _____

DEBTORS: _____ CASE NO.: _____

DEBTORS PRELIMINARY CHAPTER 13 PLAN

DATE OF PLAN _____ FIRST PAYMENT DUE TO TRUSTEE _____

INCOME $ _____ TRUSTEE PAYMENTS $ _____ FOR ____MONTHS PLAN BASE AMOUNT $ _____

EXPENSES $ _____ $ _____ FOR ____MONTHS UNSECURED % _____

SURPLUS $ _____ $ _____ FOR ____MONTHS

ADMINISTRATIVE   NOTICING FEES: # _____ + 3 X 3 X .79 = $ _____

                   ATTORNEY FEES: TOTAL _____ THRU PLAN _____

HOME MORTGAGE   Regular payments beginning _____to be paid direct. Arrearages to be paid by Trustee as follows:

	ARREARS	THRU	%	TERM	PAYMENT
1ST LIEN _____	$ _____	_____	_____	_____	$ _____
2ND LIEN _____	$ _____	_____	_____	_____	$ _____

SECURED CREDITORS	COLLATERAL	CLAIM	VALUE	%	TERM	PAYMENT
1. _____	_____	$ _____	$ _____	_____	_____	$ _____
2. _____	_____	$ _____	$ _____	_____	_____	$ _____
3. _____	_____	$ _____	$ _____	_____	_____	$ _____
4. _____	_____	$ _____	$ _____	_____	_____	$ _____
5. _____	_____	$ _____	$ _____	_____	_____	$ _____

ANY DEFICIENCY WILL AUTOMATICALLY BE "SPLIT" AND INCLUDED IN UNSECURED.

PRIORITY CREDITORS	TYPE	DISPUTED AMOUNT	CLAIM	TERM	PAYMENT
1. _____	_____	$ _____	$ _____	_____	$ _____
2. _____	_____	$ _____	$ _____	_____	$ _____

SPECIAL CLASS	BASIS	AMOUNT	TERM	PAYMENT
1. _____	_____	$ _____	_____	$ _____
2. _____	_____	$ _____	_____	$ _____

UNSECURED CREDITORS	CLAIM	CREDITORS	CLAIM	CREDITORS	CLAIM
1. _____	$ _____	6. _____	$ _____	11. _____	$ _____
2. _____	$ _____	7. _____	$ _____	12. _____	$ _____
3. _____	$ _____	8. _____	$ _____	13. _____	$ _____
4. _____	$ _____	9. _____	$ _____	14. _____	$ _____
5. _____	$ _____	10. _____	$ _____	15. _____	$ _____

TOTAL UNSECURED AND DEFICIENCIES $ _____

☐ CHECK HERE IF ADDITIONAL INFORMATION APPEARS ON REVERSE SIDE (EXECUTORY CONTRACTS? MISCELLANEOUS?)

CERTIFICATE OF SERVICE

I certify that a copy of the above and foregoing "Debtor's Preliminary Chapter 13 Plan" and an "Authorization for Preconfirmation Disbursement" was by me on this _____ day _____ of 20____ served on the trustee and all creditors listed on the original matrix and any amended matrix filed in this case by United States First Class mail.

_____

Attorney for Debtor or Pro Se Debtor

SPECIAL PROVISIONS:
(Balloon, proceeds of sale,
recovery on lawsuit, etc.)

_____
_____
_____
_____

ADDITIONAL CREDITORS:

HOME MORTGAGE:

		ARREARS	THRU	%	TERM	PAYMENT
3RD LIEN	_____	$ _____	_____	____	_____	$ _____
4TH LIEN	_____	$ _____	_____	____	_____	$ _____

SECURED CREDITORS	COLLATERAL	CLAIM	VALUE	%	TERM	PAYMENT
6. _____	_____	$ _____	$ _____	____	_____	$ _____
7. _____	_____	$ _____	$ _____	____	_____	$ _____
8. _____	_____	$ _____	$ _____	____	_____	$ _____
9. _____	_____	$ _____	$ _____	____	_____	$ _____
10. _____	_____	$ _____	$ _____	____	_____	$ _____

PRIORITY CREDITORS	DISPUTED AMOUNT	CLAIM	TERM	PAYMENT
3. _____	$ _____	$ _____	_____	$ _____
4. _____	$ _____	$ _____	_____	$ _____

SPECIAL CLASS	BASIS	AMOUNT	TERM	PAYMENT
3. _____	_____	$ _____	_____	$ _____
4. _____	_____	$ _____	_____	$ _____

UNSECURED CREDITORS	CLAIM	CREDITORS	CLAIM	CREDITORS	CLAIM
_____	$ _____	_____	$ _____	_____	$ _____
_____	$ _____	_____	$ _____	_____	$ _____
_____	$ _____	_____	$ _____	_____	$ _____
_____	$ _____	_____	$ _____	_____	$ _____

DEBTOR(S) _____ CASE NO. _____

CHAPTER 13 PLAN OR SUMMARY

I. The projected disposable income of the debtor(s) is submitted to the supervision and control of the Trustee and the Debtor(s) shall pay to the Trustee the sum of:

$ _____ ☐ Weekly ☐ Biweekly ☐ Semimonthly ☐ Monthly

☐ Direct Payment ☐ Payroll Deduction on Wages of: _____ ☐ Debtor ☐ Spouse

Length of plan is approximately _____ months, and total debt to be paid through plan is approximately $_____.

II. From the payments so received the Trustee shall make disbursements as follows:

A. <u>PRIORITY</u> payments described in 11 U.S.C. § 507 in full in deferred cash payments.

B. The holder of each allowed <u>SECURED</u> claim shall retain the lien securing such claim until a discharge is granted and such claim shall be paid in full with interest at a rate of _____% per annum in deferred cash payments as follows:

1. Mortgage Debts:

Name of Mortgage company	Home-stead Yes/No	Total amount of debt	Arrears to be paid by Trustee	Months included in arrearage amount	Postpetition –OR– payments to begin Month/Year (Direct to creditor)	Amount of regular mortgage to be paid by Trustee

2. Other Secured Debts:

				If Applicable	
Name of creditor	Total amount of debt	Debtor's value	Description of collateral	Interest factor	Debtor's Fixed Payments

C. The Debtor(s) will make direct payments as follows:

Name of creditor	Total of debt	Description of collateral	Reason for direct payment

D. Special provisions. Explanation:

_____

_____

_____

☐ This is an original plan.

☐ This is an amended plan replacing plan dated _____ .

☐ This plan proposes to pay unsecured creditors _____ %.

☐ Insurance on vehicle: ☐ Proof of Insurance attached, OR:

☐ Insurance through Trustee requested

Dated:_____   _____
                                    Signature of Debtor

Dated:_____   _____
                                    Signature of Debtor

Official Form 3
(12/03)

United States Bankruptcy Court

_____ District Of _____

In re _____,
　　　　　　　Debtor

Case No. _____

Chapter _____

APPLICATION TO PAY FILING FEE IN INSTALLMENTS

1.　　In accordance with Fed. R. Bankr. P. 1006, I apply for permission to pay the Filing Fee amounting to $_____ in installments.

2.　　I certify that I am unable to pay the Filing Fee except in installments.

3.　　I further certify that I have not paid any money or transferred any property to an attorney for services in connection with this case and that I will neither make any payment nor transfer any property for services in connection with this case until the filing fee is paid in full.

4.　　I propose the following terms for the payment of the Filing Fee.*

$ _____　　Check one ☐　With the filing of the petition, or
　　　　　　　　　　　　　　　　☐　On or before _____

$ _____　on or before _____

$ _____　on or before _____

$ _____　on or before _____

*　　The number of installments proposed shall not exceed four (4), and the final installment shall be payable not later than 120 days after filing the petition. For cause shown, the court may extend the time of any installment, provided the last installment is paid not later than 180 days after filing the petition. Fed. R. Bankr. P. 1006(b)(2).

5.　　I understand that if I fail to pay any installment when due my bankruptcy case may be dismissed and I may not receive a discharge of my debts.

_____
Signature of Attorney　　　　Date

_____
Name of Attorney

_____
Signature of Debtor　　　　　　Date
(In a joint case, both spouses must sign.)

_____
Signature of Joint Debtor (if any)　　Date

CERTIFICATION AND SIGNATURE OF NON-ATTORNEY BANKRUPTCY PETITION PREPARER (See 11 U.S.C. § 110)

I certify that I am a bankruptcy petition preparer as defined in 11 U.S.C. § 110, that I prepared this document for compensation, and that I have provided the debtor with a copy of this document. I also certify that I will not accept money or any other property from the debtor before the filing fee is paid in full.

_____
Printed or Typed Name of Bankruptcy Petition Preparer

_____
Social Security No.
(Required by 11 U.S.C. § 110(c).)

_____

_____
Address

Names and Social Security numbers of all other individuals who prepared or assisted in preparing this document:

If more than one person prepared this document, attach additional signed sheets conforming to the appropriate Official Form for each person.

x_____
Signature of Bankruptcy Petition Preparer

_____
Date

A bankruptcy petition preparer's failure to comply with the provisions of title 11 and the Federal Rules of Bankruptcy Procedure may result in fines or imprisonment or both. 11 U.S.C. § 110; 18 U.S.C. § 156.

United States Bankruptcy Court
_____ District Of _____

In re _____,
                  Debtor

Case No. _____

Chapter _____

ORDER APPROVING PAYMENT OF FILING FEE IN INSTALLMENTS

        IT IS ORDERED that the debtor(s) may pay the filing fee in installments on the terms proposed in the foregoing application.

        IT IS FURTHER ORDERED that until the filing fee is paid in full the debtor shall not pay any money for services in connection with this case, and the debtor shall not relinquish any property as payment for services in connection with this case.

BY THE COURT

Date: _____

_____
United States Bankruptcy Judge

To Whom It May Concern:

On _____, I filed a voluntary petition under Chapter 13 of the U.S. Bankruptcy Code in the Bankruptcy Court for the _____. The case number is _____. No attorney is representing me. Under 11 U.S.C. § 362(a), you may not:

- take any action against me or my property to collect any debt

- file or pursue any lawsuit against me

- place a lien on my real or personal property

- take any property to satisfy an already recorded lien

- repossess any property in my possession

- discontinue any service or benefit currently being provided to me, or

- take any action to evict me from where I live.

A violation of these prohibitions may be considered contempt of court and punished accordingly.

Very truly yours,

FORM B10 (Official Form 10) (04/04)

UNITED STATES BANKRUPTCY COURT _____ DISTRICT OF _____	PROOF OF CLAIM

Name of Debtor	Case Number	

NOTE: This form should not be used to make a claim for an administrative expense arising after the commencement of the case. A "request" for payment of an administrative expense may be filed pursuant to 11 U.S.C. § 503.

Name of Creditor (The person or other entity to whom the debtor owes money or property):

☐ Check box if you are aware that anyone else has filed a proof of claim relating to your claim. Attach copy of statement giving particulars.

Name and address where notices should be sent:

☐ Check box if you have never received any notices from the bankruptcy court in this case.

☐ Check box if the address differs from the address on the envelope sent to you by the court.

Telephone number:

THIS SPACE IS FOR COURT USE ONLY

Account or other number by which creditor identifies debtor:

Check here ☐ replaces
if this claim   a previously filed claim, dated:_____
☐ amends

1. Basis for Claim

☐ Goods sold
☐ Services performed
☐ Money loaned
☐ Personal injury/wrongful death
☐ Taxes
☐ Other _____

☐ Retiree benefits as defined in 11 U.S.C. § 1114(a)
☐ Wages, salaries, and compensation (fill out below)
Last four digits of SS #: _____
Unpaid compensation for services performed
from _____ to _____
(date)   (date)

2. Date debt was incurred:

3. If court judgment, date obtained:

4. Total Amount of Claim at Time Case Filed: $ _____ _____ _____ _____
(unsecured)   (secured)   (priority)   (Total)

If all or part of your claim is secured or entitled to priority, also complete Item 5 or 7 below.

☐ Check this box if claim includes interest or other charges in addition to the principal amount of the claim. Attach itemized statement of all interest or additional charges.

5. Secured Claim.
☐ Check this box if your claim is secured by collateral (including a right of setoff).

Brief Description of Collateral:
☐ Real Estate   ☐ Motor Vehicle
☐ Other _____

Value of Collateral: $_____

Amount of arrearage and other charges <u>at time case filed</u> included in secured claim, if any: $_____

6. Unsecured Nonpriority Claim $_____

☐ Check this box if: a) there is no collateral or lien securing your claim, or b) your claim exceeds the value of the property securing it, or if c) none or only part of your claim is entitled to priority.

7. Unsecured Priority Claim.
☐ Check this box if you have an unsecured priority claim

Amount entitled to priority $_____
Specify the priority of the claim:
☐ Wages, salaries, or commissions (up to $4,925),* earned within 90 days before filing of the bankruptcy petition or cessation of the debtor's business, whichever is earlier - 11 U.S.C. § 507(a)(3).
☐ Contributions to an employee benefit plan - 11 U.S.C. § 507(a)(4).
☐ Up to $2,225* of deposits toward purchase, lease, or rental of property or services for personal, family, or household use - 11 U.S.C. § 507(a)(6).
☐ Alimony, maintenance, or support owed to a spouse, former spouse, or child - 11 U.S.C. § 507(a)(7).
☐ Taxes or penalties owed to governmental units-11 U.S.C. § 507(a)(8).
☐ Other - Specify applicable paragraph of 11 U.S.C. § 507(a)(___).
*Amounts are subject to adjustment on 4/1/07 and every 3 years thereafter with respect to cases commenced on or after the date of adjustment.

8. Credits: The amount of all payments on this claim has been credited and deducted for the purpose of making this proof of claim.

9. Supporting Documents: *Attach copies of supporting documents,* such as promissory notes, purchase orders, invoices, itemized statements of running accounts, contracts, court judgments, mortgages, security agreements, and evidence of perfection of lien. DO NOT SEND ORIGINAL DOCUMENTS. If the documents are not available, explain. If the documents are voluminous, attach a summary.

10. Date-Stamped Copy: To receive an acknowledgment of the filing of your claim, enclose a stamped, self-addressed envelope and copy of this proof of claim

THIS SPACE IS FOR COURT USE ONLY

Date	Sign and print the name and title, if any, of the creditor or other person authorized to file this claim (attach copy of power of attorney, if any):

Penalty for presenting fraudulent claim: Fine of up to $500,000 or imprisonment for up to 5 years, or both. 18 U.S.C. §§ 152 and 3571.

INSTRUCTIONS FOR PROOF OF CLAIM FORM

The instructions and definitions below are general explanations of the law. In particular types of cases or circumstances, such as bankruptcy cases that are not filed voluntarily by a debtor, there may be exceptions to these general rules.

——— DEFINITIONS ———

Debtor

The person, corporation, or other entity that has filed a bankruptcy case is called the debtor.

Creditor

A creditor is any person, corporation, or other entity to whom the debtor owed a debt on the date that the bankruptcy case was filed.

Proof of Claim

A form telling the bankruptcy court how much the debtor owed a creditor at the time the bankruptcy case was filed (the amount of the creditor's claim). This form must be filed with the clerk of the bankruptcy court where the bankruptcy case was filed.

Secured Claim

A claim is a secured claim to the extent that the creditor has a lien on property of the debtor (collateral) that gives the creditor the right to be paid from that property before creditors who do not have liens on the property.

Examples of liens are a mortgage on real estate and a security interest in a car, truck, boat, television set, or other item of property. A lien may have been obtained through a court proceeding before the bankruptcy case began; in some states a court judgment is a lien. In addition, to the extent a creditor also owes money to the debtor (has a right of setoff), the creditor's claim may be a secured claim. (See also *Unsecured Claim*.)

Unsecured Claim

If a claim is not a secured claim it is an unsecured claim. A claim may be partly secured and partly unsecured if the property on which a creditor has a lien is not worth enough to pay the creditor in full.

Unsecured Priority Claim

Certain types of unsecured claims are given priority, so they are to be paid in bankruptcy cases before most other unsecured claims (if there is sufficient money or property available to pay these claims). The most common types of priority claims are listed on the proof of claim form. Unsecured claims that are not specifically given priority status by the bankruptcy laws are classified as *Unsecured Nonpriority Claims.*

Items to be completed in Proof of Claim form (if not already filled in)

Court, Name of Debtor, and Case Number:
Fill in the name of the federal judicial district where the bankruptcy case was filed (for example, Central District of California), the name of the debtor in the bankruptcy case, and the bankruptcy case number. If you received a notice of the case from the court, all of this information is near the top of the notice.

Information about Creditor:
Complete the section giving the name, address, and telephone number of the creditor to whom the debtor owes money or property, and the debtor's account number, if any. If anyone else has already filed a proof of claim relating to this debt, if you never received notices from the bankruptcy court about this case, if your address differs from that to which the court sent notice, or if this proof of claim replaces or changes a proof of claim that was already filed, check the appropriate box on the form.

1. Basis for Claim:
Check the type of debt for which the proof of claim is being filed. If the type of debt is not listed, check "Other" and briefly describe the type of debt. If you were an employee of the debtor, fill in the last four digits of your social security number and the dates of work for which you were not paid.

2. Date Debt Incurred:
Fill in the date when the debt first was owed by the debtor.

3. Court Judgments:
If you have a court judgment for this debt, state the date the court entered the judgment.

4. Total Amount of Claim at Time Case Filed:
Fill in the applicable amounts, including the total amount of the entire claim. If interest or other charges in addition to the principal amount of the claim are included, check the appropriate place on the form and attach an itemization of the interest and charges.

5. Secured Claim:
Check the appropriate place if the claim is a secured claim. You must state the type and value of property that is collateral for the claim, attach copies of the documentation of your lien, and state the amount past due on the claim as of the date the bankruptcy case was filed. A claim may be partly secured and partly unsecured. (See DEFINITIONS, above).

6. Unsecured Nonpriority Claim:
Check the appropriate place if you have an unsecured nonpriority claim, sometimes referred to as a "general unsecured claim". (See DEFINITIONS, above.) If your claim is partly secured and partly unsecured, state here the amount that is unsecured. If part of your claim is entitled to priority, state here the amount **not** entitled to priority.

7. Unsecured Priority Claim:
Check the appropriate place if you have an unsecured priority claim, and state the amount entitled to priority. (See DEFINITIONS, above). A claim may be partly priority and partly nonpriority if, for example, the claim is for more than the amount given priority by the law. Check the appropriate place to specify the type of priority claim.

8. Credits:
By signing this proof of claim, you are stating under oath that in calculating the amount of your claim you have given the debtor credit for all payments received from the debtor.

9. Supporting Documents:
You must attach to this proof of claim form copies of documents that show the debtor owes the debt claimed or, if the documents are too lengthy, a summary of those documents. If documents are not available, you must attach an explanation of why they are not available.

UNITED STATES BANKRUPTCY COURT

_____ DISTRICT OF _____

In re _____)
    [Set forth here all names including)
    married, maiden, and trade names used)
    by debtor within last 6 years.])
                            Debtor(s)) Case No. _____

Address _____)
)

_____) Chapter _____
)

Employer's Tax Identification (EIN) No(s). *[if any]*:)
_____)
Last four digits of Social Security No(s): _____)

AMENDMENT COVER SHEET

Presented herewith are the original and one copy of the following:

☐ Voluntary Petition (Note: Spouse may not be added or deleted subsequent to initial filing.)

☐ Schedule A—Real Property

☐ Schedule B—Personal Property

☐ Schedule C—Property Claimed as Exempt

☐ Schedule D—Creditors Holding Secured Claims

☐ Schedule E—Creditors Holding Unsecured Priority Claims

☐ Schedule F—Creditors Holding Unsecured Nonpriority Claims

☐ Schedule G—Executory Contracts and Unexpired Leases

☐ Schedule H—Codebtors

☐ Schedule I—Current Income of Individual Debtor(s)

☐ Schedule J—Current Expenditures of Individual Debtor(s)

☐ Summary of Schedules

☐ Statement of Financial Affairs

☐ I have enclosed a $20 fee because I am adding new creditors or changing addresses after the original Meeting of Creditors Notice has been sent.

_____   _____
Signature of Debtor   Signature of Debtor's Spouse

I (we) _____ and

_____, the debtor(s)

in this case, declare under penalty of perjury that the information set forth in the amendment attached hereto

consisting of _____ pages is true and correct to the best of my (our) information and belief.

Dated: _____, 20_____

_____   _____
Signature of Debtor   Signature of Debtor's Spouse

UNITED STATES BANKRUPTCY COURT

_____ DISTRICT OF _____

In re _____)   .
        [Set forth here all names including)
        married, maiden, and trade names used)
        by debtor within last 6 years.])
                                    Debtor(s))   Case No. _____
Address _____)
)
        _____)   Chapter _____
)
Employer's Tax Identification (EIN) No(s). *[if any]*:)
_____)
Last four digits of Social Security No(s): _____)

NOTICE OF CHANGE OF ADDRESS

Social Security Number (H): _____

Social Security Number (W): _____

MY (OUR) FORMER MAILING ADDRESS AND PHONE NUMBER WAS:

Name: _____

Street: _____

City: _____

State/Zip: _____

Phone: (_____) _____

PLEASE BE ADVISED THAT AS OF_____, 20_____, MY (OUR) NEW
MAILING ADDRESS AND PHONE NUMBER IS:

Name: _____

Street: _____

City: _____

State/Zip: _____

Phone: (_____) _____

_____
Signature of Debtor

_____
Signature of Debtor's Spouse

UNITED STATES BANKRUPTCY COURT

_____ DISTRICT OF _____

In re _____   )
    [Set forth here all names including   )
    married, maiden, and trade names used   )
    by debtor within last 6 years.]   )
                  Debtor(s)   ) Case No. _____

Address _____   )
)
    _____   ) Chapter 13
)

Employer's Tax Identification (EIN) No(s). [if any]:   )
_____   )
Last four digits of Social Security No(s): _____   )

PROOF OF SERVICE BY MAIL

I, _____, declare that: I am a resident or

employed in the County of _____, State of _____ .

My residence/business address is _____

_____ .

I am over the age of eighteen years and not a party to this case.

    On _____, 20___, I served the:

on _____,

by placing true and correct copies thereof enclosed in a sealed envelope with postage thereon fully prepaid

in the United States Mail at _____, address as follows:

    I declare under penalty of perjury that the foregoing is true and correct, and that this declaration was

executed on

Date: _____ , 20___ at _____

                             City and State

                             _____

                             Signature

Daily Expenses

Date: _____

Item	Cost

Date: _____

Item	Cost

Date: _____

Item	Cost

Date: _____

Item	Cost

Index

Remember:

Little publishers have big ears.
We really listen to you.

Take 2 Minutes & Give Us Your 2 cents

Your comments make a big difference in the development and revision of Nolo books and software. Please take a few minutes and register your Nolo product—and your comments—with us. Not only will your input make a difference, you'll receive special offers available only to registered owners of Nolo products on our newest books and software.
Register now by:

PHONE
1-800-728-3555

FAX
1-800-645-0895

EMAIL
cs@nolo.com

or **MAIL** us
this registration card

fold here

- -

NOLO

Registration Card

NAME _____ DATE _____

ADDRESS _____

_____

CITY _____ STATE _____ ZIP _____

PHONE _____ E-MAIL _____

WHERE DID YOU HEAR ABOUT THIS PRODUCT? _____

WHERE DID YOU PURCHASE THIS PRODUCT? _____

DID YOU CONSULT A LAWYER? (PLEASE CIRCLE ONE)   YES   NO   NOT APPLICABLE

DID YOU FIND THIS BOOK HELPFUL?   (VERY)   5   4   3   2   1   (NOT AT ALL)

COMMENTS _____

_____

_____

WAS IT EASY TO USE?   (VERY EASY)   5   4   3   2   1   (VERY DIFFICULT)

We occasionally make our mailing list available to carefully selected companies whose products may be of interest to you.

❑   If you do not wish to receive mailings from these companies, please check this box.

❑   You can quote me in future Nolo promotional materials.
Daytime phone number _____.

CHB 7.0

Nolo
in the
NEWS

"Nolo helps lay people perform legal tasks without the aid—or fees—of lawyers."

—USA TODAY

Nolo books are ..."written in plain language, free of legal mumbo jumbo, and spiced with witty personal observations."

—ASSOCIATED PRESS

"...Nolo publications...guide people simply through the how, when, where and why of law."

—WASHINGTON POST

"Increasingly, people who are not lawyers are performing tasks usually regarded as legal work... And consumers, using books like Nolo's, do routine legal work themselves."

—NEW YORK TIMES

"...All of [Nolo's] books are easy-to-understand, are updated regularly, provide pull-out forms...and are often quite moving in their sense of compassion for the struggles of the lay reader."

—SAN FRANCISCO CHRONICLE

-------------------------------- fold here --------------------------------

Place
stamp here

Nolo
950 Parker Street
Berkeley, CA 94710-9867

Attn: CHB 7.0